Rover 3500 Owners Workshop Manual

by J H Haynes
Associate Member of the Guild of Motoring Writers

and Peter Strasman
MISTC

Models covered

Rover Three Thousand Five (Automatic) 3528 cc
Rover 3500 (Automatic) 3528 cc
Rover 3500 S (Manual gearbox) 3528 cc
Also covers
Rover 3500 S (Automatic) USA import model, 215 cu in

Does not cover Rover '3½ Litre' models

ISBN 900550 85 6

Printed in England

HAYNES PUBLISHING GROUP
SPARKFORD YEOVIL SOMERSET ENGLAND
distributed in the USA by
HAYNES PUBLICATIONS INC
861 LAWRENCE DRIVE
NEWBURY PARK
CALIFORNIA, 91320
USA

Acknowledgements

Thanks are due to the Rover Company Limited (part of the specialist car division of BLMC) for their help in the provision of technical details and illustrations. Castrol Limited have supplied lubrication details and advice.

Stanley Randolph planned the layout and edited the text. The supply of illustrations and material by The Rover Company Limited does not imply that The Rover Company Limited has approved the contents of this book or is in any way responsible for the accuracy of any information printed. The copyright in illustrations and other technical material provided by The Rover Company Limited remains vested in The Rover Company Limited.

This manual and its use

This manual has been compiled by practical enthusiasts with the aim of presenting (at reasonable cost) some of the 'know-how' of car maintenance to fellow Owner/enthusiasts who prefer to carry out routine maintenance and major overhauls themselves.

It is assumed that the reader already possesses some basic knowledge of car maintenance, and it must be obvious to him at the outset that in the saving of motoring costs, the carrying out of one simple servicing operation will in itself repay more than the cost of the book.

In compiling this manual only authentic information and accurate data has been used. The authors, not content with just reading about it, have themselves undertaken in practice many of the operations described. Step-by-step photographs have been taken and are presented in conjunction with the written text. These photographs will greatly assist by actually showing what is going on.

The reader is advised not to tackle work of a major nature on this car before he has thoroughly considered the work to be done, ensuring that he is in possession of an adequate kit of tools. He must bear in mind that some overhaul work requires special 'one-off' tools. Such tools can possibly be obtained by hire/loan, or purchase from the car manufacturers or their agents. However, as this is the type of car that one would expect the enthusiast owner to retain for some years, there is no doubt that his stock of tools and servicing equipment related to this car will grow as time goes by.

On the question of purchase of servicing equipment, it is sound advice, that it is far better to buy quality, branded tools. Cheap tools are never cheap in the long run and lead to frustration on the part of the user and damage to vital parts of the car.

The book is divided into twelve chapters. Each chapter is divided into numbered sections which are headed in **bold** type between horizontal lines. Each section comprises serially numbered paragraphs and is referred to in the text as 'Chapter 1, Section 5'. If the chapter is not mentioned, the section referred to is in the same chapter in which the reference occurs.

Whenever the left or right-hand side of the car is mentioned it is assumed that one is facing forward in the direction of travel.

There are two types of illustration: Figures which are numbered in sequence within each chapter, eg Fig. 2.7 is the 7th illustration in Chapter 2; and photographs, which are given the same number as the section and paragraph number where the description occurs, eg 17.23 belongs to paragraph 23 of Section 17 in that chapter.

Whilst every care has been taken to ensure that the information in this manual is correct, changes in design and specifications for cars are a continuing process even within a given model range, and no responsibility can be accepted by the authors and publishers for any loss, damage or injury caused by any errors in or omissions from the information given.

Contents

Introduction to the Rover 3500 and model identification

First introduced to the UK in 1968 as the Three Thousand Five, this and later models are all based upon the Rover 2200 models. The V8 engine is of all aluminium construction, but many of the other components are interchangeable with those of the 2000/2200 range.

Identification
Three Thousand Five (1968 to 1970)
    Automatic transmission as standard
    Horizontally slatted grille
    Non-wrap round bumpers
    Retangular style instrumentation

3500S (October 1969 to September 1971)
This model was designed mainly for the North American market.
    Automatic transmission as standard
    Power steering

    Dual braking system
    Electrically operated windows
    Horizontally slatted grille
    Bonnet air scoops
    Wrap round bumpers

3500 (September 1970 onwards) - 'new look'
    Rectangular section grille
    Automatic transmission as standard
    Circular instrumentation
    Two raised longitudinal pressings on bonnet lid

3500S (October 1971 onwards) - 'new look'
    Rectangular section grille
    Four speed manual gearbox
    Circular instrumentation and other details as 'new look' 3500 model.

Rover Three Thousand Five — 1968 to September 1970 — Automatic transmission as standard

Rover 3500 S — October 1969 to September 1971 — Automatic transmission as standard

Buying spare parts
and vehicle identification numbers

Buying spare parts

Spare parts are available from many sources, for example: Rover garages, other garages and accessory shops, and motor factors. Our advice regarding spare part sources is as follows:

Officially appointed Rover garages - This is the best source of parts which are peculiar to your car and are otherwise not generally available (eg complete cylinder heads, internal gearbox components, badges, interior trim etc). It is also the only place at which you should buy parts if your car is still under warranty - non-Rover components may invalidate the warranty. To be sure of obtaining the correct parts it will always be necessary to give the storeman your car's engine and chassis number, and if possible, to take the 'old' part along for positive identification. Remember that many parts are available on a factory exchange scheme - any parts returned should always be clean! It obviously makes good sense to go straight to the specialists on your car for this type of part for they are best equipped to supply you.

Other garages and accessory shops - These are often very good places to buy materials and components needed for the maintenance of your car (eg oil filters, spark plugs, bulbs, fan belts, oils and greases, touch-up paint, filler paste etc). They also sell general accessories, usually have convenient opening hours, charge lower prices and can often be found not far from home.

Motor factors - Good factors will stock all of the more important components which wear out relatively quickly (eg clutch components, pistons, valves, exhaust systems, brake cylinders/pipes/hoses/seals/shoes and pads etc). Motor factors will often provide new or reconditioned components on a part exchange basis - this can save a considerable amount of money.

Vehicle identification numbers

The chassis number will be found on a plate attached to the left-hand wing valance.

The engine number is stamped on a boss which is part of the engine cylinder block casting.

The gearbox (automatic and manual) number is on a plate attached to the unit.

The final drive number is stamped on the differential casing.

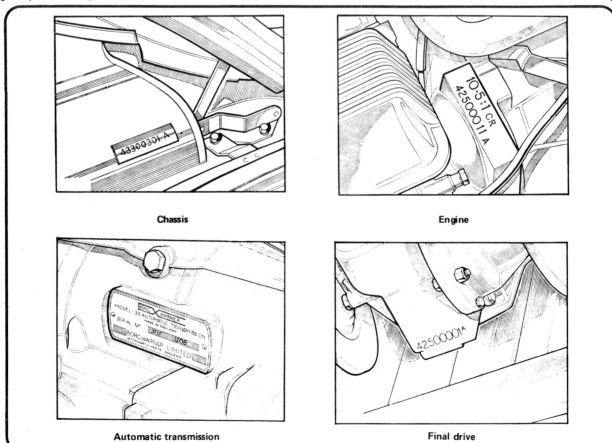

Chassis

Engine

Automatic transmission

Final drive

Rover 3500 'New Look' — September 1970 onwards — Automatic transmission as standard

Rover 3500 S — October 1971 onwards — 4-speed manual gearbox

Routine maintenance

The maintenance instructions listed are basically those recommended by the manufacturer. They are supplemented by additional maintenance tasks proven to be necessary.

The additional tasks are indicated by an asterisk (*) and are primarily of a preventative nature in that they will assist in eliminating the unexpected failure of a component due to fair wear and tear.

Maintenance instructions are repeated in certain chapters where they form part of the repair and servicing procedures.

When a new car is delivered the engine contains sufficient running-in oil for the running-in period. Providing the level is maintained between the low and high marks on the dipstick during this period, topping up is unnecessary. At the first 'Free service', the running in oil is drained and the sump replenished to the level of the high mark on the dipstick.

Every 250 miles (400 km) or weekly

1 Check the level of the coolant in the radiator and top-up if necessary to within 1 in (25.4 mm) of the filler neck. When checking with the engine hot immediately after a run, cover the filler cap with a cloth and release the cap slowly to release the pressure and to avoid scalding.
2 Check the engine oil level. Remove the dipstick, wipe clean, reinsert and again withdraw. Top up to the "FULL" mark with Castrol GTX.
3 Check the electrolyte level in the battery and - top up if necessary (distilled water only). Never inspect a battery cell with a naked light or an explosion may occur. Always wipe the top of the battery clean, and dry, after topping up.
4 Check the tyre pressures including the spare.
5* Operate all lights and flasher indicators and renew any bulbs which have 'blown'.
6* Top up the fluid in the windscreen washer reservoir.

Every 1000 miles (1600 km) or at monthly intervals

1 Check the fluid level in the clutch and brake reservoir. Use only new fluid of recommended type which has been stored in an airtight container and remained unshaken for at least 24 hours.
2 Check and top up if necessary the fluid in the power steering reservoir (if fitted).
3 Check the tension of the alternator driving belt. The correct total deflection between the crankshaft and alternator pulleys is between 0.437 and 0.562 in (11 to 14 mm).
4 Check the tension of the drive belt to the power steering pump (if fitted).
5 Check the fluid level in the automatic transmission (if fitted).

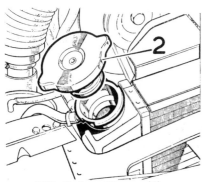

RM1. Radiator filler cap (2)

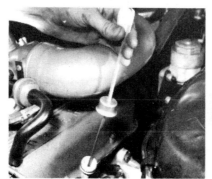

RM2. Check engine oil level

RM3. Topping up engine oil level

RM4. Battery topping up

RM5. Spare wheel location

RM6. Checking windscreen washer fluid level

RM7. Topping up brake fluid level

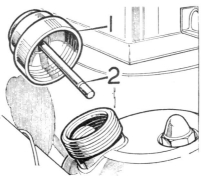

RM8. Checking power steering reservoir fluid level (1) cap (2) dipstick

RM9. Checking alternator drive belt tension

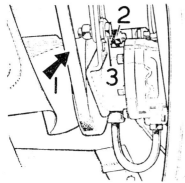

RM10. Checking power steering pump belt tension (1) belt (2) pivot bolt (3) adjustment link bolt

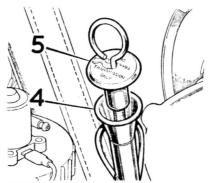

RM11. Automatic transmission dipstick location and fluid level marks (4) combined filler /dipstick tube (5) dipstick (6) HIGH mark

RM12. Engine sump drain plug

RM13. Oil filter location showing oil pressure and warning light switches

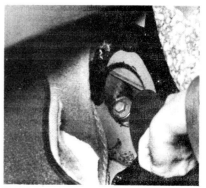

RM14. Location of gearbox filler plug within the transmission tunnel

RM15. Final drive oil level plug

RM16. Topping up carburettor damper

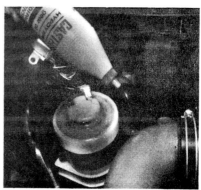

RM17. Topping up steering box

Every 6000 miles (9000 km) or at six-monthly intervals

1 Drain the engine oil and renew the oil filter, refill with Castrol GTX.
2 Check the gearbox oil level and top-up if necessary.
3 Check the 'rear axle' oil level and top-up if necessary.
4 Top up the carburettor dampers with Castrol GTX.
5 Check and top up if necessary the fluid in the steering box.
6 Lubricate the propeller shaft sliding sleeve, all locks, linkages and controls.
7 Clean and adjust the spark plugs.
8 Check and reset the distributor contact breaker points.
9* Check the security of all bolts and nuts.
10*Remove the road wheels and remove flints from the tyre treads. If the wheels have been balanced on the car refit them to their original positions on the wheel studs. If they have been balanced off the car, rotate the wheels round the car to even the rate of tread wear. Include the spare wheel in the rotational pattern.
11 Check the wear of the front and rear brake disc pads. If the thickness of the front friction pad material is less than 0.125 in (3.0 mm) or the rear 1/16 in (1.5 mm) the pads must be renewed.
12*Disconnect the leads from the battery and clean the battery terminals. Refit and fully tighten the leads to the terminals and smear the terminals with petroleum jelly to prevent corrosion.

Every 12000 miles (19000 km) or at twelve-monthly intervals

1 Drain the gearbox (not automatic transmission) when the oil is hot after a run and refill with the correct grade and quantity of oil.
2 Drain the 'rear axle' also when the oil is hot after a run and refill with the correct grade and quantity of oil.
3 Check the oil level in the De Dion tube and top up if necessary.
4 Renew the fuel filter cartridge.
5 Renew the engine flame traps (emission control).
6 Renew the air cleaner element.
7 Renew the spark plugs and contact breaker points.
8* Check the front wheel alignment. This operation is best carried out by a service station having specialised equipment.
9* Check the headlamp alignment. This again is best carried out by a service station having the necessary optical beam setting equipment.
10 Drain the cooling system and refill with fresh antifreeze mixture.
11 Check for corrosion at the HT lead connections.

Every 20000 miles (32000 km) or at eighteen-monthly intervals

1 Renew the engine breather filter.
2 Renew the windscreen wiper blades.
3* Check the condition of all hoses and drive belts and renew as necessary.
4* Examine the condition of the exhaust system and renew sections or the complete system as required.

Every 40000 miles (64000 km) or at three-yearly intervals

1 Bleed the hydraulic fluid from the braking circuits. Dismantle the master cylinder and caliper units and fit new rubber seals. Refill the system with new fluid of the specified type and bleed the brakes.
2 Check the seat belts and their anchorages for security and signs of wear.
3 Inspect the underbody (particularly under the wings) for signs of rust or corrosion. Clean and apply undersealing compound where necessary.

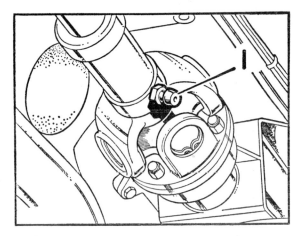

RM18. Propeller shaft sliding sleeve grease nipple (1)

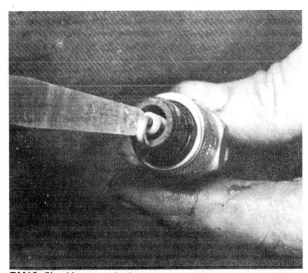

RM19. Checking a spark plug gap

RM20. Checking contact breaker points gap

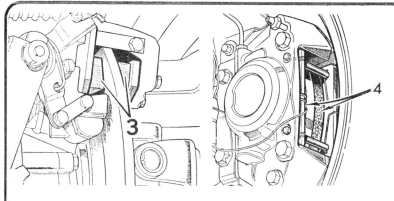

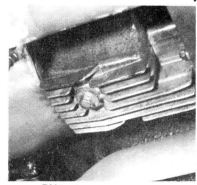

RM21. Checking disc pad wear. (3) rear pads (4) front pads

RM22. Gearbox drain plug

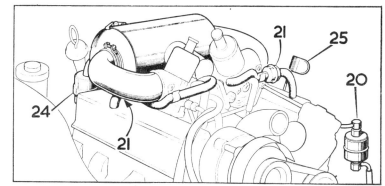

RM23. De Dion tube filler/level plug

RM24. Location of fuel filter (20) flame traps (21) and engine oil dipstick (25) breather filter (24)

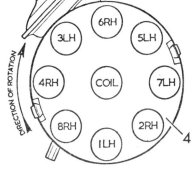

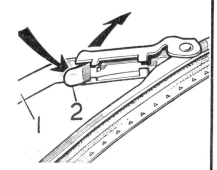

RM25. Checking HT lead connections for corrosion

RM26. Sequence of HT lead connections to spark plugs (4) distributor cap. 1 left hand (LH) and 2 right hand (RH) spark plugs are nearest radiator

RM27, Windscreen wiper blade removal (1) wiper arm (2) spring tab

Recommended lubricants and fluids

COMPONENT							TYPE OF LUBRICANT OR FLUID												CASTROL PRODUCT
ENGINE ...	...	...	...	...	...	...	Multigrade engine oil	...	...	...	...	...	...	...	...	...	...	...	Castrol GTX
GEARBOX	...	...	...	...	...	...	SAE 20W	...	...	...	...	...	...	...	...	...	...	...	Castrol GTX
DE DION TUBE							SAE 20W	...	...	...	...	...	...	...	...	...	...	...	Castrol GTX
AUTOMATIC TRANSMISSION								...	...	...	...	...	...	...	...	...	...	...	Castrol TQF
FINAL DRIVE UNIT	...	...					SAE 90 EP	...	...	...	...	...	...	...	...	...	...	...	Castrol Hypoy
STEERING BOX	...						SAE 90 EP	...	...	...	...	...	...	...	...	...	...	...	Castrol Hypoy
PROPELLER SHAFT SLIDING SPLINE								...	...	...	...	...	...	...	...	...	...	...	Castrol LM grease
FRONT AND REAR HUBS	...	...						...	...	...	...	...	...	...	...	...	...	...	Castrol LM grease
BRAKES AND CLUTCH	...	...					Hydraulic fluid	...	...	...	...	...	...	...	...	...	...	...	Castrol Girling Universal Brake and Clutch Fluid

Additionally Castrol 'Everyman' oil can be used to lubricate door, boot and bonnet hinges, locks and pivots etc.

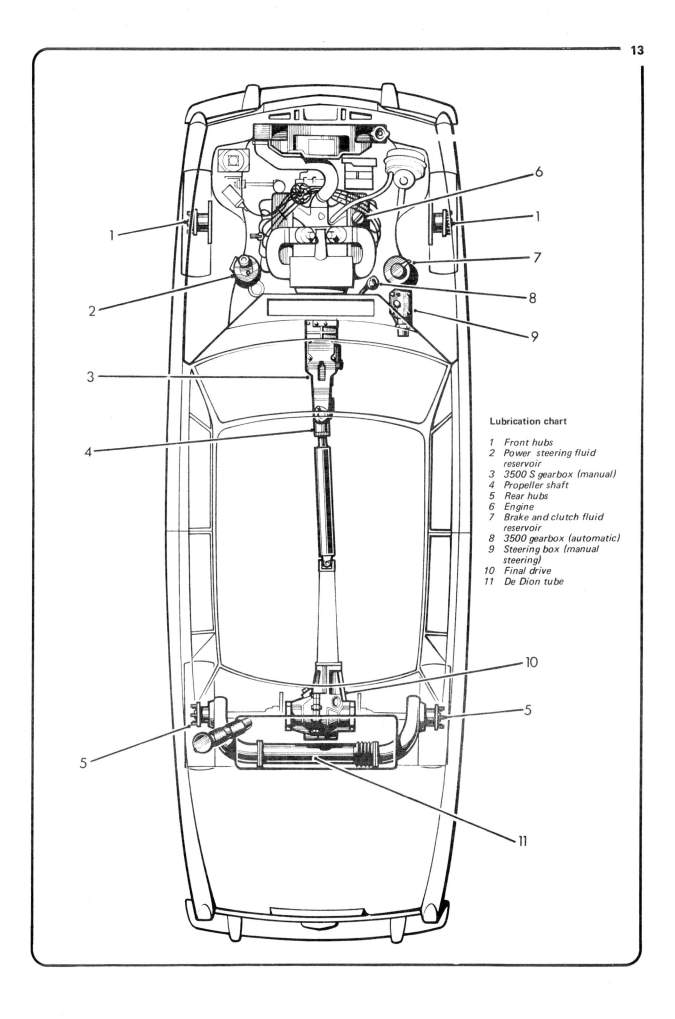

Lubrication chart

1 Front hubs
2 Power steering fluid reservoir
3 3500 S gearbox (manual)
4 Propeller shaft
5 Rear hubs
6 Engine
7 Brake and clutch fluid reservoir
8 3500 gearbox (automatic)
9 Steering box (manual steering)
10 Final drive
11 De Dion tube

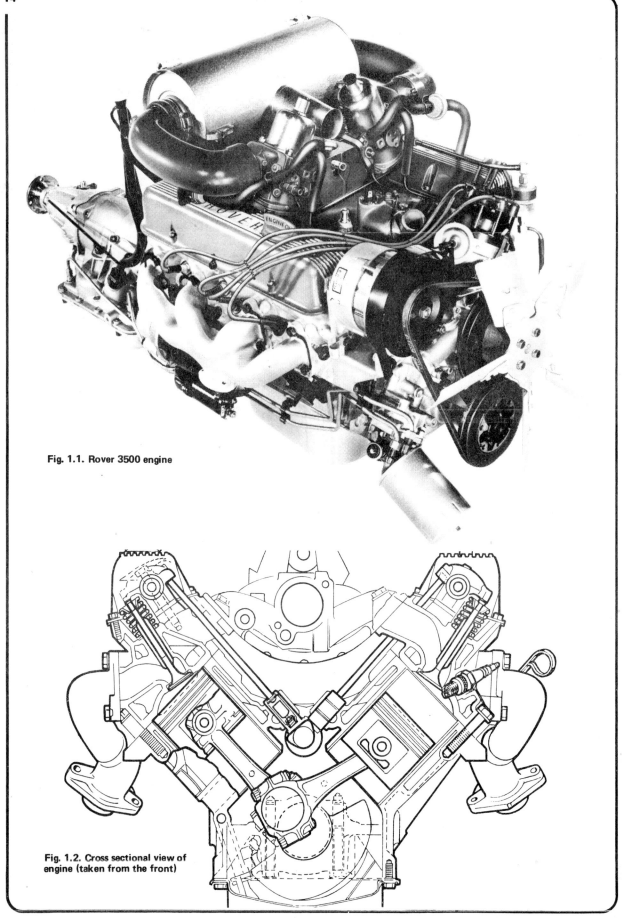

Fig. 1.1. Rover 3500 engine

Fig. 1.2. Cross sectional view of
engine (taken from the front)

Chapter 1 Engine

Contents

Specifications

Engine: general

Type	V8
Bore	88,90 mm (3.500 in.)
Stroke	71,12 mm (2.800 in.)
Number of cylinders	Eight
Cylinder capacity	3,528 cc (215 cu. in.)
* Compression ratio	10.5 : 1. Certain export territories, 8.5 : 1
BHP, 10.5 : 1	176 (131 kw) at 5,200 revs/min.
BHP, 8.5 : 1	156 (116 kw) at 5,250 revs/min.
Maximum torque, 10.5 : 1	30 mkg (220 lb ft) at 3,000 revs/min.
Maximum torque, 8.5 : 1	28 mkg (205 lb ft) at 3,000 revs/min.
Firing order	1 8 4 3 6 5 7 2

* 1974 models have re-designed pistons and a compression ratio of 9.25 : 1 for lower octane fuels.

Cylinder block:

Material	Aluminium alloy
Cylinder liner type	Dry
Liner material	Cast iron
Liner reboring limit	0.020 in. (0.50 mm)

Cylinder heads:

Material	Aluminium alloy
Type	Two heads with separate alloy inlet manifold
Inlet and exhaust valve seat material	Piston ring iron
Inlet and exhaust valve seat angle	46 + ¼ degrees

Crankshaft:

Main journal diameter　　...　...　...　...　...　...	58,400 to 58,413 mm (2.2992 to 2.2997 in.)
Minimum regrind diameter　...　...　...　...　...	57,384 to 57,396 mm (2.2592 to 2.2597 in.)
Crankpin journal diameter ...　...　...　...　...　...	50,800 to 50,812 mm (2.0000 to 2.0005 in.)
Minimum regrind diameter　...　...　...　...　...	49,784 to 49,797 mm (1.9600 to 1.9605 in.)
Crankshaft end thrust　　...　...　...　...　...	Taken on thrust faces of centre main bearing
Crankshaft end-float　　...　...　...　...　...　...	0,10 to 0,20 mm (0.004 to 0.008 in.)

Main bearings:

Number and type　...　...　...　...　...　...　...	5 Vandervell shells
Material　　...　...　...　...　...　...　...　...	Lead indium
Diametrical clearance　...　...　...　...　...　...	0,023 to 0,065 mm (0.0009 to 0.0025 in.)
Undersizes　...　...　...　...　...　...　...　...	0,254 mm, 0,508 mm, 0,762 mm, 1,016 mm
	0.010 in.　0.020 in.　0.030 in.　0.040 in.

Connecting rods:

Type ...　...　...　...　...　...　...　...　...	Horizontally split big end, plain small end
Length between centres　...　...　...　...　...	143.81 to 143.71 mm (5.662 to 5.658 in.)

Big end bearings:

Type and material　...　...　...　...　...　...	Vandervell VP lead indium
Diametrical clearance　...　...　...　...　...　...	0.015 to 0.055 mm (0.0006 to 0.0022 in.)
End-float on crankpin　...　...　...　...　...　...	0.15 to 0.37 mm (0.006 to 0.014 in.)
Undersizes ...　...　...　...　...　...　...　...	0.254 mm, 0.508 mm, 0.762 mm,　1.016 mm
	0.010 in.　0.020 in.　0.030 in.　0.040 in.

Gudgeon pins:

Length　...　...　...　...　...　...　...　...	72.67 to 72.79 mm (2.861 to 2.866 in.)
Diameter　...　...　...　...　...　...　...　...	22.215 to 22.22 mm (0.8746 to 0.8749 in.)
Fit-in con rod　...　...　...　...　...　...　...	Press fit
Clearance in piston ...　...　...　...　...　...	0.002 to 0.007 mm (0.0001 to 0.0003　in.)

Pistons:

Early type　...　...　...　...　...　...　...　... — Aluminium alloy with apertures below gudgeon pin
Clearance in bore measured at top of skirt at right angles
to gudgeon pin　...　...　...　...　...　...　... — 0.018 to 0.033 mm (0.0007 to 0.0013 in.)

Latest type　...　...　...　...　...　...　...　... — Aluminium alloy with 'W' slot skirt
Clearance in bore measured at bottom of skirt at right
angles to gudgeon pin　...　...　...　...　...　... — 0.018 to 0.033 mm (0.0007 to 0.0013 in.)

Pistons — Design 'A' (See Fig. 1.54)

Type　...　...　...　...　...　...　...　...		Aluminium alloy
Clearance:	Top land ...　...　...　...　...　...	0.65 to 0.81 mm (0.0255 to 0.0320 in.)
	Skirt top ...　...　...　...　...　...	0.018 to 0.033 mm (0.0007 to 0.0013 in.)
	Skirt bottom　...　...　...　...　...	0.008 to 0.043 mm (0.0003 to 0.0017 in.)

Pistons — Design 'B'

Type　...　...　...　...　...　...　...　...		Aluminium alloy — 'W' slot skirt
Clearance:	Top land ...　...　...　...　...　...	0.73 to 0.88 mm (0.0296 to 0.0350 in.)
	Skirt top ...　...　...　...　...　...	0.040 to 0.071 mm (0.0016 to 0.0028 in.)
	Skirt bottom　...　...　...　...　...	0.018 to 0.033 mm (0.0007 to 0.0013 in.)

Pistons are available in graded standard sizes and in ungraded oversizes of 0.25 mm (0.010 in.) and 0.50 mm (0.020 in.)
Standard pistons are graded in diameter, and the grade letter is stamped on the crown of the piston and on the cylinder block
Grade letter:

'Z'	cylinder bore diameter nominal to +0.0075 mm (0.0003 in.)
'A'	0.0075 mm (0.0003 in.) to 0.015 mm (0.0006 in.) above nominal
'B'	0.015 mm (0.0006 in.) to 0.0225 mm (0.0009 in.) above nominal
'C'	0.0225 mm (0.0009 in.) to 0.03 mm (0.0012 in.) above nominal
'D'	0.03 mm (0.0012 in.) to 0.0375 mm (0.0015 in.) above nominal
'S'	0.081 mm (0.0032 in.) to 0.088 mm (0.0035 in.) above nominal

If new pistons are required for a standard size bore, check the bore size and fit the grade of piston that provides the correct clearance
The clearance limits with new pistons and a new or rebored cylinder are 0.018 to 0.033 mm (0.0007 to 0.0013 in.)

Piston rings:

Compression ...　...　...　...　...　...　...　...	2
Number one compression ring　...　...　...　...	Chrome faced and marked 'T' or 'TOP'
Number two compression ring　...　...　...　...	Stepped 'L' shape and marked 'T' or 'TOP'
Gap in bore　...　...　...　...　...　...　...	0.44 to 0.57 mm (0.017 to 0.022 in.)
Clearance in groove　...　...　...　...　...　...	0.08 to 0.13 mm (0.003 to 0.005 in.)

Oil control 1
    Type ... ... Perfect circle, type 98
    Gap in bore ... ... 0.38 to 1.40 mm (0.015 to 0.055 in.)

Camshaft:
  Location ... ... Central
  Bearings ... ... Five non-serviceable
  Timing chain ... ... 9.52 mm (0.375 in.) pitch x 54 pitches

Valves:
  Inlet:
    Overall length ... ... 116.58 to 117.34 mm (4.590 to 4.620 in.)
    Head diameter ... ... 37.97 to 38.22 mm (1.495 to 1.505 in.)
    Angle of face 45º
    Stem diameter ... ... 8.640 to 8.666 mm (0.3402 to 0.3412 in.) at the head and
        increasing to 8.653 to 8.679 mm (0.3407 to 0.3417 in.)
    Stem to guide clearance: Top ... ... 0.02 to 0.07 mm (0.001 to 0.003 in.)
                    Bottom ... ... 0.013 to 0.063 mm (0.0005 to 0.0025 in.)
  Exhaust:
    Overall length ... ... 116.58 to 117.34 mm (4.590 to 4.620 in.)
    Head diameter ... ... 33.215 to 33.466 mm (1.3075 to 1.3175 in.)
    Angle of face 45º
    Stem diameter ... ... 8.628 to 8.654 mm (0.3397 to 0.3407 in.) at the head and
        increasing to 8.640 to 8.666 mm (0.3402 to 0.3412 in.)
    Stem to guide clearance: Top ... ... 0.038 to 0.088 mm (0.0015 to 0.0035 in.)
                    Bottom ... ... 0.05 to 0.10 mm (0.002 to 0.004 in.)
  Valve lift (both valves) ... ... 9.9 mm (0.39 in.)
  Valve spring length:
    Inner ... ... 41.4 mm (1.63 in.) under load of 9.75 to 12.02 kg (21.5 to
        26.5 lb)
    Outer ... ... 40.6 mm (1.6 in.) under load of 17.69 to 20.41 kg (39 to
        45 lb)

Valve timing:
  Inlet opens ... ... 30º BTDC
  Inlet closes ... ... 75º ABDC
  Inlet duration 285º
  Inlet peak ... ... 112.5º ATDC
  Exhaust opens ... ... 68º BBDC
  Exhaust closes ... ... 37º ATDC
  Exhaust duration 285º
  Exhaust peak ... ... 105.5º BTDC

Torque wrench settings:

	lb ft	kg m
Cylinder head bolts	65 to 70	9.0 to 9.6
Main bearing cap bolts (one to four)	50 to 55	7.0 to 7.6
Rear main bearing cap bolts	65 to 70	9.0 to 9.6
Big-end bearing cap bolts	30 to 35	4.0 to 4.9
Rocker shaft bolts	25 to 30	3.5 to 4.0
Flywheel bolts	50 to 60	7.0 to 8.5
Oil pump cover bolts	10 to 15	1.4 to 2.0
Oil pressure relief valve	30 to 35	4.0 to 4.9
Timing cover bolts	20 to 25	2.8 to 3.5
Crankshaft pulley bolt	140 to 160	19.3 to 22.3
Distributor drive gear to camshaft	40 to 45	5.5 to 6.2
Inlet manifold bolts	25 to 30	3.5 to 4.0
Inlet manifold clamp bolts	10 to 15	1.4 to 2.0
Exhaust manifold bolts	10 to 15	1.4 to 2.0
Auto. transmission drive plate to crankshaft mounting flange	50 to 60	7.0 to 8.5
Starter motor mounting bolts	30 to 35	4.0 to 4.9
Power steering pump bolts	20 to 25	2.8 to 3.5
Water pump to timing cover	6 to 8	0.8 to 1.0
Torque converter housing to engine bolts	30	4.0
Drive plate to torque converter bolts	25 to 30	3.5 to 4.0

1 General description

Two banks of four cylinders form the main cylinder block. The material used is cast aluminium and the cylinder banks are set at a 90º angle. Each bore is fitted with a cylinder liner with a maximum rebore tolerance of 0.020 in. (0.5080 mm).

The cylinder heads are also aluminium castings into which iron valve inserts and valve guides are fitted. The valves themselves are arranged in line and operate at a 10º angle above the bore centre line.

The camshaft lies between the two banks of cylinders above the crankshaft, it is driven by a single chain and is supported by five bearings. There is no chain tensioner.

To ensure quiet operation the tappets are hydraulically operated and valve clearance is automatically maintained without any adjustment being required.

The engine lubrication is conventional, the oil pressure pump being located within the timing chain cover and fitted with a normal full flow external oil filter.

IMPORTANT: Because the engine block is of aluminium construction, it is vital when tightening bolts related to the engine, that the correct torque settings specified should be strictly adhered to. It is also of equal importance that bolt lengths are noted and bolts replaced in the same location from whence removed. Where specified, always use thread lubricant and sealer.

Because of the weight and bulk of this unit it is felt that removal of the engine would be undesirable and impractical for the average home mechanic. It is fully realised that any major overhaul tasks could be greatly facilitated if the unit were out of the frame and supported on an engine stand. For those who are determined, or find it really necessary to remove the unit, the procedure is outlined in the following text. In the following sections all the items that can be tackled with the engine in position are progressively listed, and the owner must fully assess the amount of work entailed before starting work.

2 Major operations which can be performed with engine in the car

1   Removal and replacement of radiator.
2   Removal and replacement of carburettors and ancillaries.
3   Removal and replacement of alternator.
4   Removal and replacement of starter motor/solenoid.
5   Removal and replacement of distributor.
6   Removal and replacement of the cylinder heads and valve assembly.
7   Removal and replacement of the water pump.
8   Removal and replacement of the cooling fan.
9   Removal and replacement of the inlet manifold.
10 Removal and replacement of pistons and connecting rods.
11 Removal and replacement of timing chain and wheels.
12 Removal and replacement of sump and big end bearings.
13 Removal and replacement of camshaft.
14 Removal and replacement of oil pump.
15 Removal and replacement of thermostat and water temperature transmitter.
16 Removal and replacement of gearbox (S models).
17 Removal and replacement of torque converter (automatic).
18 Removal and replacement of exhaust system.

3 Operations which require removal of the engine from the car

Any internal engine work (other than listed previously) such as a replacement of crankshaft and main bearings, will require removal of the engine from the car.

4 Engine removal - general

Rover recommend that the engine is lifted complete with the gearbox or automatic transmission unit.

From a safety angle, the operator is advised to use adequate lifting tackle. He will need tackle that will give him at least three feet of lift.

At no time during the lifting operation should any part of the operator be directly beneath the suspended weight of this large heavy engine.

5 Engine removal - with manual gearbox

1   Begin the engine removal procedure by first isolating the electrical supply. Remember that the **negative** battery connection is the one that is attached to the frame (**Earth**) - this is the one to disconnect; better still detach both connections.
2   Raise bonnet and prop in normal way. Disconnect the pipe from the screen washer bottle and the jets. If the car is fitted with an under-bonnet light, disconnect the lamp heads.
3   Slacken off the four bolts securing the bonnet to the bulkhead and remove. There are plain and spring washers with these bolts, so take care. At this stage it will be necessary to enlist some assistance to support one side of the bonnet. Note that the bolts at the front end of the hinge also support the wing panel, and that the rear right-hand bolt secures the bonnet light switch. (Fig. 1.3).
4   Grip the bonnet as shown in photo, the right-hand serving to protect the car body against scratches from the pointed rear end of the bonnet. Slide the whole assembly rearwards to clear the wing panel fixing, and lift forwards. Store in a safe place.
5   To drain the radiator. Remove the radiator cap and slacken the drain plug. Make sure that you have obtained a wide brimmed container for the coolant because there will be a spread of liquid as it hits the radiator cowl. Remove the plug and drain off. (photo).
6   Drain the cylinder block. Drain taps are provided on each cylinder bank (photo). Ensure that the car heater controls are set at "HOT" otherwise water will be trapped in heater radiator and may cause air locks when refilling.
7   Whilst the block is draining move to the car interior and remove the gearbox tunnel cover.
8   Slide the seats back, out of the way, and remove the front and rear ashtrays to expose the tunnel cover securing nuts. Remove these nuts (photo).
9   Remove the two screws holding the speaker console panel, and ease the panel out. (photo).
10 Remove the two screws at the front end of the tunnel cover moulding. (photo).
11 Lift up the little flap at the front edge of the handbrake grommet and remove the screw that is hidden beneath. (photo).
12 Release the gear change knob locking piece using the correct

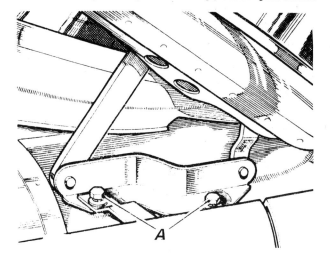

Fig. 1.3. Location of bonnet hinge bolts (A)

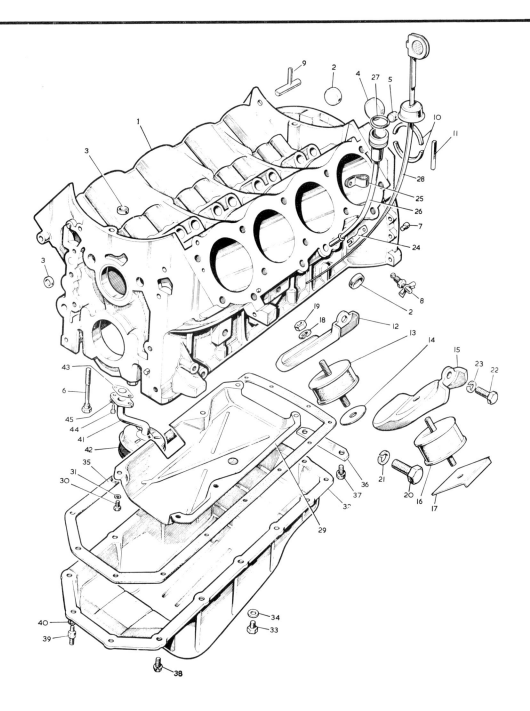

Fig. 1.4. Exploded view of the cylinder block and some associated components

1	Cylinder block assembly	18	Spring washer	33	Drain plug
2	Cup plug	19	Nut - fixing mounting rubber to plate and base unit	34	Joint washer for drain plug
3	Cup plug			35	Gasket, sump to cylinder block
4	Cup plug	20	Bolt	36	Reinforcing strip for rear of sump
5	Threaded plug for tappet oil lines	21	Spring washer	37	Special bolt and spring washer fixing reinforcing strip and sump
6	Special bolt fixing main bearing caps	22	Bolt		
7	Dowel, locating flywheel housing	23	Spring washer	38	Special bolt and spring washer fixing sump to cylinder block
8	Drain tap	24	Clamp bracket for tube		
9	Inlet pipe for crankcase breather	25	Clip for oil level rod tube	39	Shouldered stud - fixing sump and pipe brackets
10	Oil seal for crankshaft rear	26	Tube assembly for oil level rod		
11	Packing for oil seal	27	'O' ring for tube	40	Spring washer
12	Engine mounting plate	28	Oil level rod	41	Oil screen housing assembly
13	Mounting rubber	29	Sump baffle plate	42	Oil screen
14	Plain washer for mounting rubber	30	Bolt - fixing baffle plate to cylinder block	43	Gasket for oil screen housing
15	Engine mounting plate			44	Bolt - fixing oil screen housing assembly to block
16	Mounting rubber	31	Spring washer		
17	Packing plate for mounting rubber	32	Crankcase sump	45	Spring washer

5.4 Bonnet removal

5.5 Unscrewing radiator drain plug

5.6 Cylinder block drain tap

5.8 Tunnel cover securing nuts

5.9 Removing speaker console panel

5.10 Removing tunnel cover moulding screws

5.11 Tunnel screw located beneath hand-brake grommet

5.12a Unscrewing gear change knob locking piece

5.12b Gear change lever return spring

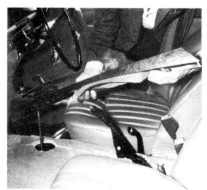
5.14 Withdrawing tunnel cover assembly

5.15 Gear change lever clamp bolts

5.18 Handbrake warning light switch

size spanner. Unscrew the gear knob followed by the chrome locking piece. Ensure that the small return spring is retained. (photos).

13 To ease the handbrake grommet away from the handbrake lever it will be found advantageous to roll back the grommet and smear both the grommet and brake lever with rubber grease or brake fluid.

14 With the brake in the 'on' position, slide the cover forwards, and upwards; allowing it to protrude into the space in the top of the console. Release the brake to the 'off' position, and withdraw the cover assembly. (photo).

15 Remove the gear change lever. Remove the bolts securing the clamp ring at base of the gear lever; the lever can now be withdrawn. (photo).

16 On cars fitted with air conditioning units, the knobs controlling temperature selection and air flow are removed by inserting a stiff piece of wire through the holes in the underside of the knob and compressing the spring loaded retaining pin - after which the knob can be withdrawn easily. To replace the tunnel cover reverse the procedure.

17 Lift the carpet from the left-hand side of the tunnel. Remove the cover plate and disconnect the speedometer drive.

18 Disconnect the electrical leads from the handbrake warning light switch (photo).

19 Now drain off the engine oil. Drain off the gear oil as well. Otherwise leave the gearbox undisturbed. Both oil draining operations are described in Routine Maintenance. Replace the drain plugs after draining.

20 Remove the hose connections to the radiator and oil cooler (automatic transmission only) (photo). Also, the hose to manifold heater (photo).

21 Remove the radiator centre fixing bolt situated just behind the bonnet catch. (photo).

22 Remove the two (one each side) radiator bracket fixing bolts. (photo).

23 Carefully lift out the radiator (photo).

24 Disconnect the electrical leads from alternator (photo).

25 Slacken the alternator belt adjustment strap and remove the fan belt. (photo).

26 Remove the three bolts attaching the alternator cradle to the cylinder block and remove the alternator, complete with cradle. (photo).

27 Remove the ring of bolts securing the fan blade assembly to the pulley boss. The fan blades will come away leaving the boss secured to the coupling spindle. (photo.).

Note: An offset locating dowel ensures that the blades cannot be refitted incorrectly.

28 Remove the air cleaner. See Routine Maintenance.

29 Disconnect and remove the heater connecting hoses. (See photo).

30 Disconnect and remove the brake servo pipe, (photo).

31 Disconnect the electrical lead from the mixture control switch which is just adjacent to the servo hose connector.

32 Disconnect the electrical lead from the water temperature transmitter which is on the front right-hand side of the cylinder block.

33 Disconnect the electrical leads from both the oil temperature and pressure transmitters. These are housed in the oil pump.

34 Disconnect both the HT and LT leads from the coil.

35 Remove the distributor cap complete with the HT harness.

36 Remove the HT harness clips, (photo).

37 Disconnect the outlet fuel pipe at the fuel reserve tap situated low down on the right-hand side of the bulkhead. Plug the fuel tap outlet to prevent leakage.

38 Disconnect the choke cable (see photos) and tie it back out of the way.

39 Disconnect the throttle linkage. Remove the split pins that pass through the nylon bush which connects the coupling rod. Remove the long vertical link rod that connects to the accelerator pedal lever. Disconnect and remove the short vertical link

5.20a Radiator top hose

5.20b Manifold heater hose

5.21 Radiator centre fixing bolt

5.22 Radiator bracket bolt

5.23 Removing radiator

5.24 Alternator leads

5.25 Removing fan belt

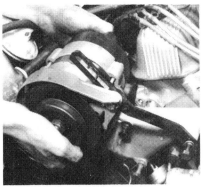
5.26 Removing the alternator

5.27 Removing fan blade assembly

5.29 Removing a heater hose

5.30 Disconnecting brake servo pipe

5.36 Removing HT lead clip

5.38a Removing choke outer cable clip

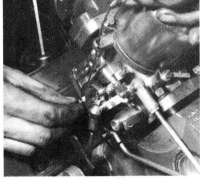
5.38b Unscrewing choke inner cable clamp bolt

5.39a Disconnecting throttle coupling rod

5.39b Removing throttle link rod

5.40 Removing emission control pipes

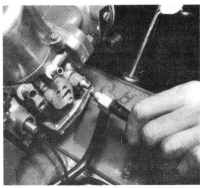
5.41 Uncoupling fuel feed and overspill pipes

rod. Remove coupling rod. Remove the carburettor cross over throttle and choke link rods (photos).

40 Remove the emission control pipes. These just pull off. (photo).

41 Disconnect and remove the fuel feed and overspill pipes. (photo).

42 Slacken and remove the carburettor flange nuts. Ease the left-hand carburettor away from the manifold and turn on one side to remove the automatic advance/retard vacuum pipe. (photo).

43 Remove the other carburettor.

44 Remove the liner and insulating gasket, (photo) from the carburettor mounting flange.

45 Remove the engine tie-rod. To remove the engine tie-rod, first slacken the lock nuts securing the rod at the engine end using two spanners. Remove the nuts, followed by the cup/guide washers and rubber bush. Carry out the same operation at the wing bracket. Withdraw the distance pieces. The rod can now be lifted through the slot in the engine bracket and withdrawn from the wing securing bracket. Adjustment is provided by the wing bracket having an oval hole for its securing bolt. To slacken this wing bracket it will be found necessary to go under the wing to slacken the securing nuts. (photos). When replacing, assemble in the correct order as shown in Fig. 1.5.

46 Remove the engine oil filter - see Routine Maintenance.

47 Remove the exhaust down pipe assembly. Slacken the centre

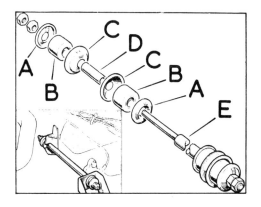

Fig. 1.5. Engine tie-rod

A Cup washer
B Rubber bush
C Guide washer
D Distance piece
E Tie-rod

5.42 Withdrawing left-hand carburettor

5.44 Carburettor mounting flange liner and gasket

5.45a Removing tie-rod from engine bracket

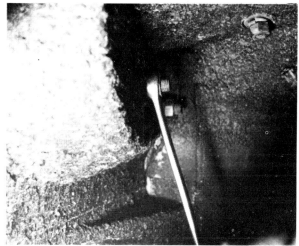

5.45b Removing tie-rod from under-wing bracket

bracket nut and washer support. Remove the manifold flange nuts (brass), disconnect the down pipe from the silencer box. Remove the centre fixing nut and lower pipes and move them clear of the car (photos).

48 Remove the propeller shaft. Before removing any coupling flange nuts, mark the sliding spline joint to ensure replacement in the same relative position. Remove the rear flange nuts and bolts and clear the propeller shaft from the car (photos).

49 Disconnect the engine earth strap. (photo).

50 Remove the fixing bolts from the clutch slave cylinder and withdraw the cylinder from the bellhousing. DO NOT disconnect the fluid pipe. Move assembly to one side and support the cylinder by tying it to the car body.

51 Disconnect the electrical leads from the starter motor solenoid.

Colour coding for leads:

WN White and Brown WY White and Yellow. (Fig. 1.6).

52 Remove the starter motor. This is not essential, but to do so will lighten the load to be lifted.

53 Remove the lower fixing from the engine front mountings.

54 Attach the engine lifting sling and take the weight with the hoist.

55 Support the gearbox with a suitable jack (photo).

56 Remove the fixing holding the gearbox cradle rear mountings, clear the mountings out of the way. (photo).

57 Lower the rear end of the gearbox and clear the jack.

58 Hoist the engine and gearbox clear of the car. If it is necessary to separate the engine from the gearbox refer to the next paragraph.

59 Remove the bellhousing cover plate - (see Fig. 1.7).

60 Remove the ring of nuts and bolts securing the bellhousing to the engine.

61 Using a mobile jack withdraw the gearbox away from the engine and lower to the floor.

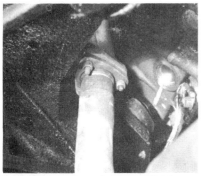
5.47a Exhaust downpipe to manifold flange

5.47b Exhaust centre mounting

5.48a Propeller shaft alignment marking

5.48b Removing propeller shaft rear flange bolts

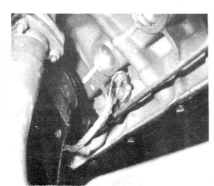
5.49 Location of engine earth strap

5.55 Gearbox support jack

5.56 Unscrewing gearbox rear mounting bolt

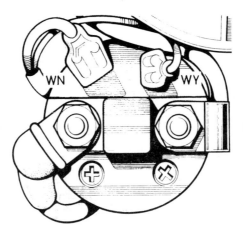
Fig. 1.6. Starter solenoid connections

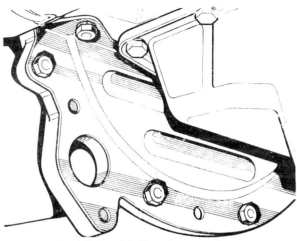

Fig. 1.7. Clutch bellhousing cover plate

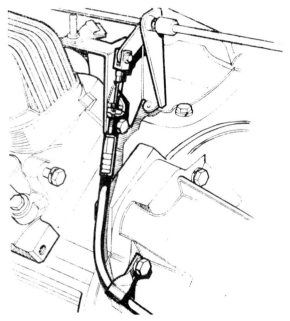

Fig. 1.8. Downshift cable connections (automatic transmission)

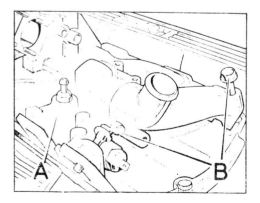

Fig. 1.9. Inlet manifold detail

A Inlet manifold
B Bolts securing manifold to cylinder head

62 On models fitted with power steering, the power steering pump must be removed and the driving belt left on the crankshaft pulley.

6 Engine removal - with automatic transmission

1 The procedure for removing an engine fitted with automatic transmission is basically identical to that for cars fitted with a manual gearbox, and will present no problems, provided that care is taken. Details of separating the automatic transmission unit from the rear of the engine will be found in Chapter 6.
2 On models fitted with automatic transmission with the fluid filler in the engine compartment, it is advised that a suitable sheet of metal be placed between the filler tube and the heater box to prevent possible damage to the heater box insulation material when lifting the engine.
3 Disconnect the speed selector linkage at the transmission housing, also the speedometer drive cable.
4 Drain the transmission fluid into a suitably large container (14 pints, 8.0 litres).

7 Ancillary engine components -removal prior to top overhaul (engine in car)

1 Drain the cooling system as outlined in Section 5.
2 Disconnect the battery at the negative terminal.
3 Remove the air cleaner - see Routine Maintenance.
4 Remove the ignition harness and clips - see Section 5.
5 Disconnect the water feed hose from the induction manifold.
6 Disconnect the throttle linkage and choke cable - see Section 5.
7 Disconnect the fuel feed pipes. Plug the pipes to prevent leakage.
8 Remove the alternator - see Section 5.
9 Remove the emission control pipes from the inlet manifold and rocker box cover - see Section 5.
10 Remove the oil level dipstick.
11 Disconnect the brake servo vacuum pipe from the manifold - see Section 5.

12 Disconnect the lead from the water temperature sender unit and mixture control switch.
13 If automatic transmission is fitted, disconnect the downshift control cable from the left-hand carburettor (Fig. 1.8).
14 Remove the six water hoses as follows:
   Radiator top hose.
   Water pump to inlet manifold.
   Pump to heater return pipe (front end).
   Heater to heater inlet pipe.
   Heater to heater return pipe.
   Pressure relief pipe radiator to inlet manifold.
15 Disconnect the advance/retard vacuum pipe from the left-hand carburettor. Also detach retaining clip on the manifold, - see Section 5.42.
16 Disconnect the engine breather from its clamp at the rear of the engine.

8 Inlet manifold - removal

1 There are twelve bolts securing the inlet manifold to the cylinder heads, these should be eased off progressively and then removed. (Fig. 1.9).
2 Note: Any bolts removed from the cylinder heads or block should have their threads cleaned with a wire brush dipped in paraffin or clean petrol.
   If this cleaning cannot be carried out immediately, it is vital that they are stored in petrol or paraffin as the sealant used when the bolts were originally fitted will tend to harden on exposure to the air making its removal difficult.
3 The third bolt from the rear of the engine retains the

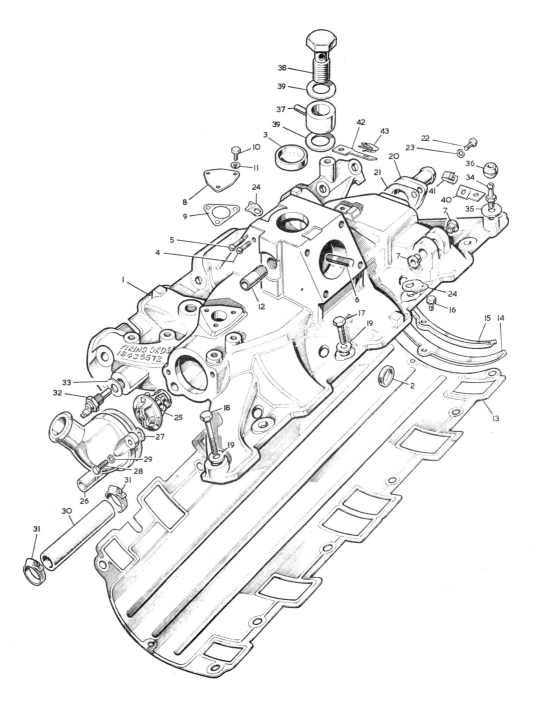

Fig. 1.10. Exploded view of the inlet manifold

1 Inlet manifold assembly	13 Gasket for inlet manifold	24 Anchor bracket for throttle return springs	33 Aluminium joint washer
2 Plug	14 Seal for gasket	25 Thermostat	34 Special stud for air cleaner fixing
3 Plug	15 Clamp	26 Water outlet elbow	35 Plain washer for special stud
4 Air bleed adaptor	16 Bolt and spring washer fixing clamp and gasket to cylinder block	27 Gasket for outlet elbow	36 Rubber grommet for stud
5 Air bleed adaptor		28 Bolt	
6 Stud	17 Bolt	29 Spring washer	37 Banjo connector
7 Bush for countershaft	18 Bolt	30 Hose for thermostat by-pass	38 Banjo bolt
8 Blanking plate	19 Plain washer		39 Joint washer
9 Joint washer for blanking plate	20 Outlet pipe for heater	31 Hose clip fixing hose to front cover and elbow	40 Bracket
10 Set screw	21 Gasket for outlet pipe		41 Clip for bracket
11 Spring washer	22 Set bolt		42 Bracket
12 Adaptor for AED delivery hose	23 Spring washer	32 Water temperature transmitter	43 Clip for bracket

brackets on to which the butterfly return springs of the carburettors are clipped. There is a bracket on each side of the engine. When reassembling, do not forget them.

4 Clear away the heater hoses and the hose from the water pump and ease the manifold away from the head.

5 On early models, there is a fibre glass insulation pad which must be lifted and discarded. DO NOT REFIT this pad but reassemble minus pad as is the case for current models.

6 Before removing the gasket clamps ensure that there is no coolant lying on top of the gasket. Remove the clamps and lift the gasket followed by the rubber gasket seals.

9 Rocker assembly - removal

1 Remove the rocker covers (four securing screws).

2 To remove the valve rocker shaft assembly: Release the four bolts that hold the rocker shaft assembly to the cylinder head. Ease them off so that the assembly rises gradually under the pressure of the valve spring. Lift the whole assembly complete with the baffle and the bolts (Fig. 1.12). **Note** If only the valve gear is to be removed, then it is advised that the pushrods are left undisturbed, to remove them may result in displacement of the hydraulic tappets.

10 Rocker shafts - dismantling

1 If dismantling of the rocker shaft assembly is intended, then it must be noted that the shafts are handed and must be correctly refitted to align the oilways.

2 Remove the split pin from one end of the rocker shaft and slide off the components carefully retaining them in the correct order of sequence for reassembly, as follows: (A) split pin; (B) plain washer; (C) wave washer; (D) rocker arm; (E) brackets; (F) springs. (Fig. 1.13).

3 If new rocker arms are being fitted ensure that the protective coating material used in storage is removed from the oil holes, and the new rocker given a smearing of clean oil before fitting to the shaft.

4 **Note:** Two different types of rocker arm are used; they **must** be fitted ensuring that the valve ends slope away from the brackets.

5 The rocker shafts are notched. This is to ensure that the oil feed holes line up correctly. The notch in each case should be uppermost. On the right-hand bank it should be located facing forwards, and on the left-hand bank it must be located to the rear of the engine. (Fig. 1.14). Use a new split pin.

11 Tappets (cam followers) and pushrods - removal and inspection

1 Withdraw the pushrods and store them in the correct sequence for reassembly. A strip of cardboard with eight holes punched to accept the rods suitably inscribed RH or LH and the holes marked 1-8, remembering that you always work from the front of the engine, numbering to the rear. Now carefully withdraw each tappet (cam follower) block in turn and examine for wear. (Fig. 1.15 and 1.16).

2 A tappet can become belled or rimmed at its lower end. In this case the tappet must be withdrawn downwards entailing the removal of the camshaft. A prominent wear pattern just above the lower end of the body need not indicate the need for renewal, unless it is decidedly grooved or scored. This condition is caused by the side thrust of the cam against the body whilst the tappet is moving vertically.

3 Retain the tappet blocks in their correct sequence of removal.

4 Examine all the surfaces of the tappet blocks for blow holes or scoring. If in doubt replace with new components.

5 Notes on tappet wear patterns (see Fig. 1.16). The tappet block **must** rotate and the circular pattern (A) is normal. If a

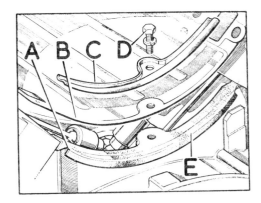

Fig. 1.11. Inlet manifold gasket detail

A Notch for locating ends of rubber seal
B Manifold gasket
C Gasket clamp
D Fixing bolt for clamp
E Rubber gasket seals

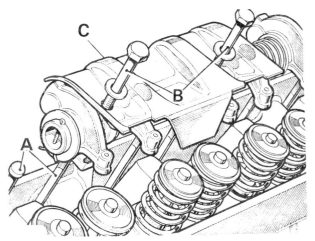

Fig. 1.12. OHV gear assembly

A Pushrods
B Rocker shaft retaining bolts
C Baffle plates

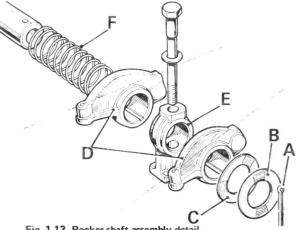

Fig. 1.13. Rocker shaft assembly detail

A Split pin
B Plain washer
C Wave washer
D Rocker arms
E Brackets
F Springs

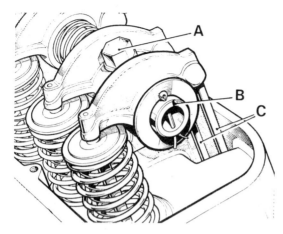

Fig. 1.14. Refitting rocker assembly

A Retaining bolt
B Notch to ensure correct alignment of oilways (Shafts are right and left-handed, care must be taken in reassembly)
C Pushrods

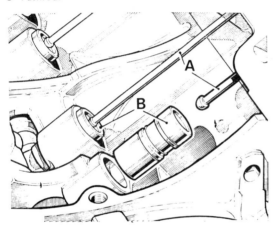

Fig. 1.15. Pushrods and hydraulic tappets

A Pushrod   B Tappet block

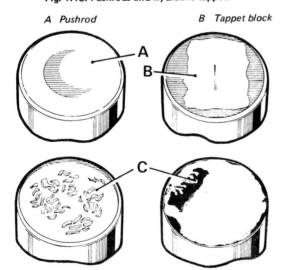

Fig. 1.16. Typical wear patterns on tappet block faces

A Normal wear, tappet rotating correctly
B Oblong pattern denoting faulty tappet rotation
C Excessive wear patterns, pitting or soft spot

tappet does not rotate then it will be shown by an oblong wear pattern (B) and it is advisable to replace with new parts.
6 In the case of any other sort of uneven wear, ie, pitting or scoring (C) being apparent, then replace with a new part.
7 Examine the area where the pushrod engages with the tappet for roughness or damage. Replace if necessary.
8 Similarly replace any pushrod so affected. Check each pushrod for straightness. A bent or distorted rod must be renewed.

12 Cylinder heads - removal

1 Proceed as previously outlined in Sections 7 to 11.
2 Disconnect the exhaust down pipe at the manifold flange (photo). Both sides.

12.2 Unscrewing exhaust downpipe flange bolt

3 Remove the engine tie-rod on the left-hand cylinder head. see Section 5.45.
4 Disconnect the fuel line filter bracket from the engine lifting hook on the left-hand cylinder head. (Fig. 1.17).

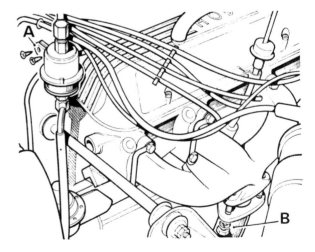

Fig. 1.17. Location of fuel line filter bracket (A) and exhaust pipe to manifold attachment (B)

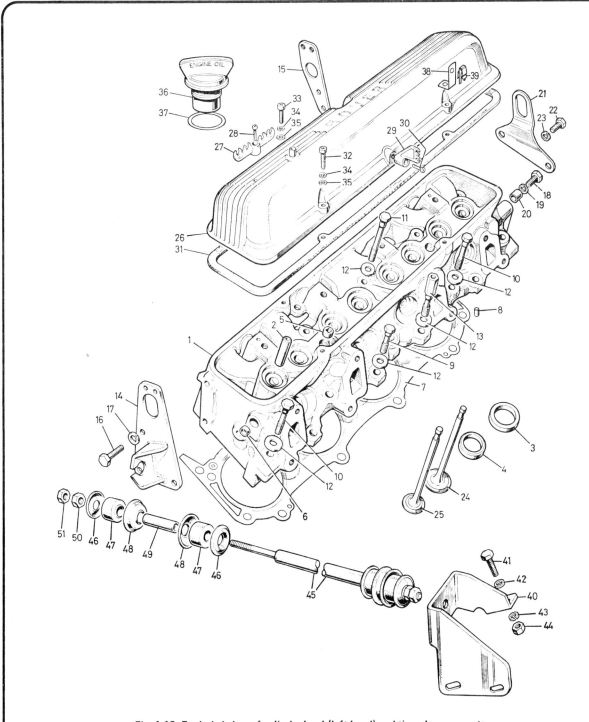

Fig. 1.18. Exploded view of cylinder head (left-hand) and tie-rod components

1	Cylinder head assembly	15	Rear lifting bracket, on RH head
2	Valve guide		
3	Valve seat insert, inlet	16	Bolt
4	Valve seat insert, exhaust	17	Spring washer
5	Core plug, threaded	18	Bolt
6	Cup plug	19	Spring washer
7	Gasket for cylinder head	20	Distance piece
8	Dowel	21	Rear lifting bracket on LH head
9	Special bolt		
10	Special bolt	22	Bolt
11	Special bolt	23	Spring washer
12	Special washer	24	Inlet valve
13	Special bolt, threaded head	25	Exhaust valve
14	Front lifting bracket on LH head	26	Rocker cover, LH
		27	Retainer for spark plug

	leads on top of rocker cover	38	Bracket on RH cylinder head for pipe clip
28	Screw fixing retainer	39	Clip for fuel spill return pipe
29	Retainer for spark plug leads on side of rocker cover, LH	40	Bracket for engine tie bar
		41	Bolt
30	Screw fixing retainer	42	Plain washer
31	Gasket	43	Spring washer
32	Screw	44	Nut
33	Screw	45	Tie bar for engine
34	Spring washer	46	Cup washer
35	Plain washer	47	Rubber bush
36	Oil filler cap for rocker cover, RH	48	Guide washer
		49	Distance piece
37	'O' ring	50	Nut
		51	Locknut

5 If both cylinder heads are being removed then they should be identity marked left or right respectively.

6 Slacken the cylinder head bolts progressively and evenly (Fig. 1.19).

7 Remember that all bolts removed from any part of the aluminium engine must be cleaned immediately.

8 Remove the cylinder heads and discard the head gaskets.

9 For easier working it may be desirable to remove the exhaust manifolds. If this is done then the manifold gaskets will have to be renewed.

10 After four repetitive cylinder head removals, then it is strongly advised that all the head bolts be replaced by new items.

11 During any servicing operations, renew any bolts that show signs of elongation.

13 Top overhaul (engine in car) - general.

1 Having removed the cylinder heads it is now assumed that a 'top overhaul' will follow.

2 For a straightforward 'decoke' (decarbonisation) which includes the regrinding of the valves, the replacement of valve springs and/or perhaps the odd suspect valve, no special tools or equipment are required, and the procedures are common knowledge to the majority of home mechanics.

3 More ambitious work to the order of replacement of the valve guides or valve seats can be tackled by the amateur possessing the necessary facilities. However, it is always found less frustrating to go to the local motor engineering works, with the cylinder heads and new valve guides. Cylinder heads of this type are expensive items easily damaged by inexperienced hands, and the comparative cost of pressing out the old guides - or valve seats and refitting the new ones, using professional equipment and know-how is worth the effort and extra outlay.

14 Valves - removal

1 Though it is recommended that the service tool spring compressor is used many standard universal valve lifting tools will do the job adequately. (Fig. 1.20 and 1.21).

2 Retain the valves in correct sequence of removal. Numbering from the front of the engine, use the same method of storing as for pushrods - see Section 11, paragraph 1.

15 Valve - servicing

1 Examine the heads of the valves for pitting and burning especially the heads of the exhaust valves. The valve seating should be examined at the same time. If the pitting on valve and seat is very slight, the marks can be removed by grinding the seats and valves together with coarse, and then fine grinding paste. Where bad pitting has occurred to the valve seats it will be necessary to recut them and fit new valves. If the valve seats are so worn that they cannot be recut then it will be necessary to fit new valve seat inserts. These latter two jobs should be entrusted to the local Rover agent. In practice it is seldom that the seats are so badly worn that they require renewal. Normally, it is the exhaust valve that is too badly worn for replacement, and the owner can easily purchase a new set of valves and match them to the seats by valve grinding.

2 Clean the valves. Remove all the hard carbon deposit from the tops and underside using a blunt knife blade. Care should be taken not to mark or score the valve seating faces. Finish off the valve cleaning with a soft wire brush, again exercising care not to touch the seat face or valve stems.

16 Cylinder heads - servicing

1 Thoroughly clean the cylinder heads using paraffin, or, a mixture of paraffin and petrol and dry off.

2 Clean the combustion chambers and ports using a brass wire brush. Draw clean rag through each valve guide bore.

3 Wash or, using a tyre pump, blow away all loose carbon particles.

17 Valves - grinding-in and refitment

1 Support the head on wooden blocks and start with No. 1 valve.

2 Smear a trace of coarse or medium carborundum paste on the seat face and apply a suction grinder tool to the valve head. With a semi-rotary motion, grind the valve head to its seat, lifting the valve occasionally to redistribute the grinding paste.

When a dull matt even surface finish is produced on both the valve seat and the valve, then wipe off the paste and repeat the process with fine carborundum paste, lifting and turning the valve to redistribute the paste as before. A light spring placed under the valve head will greatly ease this operation. When a smooth unbroken ring of light grey matt finish is produced, on both valve and valve seat faces, the grinding operation is completed.

Scrape away all carbon from the valve head and the valve stem. Carefully clean away every trace of grinding compound, taking great care to leave none in the ports or in the valve guides. Clean the valves and valve seats with a paraffin soaked rag then with a clean rag. If an air line is available, blow the valves, valve guides and valve parts clean.

3 Finally give the cylinder head a rinse in clean paraffin to remove any remaining traces of valve grinding paste. Discard this paraffin, dry the head with a clean non-fluffy rag.

4 Draw clean rag through each guide bore.

5 Refit the valves into their correct positions, oiling the stems as each valve is replaced in its respective guide.

6 Refit the valve springs; compress them, and secure the collets.

7 When all the valves and springs have been replaced, place the head face down on the bench and give each valve stem end a light tap with the butt end of a hammer handle or with a plastic headed mallet to ensure that the collets are well seated into their respective caps.

18 Cylinder heads - additional servicing hints

1 Take special care to protect the gasket faces from scoring or scratching, so after cleaning, work with the head placed on a clear bench with several layers of newspaper beneath it. Remove the top sheet as it gets dirty.

2 Destroy any rags that have been used to clean off carborundum grinding paste.

3 Have plenty of clean rag available. Do not attempt to grind-in any valves that are worn and possess sharp edges; instead, scrap and replace. It is advisable to have at least one or two spare (new or serviceable) exhaust and inlet valves to hand just in case.

4 Do not attempt work for which you do not possess adequate tools or equipment.

5 If the car has completed more than 30,000 miles (48,000 km) fit new valve springs.

6 Obtain all the aids and spares required for the job before starting. Do not try to 'make-do', especially with gaskets, seals and washers.

19 Timing cover chain and gears - removal

1 Set the engine so that no. 1 piston (one nearest radiator on left-hand bank) is at TDC (on firing stroke). This may be observed by removing the spark plug and feeling the compression being generated as the piston travels up the cylinder bore or by removing the rocker cover and checking that the valves for no. 1 cylinder are closed and in balance.

2 Disconnect the battery at the negative terminal. (Section 5.1).

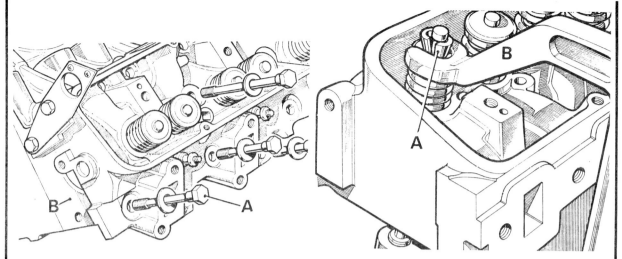

Fig. 1.19. Cylinder head bolt (A) and cylinder head (B)

Fig. 1.20. Compressing a valve spring (A) split collets

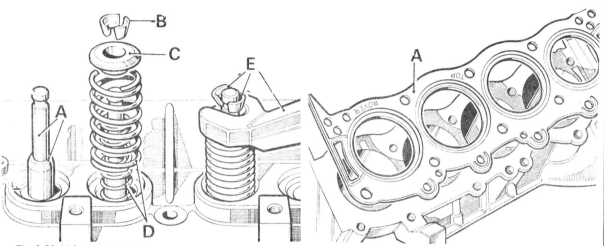

Fig. 1.21. Valve components

A   Valve stem and guide
B   Split collets
C   Cap

D   Inner and outer valve
    springs
E   Collets released by
    action of compressor

Fig. 1.22. Correct fitting of cylinder head gasket (A)

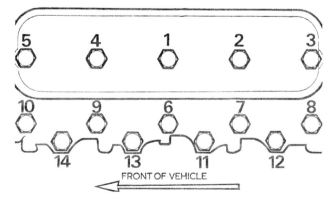

FRONT OF VEHICLE

Fig. 1.23. Cylinder head bolt tightening sequence diagram

3 Drain off the cooling system. (Section 5.5 and 5.6).
4 Remove the fan blades. (Section 5.27).
5 Remove the fan blade pulley wheel. (Fig. 1.24).
6 Release the alternator adjustment strap from the water
pump. (Section 5.25).
7 Remove the bypass hose from the thermostat housing.
8 Disconnect the heater hose from the water pump.
9 Disconnect the water pump inlet hose.
10 Remove the vacuum advance/retard pipe from the distributor.
11 Unclip the HT leads and remove the distributor cap; tying it
to one side.
12 Unclip the low tension lead from the coil, also the oil pressure
switch and oil pressure transmitter leads.
13 Release the nut and bolt retaining the fuel filter clip to the
engine lifting bracket.
14 If an AC mechanical fuel pump is fitted, remove the attaching bolts and move the pump to one side. Do not remove the
fuel lines.
15 Remove the crankshaft main pulley. (Fig. 1.25).
16 Make a mark on the distributor body to coincide with a
centre line drawn along the rotor arm (A), (Fig. 1.26).
17 If it is intended to remove the distributor body, then similar
realignment marks must be made on the body and the timing
cover (B).
18 Withdraw the timing cover bolts (including the ones attaching
to the sump). (Fig. 1.27).
19 Remove the timing cover complete.
20 All bolts removed must be cleaned immediately as described
in Section 8 paragraph 2 of this Chapter.
21 Now recheck that the engine has remained at TDC; if not,
then reposition it.
22 Slide off the oil thrower. (Fig. 1.28).
23 Remove the centre bolt retaining the distributor skew gear
and remove the gear.
24 If the car is fitted with an AC mechanical pump, withdraw
the pump operating cam.
25 The chain wheels complete with the chain can now be slid
away from their respective shafts. (Fig. 1.29).
26 If the rocker shafts are to remain in position do **not** on any
account rotate the engine, otherwise damage will be caused to
the valves and pistons.

Fig. 1.24. Cooling fan and pulley

20 Timing cover oil seals - renewal

1 Renew **both** the oil seal **and** the oil thrower.
2 Fit the new oil seal into the new thrower. (Fig. 1.31).
3 Insert the complete assembly into the recess in the front
cover ensuring that the butt ends of the seal are topmost. Stake
the oil thrower at equidistant points.
4 Rotate a hammer handle or similar rounded tool around the
face of the seal, pressing it into position until the crankshaft
pulley can be inserted.

21 Timing chain and gears - refitment

1 Assuming that care has been taken and that neither the
camshaft or crankshaft have been disturbed, proceed as follows.
2 Line up the timing marks on the timing wheels and carefully
wrap the chain around both wheels keeping the timing marks
aligned (Fig. 1.32). Note: camshaft wheel marking 'front' faces.
3 Carefully pick up the whole assembly and offer it up to the
shafts until you can just engage the keys into their respective
locations.
4 Recheck that the timing marks are still in line.
5 If all is well, push the timing wheels fully 'home'.
6 Refit the fuel pump cam ensuring that the marking 'F' is
facing outwards.
7 Refit the distributor drive skew gear and secure with the
correct washer and bolt. Tighten to a torque figure of 40 to 45
lb ft. (5.5 to 6.2 kg m),

Fig. 1.25. Crankshaft pulley (torsional vibration damper)

Fig. 1.26. Alignment marks made prior to distributor removal

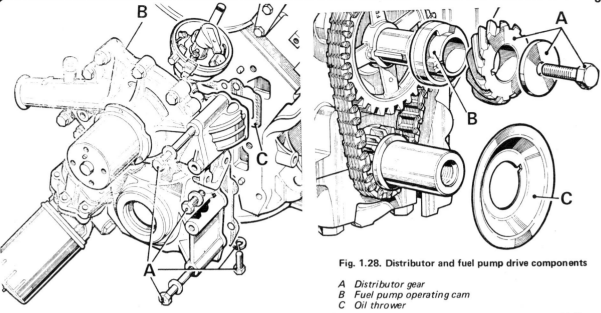

Fig. 1.28. Distributor and fuel pump drive components

A   Distributor gear
B   Fuel pump operating cam
C   Oil thrower

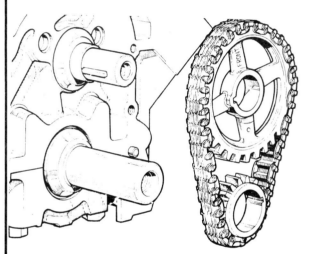

Fig. 1.27. Timing cover (B) securing bolts (A) gasket (C)

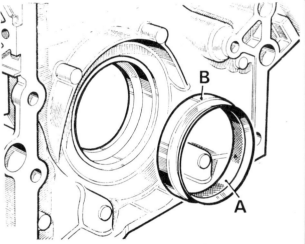

Fig. 1.30. Timing cover oil seal (A) and oil thrower ring (B)

Fig. 1.29. Timing chain and sprockets ready for fitting

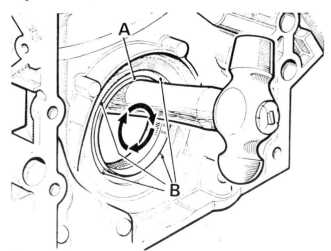

Fig. 1.31. Method of locating timing cover oil seal (A)
equidistant staking points (B)

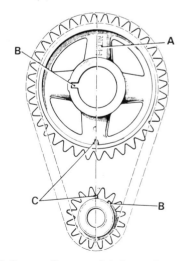

Fig. 1.32. Correct alignment of timing marks and keyways

A   'Front' marking   C   Alignment marks
B   Keyways

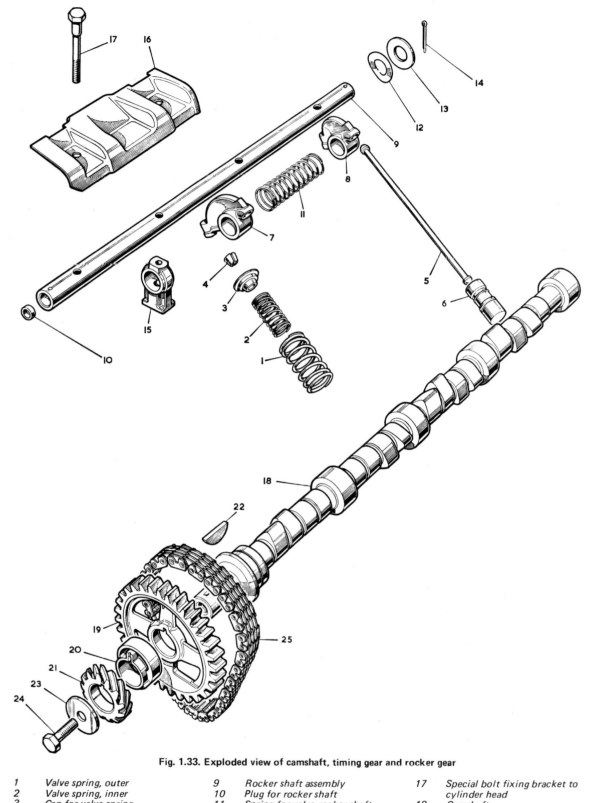

Fig. 1.33. Exploded view of camshaft, timing gear and rocker gear

1	Valve spring, outer	9	Rocker shaft assembly	17	Special bolt fixing bracket to
2	Valve spring, inner	10	Plug for rocker shaft		cylinder head
3	Cap for valve spring	11	Spring for valve rocker shaft	18	Camshaft
4	Valve cotter, half	12	Waved washer, rocker shaft end	19	Chainwheel for camshaft
5	Push rod	13	Washer	20	Cam, fuel pump drive
6	Hydraulic tappet	14	Split pin	21	Gear, distributor drive
7	Valve rocker, RH	15	Bracket for rocker shaft	22	Key
8	Valve rocker, LH	16	Oil baffle for rocker arm	23	Washer
				24	Special bolt
				25	Timing chain

8 Reposition the oil thrower with its concave side outwards and facing forwards.

22 Timing cover - refitment

1 Locate a new timing cover joint gasket and seal in position.
2 Inject engine oil through the suction port of the oil pump to prime the pump.
3 Reset the distributor rotor arm to a new position approximately 30° in advance of the final positioning mark (This will compensate for the movement that will take place as the distributor engages the skew gear on replacement).
4 Offer up the timing cover and locate in position on the crankcase.
5 Make sure that the alignment markings previously placed on the distributor, line up correctly.
6 The threads of the fixing bolts should be cleaned already. Coat these with Thread Lubricant Sealant 3M EC776, (Rover Part no. 605764).
7 Locate and screw in all the timing cover fixing bolts and tighten to a torque of between 20 to 25lb ft (2.8 to 3.5 kg m).
8 Refit the crankshaft pulley and tighten to a torque figure of between 140 to 160 lb ft (19.3 to 22.3 kg m).

23 Timing chain assembly - refitment (after disturbance)

1 Dismantle the engine top end to remove the rocker shaft assemblies. (Detailed in Section 9).
2 Set the engine, so that No. 1 piston is at TDC on the compression stroke.
3 Using the camshaft chain wheel as a temporary tool to rotate the camshaft, **fit it with the word 'front' outwards.**
4 Slowly turn the camshaft until the timing mark is exactly at six o'clock.
5 Now the timing wheel can be removed and reassembled with the chain and crankshaft timing wheel as previously detailed in Section 21.2.
6 Proceed from Section 21, paragraph 2.

24 Timing chain and gears (automatic transmission) - removal

1 The procedures are the same as for manual gearbox cars. However, to facilitate the removal of the crankshaft pulley fixings, it is possible to lock the engine by placing a suitable bar between the lower engine face and a convenient bolt head within the bellhousing, accessible by removing the bellhousing cover plate. **Do not** use the starter ring gear teeth for this purpose.

25 Camshaft - removal

1 Disconnect the battery at the **negative** terminal.
2 Drain the cooling system (Section 5.5 and 5.6).
3 Remove the radiator from the car. (Section 5.22).
4 Remove the radiator grille **early models** as described in the following paragraphs 5 to 8.
5 Release the Rover badge from the centre of the grille by tapping the knurled studs from behind. (Fig. 1.34).
6 Remove the plastic caps over the screw heads at the extreme ends of the grille by prising them off. Then remove the screws.
7 The grille is formed in two sections. Remove the sections.
8 Now remove the badge securing bracket.
9 Remove the radiator grille **late models** as described in the following paragraphs 10 to 12 (Fig. 1.35).
10 The assembly is held by self-tapping screws set into the headlamp bezels. The screws are concealed by plastic covers.
11 Remove these covers and the screws.
12 The sections of the grille can now be removed.
13 Remove the alternator (See Section 5.26).
14 Take off the air cleaner (See Routine Maintenance).

15 Remove the induction manifold. (See Section 8).
16 Remove the valve gear. (See Section 9).
17 Remove the timing chain cover. (See Sections 19.18 and 19.19).
18 Now remove the timing chain and gears. (See Section 19).
19 The camshaft can now be withdrawn.
20 Exercise extreme care when withdrawing the camshaft as any damage caused to the bearings cannot be rectified by servicing in situ.

26 Camshaft - inspection

1 Thoroughly clean the camshaft and dry off, handling with care.
2 Examine all the bearing surfaces for obvious defects, wear, score marks etc.
3 Similarly inspect the cam lobes for excessive wear.
4 Ensure that the key or keyway is not damaged or burred and that the key is a tight fit in its keyway.
5 If in doubt seek professional advice and/or replace with a new component.

27 Camshaft - refitment

1 Reverse the order of dismantling.
2 Extreme care should be taken when inserting the camshaft into the bearings for the reasons given in Section 25.20)

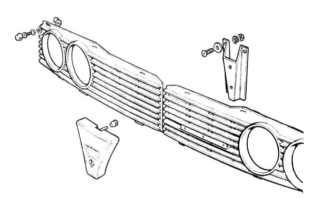

Fig. 1.34. Grille and badge attachment (early models)

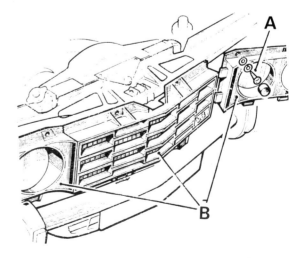

Fig. 1.35. Grille attachment (later models)

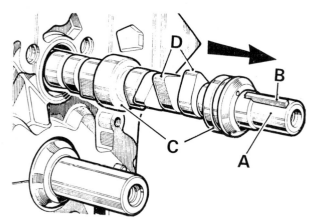

Fig. 1.36. Camshaft detail

A Camshaft   C Bearing surfaces
B Woodruff key   D Cam lobes

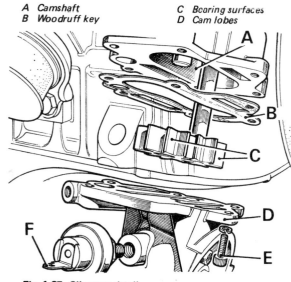

Fig. 1.37. Oil pump detail

A Pump housing   D Pump cover plate
B Gasket   E Special fixing screws
C ump gears   F Oil pressure switch

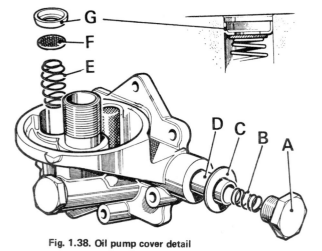

Fig. 1.38. Oil pump cover detail

A Relief valve plug   E By-pass valve spring
B Relief valve spring   F By-pass valve
C Sealing washer   G Valve seat
D Relief valve

28 Oil pump - removal

1 Unscrew the external oil filter. If it is intended to refit the same filter, do not allow it to drain.
2 Disconnect the electrical connector from the pressure switch.
3 Release the special bolts securing the pump cover. Place an oil tray underneath. Remove the bolts and cover.
4 Remove and discard the old cover gasket.
5 Slide out the pump gears. (See Fig. 1.37).

29 Oil pump - refitment

1 Use a new gasket, placing it on the pump cover.
2 Pack the pump housing with petroleum jelly (no other type of grease will do).
3 Locate the pump gears into their correct positions ensuring that the petroleum jelly is filling every visible cavity. If the pump is not completely packed with jelly then the pump may not prime itself when the engine is restarted.
4 Offer up the pump cover to the body and locate it in position. Have the special fixing bolts handy, refit them and finger tighten.
5 Finally tighten up all the securing bolts evenly, working in alternate sequence to a final torque figure of between 10 and 15 lb ft (1.4 to 2.0 kg m).
6 Replace the external oil filter and reconnect the pressure switch lead.

30 Oil pump - inspection and overhaul

If the car has covered a high mileage then be prepared to renew all the working parts contained in the oil pump.
1 First clean all the components as they are dismantled.
2 Visually check the gears for obvious scoring or chipping of the teeth. Renew if they are in poor condition.
3 Now work on the components contained within the cover.
4 Dismantle the pressure relief valve and inspect it for excessive wear and/or scoring, (Fig. 1.38).
5 Pay special attention to the relief valve pressure spring. Note whether it shows signs of wear on its sides or whether it is on the point of collapse, if not collapsed.
6 Thoroughly clean the gauze filter housed within the relief valve bore. (Fig. 1.38).
7 Test the valve in its bore in the cover; it should have no more clearance than to make it an easy sliding fit. If any side movement is obviously apparent, then the valve and/or the cover will have to be renewed.
8 If it is intended or necessary to remove the oil filter bypass valve, then prise the valve seat out using extreme care. Remove the valve and return spring.
9 Inspect the filter bypass valve for cracks chipping or warping. It should appear absolutely flat, clean and unmarked.
10 Wash the stripped casting in clean paraffin or petrol. Dry with a clean rag. Smear parts with clean engine oil before reassembly.
11 With the gears replaced in the pump housing, check the pump gear end float, (Fig. 1.40). Lay a straight edge across the two gear wheels and with a feeler gauge, measure the clearance between the straight edge and the surface of the front cover. The clearance should be between 0.0018 in. and 0.0058 in. (0.05 mm to 0.15 mm). If the measurement shows less than .0018 in. (0.05 mm) then inspect the front cover recess for signs of wear.

31 Oil pump - reassembly after overhaul

1 Use clean engine oil to lubricate the oil pressure relief valve. Fit the valve into its bore.
2 Fit the relief valve spring.
3 Fit the sealing washer to the relief valve plug, and locate and

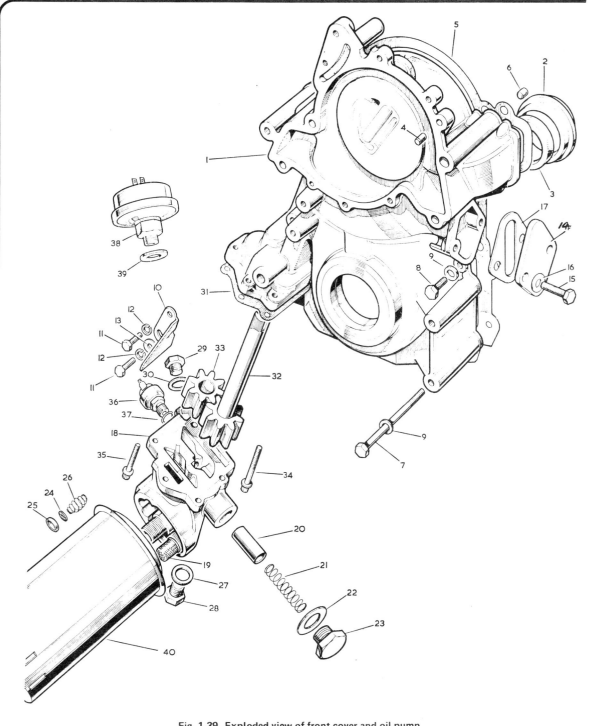

Fig. 1.39. Exploded view of front cover and oil pump

1	Front cover assembly	14	Blanking plate for front cover	27	Joint washer for blanking plug
2	Oil thrower	15	Bolt	28	Blanking plug
3	Packing for crankshaft	16	Plain washer	29	Blanking plug
4	Dowel locating water pump	17	Joint washer for blanking plate	30	Joint washer for blanking plug
5	Gasket for front cover	18	Oil pump cover	31	Gasket for oil pump cover
6	Dowel	19	Oil strainer	32	Oil pump shaft and gear
7	Bolt	20	Oil pressure relief valve	33	Oil pump idler gear
8	Bolt	21	Spring for relief valve	34	Bolt
9	Plain washer	22	Joint washer for relief valve cap	35	Bolt
10	Timing pointer	23	Cap for relief valve	36	Oil pressure switch
11	Bolt	24	Valve, oil filter by-pass	37	Joint washer for switch
12	Spring washer	25	Seat for by-pass valve	38	Oil pressure transmitter
13	Plain washer	26	Spring, oil filter by-pass	39	Washer for oil pressure transmitter
				40	Oil filter

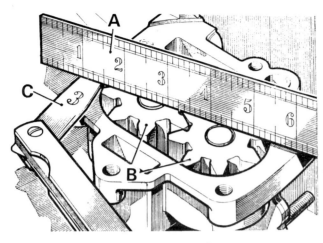

Fig. 1.40. Checking oil pump gears for wear

A Straight edge   C Feeler gauge
B Pump gears

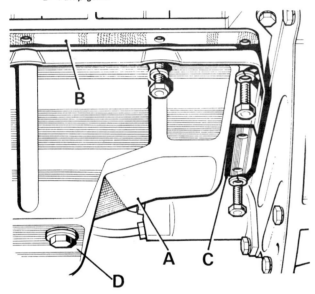

Fig. 1.41. Engine oil sump removal

A Sump   C Reinforcing strip
B Sump gasket   D Sump drain plug

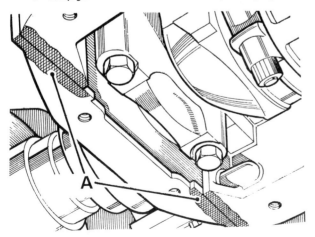

Fig. 1.42. Jointing compound application points (A)

screw up the plug. Tighten to a torque of between 30 to 35 lb ft (4.0 to 4.9 kg m).
4 Insert the bypass valve spring into the bore.
5 Place the flat valve on top of the spring, followed by the bypass valve seat - concave side outwards.
6 Press the whole assembly down to locate the valve seat into the body.
7 Press 'home' until the valve seat outer rim is approximately 0.020 to 0.040 in (0.5 to 1.00 mm) below the top edge of the main body.

32 Sump - removal

1 Drain the engine oil
2 After the oil has completely drained, refit the drain plug.
3 Slacken all securing bolts so that they are removable by hand. **Note** On automatics remove the torque converter cover plate to gain access to the rear sump fixing bolts.
4 Remove the bolts with the exception of the two remaining at diagonal corners. If the sump is stuck to its gasket remove all bolts. (Fig. 1.41).
5 It may be necessary to give the sump a few gentle taps with a mallet to free it from its gasket. **Never try prising it off** by inserting a blade or chisel between the faces, damage will most certainly result.
6 Clean all the fixing bolts in paraffin bath.
7 **Note:** On automatic models there are two retaining clips for the oil cooler pipes on the right-hand side of sump.

33 Sump - overhaul

1 Thoroughly clean off the exterior removing all traces of encrusted road dirt.
2 Wash the sump interior with paraffin brushing out any sludge which may be there.
3 With the sump now perfectly clean, carefully scrape off the remains of the sump gasket.
4 Similarly clean up the mating surface of the crankcase, paying particular attention to the joints between the timing cover and the cylinder block. (Fig. 1.42).

34 Sump - refitment

1 Use a new gasket.
2 Apply a coating of Hylomar or similar gasket cement to the faces of the timing cover to crankcase joint. (Fig. 1.42).
3 Locate the sump gasket in position on the crankcase.
4 Offer up the sump, having the fixing bolts and spring washers to-hand. Fit the bolts and tighten, working diagonally and evenly. The reinforcing strip goes under the rear fixings.
5 Refill the sump in the normal manner.
6 Allow time for the oil to drain through the engine into the sump and take reading from the oil level dipstick. **Do not overfill**
7 Run the engine and check for leaks; recheck that you have in fact tightened the drain plug.

35 Connecting rods and pistons - removal

1 Strip the engine as for top overhaul. Sections 7, 8, 9, 11 and 12.
2 The pistons complete with their connecting rods are pushed out, through the tops of the cylinder bores.
3 If working on an automatic model, remove the torque converter cover plate. This gives access to the sump rear fixings and will also enable the engine to be turned over using the drive plate as a crank.
4 Remove the engine oil sump. See Section 32.
5 Remove the baffle plate (six bolts). Have an oil drain pan

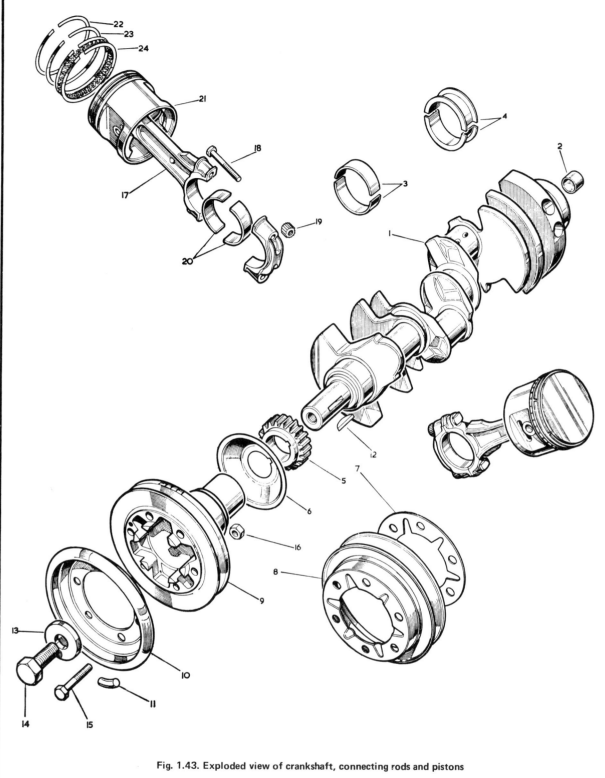

Fig. 1.43. Exploded view of crankshaft, connecting rods and pistons

1	Crankshaft assembly	9	Vibration damper and pulley	17	Connecting rod assembly
2	Bush for crankshaft	10	Balancing rim	18	Special bolt
3	Main bearing	11	Balance weight	19	Self-locking nut
4	Main bearing, flanged	12	Key	20	Connecting rod bearing, std.
5	Chainwheel on crankshaft	13	Plain washer	21	Piston assembly
6	Oil thrower on crankshaft	14	Special bolt	22	Piston ring, compression, upper
7	Reinforcing plate	15	Bolt	23	Piston ring, compression, lower
8	Pulley driving power steering pump	16	Nut	24	Piston ring, scraper

handy as the baffle will retain a quantity of engine oil.

6 Remove the sump oil strainer. (Fig. 1.44).

7 Rotate the crankshaft to gain easy access to the connecting rod (big-end) cap fixing nuts.

8 Detach the cap (big-end) from each of the connecting rods. Push the connecting rod piston partially down the bore to clear the crankshaft; then, remove the bearing shells from the caps and connectiong rods. Push the connecting rod/piston out of each bore. Ensure that the caps are returned to, and kept with the connecting rods from which they came. (Fig. 1.46).

9 Retain connecting rods, pistons, and bearing caps in their correct order of removal.

36 Pistons and connecting rods - overhaul

1 The condition of the pistons, rings, and the big end bearings and small end bushes will be governed by many factors, but principally:

a) The total mileage covered by the car.

b) The maintenance of oil level and regular oil and filter changes and usage to which the car has been subjected.

2 The home mechanic is advised that to assess the true condition of these components, he must be in possession of, or have access to, certain professional equipment and tools. For instance, the gudgeon pin has to be removed by means of an hydraulic press or ram that will exert a pressure of not less than 8 tons (8128 kg); a micrometer especially constructed for measurement of cylinder bore wear and ovality; a normal micrometer capable of encircling a piston to assess the degree of piston wear.

3 It should be noted that there are two types of piston fitted to 3500 engines. (See Fig. 1.47). The two designs though different, are not obviously so. The differences are in the relative weights which are compensated for by two different standards of crankshaft balance.

Design "A" pistons must be fitted to a crankshaft that possesses a plain face at the starter dog end, whilst design "B" pistons are always fitted to a crankshaft that has an identification groove "C" in the face of the starter dog end. If one design is to be exchanged for the other, then they must be changed as a complete set with their matching crankshaft.

4 Standard original pistons are graded in respect of diameter and the grading letter stamped on the crown, identifying with a corresponding grading letter stamped on the cylinder block. **Note: Oversize pistons are not graded in this way.**

5 Standard piston grading:

Grade letters

z Nominal bore wear to plus .0003 in (0.0075 mm).

a 0.0003 in (0.0075 mm) to 0.0006 in (0.015 mm) above nominal.

b 0.0006 in (0.015 mm) to 0.0009 in (0.0225 mm) above nominal.

c 0.0009 in (0.0225 mm) to 0.0012 in (0.03 mm) above nominal.

d 0.0012 in (0.03 mm) to 0.0015 in (0.0375 mm) above nominal.

6 If any one piston has to be renewed then the degree of bore wear must be calculated and the new piston grade selected within these limits.

7 Where the same pistons are to be refitted, then they must be marked to correspond with their respective connecting rods, and cylinder bore positions.

8 If new rings are to be fitted, this can be achieved without removing the pistons from their connecting rods.

9 Carefully remove the piston rings and retain in sequence.

10 Clean all the carbon deposits from the piston head, and clean out the ring grooves and remove any gummy deposits that have accumulated, using a suitable solvent.

11 Examine the piston carefully for any scoring of the bearing surfaces, cracking or chipping particularly at the skirt. Examine the crown for dents or marks caused by foreign objects in the combustion chamber or broken rings, plug electrodes etc. Rings that have been broken in the bore during running will have caused damage to the grooves in the piston making the rings sloppy through having excessive clearance in the grooves. Damaged or faulty pistons of this nature should be renewed. It is also possible that broken rings will have scratched the cylinder wall - in bad cases this will necessitate a rebore.

12 Remember that standard pistons are graded in sizes as previously listed in paragraph 5 of this section.

13 If the engine has been rebored then oversize pistons of .010 in (0.25 mm) and .020 in (0.50 mm) are available. **Oversize pistons are not graded.**

37 Fitting new piston rings

1 When fitting new rings it is advisable to remove the glaze from the cylinder bores. It is strongly advised that the 'deglazed' bore should have a cross hatch finish (diamond pattern) and should be carried out in such a way as not to increase the bore size in any way. This cross hatch finish provides the cylinder walls with good oil retention properties.

2 The top compression ring is surfaced with chrome material and **must** be fitted in the top groove. There are two compression rings, and it is only these two, that will need accurate gapping. Both are marked with the letter "T" (top) to indicate which side faces the piston crown.

3 The special oil control ring needs no gapping, but care must be taken to ensure that the ends of the expander, (fitted first), do not overlap but just abut each other. Fit the rails, one at a time, making sure that they locate snugly within the piston groove.

4 Fit the rings by holding them open, using both hands, thumbs at the gaps with fingers around the outer edges, easing them open enough to slip over the piston top and straight to the groove in which they belong. Use feeler gauges or strips of tin as guides to prevent the rings dropping in to the wrong groove. Do not twist the rings whilst doing this or they will snap.

5 Before fitting however, a word on gapping. Push a compression ring down the cylinder bore using a piston to position it squarely at about 1 in (25 mm) below the top of the block and measure the piston ring gap with a feeler gauge. (Fig. 1.48). The gap should be between 0.017 in and 0.022 in (0.44 and 0.57 mm). If required, file the gap using a flat 'fine cut' file. Exercise care and judgement not to overdo it. Refit the ring, square off with the piston as before and re-measure. Repeat the process until correct.

6 Once the rings have been fitted to the piston, then the vertical clearance in the groove should be checked. This will be in the region of between 0.003 and 0.005 in (0.08 to 0.13 mm). (Fig. 1.49).

7 Fit the compression rings so that the gaps in each ring are diametrically opposite, and the oil control ring so that its gaps appear on same side between gudgeon pin and the piston thrust face but staggered. Locate the rail ring gaps approximately 1 in (25 mm) either side of the expander join. (Fig. 1.51). This will ensure good compression.

38 Pistons and connecting rods - refitment

1 Make sure that all parts are scrupulously clean and smeared with clean engine oil.

2 Fit the ring compression tool, adjusting the compression rings so that their gaps are positioned as described in the preceding Section.

3 Ensure that the connecting rod/piston assembly enters the bore facing the correct way round. The identifying boss (see Fig. 1.52) must face forwards on the right-hand cylinder bank, and to the rear on the left-hand bank. This means that on each crankshaft journal the two projections or bosses on the connecting rods will face each other.

4 Rotate the crankshaft until the journal being fitted is at BDC.

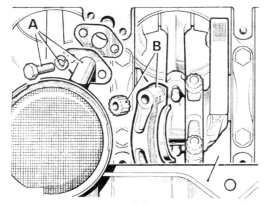

Fig. 1.44. Sump oil strainer (A) big end bearing detail (B)

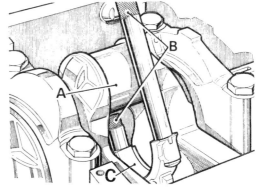

Fig. 1.45. Fitting connecting rod to crankshaft

A Crankshaft journal   C Connecting rod bearing
B Special guide bolts

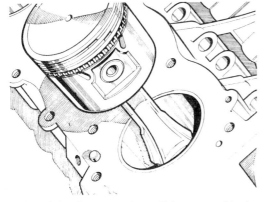

Fig. 1.46. Withdrawing connecting rod/piston assembly through top of block

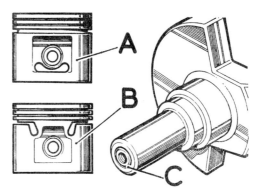

Fig. 1.47, Differing piston types (A and B) (C) crankshaft identification

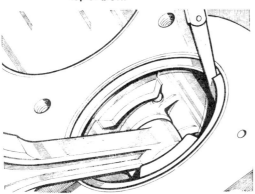

Fig. 1.48. Gapping the piston rings, using feeler gauge

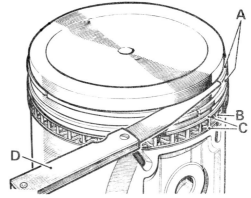

Fig. 1.49. Checking the ring clearance in groove

A Compression rings   C Ring rails of oil control
B Expander (oil control ring)   ring
                         D Feeler gauge

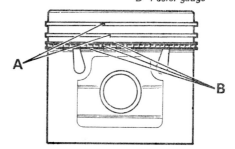

Fig. 1.51. Correct location of piston ring gaps

A Compression ring gaps on opposite sides of piston
B Oil control ring gaps staggered on same side of piston

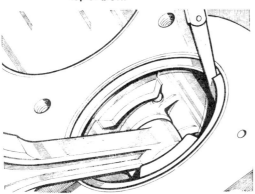

Fig. 1.50. Illustrating application of the ring compressor

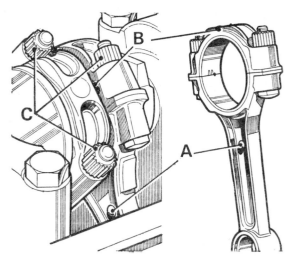

Fig. 1.52. Connecting rod and big-end bearing, identification for correct reassembly

A Boss on web   C Big-end bearing securing
B Identity rib on bearing cap   nuts

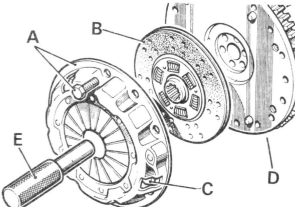

Fig. 1.53. Clutch components

A Cover and bolts   D Flywheel
B Driven plate   E Aligning tool for
C Recessed bolts (don't   refitting (see
   remove)   Chapter 5)

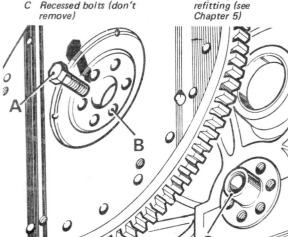

Fig. 1.54. Flywheel dismantled

A Fixing bolts   C Crankshaft flange and
B Offset hole   spigot bearing

5 Liberally lubricate the cylinder walls and big-end journals and bearings with clean engine oil.

6 Insert the pistons and connecting rods with the ring compressor attached. Use a hammer handle to gently drive the assembly into the bore.

7 Lubricate the bearing shells in both the connecting rods and caps using clean engine oil. Locate the big-end bearing on to its crankshaft journal.

8 Fit the bearing shells and caps. (**Note:** Details of inspection and renewal of bearing will be found in Sections 44 and 45). The identifying rib on the bearing cap must face the same way as the boss on the web of the connecting rod. (See Fig. 1.52).

9 Tighten the bearing cap retaining nuts evenly to a torque of between 30 and 35 lb ft (4.0 to 4.9 kg m).

39 Crankshaft - reasons and preparation for removal

1 Work on the crankshaft is not normally practicable with the engine in the car.

2 The need for removal of the crankshaft from the engine could be due to:

a) High mileage and the engine is to be completely renovated.

b) Obvious knocking noises emitted from the crankcase or sump region, indicating either a big-end failure or in the case of a knocking accompanied by rumbling noises, a failed main bearing.

3 Removal of the engine has already been covered in Sections 4, 5 and 6 of this Chapter.

4 With the engine out of the car and preferably resting on a suitable engine stand proceed as for top overhaul. (Sections 7, 8, 9, 10 and 12 of this Chapter).

5 Drain the oil from the engine sump; remove the sump, the baffle and the sump oil strainer. (See Section 32 of this Chapter).

6 Turn the engine over and remove the pistons and connecting rods. (See Section 35 of this Chapter).

7 Keep all bearings, connecting rods and pistons in correct order of removal and subsequent replacement.

8 Remove the timing gear chain and wheels, but not the camshaft. See Section 19 (or Section 24 automatic transmission).

9 Remove the clutch assembly (See Section 40).

10 Remove the flywheel (See Section 41).

11 The crankshaft will then be ready for removal. (See Section 42).

40 Clutch - removal and refitment

1 With the engine out of the car this operation is comparatively simple. It can be achieved with the engine in-situ after removing the gearbox (see Chapter 6).

2 Mark the clutch cover in relation to its position on the flywheel. (Fig. 1.53).

3 First progressively slacken the ring of bolts securing the clutch cover to the flywheel and remove them and the clutch assembly.

Warning Do not remove the three bolts located in the recesses of the clutch cover.

4 Slide out the driven plate which is sandwiched between the pressure plate and the flywheel.

5 When refitting, centralise the driven plate (Chapter 6) and align the pressure plate with the marks previously made on the cover and flywheel.

41 Flywheel - removal and refitment

1 There are six bolts securing the flywheel (or drive plate - automatic transmission) to the crankshaft flange. Slacken and remove these bolts - the flywheel can then be removed.

2 When refitting, it will be noticed that the securing bolt

positions are offset, so that incorrect fitting is impossible.

3 When refitting these bolts, fit all the bolts before final tightening. Rotate the flywheel or drive plate against the direction of engine rotation and against the leverage of the spanner used. Finally tightening to torque figure of between 50 and 60 lb ft (7.0 and 8.5 kg m).

42 Crankshaft - removal

1 With the engine stripped and out of the car as outlined in the foregoing sections, remove all the main bearing cap bolts, bearing caps and shells - retaining them in the correct sequence for refitting.

2 Carefully lift out the crankshaft.

43 Crankshaft - inspection

1 With the crankshaft suitably mounted on V blocks at No 1 and 5 journals, give a thorough visual check for scoring of, or white metal sticking to, the journals. Heavy scoring indicates that the crankshaft should be reground.

2 Check for straightness using a dial test indicator (Fig. 1.55) as follows:

a) The run out at main journals 2, 3 and 4.

b) Note the relative eccentricity of each journal to the others.

c) The maximum indication should come at nearly the same angular location on all journals.

3 With an engineer's micrometer check each journal for ovality. If this proves to be more than 0.0015 in (0.04 mm), the crankshaft must be reground.

44 Crankshaft bearings - general information and checking clearances

Crankshaft bearings (big-end and main) should only be used if they are known to have done a very low mileage only (less than 15,000 miles). As replacement bearings are relatively cheap it is false economy to replace the old ones. Where the condition of the bearings and journals was so bad that the crankshaft has to be reground, new bearings of the correct undersize will be provided by the firm which carried out the regrinding.

If replacement bearings of 'standard' size are being fitted, or

if for some reason you do not know which undersize bearings should be used - the following paragraphs detail a method of establishing bearing clearance, and therefore correct bearing size.

1 Use Plastigauge to measure the bearing clearances.

2 Before using Plastigauge all the parts to be measured must be clean, dry and free from oil.

3 With a piece of the Plastigauge laid on the top of each main bearing journal, (Fig. 1.56) refit the bearing caps as though reassembling.

4 The rear main bearing oil seals should not be fitted during this operation.

5 Tighten all bolts to correct torque (rear main bearing 65 to 70 lb ft (9.0 to 9.6 kg m).

Other main bearing cap bolts 50 to 55 lb ft (7.0 to 7.6 kg m).

6 Remove the main bearing caps - the Plastigauge will be found sticking to either the journal or the shell face: **Do not remove it.**

7 With the scale provided, measure the compressed piece of Plastigauge on each bearing at its widest point.

8 The graduation number that most closely corresponds to this width indicates the bearing clearance in thousandths of an inch.

9 The specified clearance of a new main bearing is 0.0009 in (0.023 mm) to 0.0025 in (0.065 mm).

A reading of between 0.001 in (0.025 mm) and 0.0025 in (0.065 mm) is acceptable.

10 **DO NOT** rotate the crankshaft whilst Plastigauge is in position.

11 The same procedures are adopted for checking the connecting rod big-end bearing clearances but tighten the bolts to between 30 and 35 lb ft (4.0 and 4.9 kg m).

12 Crankshaft bearings for the main journals and the connecting rod journals (big-ends) are available in the following undersizes:

    0.010 in (0.25 mm)
    0.020 in (0.50 mm)
    0.030 in (0.76 mm)
    0.040 in (1.01 mm)

13 Specified clearance for new big-end bearings is .0006 to .0022 in (0.015 to 0.055 mm).

14 A Plastigauge reading of between 0.001 in and 0.0025 in (0.025 mm and 0.065 mm) is acceptable.

15 If a bearing has seen long service, and a reading in excess of 0.003 in. (0.08 mm) is shown then it is advisable to renew it.

16 If new bearing shells are being fitted to a crankshaft with journals of unknown size it will be a matter of selective assembly, trial and error until the nearest correct assembly is achieved.

17 **Never** grind or file bearing caps to make a fitting.

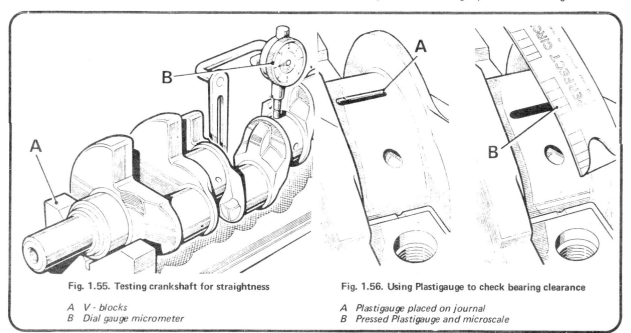

Fig. 1.55. Testing crankshaft for straightness

A V - blocks
B Dial gauge micrometer

Fig. 1.56. Using Plastigauge to check bearing clearance

A Plastigauge placed on journal
B Pressed Plastigauge and microscale

18 Having found the correct clearance, clean off all trace of the Plastigage material, and oil all surfaces to be refitted.

19 With the bearings refitted and tightened, it should be possible to freely move the connecting rods on the crank journal as allowed by the end clearance.

20 Check the end-float (side-to-side movement) of the connecting rod big-end bearings on each crank journal. (Fig. 1.57). This should be between 0.006 and 0.014 in (0.15 and 0.37 mm).

---

45 Crankshaft - refitment

1 Fit all the main bearing upper shells into position in the cylinder block. These are the ones with the oil drilling holes.

2 The flanged upper main bearing shells locate in the centre position. (Fig. 1.58). They act as the crankshaft main thrust bearing.

3 Fit a new rear oil seal leaving both ends equal and proud of the mating face of the cylinder block. (Fig. 1.59).

4 Ease the new seal down into the groove using a hammer handle or similar object to press the seal into position.

5 Leave a small projection of the seal all round (approx. 0.031 in., or 1.5 mm) above the edges of the groove.

6 Cut off the remaining ends, flush with the face of the cylinder block, using a sharp knife.

7 Place wooden blocks of about half an inch (12.5 mm) thick to fit over the upper bearing housing. These are to rest the crankshaft on before the final fitting. (Fig. 1.60).

8 Place the crankshaft into position allowing it to rest on the wooden blocks.

9 Lubricate all the bearing surfaces liberally with clean engine oil.

10 The rear oil seal should also be lubricated.

11 Draw the connecting rod bearings up into position on their crankshaft journals. Remove first one wooden block and lower the crankshaft into its upper bearing. Repeat the process for the other end.

12 Fit the connecting rod bearing caps as detailed in Section 38 of this Chapter.

13 Refit main bearing caps numbers 1 to 4, having applied clean engine oil first. Tighten the bolts only finger tight at this stage.

14 Fit new oil seals and side seals to the rear bearing cap.
Note: On early models, a 'monolithic' type seal is used with a matching cap. Later engines have a 'cruciform' type as shown in Fig. 1.61. The two different types must not be interchanged, but in an emergency the early seal may be used with the later cap.

15 Do not cut the side seals at this stage as they must project above the bearing cap mating face approximately 0.062 in (1.5 mm). Trim off the oil seal after pressing home. (See paragraph 6).

16 Lubricate the rear oil seal as before (paragraph 10).

17 Lubricate the bearing shell and side seals with engine oil.

18 Offer the bearing cap and shell to its location, fit the bolts and finger tighten them.

19 Use a blunt instrument to push in the side seals.

20 To align the thrust faces of the centre main bearing, tap the crankshaft at each end in turn - moving it in both directions to the limit of its travel.

21 Tighten the bearing caps, numbers one to four first to a torque of between 50 and 55 lb ft. (7.0 and 7.6 kg. m).

22 Finally tighten up the rear main bearing cap bolts to a torque of between 65 and 70 lb ft (9.0 and 9.6 kg m).

23 With a dial gauge, check the crankshaft end-float. This should be in the limits of 0.004 in and 0.008 in (0.10 mm to 0.20 mm). If incorrect, then examine for faulty components and/or faulty assembly.

24 Reassemble the rest of the engine by reference to the appropriate Sections, and reversing the dismantling procedure.

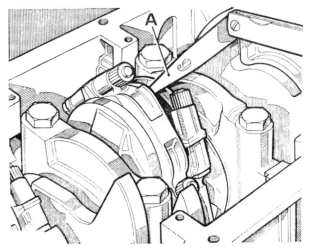

Fig. 1.57. Checking connecting rod end-float

A Feeler gauge

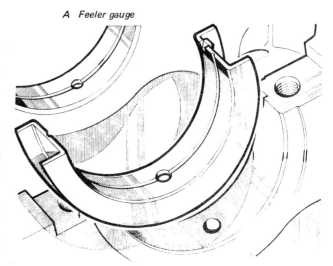

Fig. 1.58. Centre main thrust bearing — Note flange

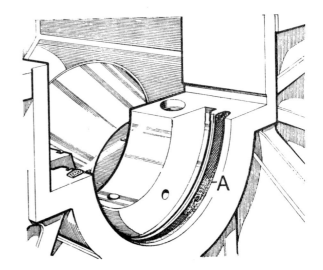

Fig. 1.59. Rear main upper bearing housing showing oil seal (A)

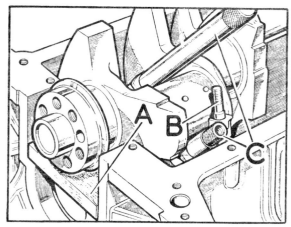

Fig. 1.60. Support for crankshaft prior to refit

A   Wooden block ½ inch
B   Connecting rod end bearing
C   Guide tool

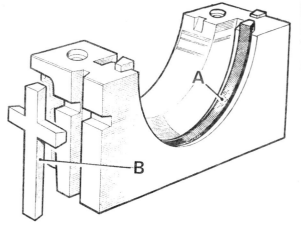

Fig. 1.61. Bottom rear main bearing showing oil seal (A) and side seal (B) — later models

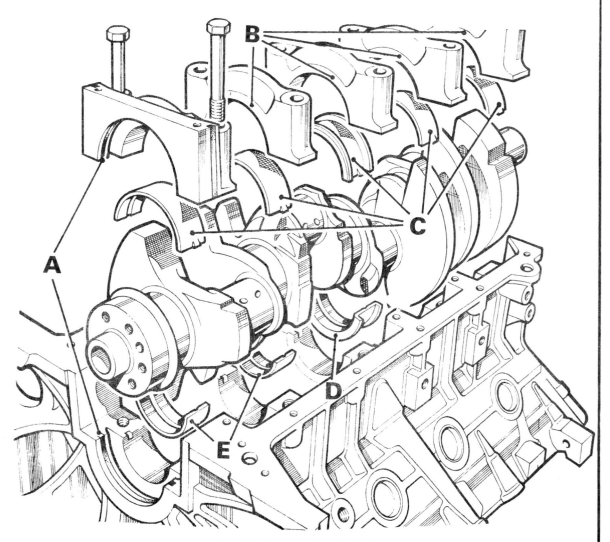

Fig. 1.62. Bottom end engine detail

A   Rear main bearing and oil seal
B   One to four main bearing caps
C   Bottom main bearing shells

D   Centre main thrust bearing (flanged)
E   Top main bearing shells

46 Starter ring gear - removal

1 Where automatic transmission is fitted (model 3500) the starter ring gear is attached to the drive plate and cannot be removed separately.   The drive plate must be renewed as an assembly. With the flywheel removed from the engine drill a small hole approximatley 0.375 in (10 mm) laterally across the starter ring gear. Take care not to allow the drill to enter or score the flywheel or flange. The hole should be made between the root of any gear teeth. This will weaken the ring gear and facilitate removal by breaking with a cold chisel. (Fig. 1.63).
2 Hold the flywheel in a soft jawed vice.
3 **Warning** Beware of flying fragments. A piece of cloth draped over the whole assembly will protect the operator from possible injury.
4 Split the starter ring gear with a hammer and chisel.

47 Starter ring gear - refitment

1 The new starter ring gear must be heated uniformally. The expansion of the metal permits it to fit over the flywheel and against the flange.Heat to between 338 degrees and 347 degrees Farenheit (170 to 175 degrees Centrigrade). **Do not exceed the specified temperature.**
2 Place the flywheel on a flat surface with the flanged side downwards.
3 Offer up the heated ring to the flywheel with the chamfered inner diameter downwards (Fig. 1.64) pressing it firmly against the flange until the ring contracts sufficiently to grip the flywheel. Allow cooling to take place naturally and do not attempt to hasten cooling in any way as this could cause weakening by setting up internal stresses in the ring gear leading to later break up.
   Where the ring gear is chamfered on both sides it may be fitted either way round.

48 Crankshaft spigot bearing - renewal

1 The spigot bearing can be renewed with the engine in the car. First remove the gearbox (Chapter 6) and clutch assembly. (Chapter 5).
2 If the engine is undergoing complete workshop overhaul and is out of the car the job is much facilitated and should be considered at this time.
3 Remove the old bearing which is a push fit into the crankshaft end flange.
4 Push in the new bearing "A" which should finish flush with the end face of the crankshaft "B". Below this level is acceptable provided it does not recess more than 0.063 in (1.6 mm). (See Fig. 1.65).
5 The inside diameter of the spigot bearing should be 0.7504 + 0.001 in (19.177 + 0.025 mm) Reamer out if necessary.

49 Engine/gearbox - installation

1 Refer to Fig. 1.66. The splined end of the gearbox input shaft, the clutch centre and the withdrawal unit abutment faces should be smeared with approved grease.

2 Line up the gearbox with the engine locating the gearbox input shaft into the clutch, ease forward until the bellhousing dowels engage. (See Chapter 5 for clutch driven plate alignment).
3 Secure the bellhousing with the correct bolts and tighten up evenly to a torque of 25 lb ft (3.5 kg m).
4 Refit the bellhousing cover plate, tighten to a torque of 8 lb ft (1.0 kg m).
5 Rotate the clutch withdrawal shaft until resistance is felt as the withdrawal sleeve contacts the clutch, (Fig. 1.67) then fit the external clutch lever in the downward vertical position. It may happen that the true vertical cannot be achieved, in which case take the nearest serration on either side of vertical.
6 Secure the lever - torque setting of 15 lb ft (2.0 kg m).
7 Before offering the unit to the car the engine/gearbox assembly must be complete with engine rubber mountings. The external clutch lever must be fitted, but do not fit the engine oil filter or the driver's gear change lever at this stage.
8 Lower the engine/gearbox unit into the car and reverse the removal and disconnection procedure described in Section 5.
9 Ensure that the speedo. cable is re-located through the gear change shaft housing before securing the rear gearbox mounting.
10 Check, and renew if necessary, the rubber mounting blocks on the gearbox mounting cradle.
11 Check and adjust the throttle linkage as follows:
   Reassemble the throttle linkage so that both carburettor throttle levers are at their stop positions. If these have been disturbed or work has been carried out on the carburettor then it will be necessary to readjust them as described in Chapter 3.
12 Refit the fan blades. It will be observed that there is an offset dowel that locates the blade assembly, this ensures that the blades are not put on back-to-front.
13 Remember to refill the gearbox with the correct grade of oil.
14 Similarly replenish the engine oil.
15 Fill the cooling system with correct mixture of antifreeze and/or inhibitor. (See Chapter 2).
16 Before starting the engine give the whole job a final and thorough check out and remove any stray spanners and other tools from the engine compartment.
17 After starting up immediately check that the oil warning light goes out. If light remains on, stop engine at once, as it will be necessary to prime the oil pump, (see this Chapter, Section 29).
18 Check the cooling system for leaks.
19 If necessary check and adjust the engine idling speed.
20 If necessary check and adjust the distributor dwell angle and ignition timing. (Chapter 4).
21 Allow the engine to cool and check coolant level in the radiator and top up as required.
22 During and after test run re-check for coolant and oil leaks.

50 Engine/automatic transmission - installation

1 Fit the automatic transmission unit to the engine as described in Chapter 6 (part 2).
2 Installation of the combined engine/transmission is similar to that described for manual gearbox types in the preceding Section.
3 Reconnect the speed selector mechanism and check for correct operation. (See Chapter 6).
4 Connect the speedometer drive cable and refill the transmission with the correct grade and quantity of fluid. .

51 Fault diagnosis - Engine

Symptom	Reason/s	Remedy
Engine fails to turn over when starter button operated	Discharged or defective battery	Charge or renew battery, push-start car (manual gearbox only).
	Dirty or loose battery leads	Clean and tighten both terminals and earth ends of earth lead.

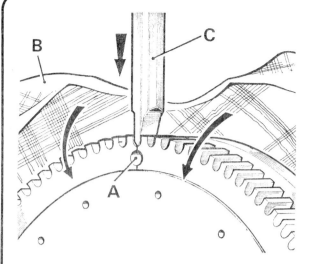

Fig. 1.63. Removing damaged starter ring gear from flywheel

A Hole drilled into ring gear to weaken
B Rag to protect operator
C Chisel

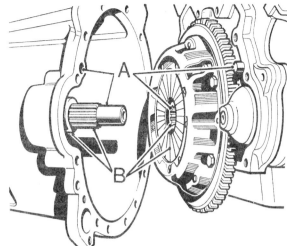

Fig. 1.66. Reassembling gearbox to engine

"A" Engage spigot into crankshaft spigot bearing. Also dowel at engine block face into hole in clutch housing
"B" Engage gearbox input shaft spline into clutch driven plate

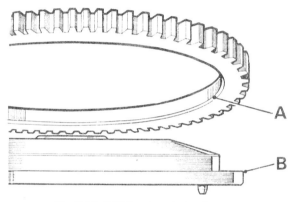

Fig. 1.64. Refitting new starter ring gear

A Chamfered inner edge
B Flywheel flange

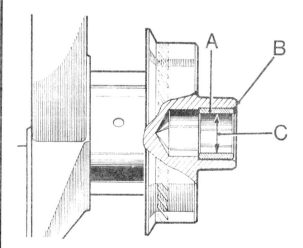

Fig. 1.65. Replacing spigot bearing

A Spigot bearing
B Crankshaft end face
C Internal diameter of bearing

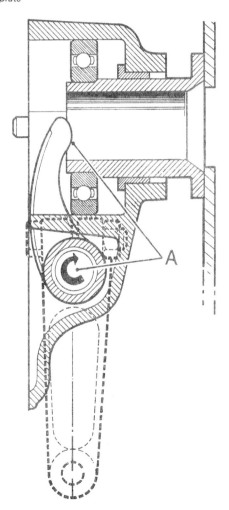

Fig. 1.67. Rotating clutch withdrawal shaft (A) in a clockwise direction

Symptom	Reason/s	Remedy
	Defective starter solenoid or switch	Run a heavy duty wire direct from the battery to the starter motor or by-pass the solenoid.
	Engine earth strap disconnected	Check and retighten strap.
	Defective starter motor	Remove and recondition.
Engine turns over but will not start	Ignition damp or wet	Wipe dry the distributor cap and ignition leads.
	Ignition leads to spark plugs loose	Check and tighten at both spark plug and distributor cap ends.
	Shorted or disconnected low tension leads	Check the wiring on the CB and SW terminals of the coil and to the distributor.
	Dirty, incorrectly set or pitted contact breaker points.	Clean, file smooth and adjust.
	Faulty condenser	Check contact breaker points for arcing, remove and fit new condenser.
	Defective ignition switch	By-pass switch with wire.
	Ignition LT leads connected wrong way round	Remove and replace leads to coil in correct order.
	Faulty coil	Remove and fit new coil.
	Contact breaker point spring earthed or broken	Check spring is not touching metal part of distributor. Check insulator washers are correctly placed. Renew points if the spring is broken.
	No petrol in petrol tank	Refill tank!
	Vapour lock in fuel line (in hot conditions or at high altitude)	Blow into petrol tank, allow engine to cool, or apply a cold wet rag to the fuel line in engine compartment.
	Blocked float chamber needle valve	Remove, clean and replace.
	Fuel pump filter blocked	Remove, clean and replace.
	Choked or blocked carburettor jets	Dismantle and clean.
	Faulty fuel pump	Remove, overhaul and replace.
	Too much choke allowing too rich a mixture to wet plugs	Remove and dry spark plugs or with wide open throttle, push-start the car (manual gearbox only)
	Float damaged or leaking or needle not seating	Remove, examine, clean and replace float and needle valve as necessary.
	Float lever incorrectly adjusted	Remove and adjust correctly.
Engine stalls and will not start	Ignition failure - sudden	Check over low and high tension circuits for breaks in wiring.
	Ignition failure - misfiring precludes total stoppage	Check contact breaker points, clean and adjust. Renew condenser if faulty.
	Ignition failure - in severe rain or after traversing water splash	Dry out ignition leads and distributor cap.
	No petrol in petrol tank	Refill tank.
	Petrol tank breather choked	Remove petrol cap and clean out breather hole or pipe.
	Sudden obstruction in carburettor	Check jets, filter, and needle valve in float chamber for blockage.
	Water in fuel system	Drain tank and blow out fuel lines.
Engine misfires or idles unevenly	Ignition leads loose	Check and tighten as necessary at spark plug and distributor cap ends.
	Battery leads loose on terminals	Check and tighten terminal leads.
	Battery earth strap loose on body attachment point	Check and tighten earth lead to body attachment point.
	Engine earth lead loose	Tighten lead.
	Low tension leads to SW and CB terminals on coil loose	Check and tighten leads if found loose.
	Low tension lead from CB terminal side to distributor loose	Check and tighten if found loose.
	Dirty, or incorrectly gapped spark plugs	Remove, clean and regap.
	Dirty, incorrectly set or pitted contact breaker points	Clean, file smooth and adjust.
	Tracking across distributor cap	Remove and fit new cap.
	Ignition too retarded	Check and adjust ignition timing.
	Faulty coil	Remove and fit new coil.

Symptom	Reason/s	Remedy
	Mixture too weak	Check jets, float chamber needle valve and filters for obstruction. Clean as necessary. Carburettor incorrectly adjusted.
	Air leak in carburettor	Remove and overhaul carburettor.
	Air leak at inlet manifold to cylinder head, or inlet manifold to carburettor	Test by pouring oil along joints. Bubbles indicate leak. Renew manifold gasket as appropriate.
Engine misfires or idles unevenly	Burnt out exhaust valves	Remove cylinder head and renew defective valves.
	Sticking or leaking valves	Remove cylinder head, clean, check and renew valves as necessary.
	Weak or broken valve springs	Check and renew as necessary.
	Worn valve guides or stems	Renew valves.
	Worn pistons and piston rings	Dismantle engine, renew pistons and rings.
Lack of power and poor compression	Burnt out exhaust valves	Remove cylinder head, renew defective valves.
	Sticking or leaking valves	Remove cylinder head, clean, check and renew valves as necessary.
	Worn valve guides and stems	Remove cylinder head and renew valves.
	Weak or broken valve springs	Remove cylinder head, renew defective springs.
	Blown cylinder head gasket (accompanied by increase in noise)	Remove cylinder head and fit new gasket.
	Worn pistons and piston rings	Dismantle engine, renew pistons and rings.
	Worn or scored cylinder bores	Dismantle engine, rebore, renew pistons and rings.
	Ignition timing wrongly set. Too advanced or retarded.	Check and reset ignition timing.
	Contact breaker points incorrectly gapped	Check and reset contact breaker points.
	Incorrectly set spark plugs	Remove, clean and regap.
	Carburettor too rich or too weak	Tune carburettor for optimum performance.
	Dirty contact breaker points	Remove, clean and replace.
	Fuel filters blocked causing top end fuel starvation	Dismantle, inspect, clean, and replace all fuel filters.
	Distributor automatic balance weights or vacuum advance and retard mechanisms not functioning correctly	Overhaul distributor.
	Faulty fuel pump giving top end fuel starvation	Remove, overhaul, or fit exchange reconditioned fuel pump.
Excessive oil consumption	Excessively worn valve stems and valve guides	Remove cylinder head and fit new valves.
	Worn piston rings	Fit oil control rings to existing pistons or purchase new pistons.
	Worn pistons and cylinder bores	Fit new pistons and rings, rebore cylinders.
	Excessive piston ring gap allowing blow-by	Fit new piston rings and set gap correctly.
	Piston oil return holes choked	Decarbonise engine and pistons.
Oil being lost due to leaks	Leaking oil filter gasket	Inspect and fit new gasket as necessary.
	Leaking rocker cover gasket	Inspect and fit new gasket as necessary.
	Leaking timing case gasket	Inspect and fit new gasket as necessary.
	Leaking sump gasket	Inspect and fit new gasket as necessary.
	Loose sump plug	Tighten, fit new gasket as necessary.
Unusual noises from engine	Worn valve gear (noisy tapping from rocker box)	Inspect and renew rocker shaft, rocker arms and ball pins as necessary.
	Worn big end bearing (regular heavy knocking)	Drop sump, if bearings broken up clean out oil pump and oilways, fit new bearings. If bearings not broken but worn fit bearing shells.
	Worn timing gears (rattling from front of engine)	Remove timing cover, fit new timing gears.
	Worn main bearings (rumbling and vibration)	Drop sump, remove crankshaft, if bearings worn but not broken up, renew. If broken up strip oil pump and clean out.
	Worn crankshaft (knocking, rumbling and vibration)	Regrind crankshaft, fit new main and big end bearings.

Chapter 2 Cooling system

Contents

Specifications

Type	Pressurised pump and fan
Cap pressure	15 lb/in^2 (1.05 kg/cm^2)
Fan:	Five bladed (Standard) Thirteen bladed, viscous unit to limit fan speed to 2,500 rev/min. (air conditioning)

Thermostat:

Type	Wax
Starts to open	80° C (176° F)

Fan belt adjustment	0.437 to 0.562 in. (11 to 14 mm) deflection
Air conditioner compressor, belt adjustment	0.187 to 0.25 in. (4 to 6 mm) deflection
Capacity (coolant)	15.25 pints (8.5 litres)

Torque wrench settings:

	lb ft	kg m
Water pump housing bolts (small)	6 to 8	0.8 to 1.0
Water pump housing bolts (large)	20 to 25	2.8 to 3.5

1 General description

1 The system is conventional, acting on the thermo-syphon, pump assisted principle and requires the minimum of general maintenance. The coolant flow is controlled by a thermostat which is fitted at the forward end of the inlet manifold casting, and behind the outlet elbow. The purpose of this thermostat is to prevent the full flow of the coolant around the system before a temperature of 173° F to 182° F (78 to 83° C) is reached (3500 models). On 3500 S models fitted with exhaust emission control, the operating temperatures of the thermostat are slightly higher, 187 to 194° F (86 to 90° C). The cooling system is designed to operate at a pressure of 15 lb/sq in. (1 kg/sq cm). A pressure relief valve is incorporated in the radiator cap. If it is necessary to remove the radiator cap when the engine is hot, it is advisable to protect the hand with a cloth draped over the cap and top of the radiator. The purpose of pressurising a cooling system in this way is to prevent the coolant from boiling at the lower normal atmospheric pressure, thus enabling the engine to work at higher and more efficient temperature ranges. Consequently, as soon as the pressure is released by removal of the radiator cap and the coolant is exposed to the lower atmospheric pressure, it is likely to boil - take care.

On the 3500 models the cooling fan is bolted directly to the pump hub, but on the S models there is a fluid drive arrangement called the 'Viscous Unit' which is interposed between the pump hub and the fan. This viscous unit cannot be repaired if damaged and must be replaced by a new unit.

2 Components of the pump and cooling fan components for both models are illustrated in Figs. 2.1 (3500 models) and 2.2 (3500 S models).

2 Draining and refilling the system

1 The procedure for draining the cooling system is fully explained in the Section dealing with Routine Maintenance, but the main points are emphasised as follows:

2 Remove the radiator cap.

3 Remove the radiator drain plug (photo). (Use a wide brimmed container).

4 Set the car heater control to fully on.

5 Drain the cylinder block. (Both sides). (photo)

6 Close both cylinder block drain taps, immediately after draining.

7 The importance of refilling with the correct mixture of anti-freeze/inhibitor and water, or inhibitor only with water cannot be over emphasised.

Recommended solutions

Anti-freeze: Anti-freeze solution conforming to British Standard No. 3150 (Castrol anti-freeze). Anti-freeze solution to

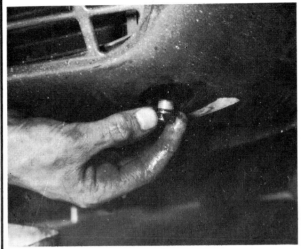

2.3 Removing the radiator drain plug

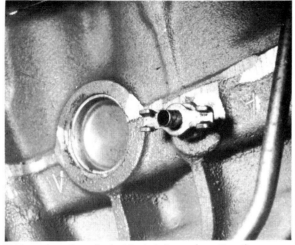

2.5 Location of a cylinder block drain tap (two fitted)

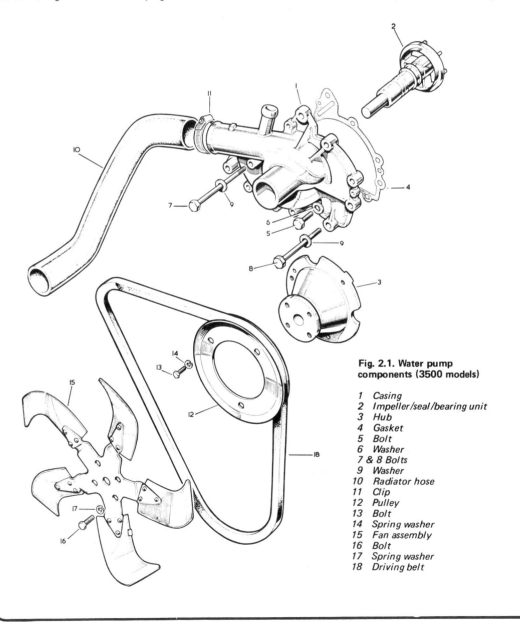

Fig. 2.1. Water pump components (3500 models)

1 Casing
2 Impeller/seal/bearing unit
3 Hub
4 Gasket
5 Bolt
6 Washer
7 & 8 Bolts
9 Washer
10 Radiator hose
11 Clip
12 Pulley
13 Bolt
14 Spring washer
15 Fan assembly
16 Bolt
17 Spring washer
18 Driving belt

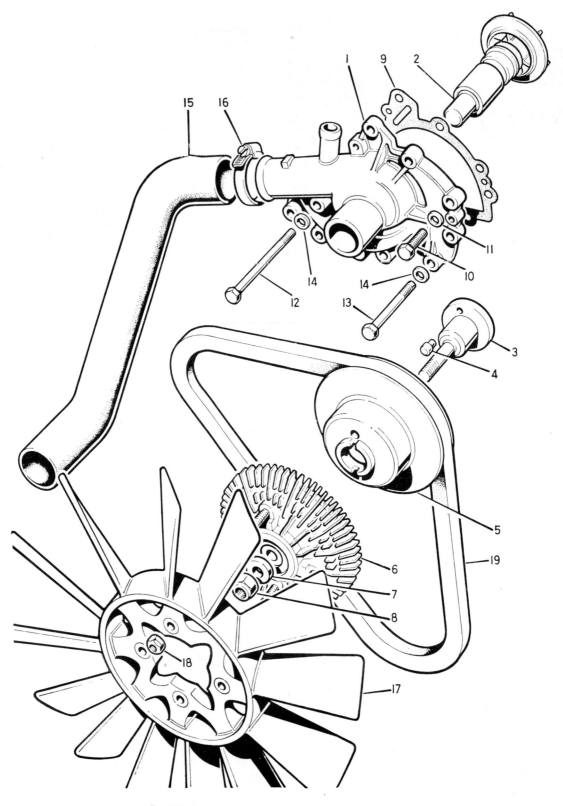

Fig. 2.2. Water pump components (3500S models)

1	Casing	6	Viscous coupling	11	Washer	16	Clip
2	Impeller	7	Washer	12	Bolts	17	Fan assembly
3	Hub	8	Self-locking nut	13	Bolts	18	Nut
4	Dowel	9	Gasket	14	Washer	19	Driving belt
5	Pulley	10	Bolt	15	Radiator hose		

MIL-E-5559 formulation.

Inhibitor: Rover approved cooling system corrosion inhibitor.

The coolant should be changed annually to ensure adequate protection.

8 When mixing water with the anti-freeze/inhibitor, or just inhibitor, it is better to use soft tap water or rain water, the mixing being carried out in a plastic bucket. It is not necessary to mix the whole amount required to fill the system, as further topping up can be done once the initial coolant mix has been poured into the radiator.

9 Use the following table to ensure adequate protection according to local climatic conditions:-

Cooling system capacity	Frost pre-caution	Proportion of anti-freeze	Anti-freeze required to raise 33.1/3% solution to 50%
15.25 UK pints	−25°F (−32°C)	33.1/3%	5.25 UK pints 3.0 litres 6.3 US pints 3.75 UK pints
8,5 litres			2,1 litres
18.5 US pints	−33°F (−36°C)	50%	7.75 UK pints 4.2 litres 9.25 US pints 4.5 US pints

10 With the exception of models exported to Canada and the USA, all cars are filled with 33.1/3% solution of anti-freeze on leaving the factory. Cars despatched to the above mentioned countries are filled with a 50% solution.

11 To increase the anti-freeze proportion from 33.1/3% to a 50% solution, all it is necessary to do, is to drain off the appropriate proportion of the original solution, then add the same quantity of neat anti-freeze, thus compensating for the anti-freeze lost when the radiator was partially drained.

12 If anti-freeze conditions are not likely to prevail, then the system should be filled with a solution of water plus inhibitor, in the proportion of 3 fluid ounces (19 cc) of inhibitor for each gallon of water held in the system.

13 Where prior to refilling, the system is to be flushed out, (and it is advisable to do so) refer to the next Section.

14 Before refilling, ensure that all taps are shut, the car heater is set at the fully on position, and that you have replaced the radiator drain plug.

15 After filling, run the engine to thoroughly circulate the mixture and visually check for leaks.

16 Check the level of coolant in the radiator and top up as required.

3 Flushing the cooling system

1 There are certain conditions and circumstances when the system **must** be flushed out, for example, when a change of make or type of anti-freeze is made.

2 Proceed as follows: Empty the cooling system completely. Refill with clean water and run the engine to circulate. Stop the engine and drain off. Repeat the operation.

3 It often happens that the cylinder block taps may become choked and with this type of tap it is impossible to poke a piece of wire through to clear them, so it will become necessary to remove the taps by unscrewing them from the cylinder block.

4 With the taps open or removed and a hose pipe inserted into the radiator filler neck, run water through the system for at least 15 minutes.

5 If the system is very dirty, or on an older car where there has been lack of maintenance, it may be advisable to remove the radiator (Section 7) from the car and run water through from the bottom tank letting it run out through the filler cap. An occasional vigorous physical shake, with water filling the core will dislodge any sediment. This operation is known as back flushing.

6 Close all the taps; replace the radiator drain plug and refill with recommended anti-freeze or inhibitor.

4 Water pump - removal

1 Drain the coolant, using a clean container if the coolant is to be re-used. Move the screen wash reservoir to one side.

2 Remove the fan guard and cowl if fitted (Fig. 2.3).

3 Remove the radiator (Chapter 1, Section 5).

4 Remove the cooling fan. (Chapter 1, Section 5).

5 On 3500 S models, release the bolts securing the fan pulley.

6 On 3500 S models fitted with a viscous unit, remove the fan blades and slacken the nut and washer securing the viscous coupling.

7 Slacken the alternator fixings to remove the fan belt.

8 Remove the adjustment bolt from the alternator strap and move the alternator to one side.

9 Disconnect the hoses from the water pump (photos).

10 On cars fitted with power steering, remove the power steering pump bracket.

4.9a Detaching radiator bottom hose from water pump

4.9b Detaching a heater hose from inlet manifold

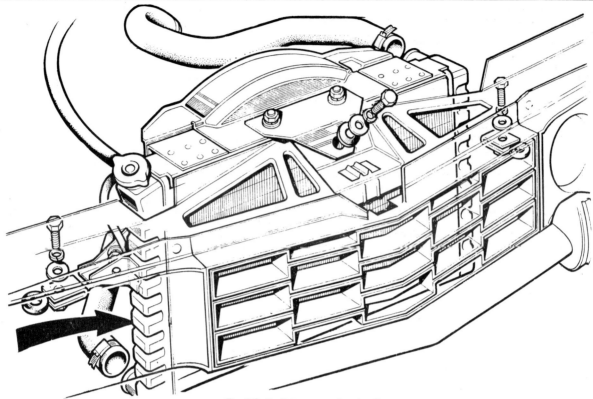

Fig. 2.3. Radiator mounting detail

11 Remove the nut and washer holding the viscous unit (if fitted) and withdraw the unit.

12 Progressively release all the water pump securing bolts and remove. Treat bolts in the same manner as described in Chapter 1, Section 7.

13 The pump can now be removed with its gasket.

14 On cars fitted with air conditioning, the compressor must be moved to one side out of the way. **On no account should the refrigeration pipes be disconnected.** Slacken the mounting pivot and adjustment bolts to remove the compressor driving belt. Slacken the pinch bolt securing the idler pulley driving the compressor and remove the pulley.

15 Remove the engine tie-rod (Chapter 1, Section 5).

16 Remove the windscreen washer reservoir from its bracket and place to one side. Disconnect the electrical lead from the compressor clutch.

17 It is in most cases cheaper and less frustrating to replace worn assemblies with an exchange unit. The water pump is no exception to this rule and though it is possible to replace bearings, shaft and seals, it is advised that the former course is adopted.

5 Water pump - refitment

1 Refitment is mainly a matter of reversing the removal procedure. However, there are one or two points to watch for during the operation.

2 Ensure that the mating surfaces of pump and engine front cover are scrupulously clean.

3 Using a smear of light grease, secure the **new** gasket to the pump body.

4 Apply a light smear of grease to the other gasket surface and offer the unit to the engine.

5 The pump securing bolts should be cleaned, and treated with lubricant sealant 3M EC776.

6 The securing bolts that protrude through the timing chain cover into the cylinder block are tightened to a torque figure

of 20 to 50 lb ft (2.8 to 3.5 kg m). The bolts which only secure to the timing chain cover should be tightened to a torque figure of 6 to 8 lb ft (0.8 to 1 kg m).

7 On units fitted with viscous drive, ensure that the fan blades are fitted correctly. The larger diameter of the moulded bosses must face to the front of the car. Adjust the fan belt as described in Section 8.

6 Thermostat - removal, testing, refitment

1 If the engine tends to overheat, the cause is most likely to be due to a faulty thermostat that is failing to open at its predetermined temperature setting.

2 Conversely, where the thermostat is stuck permanently

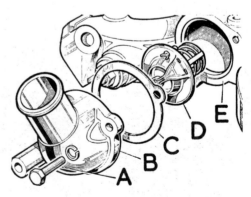

Fig. 2.4. Thermostat components

A Securing bolt	C Gasket
B Cover/elbow	D Thermostat
	E Inlet manifold

open, it will be found that the engine takes a long time to warm-up. In cold weather, this results in having to drive considerable distances using the choke, with of course, the attendant costly fuel bill. If in doubt take out the thermostat and test it.

3 There is no need to drain the whole system, but simply drain coolant from the radiator until the level of the coolant is down to the top of the cylinder block. This level will have to be achieved by trial and error. Drain off some coolant, and replace the radiator drain plug. Carefully remove the engine outlet hose at the elbow. If water is present, replace the hose quickly and drain some more coolant. (photo)

4 Once the coolant has reached a suitably low level then the elbow can be removed and the thermostat exposed.

5 There are two bolts securing the thermostat housing elbow to the front of the engine. These should be removed, and the housing elbow lifted off. (photo)

6 Remember to have a new gasket ready for replacement.

7 Carefully remove the thermostat which should just lift out.

8 Examine it to ascertain whether or not it is stuck open, assuming a cold engine. If so, there is no point in further tests; it should be renewed.

9 If the thermostat looks normal then proceed as follows:

10 Place the unit in a saucepan of cold water. Do not allow it to touch the bottom. Suspend it or support it with a piece of wire or string.

11 Heat the saucepan and raise the temperature to that at which the thermostat is specified to open.

12 If it fails to operate correctly, renew it with one of the correct type.

13 If it happens that you do not have a spare, the car will run quite well for the next day or so without a thermostat until a replacement can be obtained, but will take much longer to reach operating temperature.

14 Refit the elbow and thermostat housing cover and reconnect the hose. The radiator must be topped up and checked for leaks.

15 One more point, when fitting the new thermostat, make sure that the small split pin, called a jiggle pin, which pokes through the valve face, is placed at the 12 o'clock position in the housing. This will prevent air locks occurring in this area.

7 Water temperature gauge and transmitter - testing

The water temperature transmitter is located adjacent to the thermostat housing. It is connected to the gauge on the instrument panel by a cable in the main ignition feed circuit and a special bimetal voltage stabiliser.

If unsatisfactory gauge readings are being obtained the transmitter may be tested by removing the cable connection on the transmitter and placing the cable metal end onto a good earthing point, for example, a paint-free part of the cylinder head. Switch on the ignition and note the movement of the gauge needle. If the needle moves into the hot sector a new thermal transmitter should be fitted. If the needle fails to move, then a break in the wiring or a fault in the gauge (which is tested by substitution) will be the cause of the trouble.

To remove the thermal transmitter, partially drain the cooling system and unscrew the transmitter from the cylinder head. Refitment is the reverse procedure to removal. Always fit a new joint washer.

8 Fan belt - adjustment

1 The maintenance of correct fan belt tension is essential to ensure correct coolant temperature and to maintain the proper

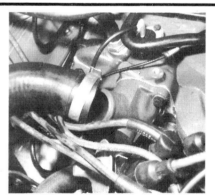

6.3 Removing hose from thermostat elbow

6.5 Withdrawing thermostat housing cover

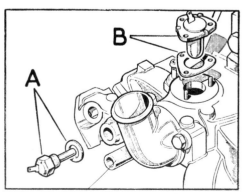

Fig. 2.5. Water temperature transmitter (A) and mixture control switch (B) (early models)

Fig. 2.6. Fan belt adjustment diagram

1 Belt deflection measuring point
2 Alternator mounting bolt
3 Adjuster strap bolt

operation of the electrical charging system.

2 After slackening the alternator mounting bolts and adjustment strap bolts, move the alternator in or out until the deflection of the belt when pressed in by the thumb at a point midway between the alternator and crankshaft pulleys is approximately ½ in. (11 to 14 mm).

9 Fault diagnosis - Cooling system

Symptom	Reason/s	Remedy
Overheating	Insufficient water in cooling system	Top up radiator.
	Fan belt slipping (accompanied by a shrieking noise on rapid engine acceleration)	Tighten fan belt to recommended tension or replace if worn.
	Radiator core blocked or radiator grille restricted	Reverse flush radiator, remove obstructions.
	Bottom water hose collapsed, impeding flow	Remove and fit new hose.
	Thermostat not opening properly	Remove and fit new thermostat.
	Ignition advance and retard incorrectly set (accompanied by loss of power, and perhaps misfiring)	Check and reset ignition timing.
	Carburettor incorrectly adjusted (mixture too weak)	Tune carburettor.
	Exhaust system partially blocked	Check exhaust pipe for constrictive dents and blockages.
	Oil level in sump too low	Top up sump to full mark on dipstick.
	Blown cylinder head gasket (water/steam being forced down the radiator overflow pipe under pressure)	Remove cylinder head, fit new gasket.
	Engine not yet run-in	Run-in slowly and carefully.
	Brakes binding	Check and adjust brakes if necessary.
Underheating	Thermostat jammed open	Remove and renew thermostat.
	Incorrect thermostat fitted allowing premature opening of valve	Remove and replace with new thermostat which opens at a higher temperature.
	Thermostat missing	Check and fit correct thermostat.
Loss of cooling water	Loose clips on water hoses	Check and tighten clips if necessary.
	Top, bottom, or by-pass water hoses perished and leaking	Check and replace any faulty hoses.
	Radiator core leaking	Remove radiator and repair.
	Thermostat gasket leaking	Inspect and renew gasket.
	Radiator pressure cap spring worn or seal ineffective	Renew radiator pressure cap.
	Blown cylinder head gasket (pressure in system forcing water/steam down overflow pipe	Remove cylinder head and fit new gasket.
	Cylinder wall or head cracked	Dismantle engine, despatch to engineering works for repair.

Chapter 3
Carburation, emission control and exhaust system

Contents

Specifications

Fuel pump:

Type	AC mechanical (standard)
	Bendix electric (fitted for air conditioning)
Pressure range	3.5 to 5.0 lbf/in^2 (0.246 to 0.351 kgf/cm^2)

Carburettors:

Type	Twin SU	
Model	**HIF6**	**HS6** (fitted to early models)
Needle	BBG	BAK (early KO)
Bore	1.75 in. (44.45 mm)	1.75 in. (44.45 mm)
Jet size	0.100 in. (2.54 mm)	0.100 in. (2.54 mm)
Float level	0.062/0.187 in. (3.0/4.5 mm)	0.125/0.187 in. (3.0/4.5 mm)
Damper oil	SAE 20	SAE 20

Idling speeds

With emission control	700/750 rev/min.
Without emission control	600/650 rev/min.
Without emission control but with air conditioning	700/750 rev/min.
Fast idle (all models)	1100/1200 rev/min.

C,O. emission 4%

Air cleaner type: ... ... Paper element - disposable

Fuel tank capacity ... ... 15 gals (includes 2.5 gals. reserve)
(68 litres)   (12 litres)

Torque wrench setting:	lb ft	kg m
Exhaust manifold bolts (HOT)	15	2.0

1 General description

Although giving an impression of complexity at first glance (particularly those cars fitted with emission control), the fuel and carburation system is basically conventional.

Using the best components available, the system can be said to be extremely reliable requiring the minimum of attention in service. Detail differences are found in the positioning of the fuel reserve tap - on the earlier models this was cable operated and located beneath the tank unit.

On models equipped with air conditioning plant, the conventional AC mechanical pump is replaced by a Bendix electrical pump which is mounted underneath the body on the rear right-hand wing valance. Cold starting on early models is assisted by the inclusion of an automatic enrichment device working separately as an auxiliary carburettor and governed by the engine temperature. Current cars are not fitted with this device. The d-i-y mechanic is warned that the carburettor mixture ratio settings are carried out at the Rover factory and sealed. Any alteration to these settings is not advised, unless the owner has access to the specialised equipment needed to reset to the correct standard.

Adjustments to engine idling speed and fast idle speed can be undertaken provided that the contact breaker dwell angle, ignition timing and automatic advance/retard have been checked out, and accurately reset as required. Before adjustments of this nature are carried out the owner should ensure that he has the

means of accurately recording the engine speed by the use of a separate and independent tachometer.

Removal, overhaul, and replacement of worn carburettor parts, gaskets etc., are all within the scope of the d-i-y mechanic but do not be tempted to remove the jet bearing assembly.

Identification of parts and layout of the fuel tank, gauge unit, reserve tap, fuel pipes and fixings for standard models are clearly shown in Fig. 3.1 and in Fig. 3.2 for models fitted with emission control.

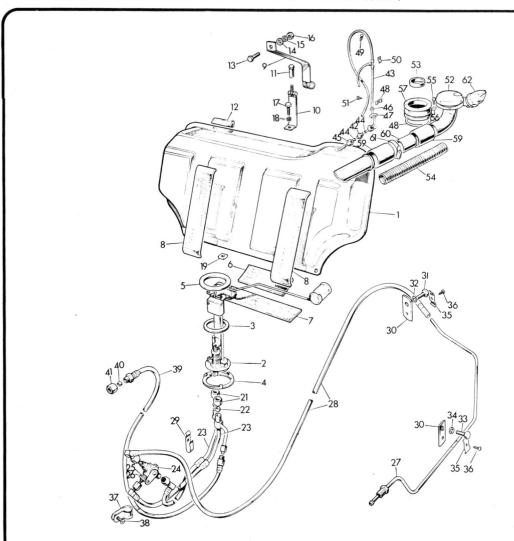

Fig. 3.1. Fuel tank and connections (non emission control models)

1	Tank	16	Nut	31	Bolt	47	Grommet
2	Fuel level unit	17	Bolt	32	Spring washer	48	Clip
3	Seal	18	Spring washer	33	Bolt	49	Clip
4	Locking ring	19	Strap adjustment nut	34	Spring washer	50	Clip
5	Seal	20	Olive	35	Clip	51	Screw
6	Insulation strip	21	Union nut	36	Self-tapping screw	52	Filler cap and pipe
7	Insulation strip	22	Fuel pipe	37	Clip	53	Seal
8	Insulation strip	23	Fuel pipe	38	Screw	54	Flexible inner filler pipe
9	Retaining strap	24	Reserve tap	39	Fuel pipe	55	Screw
10	Retaining strap	25	Lockwasher	40	Olive	56	Nut
11	Nut	26	Nut	41	Union nut	57	Grommet
12	Rubber pad	27	Fuel pipe	42	Breather pipe connector	58	Grommet retainer
13	Bolt	28	Fuel pipe	43	Breather/drain pipe	59	Flexible connector
14	Washer	29	Clip	44	Olive	60	Spacer tube
15	Spring washer	30	Bracket	45	Union nut	61	Hose clips
				46	Grommet	62	Cap lock

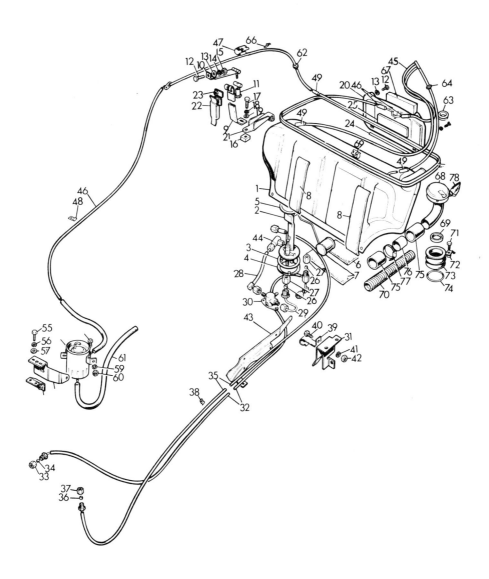

Fig. 3.2. Fuel tank and connections (emission control models)

1 Tank	21 Bracket	41 Spring	60 Nut
2 Fuel level unit	22 Bracket	42 Nut	61 Hose
3 Seal	23 Nut	43 Shield	62 Grommet
4 Locking ring	24 Plastic moulding	44 Fuel tap	63 Grommet
5 Seal	25 Felt strip	45 Breather tube assembly	64 Grommet
6 Insulation strip	26 Olive	46 Connector	65 Clip
7 Insulation strip	27 Union nut	47 Clip	66 Clip
8 Insulation strip	28 Fuel pipe	48 Clip	67 Rubber pad
9 Retaining strap	29 Fuel pipe	49 Connector	68 Filler pipe and cap
10 Retaining strap	30 Reserve tap	50 Evaporator pipes	69 Seal
11 Nut	31 Bracket	51 Hose	70 Flexible inner filler pipe
12 Bolt	32 Fuel pipe	52 Charcoal canister	71 Screw
13 Washer	33 Union nut	53 Bracket	72 Nut
14 Spring washer	34 Olive	54 Reinforcement plate	73 Grommet
15 Nut	35 Fuel pipe	55 Bolt	74 Grommet retainer
16 Plate	36 Olive	56 Spring washer	75 Hose
17 Bolt	37 Union nut	57 Washer	76 Spacer tube
18 Spring washer	38 Clip	58 Bolt	77 Hose clip
19 Washer	39 Clip	59 Spring washer	78 Filler cap lock
20 Expansion tank	40 Bolt		

2 Fuel pump (AC mechanical) - removal, overhaul and replacement

1 The AC mechanical fuel pump is situated on the left-hand side of the engine (Fig. 3.3).

2 Disconnect the fuel supply pipe at the reserve tap located behind the right-hand side (rear) of the engine. Plug the outlet at the tap to prevent leaks. (Thread size 7/16 in. UNF).

3 Disconnect both fuel inlet and outlet pipes from the pump unit.

4 Remove the fixing bolts holding the pump to the engine and withdraw the pump complete with its gasket washer.

5 The AC mechanical pump has been with us for many years, and has become noted for its trouble free long service, requiring the very minimum of maintenance. The pump's weakest point is undoubtedly its diaphragm. Other potential failings due to long service can be listed as follows: weakening or breakage of the main diaphragm spring; weak valve springs; worn or warped valves; worn rocker arm pivot points; leaking gasket beneath the cover.

   If the pump is to be overhauled for any of these reasons, then the owner must obtain the necessary service overhaul kit. Such kits are obtainable either from Rover agents or any other AC stockists.

6 Before dismantling the pump, mark the edges of the pump body and the valve chamber to ensure that on reassembly they are joined in the same relative position.

7 Remove the flange screws and separate the two halves of the pump. If they are stuck fast, **do not** prise them apart with a blade but rap smartly with a soft headed mallet.

8 Unscrew the centre bolt holding the diaphragm cover and remove the cover. Discard the old gasket washer.

9 Scrape off the burrs produced by staking the valves and drive out the valves and gaskets from their housings.

10 To remove the diaphragm and pull rod, jam the link rod in a position at its limit towards the diaphragm with a thin screwdriver blade. Press on the diaphragm centre until the slotted end of the pull rod just touches the blocked link. Tilt the diaphragm away from the body flange and exert side pressure on the pull rod, away from the mounting flange. Whilst exerting this pressure, tilt the diaphragm toward the mounting flange and unhook the slotted end of the pull rod from the link. The diaphragm and pull rod can now be removed with the diaphragm spring.

11 If only renewing the diaphragm, it is not necessary to remove the rocker arm assembly. However it is advised that on a high mileage car it would be desirable to obtain a repair kit that included a new rocker arm pin and link.

12 To remove the rocker arm assembly proceed as follows: Grind, file or drill off the riveted end of the pivot pin flush with the flat steel washer. Tap out the pin with a pin punch and a

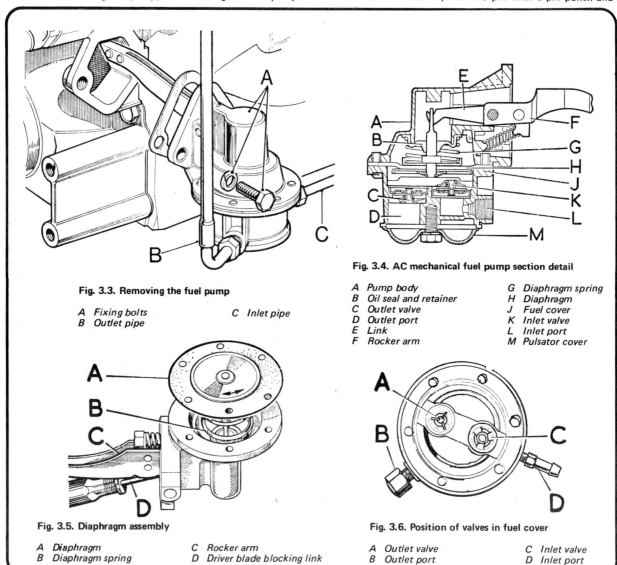

Fig. 3.3. Removing the fuel pump

A *Fixing bolts*
B *Outlet pipe*   C *Inlet pipe*

Fig. 3.4. AC mechanical fuel pump section detail

A *Pump body*   G *Diaphragm spring*
B *Oil seal and retainer*   H *Diaphragm*
C *Outlet valve*   J *Fuel cover*
D *Outlet port*   K *Inlet valve*
E *Link*   L *Inlet port*
F *Rocker arm*   M *Pulsator cover*

Fig. 3.5. Diaphragm assembly

A *Diaphragm*   C *Rocker arm*
B *Diaphragm spring*   D *Driver blade blocking link*

Fig. 3.6. Position of valves in fuel cover

A *Outlet valve*   C *Inlet valve*
B *Outlet port*   D *Inlet port*

light hammer.

13 Remove the rocker arm, the spring and link assembly from the pump body.

14 All the parts that are to be used again should now be thoroughly cleaned in a suitable solvent and the passages and holes blown out with a tyre pump.

15 Visually check for damage or cracks in the body and valve chamber parts. Distorted or damaged flange faces or stripped or crossed threads in the screw holes would necessitate exchanging the complete pump.

16 Check the rocker assembly for wear at the fulcrum pin, side play and wear at the pad contact of rocker arm and link.

17 If damage to the pump body is found it is advisable to renew the pump.

Reassembly:

18 Always use new parts from a service replacement kit - as, often, all the wear in the old ones is not always obvious to the eye.

19 If the rocker arm and link are to be renewed; locate the new rocker arm and spring link roughly in position. Use a pin punch or undersize rod to line up the holes. Push in the new fulcrum pin behind the locating rod. Fit a new steel washer and supporting the head of the pin peen the end to retain the pin against the washer.

20 Fit the new oil seal into its retainer and drive home into the pump body using a 7/8ths in. diameter drift. Stake at four points around the retainer.

21 Block the link as for dismantling. Place the diaphragm spring in position not forgetting to place the cup washer on the ends of the spring. Push the diaphragm pull rod through this assembly with the flats of the rod at a 90° angle to the link in the body. Hook the pull rod over the end of the link.

22 Place the new valve gaskets into position in the valve housings. The valve with the spring cage facing upwards goes in the housing nearest to the inlet connector. The other valve fits the outlet valve housing with its spring cage facing **downwards**.

23 Seat the valves down firmly against their respective gaskets and stake the cover in four places.

24 Bring the two halves of the pump body together, lining them up to the marks previously inscribed. Locate all the retaining screws and lock washers taking care not to damage the fabric of the diaphragm when inserting the screws.

25 Tighten the screws alternately and evenly. Remembering that the pump body is aluminium alloy - do not overtighten. Replace the diaphragm cover using a new gasket.

26 A rough test for the pump before refitting to the car can be carried out, checking that it does in fact suck at the inlet and blow at the outlet by operating the actuating lever. More advanced testing cannot be carried out without access to specialist equipment.

27 Replacement of the pump is a straightforward reversal of the removal procedure.

3 Fuel pump (Bendix electric) - removal, cleaning and replacement

1 Removing the pump to clean the filter - proceed as follows: Disconnect the fuel return pipe at the left-hand carburettor thus preventing draining due to syphoning.

2 Remove the rear trim panel within the boot and disconnect the electrical supply lead to the pump at the snap connector.

3 Jack up the car for easier access.

4 Push in the fuel cut-off valve "F" (Fig. 3.7).

5 Disconnect the inlet and outlet fuel pipes from the pump.

6 Remove the fixing bolts securing the pump to its bracket.

7 As the pump is withdrawn, the electrical supply wire can be drawn down through the grommet in the boot floor.

Cleaning:

8 With the pump removed from the car, remove the inlet and outlet unions (Fig. 3.7a).

9 Remove the nylon clips that retain the sponge rubber cover.

10 Ease the rubber covering away from the pump body.

11 The end cover is held by a bayonet type lock. Use a 5/8ths AF spanner to turn it anticlockwise to release.

12 Remove the filter and clean in petrol, finishing off with a pressure air jet from inside the filter.

13 Remove the magnetic pick-up from the end cover and clean; replace in the centre of the end cover.

14 Replace all the parts of the pump by reverse procedure and refit to the car. Use a new gasket under the end cover if necessary.

15 To refit the pump, reverse the removal procedure. **Note:** Ensure that the earth wire and earth strip are refitted correctly to the bolts securing the pump to its mounting bracket.

4 Fuel tank indicator unit - removal and refitment

1 Disconnect the battery at the negative terminal.

2 To remove, first drain off the fuel by disconnecting the fuel

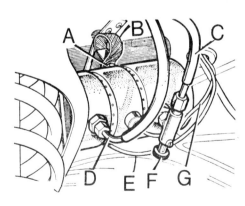

Fig. 3.7. Removing electric fuel pump

A Fixings, pump to   D Outlet pipe
   bracket   E Earth wire
B Earth strap   F Fuel cut-off valve
C Inlet pipe   G Electrical supply wire

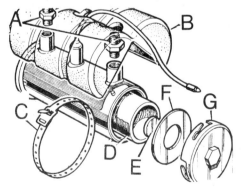

Fig. 3.7a. Servicing the filter

A Inlet and outlet unions   E Magnetic pick-up
B Sponge rubber casing   F End cover gasket
C Nylon retaining clips   G End cover with
D Filter   bayonet locks

pipes on the underside of the fuel tank indicator unit. (photo)

3   Disconnect the electrical leads from the tank unit noting the colour code position for replacement.

4   It will be necessary to use a special spanner to release the locking ring. The ring should be turned in an anticlockwise direction to release it. (Fig. 3.8).

5   Withdraw the tank unit, removing the sealing ring.

6   The retaining spring for the filter should be released and the filter removed.

7   Clean the nylon filter by washing in petrol and blowing from inside with an air jet.

8   If fitting new unions, place the nut over the pipe first followed by the olive, then secure to the union.

Refitting:

9   Fit the nylon filter over the reserve outlet and secure with the spring.

10 Locate the large rubber washer onto the tank unit, and offer up the complete assembly to the fuel tank.

11 Hold in position and locate the locking ring, engaging the correct threads. Tighten up with special locking ring tool.

12 Reconnect the fuel lines to the unit. (The long union should receive the main fuel pipe).

13 Reconnect the electrical leads having previously noted the colour coding.

14 Refill the tank and examine for leaks.

15 Reconnect the battery, switch on the ignition and check the operation of the fuel gauge.

16 Fig. 3.9 shows the tank unit and reserve tap layout fitted to early 3500 S models. On early 3500 models and current 3500 S the reserve tap arrangement is as shown in Fig. 3.10.

---

5   Fuel tank - removal and refitment

1   **Disconnect the battery** at the negative terminal.

2   Disconnect the electrical leads from the tank unit and drain tank as described in Section 4.

3   Remove the spare wheel from the boot.

4   Spring the trim board from its clips and remove from the boot.

5   Release the hose clips securing the upper hose and pull it off.

6   Remove the four screws securing the filler pipe and remove the filler neck complete with its corrugated inner tube.

7   There are two pipe connections for the tank breather system on the main tank, and two connections on the expansion tank, plus a connection adjacent to the right-hand side of the main tank. These should be disconnected. (Fig. 3.11).

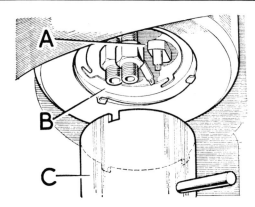

Fig. 3.8. Special tool to remove tank unit lock ring

A   Tank unit
B   Lock ring
C   Special ring

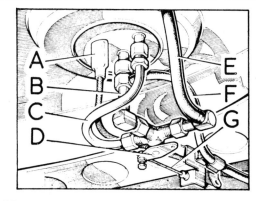

Fig. 3.9. Tank unit and reserve tap fitted to early 3500 S models

A   Electrical leads to fuel gauge
B   Fuel reserve tap
C   Main fuel pipe
D   Reserve tap
E   Outlet to fuel pump
F   Fuel circulation pipe
G   Operating cable, reserve tap

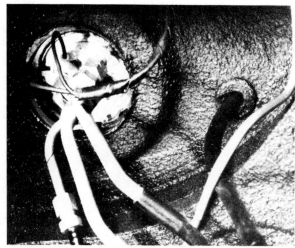

4.2 Fuel tank level indicator unit

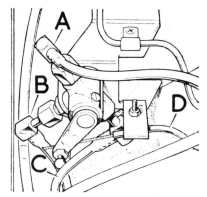

Fig. 3.10. Reserve tap fitted to early 3500 models and current 3500 S models

A   Outlet to fuel pump
B   Reserve supply
C   Main supply
D   Operating cable

8 Four bolts secure the expansion tank to the main tank. These must be removed, and the expansion tank removed.
9 Release the screws securing the two clamping straps and lift the tank clear.
10 **Refitting the fuel tank:** Reverse the removal procedure. Fit a new hose and secure with Bostik 1753.
11 Check that all is secure before filling tank.
12 Refill tank, filtering the fuel previously removed through a gauze mesh funnel.
13 For tanks fitted with evaporative emission control, refer to Section 20 and to Fig. 3.2.
14 Restore all electrical connections.

6 Choke control cable - removal and refitment

1 Disconnect the battery at the negative terminal.
2 Disconnect the choke cable at the carburettor (Chapter 1, Section 7).
3 Remove the console speaker panel. (Chapter 1, Section 5).

4 Disconnect the electrical leads from the cold start switch.
5 Release the cable clamping bolt and remove the switch.
6 Remove the nut securing the outer cable to the panel.
7 Withdraw the cable assembly through the panel (Figs. 3.12, 3.13, 3.14).
8 **Reassembly - points to watch:**
a) Make sure that the panel nut and spring washer are in place before refitting.
b) Use MS4 silicone grease to assist in passing cable through the grommets.
9 Reverse the procedure described in paragraphs 3 to 7.
10 Fix the outer casing of the choke cable to the carburettor body using the spring clip.
11 Pass the inner cable through the trunnion of the left-hand choke cam.
12 Ensure that the choke is in the closed position before tightening the trunnion bolt.
13 Reconnect the negative battery lead; start the engine, checking that the choke control is working correctly.
14 Finally, cut off any excess of inner cable, leaving about half an inch protruding beyond the trunnion bolt.

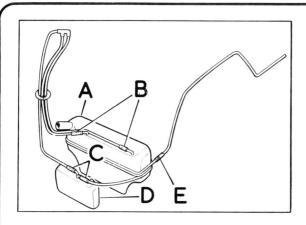

Fig. 3.11. Connecting pipes, fuel tank breather system (emission control)

A   Main tank
B   Breather connections at main tank
C   Breather connections at expansion tank
D   Expansion tank
E   Connection for pipe to charcoal canister

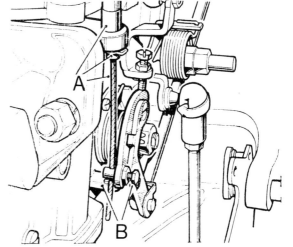

Fig. 3.12. Choke control fixings at carburettor

A   Outer and inner cables and spring clip fixing
B   Trunnion and trunnion bolt

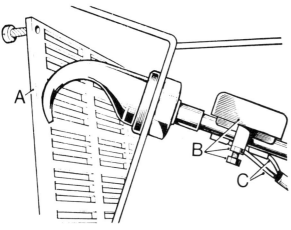

Fig. 3.13. Choke control at console panel

A   Speaker panel
B   Cold start switch and clamp bolts
C   Electrical switch leads

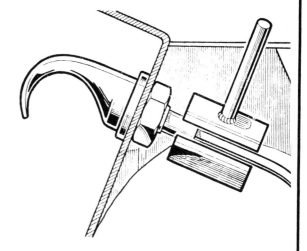

Fig. 3.14. Removal of panel nut using split type box spanner

7 Carburettor adjustments - general

1 The carburettor mixture ratio has been preset at the Rover works and should not be interfered with.

2 However, adjustment can be carried out to the engine idle speed and fast idle speed, without great difficulty.

3 In order to obtain accurate results, the following points must be strictly observed:

a) The ignition timing, dwell angle, contact breaker points and automatic advance should all be checked for correct settings.

b) To produce 'spot on' results, an independent and 'accuracy checked' tachometer should be used. The instrument fitted to the car is **not** suitable.

c) Ideally, any adjustments to carburettor settings should be carried out wherever possible in an ambient air temperature of between 60°F and 80°F (15.5 to 26.5°C).

4 The engine idle speed for standard models is 600 to 650 rev/min. For models fitted with air conditioning, with the compressor isolation switch disengaged, the idle speed is 700 to 750 rev/min. Similarly for models fitted with emission control, the engine idle speed is 700 to 750 rev/min. Fast idle speeds for all models is 1100 to 1200 rev/min.

5 Before attempting any checks upon the settings, a thorough visual and physical examination should be carried out on the throttle control linkages, particularly between the pedal and carburettors to ensure that there is no tendency to jerky action or sticking. Ensure that the choke control is operating to its full extent.

6 If it should become necessary to adjust the throttle linkage on cars fitted with automatic transmission, then it must follow that an additional check and possible re-adjustment may have to be carried out on the downshift cable, so ensuring, that the downshift cable has not suffered any movement or change in relation to the new linkage adjustment. **Note:** Incorrect setting of the downshift cable will result in the wrong oil pressure, which in turn will give rise to possible transmission clutch failure.

7 Before commencing operations upon the engine idle adjustment, the engine should be warmed up to the point when the thermostat has fully opened. Continue running for about 5 minutes, after which, the car should be taken for a run of at least 10 minutes duration, during which, the rev/min. should remain as near as possible to around the 2500 mark. This warming up cycle may be repeated as often as required during idle adjustments, but the driver is warned against overheating the engine which will cause erratic results.

8 On early models fitted with automatic choke or enrichment device, it should be noted that the device should be rendered inoperative before carrying out idle adjustments. This is achieved by means of the cut-off valve provided. To operate this valve, turn the tap clockwise to release it from its retaining thread, then push it inwards. (Fig. 3.14a).

8 SU HIF6 carburettors (standard and emission control) - idling adjustment

1 For automatic cars, move the gear selector lever into the "P" (park) position.

2 Warm up the engine as outlined in the preceding Section.

3 Stop the engine, and remove the air cleaner. (photo) See Chapter 1, Section 7.

4 Release the screws "A" holding the throttle lever to the carburettor lever on both carburettors (Fig. 3.16). This will allow independent adjustment of the carburettors.

5 With the engine running, use the special tool (Fig. 3.15) to slacken off the idle adjusting screw locknuts "B". (Fig. 3.16).

6 Adjust the idle screws equally to obtain the correct engine speeds given in the preceding Section.

7 When both carburettors have been adjusted satisfactorily, lock up the adjusting screw locknuts - holding the adjusting

screw in its position with a screwdriver.

9 SU HIF6 carburettors (standard and emission control) - fast idle adjustment

1 Pull out the mixture control to the point where the mark on the fast idle cam "D" is opposite the centre line of the fast idle adjusting screw "C". (Fig. 3.16).

2 Use the special locknut spanner to release the locknut.

3 Adjust the fast idle screw until a reading of 1100 to 1200 rev/min. is obtained on the tachometer.

10 SU HIF6 carburettors - balancing (synchronisation) using flow meter

1 Zero the gauge pointer by means of the adjusting screw.

2 Fit the balancing flow meter to the carburettor intakes making sure that there are no air leaks (Fig. 3.17).

3. With the engine running, note the reading on the gauge. If the pointer remains or settles in the zero area of the scale, then no adjustment is necessary. If needle moves to the right, reduce the air flow entering the left-hand carburettor by **unscrewing** the idle adjustment screw. Alternatively increase the air flow through right-hand carburettor by **screwing up** the idle adjuster on that carburettor. If conversely, the needle moves to the left, then reverse the procedure.

4 If the idling speed rises too high or drops during these checks, adjust to the correct idle speed, maintaining the gauge needle in the zero area.

5 The difference in engine speeds set with and/or without the balancer in position will be negligible, being in the region of plus or minus 25 rev/min. However, a wide variation in speeds would indicate a basic carburettor fault that may only be remedied by an overhaul, or replacement units. It should be borne in mind that with the SU HIF6, only limited overhaul is possible. (see Section 17 of this Chapter).

6 Place an 0.006 in. (0.15 mm) feeler gauge between the right leg of the fork of the adjusting lever and the pin of the throttle lever of the right-hand carburettor. (Fig. 3.18).

7 Clamp the feeler in position by light pressure to the linkage and at the same time tighten the throttle lever fixing screws.

8 Stop the engine, and replace the air cleaner.

9 On automatics, check that the downshift cable setting is correct. (see Chapter 6, Part 2).

11 SU HS6 (manual choke carburettors) - adjustments

1 In order to obtain accurate results with this type of carburettor, it is desirable to have the use of the air flow balancer device (part No. 605330). Though intended primarily to indicate the air flow into the carburettors, it also serves as an excellent guide to the mixture settings. If when the balancer is fitted the existing mixture setting is too rich, there will be a drop in rev/min or complete stalling of the engine. Conversely, if the mixture setting is on the weak side, then a considerable increase of rev/min. can be expected. It is therefore important that before attempting to balance the carburettors the following procedures are carried out.

2 Move the gear lever or gear selector to neutral or park position.

3 Check for jerkiness or sticking of the throttle pedal to carburettor control linkages.

4 Check the action of the throttle control to ensure that, with the pedal released, there is no starting of movement at the carburettor end. Movement should, however, start with the minimum of pressure on the throttle pedal. So check for free play in the linkage, that could be due to wear at the various couplings.

5 Run the engine as outlined in Section 7, paragraph 7, of this Chapter.

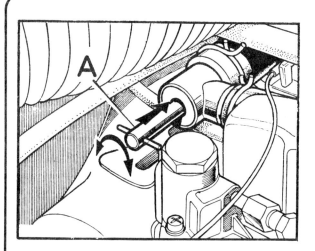

Fig. 3.14a Cut-off valve for automatic enrichment device

A Plunger and tap

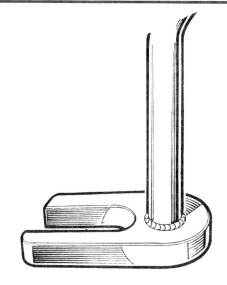

Fig. 3.15. Special tool for carburettor idle adjustment

8.3 Carburettor throttle and choke linkage with air cleaner removed

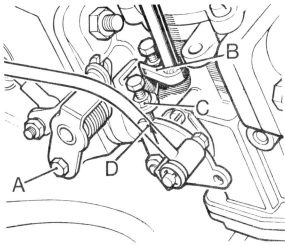

Fig. 3.16. Engine idle adjustment points

A Throttle lever screw   C Fast idle screw
B Idle screw locknut   D Fast idle cam mark

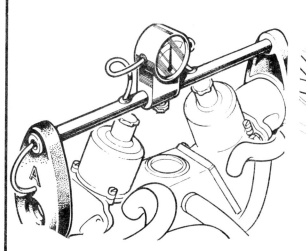

Fig. 3.17. Gray-Horwood type air flow meter

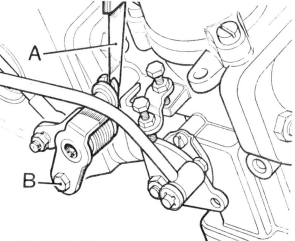

Fig. 3.18. Locking up after idle adjustments

A Feeler gauge   B Throttle lever screw

6 Pivot the air cleaner upwards out of the way to give access to the rear of the carburettors.

7 Release the throttle adjusting lever screws "A" on both carburettors. (Fig. 3.19).

8 Using the independent tachometer, (the instrument fitted to the car is not suitable), check the idle speed, which should be between 600 and 650 rev/min. If incorrect adjust by moving the throttle stop screws, first releasing the locknuts with a suitably modified spanner or tool. (Fig. 3.20).

9 To check the mixture setting of each carburettor separately, lift the piston about 0.040 in. (1 mm). Should the engine revs rise at once then the mixture is on the rich side. Conversely an immediate drop in revolutions will indicate a weak mixture.

10 See Fig. 3.21 for mixture adjustment. Screw the nut **IN** to weaken and/or **OUT** to enrich.

11 Once the engine speed remains constant, the correct mixture is achieved. As the piston is lifted, the engine speed may drop slightly but slowly.

12 Now take off the air cleaner. (See Chapter 1, Section 7).

13 Zero the pointer on the balancing gauge.

14 Fit the balancer to the carburettors making sure that there are no air leaks.

15 If the result of fitting the balancer is abnormal refer to paragraph 1 in this Section and rectify as instructed.

16 The gauge, with the engine running at its recommended idle speed of 600 to 650 rev/min. should read in the zero sector. In this case no further adjustment is required. If it reads to the right of the scale, then adjust by unscrewing the throttle stop on the

left-hand carburettor, thus decreasing the air flow through this carburettor. Alternatively, increase the air flow through the right-hand carburettor by screwing in the throttle stop screw. Should the pointer read to the left of the scale, then simply reverse the procedure.

17 Once the correct adjustment has been arrived at, the balancer can be removed. There will be a marginal plus or minus variation of about 25 rev/min. when the balancer is removed. This can be ignored.

18 Switch off the engine, and place a 0.006 in. (0.15 mm) feeler gauge between the right leg of the fork of the adjusting lever, and the pin of the throttle lever (Fig. 3.22) on the right-hand carburettor.

19 Clamp the feeler in position by applying light pressure to the linkage, and at the same time tighten up the throttle fixing screw. Remove the feeler.

20 To similarly hold the throttle lever position on the left-hand carburettor, bear upon the throttle lever to hold it lightly against the roller of the countershaft lever (Fig. 3.23), and tighten up the fixing screw. Release the pressure on the throttle lever.

21 As previously mentioned, if automatic transmission is fitted, check the adjustment of the downshift cable.

12 Choke (manual) - checking and adjustment

1 Release the choke inner cable at the carburettor end by slackening the ferrule nut.

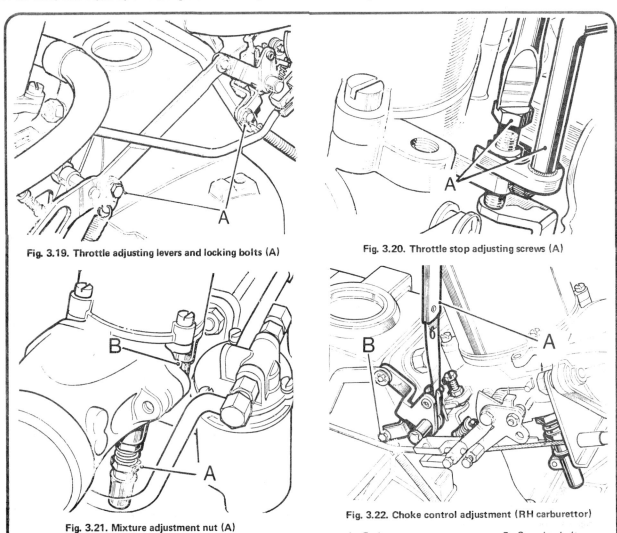

Fig. 3.19. Throttle adjusting levers and locking bolts (A)

Fig. 3.20. Throttle stop adjusting screws (A)

Fig. 3.21. Mixture adjustment nut (A)

Fig. 3.22. Choke control adjustment (RH carburettor)

A *Feeler gauge*   B *Securing bolt*

2 Test the operation of the interconnecting rod (Fig. 3.24) that actuates the cam levers, to ensure that the carburettor jets drop to their full extent.

3 Release the trunnion screw securing the rod, and operate the left-hand choke lever. Note that the right-hand lever is still operative even with the trunnion screw loose.

4 Line up and adjust the position of the connecting rod related to the right-hand choke lever, so that both carburettor jets are synchronised in their initial movement, when the mechanism is actuated.

5 When synchronisation is achieved, tighten the trunnion screw.

6 To set the operating cable correctly, pull out the choke knob approximately 6/10 inch (14 to 16 mm).

7 Manually operate the choke lever at the carburettor until the jets begin to lower.

8 Ensure that the outer choke cable is secure against its abutment bracket, and that the inner cable slides freely in the ferrule.

9 Secure the ferrule to the cable making sure that the cable is

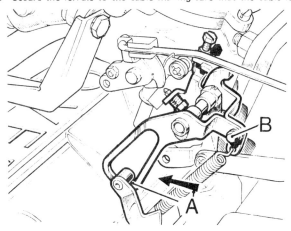

Fig. 3.23. Choke control adjustment (LH carburettor)

A Lever roller   *B Fixing bolt*

taut with the cable set as described in paragraph 6.

10 Make sure that the maximum jet drop is in fact obtainable and that the jets return to their normal slow-running position as the control knob is pushed fully 'home'.

11 Start up the engine and run to normal working temperature.

12 Pull the choke knob out and then return it to the fast idle position (ie, 6/10 inch, 14 to 16 mm) and lock in this position.

13 Release both fast idle adjusting screws until the pins are just clear of the cams.

14 Adjust the fast idle speed by screwing in the fast idle screws until a point where the engine is running at its recommended 1200 to 1400 rev/min. is reached.

15 Lubrication of the cams should be carried out using an oil based graphite or molybdenum disulphide preparation.

16 Refit the air cleaner and road test the car.

13 SU HS6 (emission control) carburettor - adjustments

1 **Note:** Cars fitted with emission control have the jet nuts controlling the mixture set at their richest permitted setting to comply with the regulations. Fitted with locking devices which only allow approximately 3 flats of total movement, (Fig. 3.25) means that the mixture can only be weakened by any intended adjustments. In the case of available adjustment being insufficient to attain the required idling speed (ie, 700 to 750 rev/min.) the only course may be to fit replacement carburettors or carry out an overhaul of the existing ones. Overhaul however is restricted to some degree by the very nature of the emission control requirements. This is dealt with in a later Section of this Chapter.

2 On no account must the mixture locking devices be interfered with as to do so would cause the car to fail in meeting the legal requirements relating to air pollution.

3 There are also sealed locknuts fitted to the idle adjustment screws to prevent careless or inexperienced tampering. These may be unlocked to adjust; but, having done so it is advised that they are subsequently securely tightened and resealed.

4 Apart from the foregoing observations and advices, the procedures are the same as outlined in Section 11 of this Chapter. **Note: The engine idle speed for emission controlled models is between 700 and 750 rev/min.**

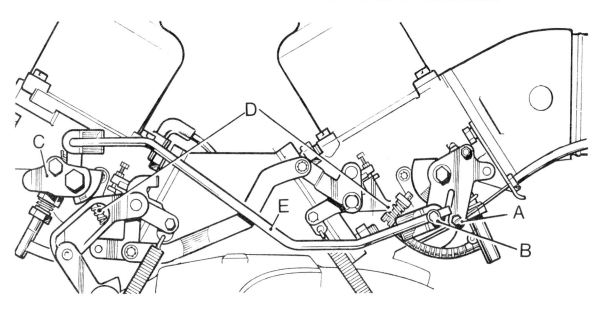

Fig. 3.24. Choke and fast idle adjustment for type HS6 carburettor

A Choke pinch bolt   *B Trunnion screw*   *C LH choke lever*   *D Mixture control screws*
E Interconnecting rod

16.4 Removing the suction chamber

16.6 Carefully remove the piston assembly

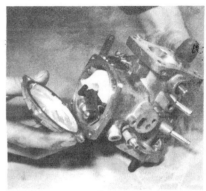

16.9 Bottom cover plate removed

16.11a Removing bimetal strip and jet assembly

16.11b How to separate jet from bimetal strip

16.12 Removing the float hinge pin

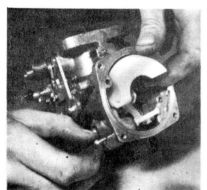

16.13a Removing the float

16.13b Removing the needle valve

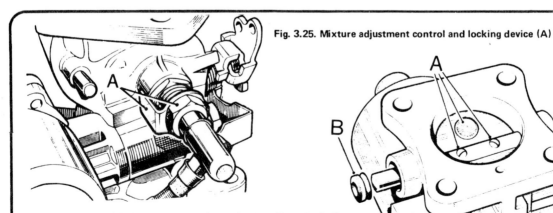

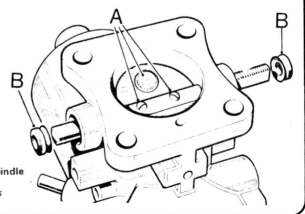

Fig. 3.25. Mixture adjustment control and locking device (A)

Fig. 3.26. Reassembly of throttle butterfly and spindle

A   Poppet valve   B   Rubber seals

14 Carburettors - removal

Refer to Chapter 1, Section 5.

15 Filters, breathers and flame traps - servicing

Full maintenance and servicing instructions are given in the Routine Maintenance Section for the following components:
Crankcase emission breather filter.
Fuel line filter.
Rocker cover fume emission flame traps.

16 SU HIF6 (standard emission control) carburettors - overhaul

1 Remove the carburettors from the car. (See Chapter 1, Section 7).
2 Give both carburettors a preliminary clean-up by washing in a clean petrol bath. Wipe dry with a clean rag.
3 Remove the oil cap and withdraw the damper rod - do not lose the sealing washer (Fig. 3.28).
4 Remove the suction chamber (dashpot) by removing the fixing screws and identity tag. Do not tilt the chamber when withdrawing. (photo)
5 Remove the piston return spring.
6 Carefully withdraw the piston assembly and empty the oil in the piston rod. (photo)
7 To remove the jet needle, remove the needle locking screw and withdraw the needle complete with the spring and guide.
8 Remove the circlip holding the piston lift pin and remove the pin and spring.
9 Remove the screws holding the bottom cover plate and remove the plate with its sealing ring. (photo)
10 Remove the spring loaded screw securing the bimetal strip and adjusting lever.
11 Withdraw the bimetal strip and jet assembly; disengage the jet from the bimetal strip. (photos)
12 Remove the pivot pin for the float spindle. Note the sealing washer. (photo)
13 Remove the float, and the needle, fuel control valve. (photos)
14 Remove the float needle valve seating.
15 Unscrew the locknut for the jet bearing, and withdraw the jet bearing complete with its sealing washer.
16 Remove the end nut on the choke cam spindle, and remove the cam assembly. Take note of the positions of the spring, spacers and washers.
17 Dismantle the cold start assembly.
18 Dismantle the throttle lever assembly. Start at the lever end by removing the long spindle extended nut that retains the levers to the butterfly shaft.
19 Remove the throttle butterfly by removing its two retaining screws.
20 Withdraw the spindle from the carburettor body complete with the end seals.
21 This is as far as the dismantling should go to effect an overhaul. It is emphasised, that on no account, should the jet height setting be altered. This setting is preset at the factory using special flow test rigs. It is for this reason that the access hole to the jet adjustment screw is plugged. All other parts can be renewed from the service spares kit available from any Rover dealer or SU stockist - with the exception of the jet adjustment screw. If after overhaul, the carburation still proves to be un-satisfactory, a complete replacement unit will be advisable.
22 Clean all the parts thoroughly in methylated spirit or other suitable solvent.
23 All the seals should be renewed during the rebuild and if the car has covered a high mileage, then it is advised that the jet metering needle be renewed also. Similarly should the throttle butterfly spindle and its bearings be regarded with a degree of suspicion, it is advisable to have all these new parts to hand, possibly on a 'use-or-return' basis, by arrangement with your

local stockist.
24 Plug the transfer holes in the piston assembly and reassemble the piston into the suction chamber, refitting the damper and sealing washer. Turn the whole assembly up-side-down and estimate the time taken for the piston to drop down into the suction chamber. It should take five to seven seconds for HIF6 with 1.750 in. (44.5 mm) bore. If a longer time is taken, then re-examine for congealed, or thick oil remaining on the piston rod the piston itself or the suction chamber. Re-clean and carry out the test once more.
25 Reassemble the butterfly spindle and butterfly (Fig. 3.26) ensuring that the threaded end protrudes from the cold start side of the carburettor body. Note that the edges of the butterfly are chamfered. The butterfly should fit so that the bottom edge moves away from the manifold fitting flange when the throttle is opened. Make sure that the chamfered edges are a good mating fit to the bore.
26 Refit the butterfly securing screws (which should be new), but do not tighten fully at this stage.
27 **Note:** Emission controlled cars are fitted with a butterfly that has a poppet valve set into the butterfly face.
28 Operate the throttle spindle several times to centralise the butterfly; then, fully tighten the screws. Lock by gently peening over the protruding ends of the screws. Take great care not to bend the shaft.
29 Replace the new spindle seals with the dished ends towards the throttle. Push the seals in to within 0.035 in. (0.9 mm) below the surface of the spindle housing flange.
30 With the throttle closed, refit the throttle return, and throttle levers (Fig. 3.27).
31 The bush is fitted with its spigot end through the throttle lever.
32 Fit the tab washer; tighten the retaining nut and lock up with the tab washer.
33 To refit the cold start assembly. First, oil the 'O' ring and fit it to the valve body (Fig. 3.29). Insert the spindle into the valve body from the 'O' ring end. Locate the oil seal with the dished end leading.
34 Turn the carburettor onto its side and support it to give free access to the cold start valve bore. Place the valve gasket (Fig. 3.30) in position with its 'cut-out' slot nearest the top screw hole.
35 Offer up the cold start assembly to the housing ensuring that the 'cut-out' slot in the valve flange lines up with that of the gasket.
36 Assemble the end seal to the cover and fit the retaining plate

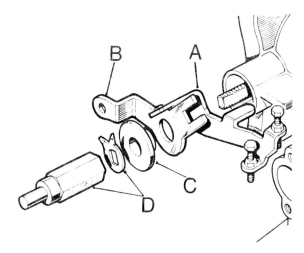

Fig. 3.27. Throttle lever assembly

A Throttle return lever   C Bush
B Throttle lever   D Tab washer and nut

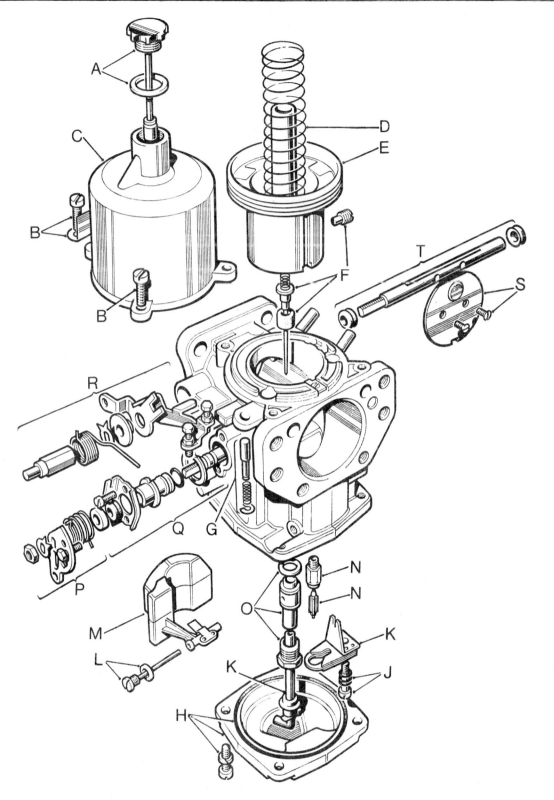

Fig. 3.28. Exploded view of SU type HIF 6 carburettor

A Oil cap, damper with gasket
B Suction chamber securing screws
C Suction chamber
D Piston spring
E Piston
F Jet metering needle and securing screw assembly
G Piston lift pin
H Float chamber cover and securing screws
J Securing screw for the bi-metal blade assembly
K Bi-metal blade and jet assembly
L Hinge pin for float
M Float assembly
N Fuel control valve seat and needle valve
O Jet bearing, lock nut and sealing washer
P Cam lever and spring
Q Cold start assembly
R Throttle levers
S Throttle butterfly
T Throttle spindle and seals

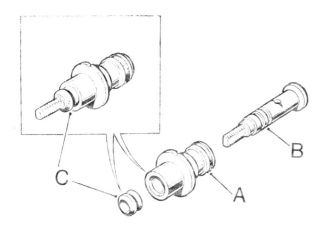

Fig. 3.29. Cold start valve reassembly

A 'O' ring   C Spindle shoulder
B Spindle   end seal

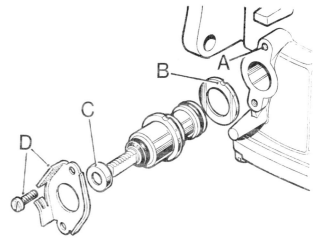

Fig. 3.30. Components of cold starting device

A Carburettor body   C End seal cover
B Gasket   D Retaining plate

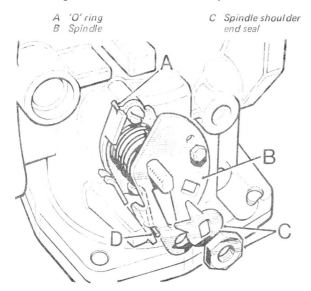

Fig. 3.31. Cold start device assembled

A Cam return spring   C Tab washer and nut
B Cam lever   D End of cam return spring

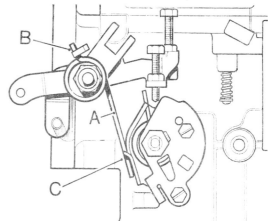

Fig. 3.32. Throttle lever and cam correctly positioned

A Throttle return spring C Long spring end
B Short spring end

with the slotted flange facing towards the throttle spindle. Tighten the screws evenly. Do not overtighten.

37 Locate the cam return spring. The straight end, slots into the top 'cut-out' in the retaining bracket (Fig. 3.31).

38 Offer the cam lever to the spindle with the right-angled extension towards the carburettor body and opposite the casting stop piece.

39 Lock up with the tab washer and nut.

40 Use a wire hook to locate the spring end under the extended tab on the cam lever.

41 Locate the throttle return spring with the long extension of the spring inwards. The short extension locates into the slotted right-angled extension of the throttle lever. The long end of the spring abuts against the bottom slot on the cold start retaining bracket (Fig. 3.32).

42 Refit the jet bearing assembly into the carburettor body, not forgetting to fit the fibre washer, then tighten the locking nut (Fig. 3.33).

43 Refit the float chamber fuel control needle valve seating and tighten.

44 Support the carburettor body for two handed access to the float chamber. Place the needle valve into position in the valve seating - pointed end first. Offer up the float to the float

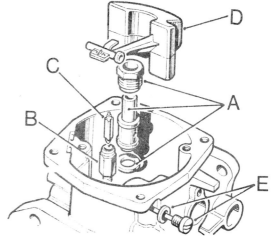

Fig. 3.33. Float components

A Jet assembly   C Needle valve
B Needle valve seating   D Float
                           E Float pivot spindle

chamber with the "Part No." lettering uppermost, and the hinged tab abutting against the needle valve. Locate the pivot pin into the carburettor body engaging it through the float hinge. Do not forget the fibre sealing washer. Tighten the pivot pin.

45 To check the correct positioning of the float in relation to the float chamber proceed as follows: With the carburettor supported with the float chamber uppermost, the needle valve closed by the weight of the float alone, lay a straight edge across carburettor body flange face and measure with a feeler gauge the clearance between the straight edge and the centre of the float ridge. (Fig. 3.34). The clearances should read 0.040 in. plus-or-minus, 0.20 in. (1.0 mm ± 0.5 mm). If required, bend the float hinge tab to adjust to the correct height.

46 Assemble the bimetal strip, the jet and position jet into the jet bearing (Fig. 3.35) - the jet head should run parallel with the longer arm of the bimetal strip. The longer arm must engage over the head of the jet adjusting screw. Engage the pivot screw and spring and tighten carefully until the shoulder is tight against the body.

47 Refit the float chamber bottom cover plate "A", not forgetting the sealing washer "B" which fits into the groove in the cover plate. Ensure that the cut-out section of the plate lines up with carburettor inlet fitting flange (Fig. 3.36).

48 Refit the piston lifting pin, spring and circlip assembly.

49 Refitting the jet needle to the piston: Locate the spring on the top end of the needle ensuring that it fits snugly into the annular groove (Fig. 3.37). Insert the needle through its guide, from the end of the guide carrying the small protrusion. Offer up the complete assembly to the piston, positioning the guide so that the etching marked on its bottom face aligns centrally to the slot between the air holes in the piston (Fig. 3.38). Push the guide into the recess in the piston until the guide face is level with the bottom face of the slot. Lock in this position with the locking screw.

50 Carefully locate the piston assembly onto the carburettor body, and lightly oil the surface of the piston rod (Fig. 3.39). Replace the spring "B", and by first visually lining up the position, fit the suction chamber without rotation or tilting. The identification tag goes under the rear screw. Tighten the retaining screws evenly - do not overtighten.

51 The damper oil can be introduced at this stage or left until the carburettors are refitted to the car. In either event do not forget the sealing washer under the oil cap.

52 Finally check the free movement of the piston before refitting the carburettor to the car.

---

17 SU HS6 (emission control) carburettors - overhaul

---

1 The observations and recommendations as to jet height and mixture setting are the same as for carburettor HIF6 which is fully covered in the preceding Section. The dismantling procedures are similar in practice though the HS6 is in fact an instrument of earlier design and not so compact as the later model HIF6.

2 With the carburettors removed from the car, give them a clean-up before dismantling. In the same way as for the HIF6 dismantle the damper, the suction chamber and piston assembly. Remove the jet needle if necessary (Fig. 3.40).

3 The obvious difference between the HIF6 and this carburettor is the placing of the float chamber. This should present no particular problems during dismantling or reassembly (Fig. 3.41).

4 To dismantle the pick up lever and return spring (Fig. 3.42), apply some pressure to the cam lever "A" and remove the screw from the jet head base thus releasing the pick-up link. Removal of the bolt "C" holding the pick-up assembly "B" will allow the release of the return spring, followed by the rest of the assembly.

5 Disconnect the flexible pipe from the float chamber and remove the gland and metal washer (Fig. 3.43).

6 Carefully remove the jet tube and flexible pipe together, from the carburettor body.

7 **On no account should the jet bearing assembly be removed.**

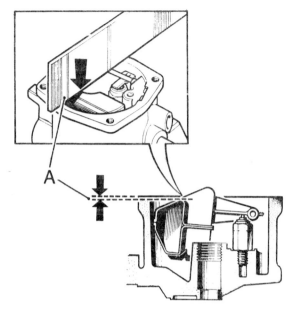

Fig. 3.34. Testing float adjustment, gap (A) 0.040 in. (1.0 mm)

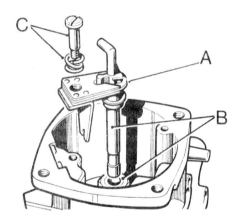

Fig. 3.35. Bi-metal and jet assembly

A Jet head in bi-metal cut-out   C Pivot pin and
B Jet and jet bearing   spring

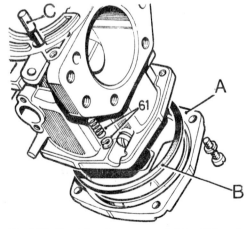

Fig. 3.36. Float chamber cover and piston lifting pin

A Cover plate   C Piston lifting pin
B Sealing ring

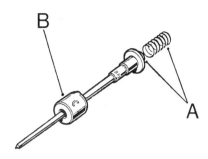

Fig. 3.37. Jet metering assembly

A Jet needle and spring   B Needle guide

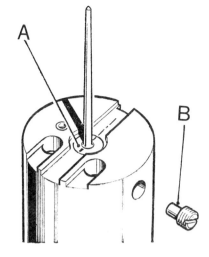

Fig. 3.38. Fitting needle to piston

A Needle/guide assembly   B Locking screw

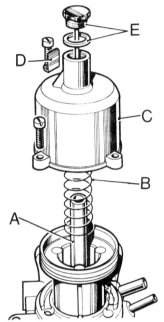

Fig. 3.39. Piston and suction chamber

A Piston assembly   D Carburettor identification
B Spring   tag
C Chamber   E Damper

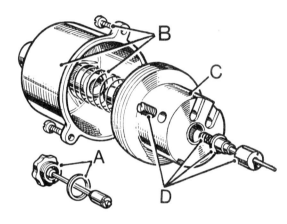

Fig. 3.40. Piston and suction chamber detail

A Damper, cap and washer   C Piston
B Suction chamber   D Jet metering needle
                                 assembly

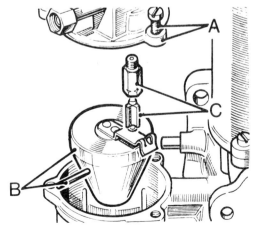

Fig. 3.41. Float and float valve detail

A Chamber lid and retain-   C Fuel control valve seat
   ing screws   and needle valve
B Float and pivot pin

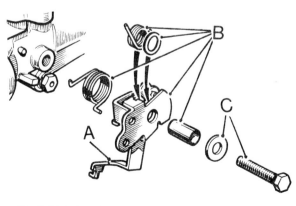

Fig. 3.42. Pick-up link assembly

A Cam lever   C Retaining bolt and
B Pick-up link assembly   washer

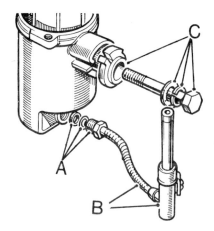

Fig. 3.43. Float chamber components

A Union   C Bolt assembly
R Flexible pipe and jet tube

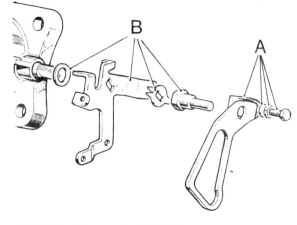

Fig. 3.44. LH carburettor throttle linkage

A Throttle lever secured by   B Spindle extension nut,
   bolt, spring washer and   tab washer, lever link
   brass washer   and brass washer

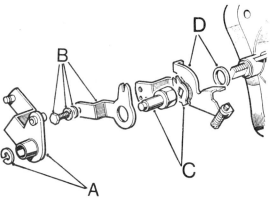

Fig. 3.45. RH carburettor throttle linkage

A Circlip and RH throttle   C Spindle extension nut and
  lever   tab washer
B Adjusting bolt and lever   D Carburettor lever and
                           brass washer

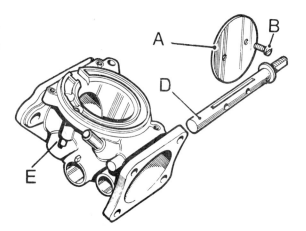

Fig. 3.46. Butterfly and throttle spindle

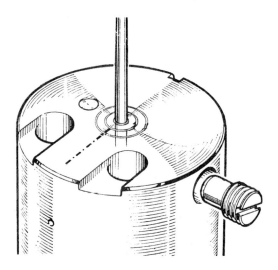

Fig. 3.47. Refitting the jet needle

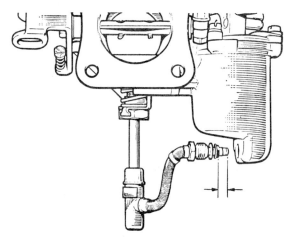

Fig. 3.48. Reassembly of jet tube to carburettor

8 Release the bolt and detach the float chamber from the carburettor body.

9 Disconnect the throttle link of the right-hand carburettor.

10 For the throttle lever assembly (left-hand carburettor) see Fig. 3.44, and for right-hand carburettor see Fig. 3.45.

11 To remove the butterfly spindle, (Fig. 3.46) first remove the butterfly "A" by removing the two brass screws 'B', (which should be discarded to be replaced by new screws), slide the butterfly out of its slot in the spindle. On reassembly, the plain end "D" should be on the float chamber side.

12 Inspection for wear: Thoroughly clean all the parts and critically examine the following items for signs of wear, or damage: The throttle spindle and bearing surfaces in the carburettor body. All linkages and levers for excessive movement which will indicate wear. Clean and examine the inside surface of the suction chamber for wear patterns, scoring etc. Similarly examine the bearing surface of the piston and piston rod. The jet needle and jet bearing. On a high mileage car, most of these parts are bound to show varying degrees of wear, and the d-i-y owner must decide depending upon his previous knowledge of the car's history as to what and when to replace in the way of component parts. The advice given in paragraph 23 of the preceding Section applies.

13 The piston lift pin can be removed if required in the same manner as for the model HIF6 carburettor.

14 Points for reassembly: Refit the spindle and butterfly in the same manner as for the HIF6 carburettor, with the exception that there are no spindle end seals, and no alternative butterfly, for emission control. Refit the throttle lever and link levers in reverse order of dismantling. Replace the brass washer on the throttle spindle making sure that it fits over the thick portion of the spindle - which will be just protruding, from the carburettor body. Do not fully tighten the adjusting screws or nuts on any throttle linkage that will obviously need re-adjusting when finally refitted to the car.

15 Refitting the jet metering needle to the piston: Fit the spring and bias sleeve and insert the assembly into its position in the piston so that the shoulder on the shank is flush with the face of the piston. In the event of an alignment mark being provided, the marks must line up as shown in Fig. 3.47. On later versions of this carburettor, a full length locating flat is provided for positioning the needle retaining screw. Locate the locking screw and tighten.

16 Reassemble the piston and suction chamber in the same manner as for the HIF6 carburettor.

17 Check that the piston has complete free fall to its limits so that it rests back on to the bridge of the carburettor body, after being lifted by the piston lift pin. Also ensure that the jet needle is not fouling or sticking in the jet bearing.

18 Reassemble the jet tube and flexible pipe to the float chamber using a new gland (Fig. 3.48). Do not tighten at this stage. Make sure that at least 0.187 in. (4.7 mm) of tube projects before fitting.

19 Assemble the float chamber, and locate the jet tube together to the carburettor body. Locate the retaining bolt for the float chamber and secure.

20 Reassemble the pick up lever and cam link assembly to carburettor body. (Figs. 3.49, 3.50, 3.51).

21 Tighten the gland nut retaining the flexible pipe to the float chamber.

22 Reassembly of the float and float needle valve: Fit the valve seat to the chamber cover and replace the valve - pointed end in first (Fig. 3.52). Fit the float in position securing it with its pivot pin.

23 Check the float level with the chamber cover inverted and the valve head closed by only the weight of the float; a check can be made by measuring the gap between the float and the rim of the chamber cover. The gap should be between 0.125 in. and 0.187 in. (3 and 4.5 mm). For later models where the float and arm are integral, and not riveted, the measurement should be taken between the lid register and the nearest point on the float. On this type of float, there is no means of adjusting and error in float level will have been caused by damage to the assembly. The

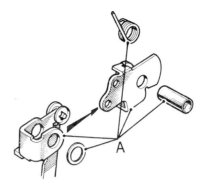

Fig. 3.49. Reassembly of pick-up lever and cam

A Cam lever, pick-up lever and link, spacing tube, spring and shim washers

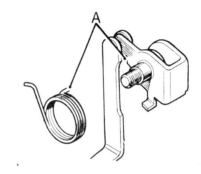

Fig. 3.50. Locating spring end "A" in slot provided

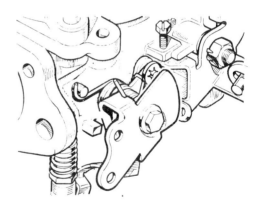

Fig. 3.51. Pick-up lever and cam reassembled to carburettor

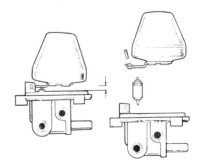

Fig. 3.52. Checking float height

damaged or faulty part must be identified and renewed.

24 Refit the chamber cover with a new gasket and tighten evenly.

25 The damper can be refilled at this stage with SAE 20 oil to within ½ in. (12 mm) of the top of the hollow piston rod, or it can be left until the carburettors are refitted to the car.

---

18 SU HS6 carburettors - throttle linkage

1   Fig. 3.53 illustrates the layout of the throttle linkage for type HS6 carburettors. Necessary points to watch are covered in the text under carburettor adjustments HS6.

---

19 SU HIF6 carburettors - throttle linkage and choke controls

1   Fig. 3.54 illustrates the layout of the throttle and choke

control linkage fitted to SU carburettor type HIF6.

2   Dismantling of the throttle control linkage is covered in Chapter 1, Section 7. The layout is shown in Fig. 3.55.

3   If any of the link-rod ball joints have been disturbed during carburettor overhaul, then reset the distances between the centres of the ball joints (Fig. 3.56) as follows:

For the long vertical rod:
Right-hand drive   7.635 in. (193.6 mm)
Left-hand drive   7.968 in. (202.3 mm)

For the short vertical rod:
3.922 in. $\pm$ 0.030 in.
(96.6 mm $\pm$ 0.7 mm)

Carburettor link rod:
5.070 in. $\pm$ 0.030 in.
(128.7 mm $\pm$ 0.7 mm)

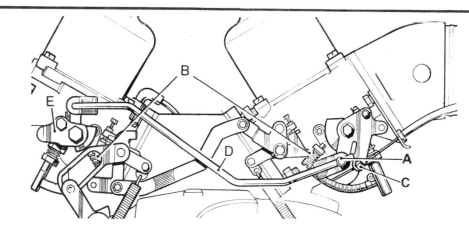

Fig. 3.53. Throttle linkage for SU HS6 carburettor - general layout

A   Trunnion and trunnion
    bolt
B   Throttle adjusting screws
C   Ferrule screw securing
    choke inner cable
D   Interconnecting rod
E   Left-hand choke lever

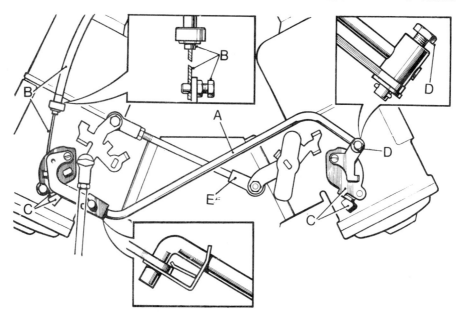

Fig. 3.54. Throttle and choke linkage layout detail for SU HIF6 carburettor

A   Choke link rod
B   Choke control cable
(inset shows fixing detail)
C   Choke control arms
D   and inset, trunnion and
    securing bolt for choke
link rod
E   Throttle linkage

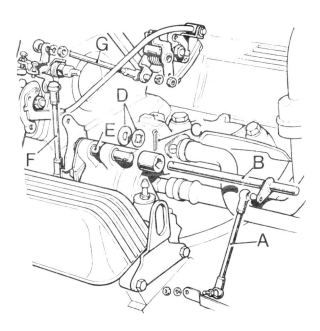

Fig. 3.55. Throttle control linkage layout

A   Long vertical link rod
B   Coupling rod
C   Split pin securing nylon coupling
D   Clip and plain washers
E   Countershaft
F   Short vertical link rod
G   Throttle link rod

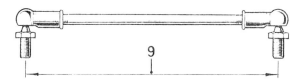

Fig. 3.56. Throttle link rod to ball joint centres adjustment diagram

20 Emission control - general

1 Where Rover cars are supplied to countries that enforce emission control regulations, the cars are equipped and tuned to conform with the current regulations in force at the time of their manufacture. But due to the varying regulations dependent upon the particular country or state concerned, the degree of emission control equipment and adjustment incorporated in any specific car may vary from that of another. It will therefore become the responsibility of the owner to ensure that his car does in fact conform to the regulations concerning air pollution in the country or state in which the car is to be used.

2 **Crankcase emission control:** All Rover 3500 and 3500 S models are equipped with crankcase emission control breathing, in which the crankcase fumes are recirculated through the inlet manifold to be burned during the normal combustion process, instead of being emitted directly into the atmosphere.

3 The breathing cycle is illustrated in Fig. 3.57. Clean air is taken from the rear end of the air cleaner and fed through the engine breather filter into the rear of the crankcase. Crankcase fumes rise via the pushrod tubes into the rocker cover space. From here the fumes are drawn through the flame traps into the carburettor intake adapters and so into the normal engine combustion cycle; they are burned with the fuel and exhausted through the exhaust system.

4 Maintenance of the crankcase emission control system is covered in the Routine Maintenance Section at the front of this manual.

5 3500 and 3500 S models supplied to countries or states in which emission control regulations are enforced, are specially equipped to control the emission of hydrocarbons and carbon monoxide from the exhaust system. Conformity to the regulations is achieved by alteration to the carburation, and cylinder combustion characteristics of the engine.

6 The jet metering needle within the carburettor is fitted with a spring loaded mechanism, the needle being biased against its retainer by the spring, thus, maintaining the jet needle at all times in correct relationship to the carburettor jet. This innovation to carburation has been found to greatly improve the control of gas emission (Fig. 3.58).

7 Another innovation directed to this same end, is the introduction of a poppet valve incorporated into the throttle butterfly. The purpose and action of this valve is to compensate, by supplementing the volume of air in the fuel mixture under high depression conditions existing in the manifold when the accelerator pedal is released and the throttle butterfly shut during the 'over-run' periods of driving. Under normal driving when the car is under power and the manifold depression is low, the valve remains shut (Fig. 3.59).

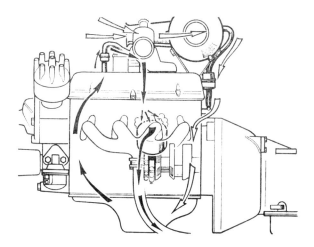

Fig. 3.57. Crankcase emission control system

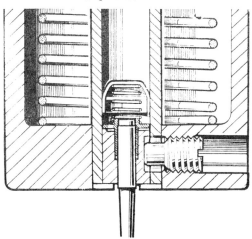

Fig. 3.58. Exhaust emission control valve

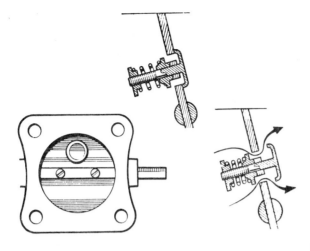

Fig. 3.59. Butterfly poppet valve (emission control)

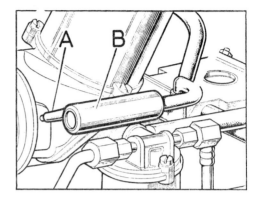

Fig. 3.60. Carburettor temperature compensator (emission control)

A Connecting pipes   B Compensator

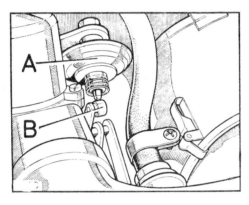

Fig. 3.61. Throttle damper (emission control)

A Damper   B Throttle control spindle

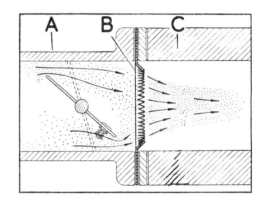

Fig. 3.62. Fuel deflector (emission control)

A Carburettor   C Inlet manifold
B Deflector

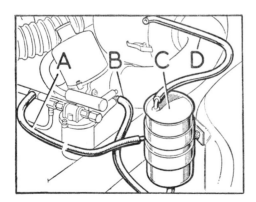

Fig. 3.63. Charcoal canister (carburettor evaporative emission control)

A, B, D Connecting pipes   C Canister

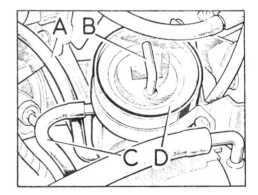

Fig. 3.64. Charcoal canister (fuel tank evaporative emission control)

A, B, C Connections   D Canister

8 It is emphasised that correct ignition timing and dwell angle as well as carburettor settings must be maintained to ensure continued compliance with the exhaust emission control regulations. Therefore, strict observance of the recommendations set out in this manual should be adhered to, if the car is to meet the legal requirements, in respect of air pollution.

9 **Carburettor temperature compensator:** Each carburettor has an independent temperature compensator "B" (Fig. 3.60). The unit contains a bimetallic valve which being sensitive to intake temperatures, actuates a jet bypass air bleed to give weaker mixtures at high air intake temperatures.

10 **Throttle damper:** This device "A" (Fig. 3.61) prevents the throttle plate snapping shut when the throttle pedal is suddenly released. It is pneumatically actuated and its action reduces hydrocarbon emission during rapid deceleration.

11 **Fuel deflector:** This deflector "B" (Fig. 3.62) is fitted between the carburettor and the inlet manifold at the mounting flange. Its design permits better atomising of the fuel/air mixture and so prevents fuel condensation on the manifold walls - this enables the engine to operate on weaker fuel/air mixtures.

12 **Evaporative emission control:** On later models where this system is installed, a charcoal filled canister is fitted to absorb vapour from the carburettor float chambers and another to absorb vapour from the fuel tank (Fig. 3.63 and 3.64).

13 These canisters are disposable and should be renewed at intervals of 24,000 miles (40,000 km) or immediately should flooding of the carburettor or fuel tank have taken place.

14 Normal maintenance consists of checking the security of all connecting hoses so that the system of purging the canisters of fuel vapour by the induction of the engine, when it is operating, may be positive and continuous. Do not attempt to clean the canisters by blowing compressed air into them, this could cause the charcoal to ignite!

21 Throttle linkage - removal, adjustment and refitment

1 The accelerator linkage varies slightly according to model and is shown in component form in Figs. 3.65 and 3.66.

2 To dismantle the linkage, detach the two ball joints which

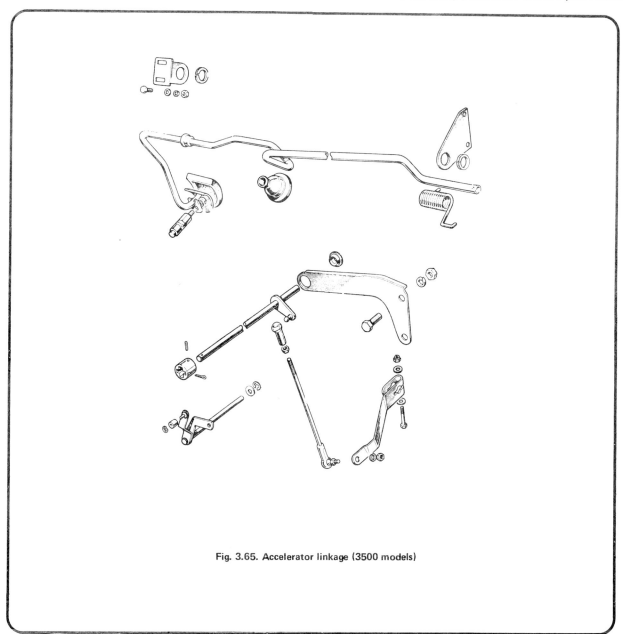

Fig. 3.65. Accelerator linkage (3500 models)

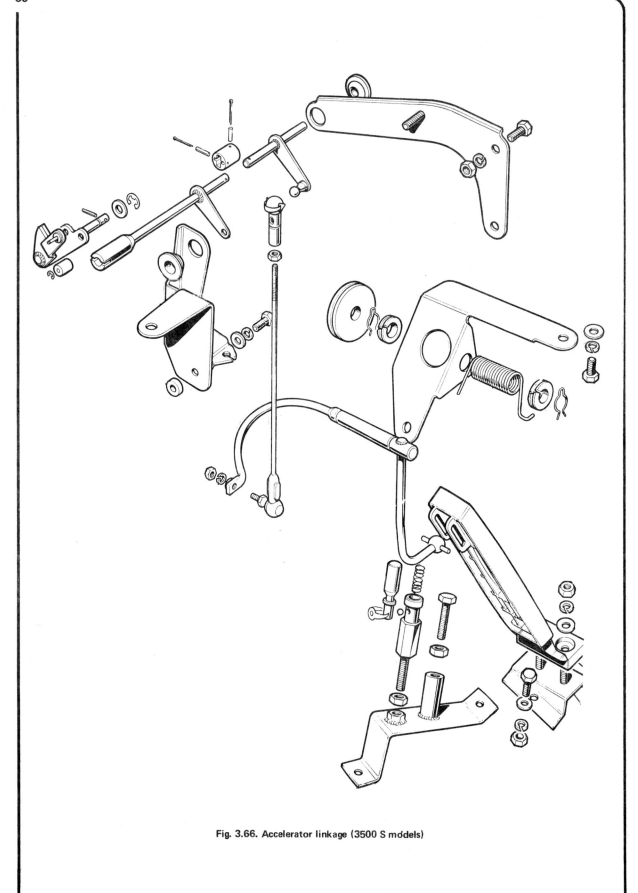

Fig. 3.66. Accelerator linkage (3500 S models)

secure the vertical rod and remove the rod assembly.

3 Detach the split pin from the nylon coupling and rod (bulkhead to carburettor) and lift off the coupling rod.

4 Remove the lever return spring.

5 Remove the accelerator pedal bracket (nuts located under front wing).

6 Remove the pinch bolt which secures the lever to the cross-shaft and detach the lever.

7 Remove the cross-shaft mounting bracket.

8 Detach the brake pedal return spring and withdraw the accelerator cross-shaft and pedal assembly through the bulkhead into the interior of the car.

9 Re-fitting is a reversal of removal, but the following adjustment must then be carried out: Hold the accelerator pedal hard down to the floor and have an assistant tighten the locknut on the lower ball joint of the vertical rod. Hold the accelerator coupling shaft in the full throttle position and adjust the upper ball joint by turning it on the control rod until it will just slip over the ball on the coupling shaft. Assemble the ball joint and secure the locknut.

10 Check for full movement of the accelerator pedal and that the carburettor butterfly is fully open when the pedal is fully depressed.

22 Exhaust system - general

1 The exhaust system varies slightly in design according to model and date of manufacture. A typical layout with mounting arrangements is shown in Fig. 3.67.

2 The system is in sections with flanged connections for easy renewal of corroded or damaged portions. (photo) Always apply penetrating oil to the flange bolts before unscrewing them, and obtain new bolts and joint gaskets before fitting the new exhaust components.

3 Examine the rubber mountings and renew them if they have perished due to oil or heat.

4 The exhaust manifold bolts are secured with locking plates. When fitting the manifolds, run the engine to normal operating temperature and finally tighten the bolts to a torque of 15 lb/ft (2.0 kg/m) **before** bending over the tabs of the locking plates.

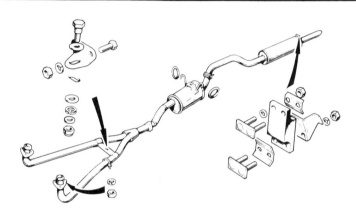

Fig. 3.67. Exhaust system and mountings (manual gearbox)

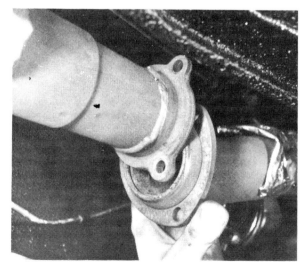

22.2 Disconnecting an exhaust system section

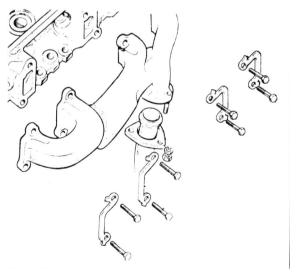

Fig. 3.68. Exhaust manifold showing bolts and locking plates

23 Fault diagnosis - carburation and fuel system

Symptom	Reason/s	Remedy
Carburation and ignition faults	Air cleaner choked and dirty giving rich mixture	Remove, clean and replace air cleaner.
	Fuel leaking from carburettor/s, fuel pumps, or fuel lines	Check for and eliminate all fuel leaks. Tighten fuel line union nuts.
	Float chamber flooding	Check and adjust float level.
	Generally worn carburettor/s.	Remove, overhaul and replace.
	Distributor condenser faulty	Remove, and fit new unit.
	Balance weights or vacuum advance mechanism in distributor faulty.	Remove, and overhaul distributor.
Incorrect adjustment	Carburettor/s incorrectly adjusted, mixture too rich	Tune and adjust carburettor/s
	Idling speed too high	Adjust idling speed.
	Contact breaker gap incorrect	Check and reset gap.
	Valve clearances incorrect	Check rocker arm to valve stem clearances and adjust as necessary.
	Incorrectly set spark plugs	Remove, clean and regap.
	Tyres under-inflated	Check tyre pressures and inflate if necessary.
	Wrong spark plugs fitted	Remove and replace with correct units.
	Brakes dragging	Check and adjust brakes.
Dirt in system	Petrol tank air vent restricted	Remove petrol cap and clean out air vent.
	Partially clogged filters in pump and carburettor/s	Remove and clean filters.
	Dirt lodged in float chamber needle housing	Remove and clean out float chamber and needle valve assembly.
	Incorrectly seating valves in fuel pump	Remove, dismantle, and clean out fuel pump.
Fuel pump faults	Fuel pump diaphragm leaking or damaged	Remove, and overhaul fuel pump.
	Gasket in fuel pump damaged	Remove, and overhaul fuel pump.
	Fuel pump valves sticking due to petrol gumming	Remove, and thoroughly clean fuel pump.
Air leaks	Too little fuel in fuel tank (prevalent when climbing steep hills)	Refill fuel tank.
	Union joints on pipe connections loose	Tighten joints and check for air leaks.
	Split in fuel pipe on suction side of fuel pump	Examine, locate, and repair.
	Inlet manifold to block or inlet manifold to carburettor/s gasket leaking	Test by pouring oil along joints — bubbles indicate leak. Renew gasket as appropriate.

Chapter 4 Ignition system

Contents

Specifications

Distributor:

Make and type	Lucas 35 D8/1569
Rotation of rotor	Anticlockwise
Dwell angle	26° to 28°
Contact breaker gap	0.014 to 0.016 in. (0.36 to 0.40 mm)
Condenser capacity	0.18 to 0.25 microfarad

Ignition timing:

10.5 : 1 compression ratio	100 octane fuel	6° BTDC static and dynamic (600 rev/min)
	96 octane fuel	TDC static and dynamic (600 rev/min)
8.5 : 1 compression ratio	90 octane fuel	6° BTDC static and dynamic (600 rev/min)
Vehicles fitted with emission control:	96 octane fuel	TDC static and dynamic (700-750 rev/min)

Centrifugal advance — decelerating check with vacuum unit disconnected
Early models with Lucas No. 41176 or 4278 stamped on the distributor body

	Crankshaft angle	Engine rev/min.
Ignition timing	6° BTDC	
	30° to 34°	4800
	26° to 30°	3800
	18° to 22°	1800
	14° to 18°	1400
	8° to 12°	1000
	6°	Below 600

Vacuum advance:
Starts	101 mm (4 in.) Hg
Finishes	508 mm (20 in.) Hg

Models with Lucas No. 41317 stamped on the distributor body

	Crankshaft angle		Engine rev/min.
Ignition timing	6° BTDC	TDC	
	30° to 34°	24° to 28°	4800
	26° to 30°	20° to 24°	3800
	20° to 24°	14° to 18°	2400
	16° to 20°	10° to 14°	1800
	9° to 12°	3° to 6°	1200
	6° to 9°	0° to 3°	900
	6°	0°	Below 700

Vacuum advance:
Starts	101 mm (4 in.) Hg
Finishes	508 mm (20 in.) Hg

Models with Lucas No. 41392 stamped on the distributor body

Ignition timing	Crankshaft angle	Engine rev/min.
	6° BTDC	
	25° to 29°	4400
	20° to 24°	2600
	15° to 20°	1800
	8° to 12°	1200
	6°	Below 600

Vacuum advance:
  Starts ... ...   101 mm (4 in.) Hg
  Finishes ... ...   381 mm (15 in.) Hg

Spark plugs:
  Make ... ...   Champion
  Type ... ...   L87Y (L92Y after January 1972)
  Gap ... ...   0.60 mm (0.025 in.)

Ignition coil:
  Make/type ... ...   Lucas 16 C 6 with ballast resistor
  Primary resistance at 20° C (68° F) ... ...   1.2 to 1.4 ohms
  Consumption — ignition on at 2000 rev/min. ... ...   1 amp

1 General description

The ignition system on all models consists of an ignition coil and distributor and draws its low tension supply from the 12 volt battery.

Two essential modifications to this otherwise conventional system have been introduced in the interests of emission control and air pollution regulations, where applied. These modifications are described later in this Section.

Any ignition system fitted to an internal combustion engine must have one ultimate aim, and that is to provide the combustion-igniting spark at the right place (ie. the spark plug points), at the right moment in time (between 6° BTDC and TDC of the combustion stroke) in the right order of firing; one might add also, in sufficient strength to create the necessary spark under compression at the plug points.

In an ignition coil/distributor system there are two separate electrical circuits, the primary or low tension circuit (LT) and the secondary or high tension (HT) circuit. The high tension circuit is entirely dependent upon the degree of working efficiency of the primary circuits and equipment for its ultimate performance. In the primary circuit, a transformer or coil as it is better known, is placed into circuit with the 12 volt supply when the ignition switch is operated. A further automatic switch called the contact breaker, driven indirectly by the camshaft interrupts the LT supply. The contact breaker is so arranged by integral design with the engine to operate 'open' coinciding with the TDC of any given piston on its compression stroke. The contact breaker is opened by a series of cam lobes (eight in this case) fitted to a spindle or shaft that is driven by a skew gear from the engine camshaft. It follows that there must be eight openings of the contact breaker to one complete revolution of the distributor cam, and the distributor cam will revolve once for every two revolutions of the engine crankshaft. The resulting break in the low tension supply will cause the electro-magnetic field, that has been built up by energising the primary windings to collapse. The field or flux cuts through the multi windings of the secondary coil inducing in it a very high voltage of the order of some twelve to eighteen thousand volts. This high voltage or tension is tapped by the coil HT lead and led by the distributor to the relevant spark plugs.

During this phenomena there is a considerable back surge of electricity in the primary circuit. This is known as back EMF. This back EMF would very quickly burn out the points by arcing if they were not protected by the condenser (capacitor). This piece of equipment, housed within the distributor body and connected across the contact breaker points, soaks up (by becoming charged) all this back EMF that is present across the points. A test for condenser serviceability is to part the points with the ignition "ON" observing the degree of arcing present. If

the arcing is heavy then the condenser may be faulty. Without the condenser the engine will not run.

The rotor arm is fitted to the end of the cam spindle, and so placed, is synchronised with the cam and engine crankshaft movement. The result is that the end of the rotor is correctly placed in rotation opposite a contact segment (any one of eight housed within the distributor cap) at the moment of opening of the contact breaker points. Each of the eight segments is connected to a plug lead, also heavily insulated, which in turn is connected to its relevant spark plug. The leads are arranged in the correct firing order of 1 8 4 3 6 5 7 2. The odd numbers 1 3 5 7 being in the left-hand cylinder bank, and the even numbers 2 4 6 8 in the right-hand bank. (Fig. 4.1), as viewed from the rear of the engine.

The innovations for emission control, mentioned earlier in this Section consist of a thermostatically operated vacuum control valve which is fitted to early 3500 S models. The device lies adjacent to the automatic enrichment unit. It senses the engine coolant temperature allowing an air bleed at high temperatures to the distributor vacuum retard control, so advancing the ignition at small throttle openings. The advantage of this can be appreciated under heavy traffic driving conditions. The other device (3500 S models only) which assists in the setting of the ignition to each individual engine's requirements, is an adjusting screw and locknut set into the distributor vacuum unit. The adjustment is set in production and must not be interfered with. Should it become loosened or damaged, then a replacement distributor will have to be fitted. The adjustment screw cannot be reset, once disturbed.

2 Distributor - removal, refitment and retiming

1 **Note:** For all normal maintenance see Routine Maintenance Section.
2 Disconnect the battery at the negative terminal.
3 Disconnect the LT lead at the distributor body and remove the suction pipe from the advance retard vacuum capsule.
4 Unclip the distributor cap and place it to one side.
5 Now mark the distributor body in relation to the centre line of the rotor arm. (Fig. 4.2).
6 Mark the distributor body in relation to its position on the engine front cover.
7 Remove the clamping bolt and clamp. (Fig. 4.3).
8 Carefully withdraw the distributor. **Note:** If the engine is turned with the distributor removed, it will be necessary to follow the complete retiming procedure.
Refitment
1 If the distributor is being replaced by a new or service unit then the new unit will have to be marked in the same relative

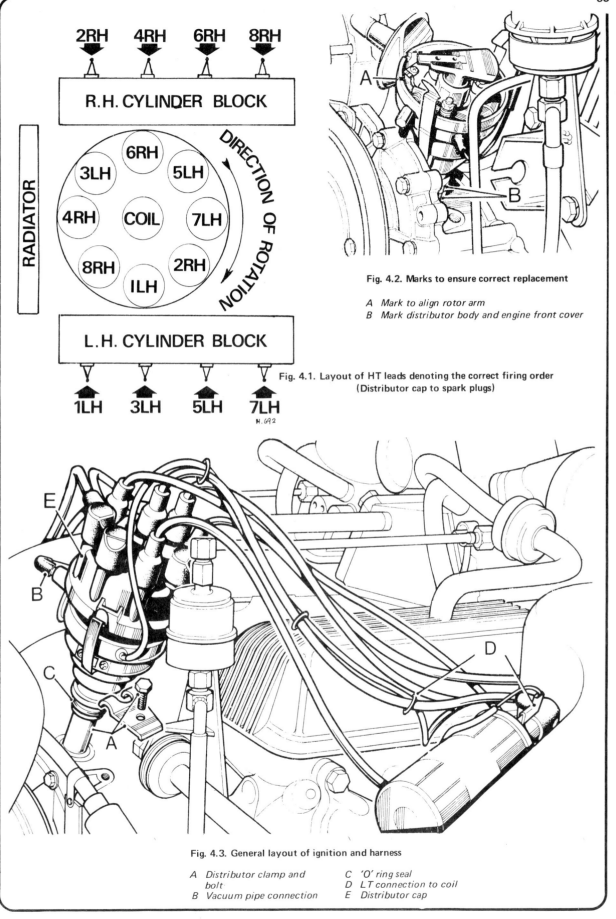

2RH 4RH 6RH 8RH

R.H. CYLINDER BLOCK

RADIATOR

6RH
3LH   5LH
4RH   COIL   7LH
8RH   2RH
1LH

DIRECTION OF ROTATION

L.H. CYLINDER BLOCK

1LH 3LH 5LH 7LH

H.692

Fig. 4.2. Marks to ensure correct replacement

A Mark to align rotor arm
B Mark distributor body and engine front cover

Fig. 4.1. Layout of HT leads denoting the correct firing order
(Distributor cap to spark plugs)

Fig. 4.3. General layout of ignition and harness

A Distributor clamp and bolt
B Vacuum pipe connection
C 'O' ring seal
D LT connection to coil
E Distributor cap

positions as the original unit.

2 Ensure that the plug leads are correctly connected to the distributor cap.

3 Provided that the engine has not been turned whilst the distributor has been removed, the refitment is as follows:

4 It is advisable to fit a new 'O' ring seal to the distributor body.

5 Rotate the rotor arm drive shaft until the centre line of the rotor arm is approximately 30° anticlockwise from the mark previously made on the rim of the distributor body (Fig. 4.4).

6 Refit the distributor, lining up the markings previously made on the engine front cover and distributor body.

7 It may be found that the oil pump drive shaft will need to be aligned to engage the distributor drive shaft into its slot.

8 Refit the clamp and clamp bolt ensuring that the distributor is in exactly the same position that it occupied before removal.

9 Reconnect the vacuum pipe and LT lead; fit the distributor cap.

10 Check that all the plug leads are correctly positioned, and that all the connectors are secured.

11 Reconnect the battery and test.

12 If the engine has been turned whilst the distributor has been removed then follow the operations described in paragraphs 13 to 21.

13 Turn the engine over to set No. 1 piston at 6° BTDC on the compression stroke.

14 Set up the distributor to align the rotor arm with No. 1 plug lead, then turn back the rotor approximately 30° anticlockwise.

15 Fit the distributor to the engine making sure that the centre line of the rotor arm now coincides with the mark corresponding with the No. 1 plug lead segment. Reposition if not correct.

16 If the distributor drive does not engage in its slot then it may be necessary to re-engage the oil pump drive by lightly pressing down on the distributor at the same time as the engine is gently turned.

17 Refit the clamp bolt, but do not tighten at this stage.

18 Turn the engine back until the 6° mark on the crank pulley passes the pointer, then gently ease the engine over, forwards this time, to align pointer with the 6° mark. (photo)

19 Rotate the distributor body in an anticlockwise direction until the points are just starting to open. At this stage lock the distributor in position by tightening up the clamp bolt.

20 Reconnect the vacuum pipe and LT supply. Refit the distributor cap checking first that the rotor arm is in place.

21 Reconnect the battery and test.

22 If suitable equipment is available then the dwell angle and ignition timing settings may be set as shown in specifications.

23 It is strongly advised that the following procedures are strictly observed, as incorrect timing of this type of engine can lead to rapid deterioration and engine damage.

24 Before running the engine to set the dwell angle, ensure that the elementary checks have been made by using the basic 'lamp method'. (Section 5).

25 Run the engine to warm-up so that it will run evenly. If the car is fitted with air conditioning equipment, the compressor must be disconnected.

26 With the engine running, set the carburation to an idling speed of 600 to 650 rev/min. (For emission controlled or air conditioning models set to 700 to 750 rev/min.)

27 Using a tach-dwell meter, set the switches to the DWELL and CALIBRATE positions. Set the calibration (with the test leads disconnected from the engine), so that the pointer shows on the SET LINE.

28 Follow the manufacturer's instructions and couple the meter to the engine.

29 To get the best reading of dwell angle it is advised that the reading be reduced to 26°, so that an initial higher reading is desirable. Adjust down from 30° to 26° to 28°.

30 Remembering to set the selector knob on the meter to the eight cylinder position and the tach-dwell selector knob to 'dwell', adjust the dwell angle by turning the hexagon headed adjusting screw on the distributor body (Fig. 4.5) until a meter scale reading of 26° to 28° is achieved.

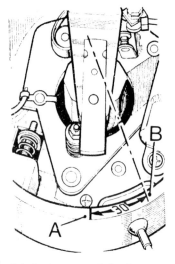

Fig. 4.4. Replacement of distributor to engine

A   Set drive 30° in advance of mark
B   Correct alignment of marks

2.18 Timing marks on the crankshaft pulley and relative pointer

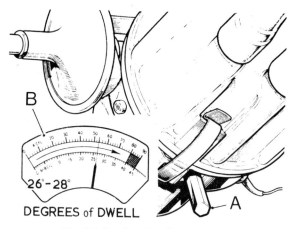

Fig. 4.5. Dwell angle adjustment

A   Hexagon headed adjusting screw
B   Select the eight cylinder scale

31 If the meter used does not have an eight cylinder scale, then the four cylinder scale can be used by doubling the readings, ie. 52° to 56°.

32 Disconnect the tach-dwell meter.

33 Now the ignition timing will have to be accurately set as follows:

34 Connect up the stroboscopic timing lamp according to the manufacturer's instructions, with the high tension lead connected into the plug lead serving to No. 1 cylinder.

35 Disconnect the vacuum pipe at the distributor and block the pipe to prevent uneven running. (photo)

36 Check that the engine idle speed is set at 600 rev/min. (all models). This can be achieved by slightly lifting the piston in one only of the carburettors. It is of paramount importance that the engine idle speed of 600 rev/min. is observed, as deviation from this, particularly in an upward direction would result in wrongly timed ignition.

37 To check the timing, ensure that the stroboscopic lamp synchronises with the pointer on the front of the engine and the 6° mark on the crankshaft pulley, or in the event of 96 octane fuel being used, or the car being emission controlled, the synchronisation should be made at the TDC mark.

38 If it is necessary to adjust the timing then the clamp bolt should be slackened and the distributor turned until the correct timing is achieved; clockwise to retard, and anticlockwise to advance.

39 Tighten the clamp bolt, replace the vacuum pipe not forgetting to remove the plug. Disconnect the strobe lamp and if the car is air conditioned, switch in the compressor.

40 Test run the car.

2.35 Detaching vacuum pipe (carburettor removed in the interest of clarity)

3 Contact breaker points gap - checking and adjustment

1 To check the contact breaker points so that the correct gap is obtained, first release the two clips securing the distributor cap to the distributor body, and lift away the cap. Clean the inside and outside of the cap with a dry cloth. It is unlikely that the eight segments will be badly burned or scored, but if they are the cap must be renewed. If a small deposit only is found on the segments, it may be scraped away using a small screwdriver.

2 Push in the carbon brush located in the top of the cap several times to ensure that it moves freely. The brush should protrude by at least ¼ inch (6.35 mm).

3 Gently prise the contact breaker points (Fig. 4.6) open to examine the condition of their faces. If they are rough, pitted or dirty, it will be necessary to remove them for refacing or for replacement points to be fitted.

4 Presuming the points are satisfactory, or that they have been cleaned or replaced, measure the gap between the points by turning the engine over until the contact breaker arm contact is on the peak of one of the cam lobes. An 0.015 in. (0.3810 mm) feeler gauge should now just fit between the points.

5 If the gap varies from this amount, turn the adjusting nut 'B' (Fig. 4.7) clockwise to increase or anticlockwise to decrease the gap.

6 Replace the rotor arm and distributor cap and clip the spring blade retainers in position.

7 Regard this method as emergency setting and re-check by dwell angle and tach-meter as soon as possible.

4 Contact breaker points - removal, servicing and refitment

1 If the contact breaker points are burned, pitted or badly worn they must be removed and either renewed or their faces ground smooth.

2 To remove the points, unscrew the terminal nut and remove it, together with the washer under its head. Remove the flanged nylon bush and then the condenser lead and the low tension lead from the terminal post. Lift off the contact breaker arm and then remove the large fibre washer from the terminal post.

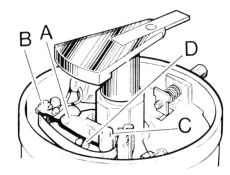

Fig. 4.6. Distributor contact breaker points

A Points
B Spring securing post making LT contact with points
C Contact breaker arm pivot post
D Contact breaker plate securing screw

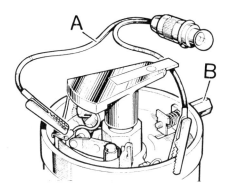

Fig. 4.7. Contact breaker points adjustment - timing light method

A Timing light and leads
B Contact breaker points adjustment screw

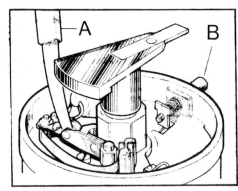

Fig. 4.8. Contact breaker points gap adjustment

A Feeler gauge   *B Adjustment screw*

3 The adjustable contact breaker plate is removed by unscrewing one holding down screw and removing it, complete with spring and flat washer.
4 To reface the points: rub the faces on a fine carborundum stone, or on fine emery paper. It is important that the faces are rubbed flat and parallel to each other, so that there will be complete face to face contact when the points are closed. After normal service intervals, one point will be pitted and the other will have deposits on it. Remove all 'pips' or 'craters'.
5 To refit the points, first position the adjustable contact breaker plate, and secure it with its screw, spring and flat washer. Fit the fibre washer to the terminal post and fit the contact breaker arm over it. Insert the flanged nylon bush with the condenser lead immediately under its head, and the low tension lead under that, over the terminal post. Fit the steel flat washer and screw on the securing nut.
6 The points are now reassembled and the gap should be set initially as described in Section 3 and the timing checked as described in Section 5.

5 Ignition timing (static) - checking and adjustment (using lamp method)

1 Remove the distributor cap.
2 Turn the engine over (using a 15/16th in. (0.937 mm) AF socket spanner applied to the crankshaft pulley nut), to a point where the contact breaker points are fully opened, with No. 1 cylinder on its firing stroke. The heel of the contact breaker arm should be resting at the peak of the cam lobe.
3 Connect the 12 volt lamp (or voltmeter) across the breaker lead terminal and an earthing point.
4 Switch on the ignition.
5 Now turn the hexagon headed adjusting nut in an anti-clockwise direction until the timing light just goes out or the voltmeter ceases to register.
6 Make a further two turns of the adjusting screw in the same anticlockwise direction. To assist the helical return spring during this operation, it is recommended that the adjustment nut is pressed inwards with the thumb as it is turned.
7 Now turn the adjusting nut slowly in a clockwise direction until the light just comes on (or the voltmeter begins to register).
8 Make a note of the position of the flats of the adjusting nut and continue in a clockwise direction for a further **five** flats.
9 Switch off the ignition and remove the timing light (or meter).
10 Replace the distributor cap ensuring that the rotor arm is in place.
11 The above operation can be regarded as a simple basic and rough setting and the owner is advised that the dwell angle should be finally and accurately set, using a specialised dwell angle and tach-meter.

6 Condenser - testing, removal and refitment

1 The purpose of the condenser, (sometimes known as a capacitor), is to ensure that when the contact breaker points are open there is no sparking across them - which would waste voltage and cause wear.
2 The condenser is fitted in parallel with the contact breaker points. If it develops a short circuit, it will cause ignition failure as the points will be prevented from interrupting the low tension circuit and serious arcing will occur.
3 If the engine becomes very difficult to start or begins to miss after several miles running, and the contact breaker points show signs of excessive burning or overheating, then the condition of the condenser must be suspect. A further test can be made by separating the points by hand with the ignition switched on. If this is accompanied by a flash it is indicative that the condenser has failed.
4 Without special test equipment the only sure way to diagnose condenser trouble is to replace a suspected unit with a new one and note if there is any improvement.
5 To remove the condenser from the distributor, remove the distributor cap and the rotor arm. Unscrew the contact breaker arm terminal nut, and remove the nut, washer and flanged nylon bush and release the condenser. Refitment of the condenser is simply a reversal of the removal process. Take particular care that the condenser lead does not short circuit against any portion of the contact breaker plate.
6 If severe burning of the contact points or even melting of the actuating heel is evident, carry out the following checks:
7 Check the serviceability of the voltage regulator as described in Chapter 10.
8 Check the ballast resistance wire. On early model cars this was wired independently but on later models, it is incorporated in the main dash harness. Stop the engine, switch on the ignition, and check that the contact points are closed (turn the engine if necessary). Connect a voltmeter between the coil + terminal and earth. If 12 volts (full battery voltage) is indicated then the ballast resistance wire will require renewal as the correct voltage permitted to pass across the contact points is between 6 and 7 volts.

7 Spark plugs and HT leads

1 The correct functioning of the spark plugs is vital for the correct running and efficiency of the engine.
2 At intervals of 5,000 miles (8,000 km) the plugs should be removed, examined, cleaned and if the electrodes are worn, renewed. The spark plugs should be renewed in any event every 10,000 miles (16,000 km). The spark plugs fitted as standard are Champion L87Y (but see 'modifications' Section 13).
3 The condition of the spark plugs will also tell much about the overall condition of the engine (see Fig. 3.19).
4 If the insulator nose of the spark plug is clean and white, with no deposits, this is indicative of a weak mixture, or too hot a plug (a hot plug transfers heat away from the electrode slowly a cold plug transfers heat away quickly).
5 If the top and insulator nose is covered with hard black deposits, then this is indicative that the mixture is too rich. Should the plug be black and oily, then it is likely that the engine is fairly worn, as well as the mixture being too rich.
6 If the insulator nose is covered with light tan to greyish brown deposits, then the mixture is correct and it is likely that the engine is in good condition.
7 If there are any traces of long brown tapering stains on the outside of the white portion of the plug, then the plug will have to be renewed, as this shows that there is a faulty joint between the plug body and the insulator and compression is being allowed to leak away.
8 Plugs should be cleaned by a sand blasting machine, which will free them from carbon better than cleaning by hand with a wire brush. The machine will also test the condition of the plugs

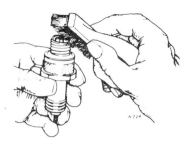

Cleaning deposits from electrodes and surrounding area using a fine wire brush.

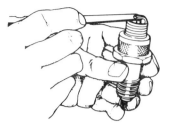

Checking plug gap with feeler gauges

Altering the plug gap. Note use of correct tool.

Spark plug maintenance

White deposits and damaged porcelain insulation indicating overheating

Broken porcelain insulation due to bent central electrode

Electrodes burnt away due to wrong heat value or chronic pre-ignition (pinking)

Excessive black deposits caused by over-rich mixture or wrong heat value

Mild white deposits and electrode burnt indicating too weak a fuel mixture

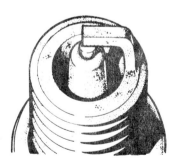

Plug in sound condition with light greyish brown deposits

Fig. 4.9. Spark plug conditions

under compression. Any plug that fails to spark at the recommended pressure should be renewed.

9   The spark plug gap is of considerable importance, as, if it is too large or too small, the size of the spark and its efficiency will be seriously impaired. The spark plug gap should be set to 0.025 in. (0.60 mm) for the best results.

10 To set it, measure the gap with a feeler gauge, and then bend open, or close, the outer plug electrode until the correct gap is achieved. The centre electrode should never be bent as this may crack the insulation and cause plug failure, if nothing worse.

11 When replacing the plugs, remember to use new washers. Replace the distributor HT leads in the correct firing order, which is 1 8 4 3 6 5 7 2; No. 1 cylinder being the one nearest the radiator in the left-hand cylinder bank.

12 The plug leads require no routine maintenance other than being kept clean and wiped over regularly. At intervals of 5,000 miles (8,000 km) however, pull the lead off each plug in turn and remove them from the distributor by slackening the screws located inside the cap. Moisture can seep down these joints giving rise to a white corrosive deposit which must be carefully removed from the end of each cable.

8 Distributor - dismantling, overhaul and reassembly

1   Remove the distributor as detailed in Section 2 of this Chapter.
2   Clean off all the road dirt and oil from the exterior of the distributor body.
3   Work on a clear clean bench making sure that you have suitable receptacles in which to place the various parts as they are removed.
4   It is assumed that the distributor cap and the rotor arm have been removed before the distributor was taken from the car. The checking of these two components will be covered at the end of this Section.
5   Remove the felt lubricating pad from the hollow centre of the spindle where the rotor arm normally sits.
6   Remove the nut and insulating washer securing the LT and condenser leads to the moving contact. If a two piece contact breaker is fitted, remove the moving contact.
7   Remove the large headed screw holding the fixed contact plate and remove the fixed contact. If a one piece assembly is fitted, remove the whole assembly.
8   Examine the contact points with a view to possible renewal. See Sections 3 and 4 of this Chapter.
9   Remove the crosshead screw holding the condenser and remove the condenser.
10 Remove the nut, plain washer and the spring from the contact breaker baseplate pivot post.
11 Unscrew the dwell angle adjustment screw, removing the screw and the spring.
12 Remove the crosshead screw that retains the earthing lead to the contact breaker baseplate, and remove the baseplate.
13 Remove the crosshead screws holding the vacuum advance/retard unit to the distributor body, and remove the unit and the grommet.
14 Remove the other two screws holding the centrifugal advance cover plate to the distributor body, and lift the plate out.
15 The centrifugal advance unit is now exposed, and the return springs must be carefully eased from the locating grooves in their respective posts.
16 Care must be taken when removing the springs, that they are not stretched or distorted in any way, as any such damage will adversely affect the operation of the unit.
17 Remove the screw from within the recess in the centre of the cam spindle and withdraw the cam piece and foot from the spindle.
18 Lift out the counterbalance weights.
19 The driving gear at the bottom of the spindle is secured by a taper pin which must be located and carefully driven out, taking

care not to damage the gear teeth or bend the actual shaft. It is not essential that the driving spindle is removed unless excessive wear is suspected. However, a word of warning: If the parts are to be cleaned in a paraffin or petrol bath, care must be taken to ensure that the spindle and its bearings are not washed clean of lubricant which will result in seizure of these parts when refitted to the car. Whether or not the spindle is removed, in either case ensure that the rebuilt spindle assembly is adequately lubricated before refitting to the car.

20 Inspection and repair: Check that the contact breaker points are up to standard as described in Section 4. Also check the distributor cap for signs of tracking, indicated by a thin hair line running between the segments. Examine the segments for excessive burning or pitting. A crack in the cap is not an unusual fault and should be carefully looked for. Any of the above faults will justify the renewal of the cap.
21 Examine the rotor arm for excessive burning at the tip of the brass strip, also check the security of the metal piece and its bonding to the plastic; if loose, replace. In the same way that a hair line crack in the distributor cap will cause elusive trouble, the same condition can exist within the moulding of the rotor arm, resulting in tracking of the HT voltage being short circuited to earth via the drive spindle. Careful examination of the rotor arm is advised. Some slight burning can be expected at the brass tip and this can be cleaned with a fine toothed file or very fine emery paper.
22 Make sure that the carbon brush moves freely in its recess in the cap and that it is attached to its spring. The carbon should protrude far enough to bear on the centre of the brass strip of the rotor arm.
23 Examine the fit of the contact breaker plate to the bearing plate and also check the breaker arm for wear or looseness and renew as necessary.
24 Examine the balance weights and pivots for wear. Check the fit of the cam piece on the spindle and replace if found to be a sloppy fit. If in doubt, compare these parts against a new unit and renew as indicated.
25 If the drive spindle is found to be a loose fit in the distributor body and on removal can be seen to be worn then it will be necessary to fit new bushes and spindle.
26 If the drive spindle has been removed, lubricate liberally before replacement.
27 Check that the balance weight springs have not been stretched in any way. If in doubt check against new springs. If they are in fact stretched, then renew.
28 If the car is fitted with emission control equipment, this fact must be made clear when ordering spare parts. Many of the parts are modified to emission control requirements and differ in specification from those parts fitted to standard models.
29 If a distributor is found to be suffering from excessive wear in all components, it may be more advantageous to obtain a completely reconditioned exchange unit.
30 Reassembly is a reversal of the dismantling process, but there are several points which should be noted in addition to those already given in Section 8.
31 Lubricate the balance weights and other parts of the mechanical advance mechanism, the distributor shaft and the portion of the shaft on which the cam bears, with SAE 20 engine oil, during reassembly. Do not oil excessively but ensure that these parts are adequately lubricated.
32 Check the action of the weights in the fully advanced and retarded positions and ensure that they are not binding by holding the shaft and action plate and rotating the cam.
33 Set the contact breaker gap to the correct clearance.

9 Ignition system - fault finding

By far the majority of breakdown running troubles are caused by faults in the ignition system, either in the low tension or high tension circuits.

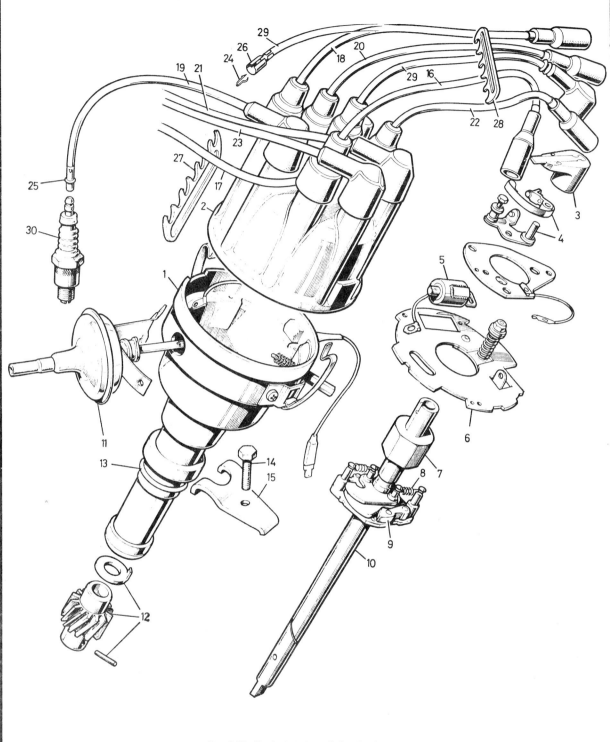

Fig. 4.10. Exploded view of the distributor

1	Distributor complete	11	Vacuum unit and grommet	18	Plug lead No. 3
2	Distributor cap	12	Driving gear, pin and thrust	19	Plug lead No. 4
3	Rotor arm		washer	20	Plug lead No. 5
4	Contact points	13	Sealing ring	21	Plug lead No. 6
5	Condenser	14	Bolt (3/8 in. UNC x 1 in.	22	Plug lead No. 7
6	Base plate		long) fixing distributor to	23	Plug lead No. 8
7	Cam		cover	24	Staple pin for plug
8	Auto advance spring set	15	Clamp for distributor		lead
9	Auto advance weight	16	Plug lead No. 1	25	Connector for lead, plug
10	Shaft and action plate	17	Plug lead No. 2		end

26	Connector for lead, distributor end
27	Retainer, large, for spark plug leads
28	Retainer, small, for spark plug leads
29	Lead, HT, coil to distributor
30	Spark plug

10 Ignition system - fault symptoms

There are two main symptoms indicating ignition faults - either the engine will not start or fire, or the engine is difficult to start and misfires. If it is a regular misfire (ie. the engine is only running on 5 or 6 cylinders) the fault is almost sure to be in the secondary, or high tension circuit. If the misfiring is intermittent, the fault could be in either, the high, or low tension circuits. If the engine stops suddenly, or will not start at all, it is likely that the fault is in the low tension circuit. Loss of power and overheating, apart from faulty carburation settings, are normally due to faults in the distributor or incorrect ignition timing.

11 Fault diagnosis - engine fails to start

1   If the engine fails to start and it was running normally when it was last used, first check there is fuel in the petrol tank. If the engine turns over normally on the starter motor and the battery is evidently well charged, then the fault may be either in the high or low tension circuits. First check the HT circuit. **Note:** If the battery is known to be fully charged, the ignition comes on, and the starter motor fails to turn the engine, **check the tightness of the leads on the battery terminals** and also the security of the earth lead at its **connection to the body.** It is quite common for the leads to have worked loose, even if they look and feel secure If one of the battery terminal posts gets very hot while trying to work the starter motor, this is a sure indication of a faulty connection to that terminal.
2   One of the most common reasons for bad starting is wet or damp spark plug leads and/or distributor. Remove the distributor cap. If condensation is visible internally, dry the cap with a rag and also wipe over the leads. Replace the cap.
3   If the engine still fails to start, check that current is reaching the plugs, by disconnecting each plug lead in turn at the spark plug end, and holding the end of the cable about 3/16 in. (4.8 mm) away from the cylinder block. Spin the engine on the starter motor, by pressing the rubber button on the starter solenoid switch (under the bonnet).

In the interests of safety - on cars fitted with automatic transmission the starter solenoid switch is specially blanked off so that the engine may not be started from under the bonnet.
4   Sparking between the end of the cable and the block should be fairly strong with a regular blue spark (hold the lead with rubber to avoid electric shocks). If current is reaching the plugs, then remove them and clean and regap them to 0.025 in. (0.6350 mm). The engine should now start.
5   If there are no sparks at the plugs disconnect the cable from the centre of the distributor and hold about 3/16 in. (4.8 mm) from the block. Spin the engine as before, a rapid succession of loose sparks between the end of the lead and the block indicates that the coil is in order, and that either the distributor cap is cracked, the carbon brush is stuck or worn, the rotor arm is faulty, or the contact points are burnt, pitted or dirty. If the points are in bad shape, clean and reset them as described in Section 4.
6   If there are no sparks at the end of this lead from the coil, then check the connections at the lead to the coil and distributor head and if they are in order, check the low tension circuit starting with the battery.
7   Switch on the ignition and turn the crankshaft so that the contact breaker points have fully opened. Then, with either a 20 volt voltmeter or bulb and length of wire, check that current from the battery is reaching the starter solenoid switch. No reading indicates that there is a fault in the cable to the switch, or in the connections at the switch or at the battery terminals. Alternatively, the battery earth lead may not be properly earthed to the body.
8   If a reading is obtained at the contact breaker terminal, then check the wire from the coil to the side of the distributor for loose connections etc. This cable is coloured white with a black

tracer. If a reading is obtained, then the final check on the low tension circuit is across the contact breaker point. No reading means a broken condenser which, when renewed will enable the car to finally start.

12 Fault diagnosis - engine misfires

1   If the engine misfires regularly, run it at a fast idling speed, and short out each plug in turn by placing a short screwdriver across from the plug terminal to the cylinder block. Ensure that the screwdriver has a **wooden or plastic, insulated handle.**
2   No difference in engine running will be noticed when the plug in the defective cylinder is short circuited. Short circuiting the working plugs will accentuate the misfire.
3   Remove the plug lead from the end of the defective plug and hold it about 3/16 in. (4.8 mm) away from the block. Restart the engine. If the sparking is fairly strong and regular the fault must lie in the spark plug.
4   The plug may be loose, the insulation may be cracked, or the points may have burnt away giving too wide a gap for the spark to jump. Worse still, one of the points may have broken off. Either renew the plug, or clean it, reset the gap, and then test it.
5   If there is no spark at the end of the plug lead, or if it is weak and intermittent, check the ignition lead from the distributor to the plug. If the insulation is cracked or perished, renew the lead. Check the connections at the distributor cap.
6   If there is still no spark, examine the distributor cap carefully for tracking. This can be recognised by a very thin black line running between two or more electrodes, or between an electrode and some other part of the distributor. These lines are paths which now conduct electricity across the cap, thus letting it run to earth. The only answer is a new distributor cap.
7   Apart from the ignition timing being incorrect other causes of misfiring have already been described under the section dealing with the failure of the engine to start.
8   If the ignition timing is too far retarded, it should be noted that the engine will tend to overheat, and there will be quite a noticeable drop in power. If the engine is overheating and the power is down, and the ignition timing is correct, then the carburettor should be checked as it is likely that this is where the fault lies. See Chapter 3 for details.

13 Modifications

1   On early models there was the possibility of trouble being caused by a poor moulding of the right angled boot on the coil to distributor HT lead. This fault has been corrected and the later type of boot now carries a moulding number to facilitate identity. Attention is also drawn to the fact that there is an improved distributor now available.
2   The correct fitment of HT leads is another point that is strongly stressed. If any two HT leads are misplaced so as to lie alongside or above one another, there is a real possibility that cross firing may be induced between them with the result that one or more cylinders will fire out of order. In the event of misfiring occurring, it is advised that the first checks should be in this area. The correct layout for the HT leads is illustrated in Fig. 4.11. The plug lead retainers are shown at "A" on the diagram.
3   To overcome misfire problems experienced in the earlier models the original champion plug L-87Y has been replaced by type L-92Y. The change of plug applies to all V8 models produced since January 1972. For models produced before 1972, the original plug L-87Y is still recommended.

14 Thermostatic vacuum control valve (early 3500 S models)

1   This valve is fitted adjacent to the automatic enrichment device. The valve senses the engine coolant temperature and permits a metered air bleed to enter the distributor vacuum capsule at high engine coolant temperatures. This action causes

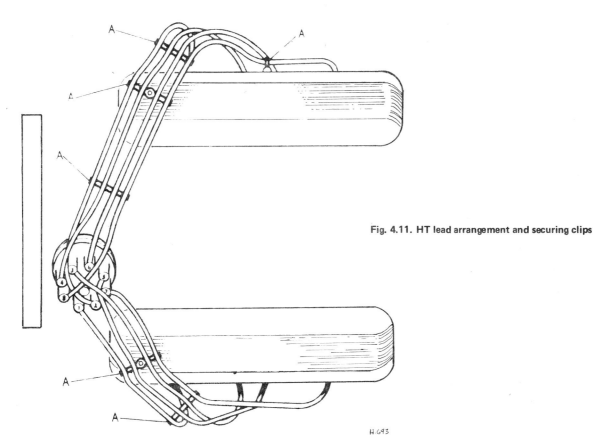

Fig. 4.11. HT lead arrangement and securing clips

H.693

the ignition to advance and the coolant temperature is lowered, so preventing overheating at small throttle openings in heavy traffic concentrations.

2 The valve is designed to operate within a temperature range of between 220° F ($\pm$ 3°) (104.4° C ($\pm$ 1.5°)).

3 The unit cannot be repaired and must be renewed as a complete component if faulty.

---

15 Vacuum switch - emission control type distributors

---

1 Cars equipped with full emission control systems have a throttle controlled vaccum switch installed to improve idling and over-run fume emission characteristics.

2 The vacuum switch "A" (Fig. 4.12) is actuated by a lever "B" attached to the throttle spindle and is adjusted to cut out all vacuum retard at approximately 3000 rev/min. on a free running engine (in neutral).

3 The unit enables normal advance characteristics to be maintained during starting and heavy acceleration conditions but retards the ignition setting under part load conditions. These arrangements ensure that emission control regulations are complied with.

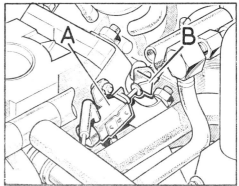

Fig. 4.12. Vacuum switch (emission control)

A Switch
B Throttle spindle lever

Chapter 5 Clutch

Contents

Specifications

Type	Borg and Beck, diaphragm spring, single dry plate, hydraulically operated
Clutch driven plate diameter	9.5 in. (241.3 mm)
Driven plate cushion springs (number)	6
(colour)	Brown/cream
Clutch pedal height	6.5 in. (165 mm)
Fluid	Castrol Girling Universal Brake and Clutch Fluid

Torque wrench settings:	lb ft	kg m
Cover bolts	20	2.8
Slave cylinder bolts	25	3.5
Clutch withdrawal unit bolts	15	2.0
Cross-shaft end cover bolts	8	1.0
External clutch lever nut	15	2.0

1 General description

The clutch fitted in conjunction with the manual gearbox on post October 1971 3500 S models is of single dry plate diaphragm spring type. The diameter of the clutch driven plate is 9.5 in. (240 mm) and it is operated hydraulically.

The unit comprises a steel cover which is dowelled and bolted to the rear face of the flywheel and contains the pressure plate, diaphragm spring and fulcrum rings.

The clutch disc is free to slide along the splined first motion shaft and is held in position between the flywheel and the pressure plate by the pressure of the pressure plate spring. Friction lining material is riveted to the clutch disc and it has a spring cushioned hub to absorb transmission shocks and to help ensure a smooth take off.

The circular diaphragm spring is mounted on shoulder pins and held in place in the cover by two fulcrum rings. The spring is also held to the pressure plate by three spring steel clips which are riveted in position.

The clutch release mechanism consists of a hydraulic master cylinder and slave cylinder and the interconnecting pipework, a release fork and sealed ball type release bearing - the latter being in permanent contact with the fingers of the pressure plate assembly.

Provided that the clutch pedal arm, the pedal stop and the master cylinder operating rod are all correctly set as described later in this Chapter, clutch adjustment to compensate for wear in the friction linings and release bearing face will be automatic. Depressing the clutch pedal actuates the clutch release arm by means of hydraulic pressure. The release arm pushes the release bearing forwards to bear against the release fingers, so moving the centre of the diaphragm spring inwards. The spring is sandwiched between two annular rings which act as fulcrum points. As the centre of the spring is pushed in, the outside of the spring is pushed out, so moving the pressure place backwards and disengaging the pressure plate from the clutch disc.

When the clutch pedal is released the diaphragm spring forces the pressure plate into contact with the high friction linings on the clutch disc and at the same time pushes the clutch disc a fraction of an inch forwards on its splines so engaging the clutch disc with the flywheel. The clutch disc is now firmly sandwiched between the pressure plate and the flywheel so the drive is taken up.

2 Maintenance

1 This comprises occasionally checking the security of the bolts which retain the master and slave cylinders and applying a little engine oil to the operating rod clevis joints.

2 Periodically check the hydraulic pipes and unions for leaks or

corrosion or deterioration.
3   Maintain the fluid level in the hydraulic reservoir as described in the Routine Maintenance Section.

3   Master cylinder - removal and refitment

1   Remove the air cleaner as described in Chapter 1.
2   Clamp the flexible pipe which runs between the reservoir and the master cylinder, to prevent loss of fluid (Fig. 5.1).
3   Disconnect the inlet pipe at the union which is located at the top of the master cylinder.
4   Disconnect the fluid outlet pipe from the master cylinder.
5   Disconnect the master cylinder operating rod from the pedal arm by withdrawing the split pin and clevis pin. On right-hand drive cars this operation is carried out within the engine compartment, but on left-hand drive cars the clevis is located within the car interior.
6   Loosen the locknut and unscrew the clevis from the master cylinder operating rod.
7   Unscrew the master cylinder securing nuts and withdraw the unit from its mounting bracket.
8   Refitment is a reversal of removal but the length of the pushrod (fully extended) must be reset to 4.750 in. (120 mm) as shown in Fig. 5.2.
9   When installation is complete, bleed the system as described in Section 9.

4   Master cylinder - overhaul

1   Remove the master cylinder as described in the previous Section.
2   See Fig. 5.3 and remove the circlip at "A" when the pushrod and retaining washer can be withdrawn from the cylinder.
3   Removal of the piston assembly may be facilitated by the application of a low pressure air line to the outlet port (Fig. 5.4).
4   Prise up the locking prong that retains the spring and separate it from the piston (Fig. 5.5).
5   Remove the piston seal and discard it.
6   Compress the spring so that the valve stem is in line with the larger hole in the spring retainer (Fig. 5.6), and remove the spring and retainer.
7   Remove the valve spacer and spring washer from the valve stem.
8   Remove the valve seal and discard it.
9   Obtain a repair kit which includes new seals and other components.
10 Examine all components for scores or 'bright' wear areas and if evident, renew the complete master cylinder. Wash all components in methylated spirit or clean hydraulic fluid.
11 Reassembly: Use Castrol-Girling rubber grease to coat the new seals. The remaining parts should be smeared with Castrol-Girling Brake and Clutch Fluid.
12 The new valve seal should be fitted (flat side on first) to the

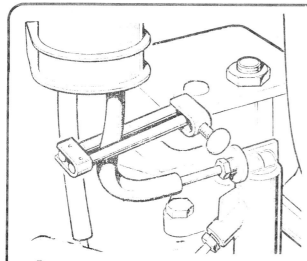

Fig. 5.1. Reservoir hose clamped to prevent fluid loss

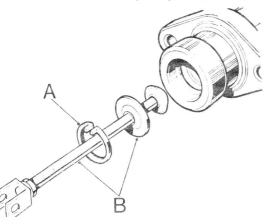

Fig. 5.3. Dismantling master cylinder

A   Circlip   B   Push-rod and
                                    retaining washer

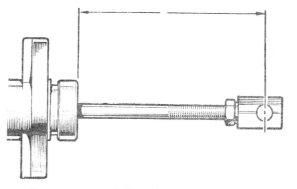

Fig. 5.2. Master cylinder push-rod setting diagram

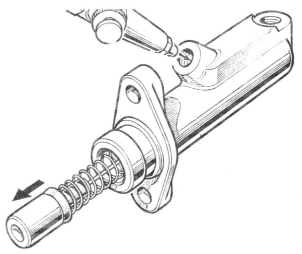

Fig. 5.4. Expelling piston from master cylinder

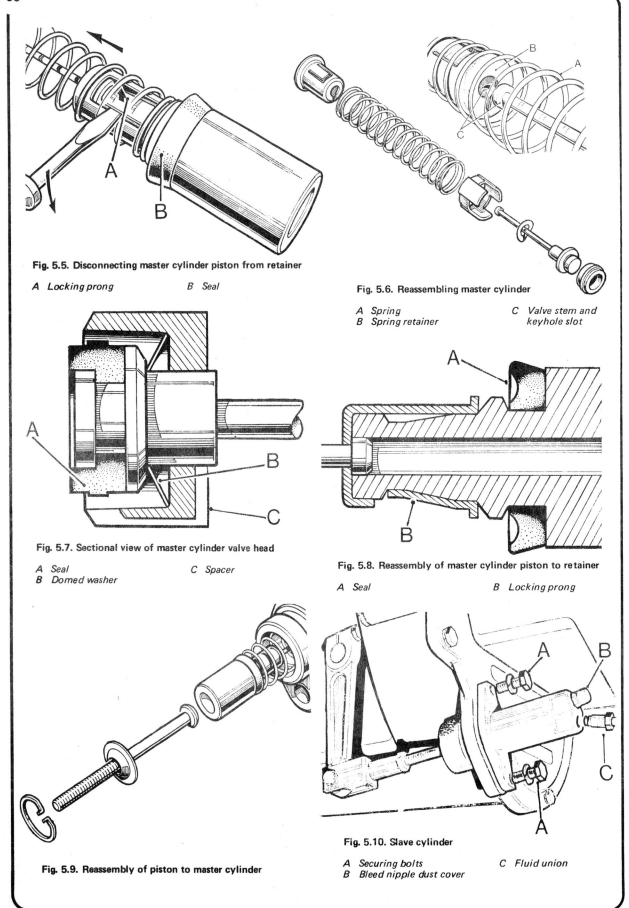

Fig. 5.5. Disconnecting master cylinder piston from retainer

A   Locking prong   B   Seal

Fig. 5.6. Reassembling master cylinder

A   Spring   C   Valve stem and
B   Spring retainer   keyhole slot

Fig. 5.7. Sectional view of master cylinder valve head

A   Seal   C   Spacer
B   Domed washer

Fig. 5.8. Reassembly of master cylinder piston to retainer

A   Seal   B   Locking prong

Fig. 5.9. Reassembly of piston to master cylinder

Fig. 5.10. Slave cylinder

A   Securing bolts   C   Fluid union
B   Bleed nipple dust cover

end of the valve stem (Fig. 5.7).

13 The spring washer fits over the small end of the stem **domed side first.**

14 Now fit the spacer, again over the small end, **legs first.**

15 Place the spring in position on the valve stem and insert the retainer into the spring. Compress the spring holding the retainer and engage the valve stem into the keyhole slot in the retainer.

16 Fit the new piston seal to the piston making sure that the larger diameter goes on last (Fig. 5.8).

17 Bring the piston and the spring retainer together inserting the piston into the retainer until the locking prong engages.

18 Apply Castrol-Girling rubber grease to the piston and seal, and insert the whole assembly, valve in first, into the cylinder.

19 Refit the pushrod and secure with its retaining washer and circlip. (Fig. 5.9)

20 Having re-checked that all the operations have been correctly carried out and that there are no bits left on the bench, the unit can now be refitted to the car.

5 Clutch slave cylinder - removal and refitment

1 It is not necessary to drain the reservoir or clutch master cylinder when removing the slave cylinder, but some means of preventing the fluid from draining through the system must be implemented.

2 One method is to clamp the flexible hose which runs between the fluid reservoir and the master cylinder.

3 Another way that draining can be prevented is to seal off the breather hole in the reservoir filler cap using a piece of plastic sheet placed over the filler hole and the filler cap screwed on over the plastic sheet.

4 Drain off the fluid from the slave cylinder by opening the bleed valve. This fluid can be collected in a suitable drain tin.

5 Disconnect the fluid pipe to the slave cylinder, and plug it to prevent possible leakage.

6 Remove the securing bolts holding the cylinder to the engine backplate and draw the cylinder away from the pushrod which can be left in position on the clutch arm (Fig. 5.10)

7 Absolute cleanliness is essential when working on hydraulic systems. Externally clean before dismantling using clean rag. Clean and cover pipe ends to prevent the ingress of dirt or grit. Remember that the introduction of any foreign matter into a hydraulic system will have disastrous results.

8 Commence refitting by locating the pushrod through the rubber dust cover of the slave cylinder. Position the cylinder and locate the securing bolts. (photo) Tighten the bolts evenly to a torque of 30 lb ft (4 kg/m).

9 Reconnect the fluid pipe. Do not forget to remove the plug.

10 Remove the hose clamp or sheeting used to prevent leakage.

11 Bleed the system as outlined in Section 9 of this Chapter.

6 Slave cylinder - overhaul

1 Remove the cylinder as outlined in the previous Section.

2 Clean-up the exterior of the unit using clean brake fluid or methylated spirit.

3 Procure the necessary servicing kit of spares which will include the required seals and dust cover. In the case of a high mileage car, the piston return spring should be renewed.

4 Dismantle the unit by first removing the dust cover, followed by the circlip after which the piston can usually be shaken out (Fig. 5.11). On no account should the unit be banged onto a hard surface. If difficulty is experienced a low pressure air line applied to the fluid inlet will expel the piston.

5 Withdraw the spring and unscrew the bleed valve from the cylinder body.

6 Clean all components in hydraulic fluid or methylated spirit. Discard all rubber seals.

7 Examine the piston surface and cylinder bore for scoring or 'bright' wear areas. If these are evident, renew the complete unit.

8 Treat the seal with a smear of Castrol-Girling rubber grease, and to the remainder of the internal parts apply a film of clean hydraulic fluid.

9 Fit the seal (smaller diameter first) to the piston.

10 Locate the spring, again with the smaller diameter toward the piston.

11 Apply a smear of Castrol-Girling rubber grease to the piston assembly and insert (spring first) into the slave cylinder body.

12 Refit the circlip.

13 Fill the inside of the dust cover with Castrol-Girling rubber grease and refit it to the unit.

7 Clutch pedal assembly - removal and refitment

1 Remove the air cleaner and disconnect the master cylinder pushrod from the foot pedal arm as described in Section 3.

2 Remove the clutch pedal lever as shown in Fig. 5.12.

3 After the retaining nut has been removed, the following parts can be taken off (when it comes to reassembly, reverse the order):- Spring washer; flat washer; the pedal lever; 1st shim washer; felt washer and 2nd shim washer.

4 Remove the inlet and outlet pipes from the **brake** master cylinder but not before making sure that measures have been taken to prevent leakage of the fluid from the reservoir. See

5.8 Fitting slave cylinder

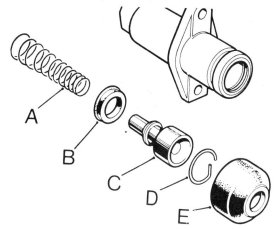

Fig. 5.11. Exploded view of slave cylinder

A Spring
B Seal
C Piston

D Circlip
E Dust excluding boot

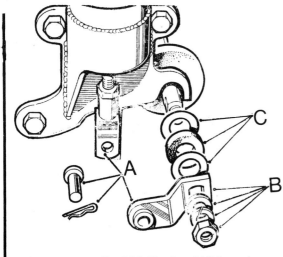

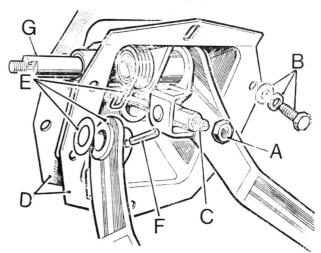

Fig. 5.12. Clutch pedal linkage

A *Clevis pin*
B *Lever components*
C *Shims and felt washer*

Fig. 5.13. Clutch and brake pedal support housing

A *Locknut*
B *Housing bolt*
C *Master cylinder push-rod*
D *Housing and gasket*

E *Pedal arm and return
   spring*
F *Tension pin*
G *Cross-shaft*

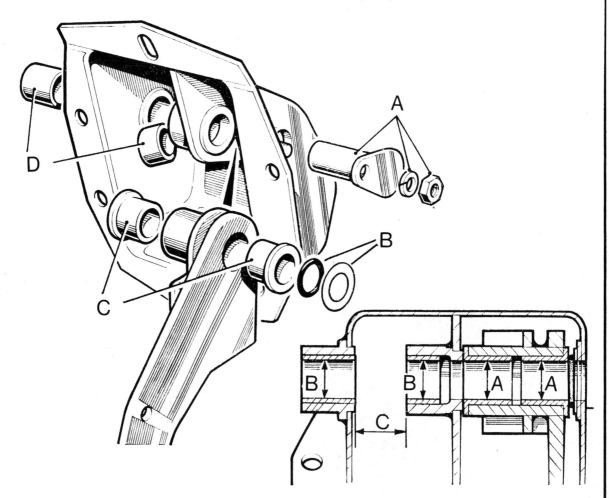

Fig. 5.14. Foot pedal bush arrangement

A *Brake cross-shaft*
B *Shim and 'O' ring*

C *Brake pedal bushes*
D *Clutch pedal bushes (inset) sectional view of cross-shaft bush
   arrangement*

Section 3.

5 Remove the two bolts holding the **brake** master cylinder to the bulkhead.

6 Release the fixings for the mounting bracket of the accelerator cross shaft. These are accessible from under the right-hand wing valance.

7 **LH drive cars only:** Disconnect the fluid pipes from the clutch master cylinder, and remove the securing bolts from the bulkhead. There are spring washers under these bolts.

8 The way is now clear to move into the driving compartment to remove the pedal box assembly. Clear the carpet back out of the way.

9 Refer to Fig. 5.13 for the following operations: Remove the brake pedal pushrod locknut and screw the pushrod forward to clear the threaded trunnion and remove the brake master cylinder from the engine compartment.

10 In the case of left-hand drive cars, similarly remove the clutch pushrod fixings at the pedal, and remove the clutch master cylinder.

11 Remove the bolts holding the pedal box to the bulkhead, and remove the pedal box assembly from the car. Note the gasket.

12 The clutch pedal is secured to the pedal shaft by a roll-pin secured by a wire-lock. Remove the wire-lock and drive out the pin.

13 The shaft may now be withdrawn and the pedal freed. Take note of the correct replacement sequence of the shim and return spring.

14 If it is required to remove the brake pedal for overhaul or replacement, remove the brake pedal shaft, shim and 'O' ring when the pedal and its return spring may be withdrawn (Fig. 5.14).

15 On a high mileage car the bushes in both the pedal box and the pedal pivot points will undoubtably be worn.

16 Refitment is a reversal of removal sequence but the following points should be observed. The bushes should be lightly oiled before reassembly. The 'O' ring should be greased. Use a new roll-pin and make sure that it is wire-locked in position. Secure the pedal box gasket with a suitable adhesive such as Bostik, securing it to the pedal box but not to the bulkhead of the car. Do not forget to refit the clutch pedal stop to the bottom left of the pedal box. The felt washer for the clutch pedal shaft should be soaked with SAE 30 oil, and the exposed end of the clutch pedal shaft should be greased. The pedal lever retaining nut should be tightened to a torque figure of 30 lb ft (4.1 kg/m).

17 Check the correct operation and adjustment of the pedal linkage, observing the details given in Sections 3 and 7.

18 Finally bleed the hydraulic systems that have been disconnected.

8 Clutch pedal linkage - checking and adjustment

1 After removal or installation of the clutch actuating components, check and adjust if necessary the clutch operating mechanism to ensure that the height of the clutch pedal pad is the same as that of the brake pedal pad.

2 Remove the carpet from the driver's side of the car.

3 Measure the distance between the tip of the footbrake pedal and the steel floor of the car. The distance measured should be 6.5 in. (165 mm).

4 If required, reset the brake pedal to the correct dimension by slackening the locknut (inset Fig. 5.15). Use a screwdriver to adjust the pushrod by screwing in, or out, as the case might be.

5 When the correct pedal height has been achieved, tighten up the locknut to secure.

6 Now check that the clutch pedal is level with the new adjustment made to the brake pedal.

7 If the clutch pedal needs adjustment, slacken the locknut on the master cylinder pushrod and screw the pushrod in or out of the clevis jaw whichever way is required, to achieve the required adjustment (Fig. 5.15 - lower inset).

8 Once the correct pedal height is achieved, tighten the locknut to secure.

9 To check and adjust the clutch linkage at the slave cylinder

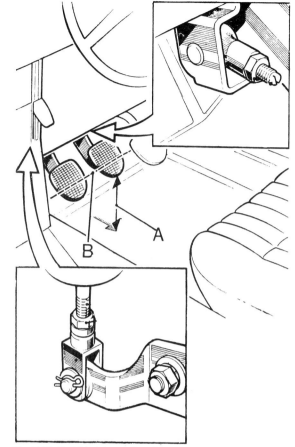

Fig. 5.15. Pedal height setting diagram

A Tip of pedal pad to steel floor pan 6.5 in (165 mm)
B Upper pedal surface alignment
Upper inset. Locknut and screw for brake pedal height adjustment
Lower inset. Adjustment point for master cylinder

and clutch lever end proceed as follows:

10 Check the correct alignment of the clutch external lever by disconnecting the slave cylinder pushrod (Fig. 5.16).

11 The lever should occupy a vertical position when the lever is bearing up against the clutch release mechanism (Fig. 5.16A). If it is not, it will be necessary to remove the lever from its splined shaft and refit in the vertical position. If a dead vertical spot cannot be found then set the lever onto the splines in the nearest serration either side of vertical.

12 Secure the lever tightening the pinch bolt to a torque of 15 lb ft (2.0 kg/m).

13 Reconnect the clevis joint of the pushrod to the lever.

14 To check the correct adjustment of the slave cylinder pushrod proceed as follows:

15 Release the clutch pedal stop by releasing the locknut and screwing the stop fully down (Fig. 5.17).

16 Pull the rubber dustcap of the slave cylinder away from the body of the unit so that the piston and pushrod end are exposed. (Fig. 5.18).

17 Measure the distance between the rear face of the piston and the inner face of the retaining circlip, this should be 0.790 in. (20 mm).

18 To adjust to obtain the correct dimension, slacken the locknut on the slave cylinder pushrod and screw the pushrod in or out of its clevis jaw depending upon which way the adjustment is required.

19 Once the correct dimension is obtained, tighten up the locknut to secure.

20 All that is necessary now is to secure the clutch pedal stop

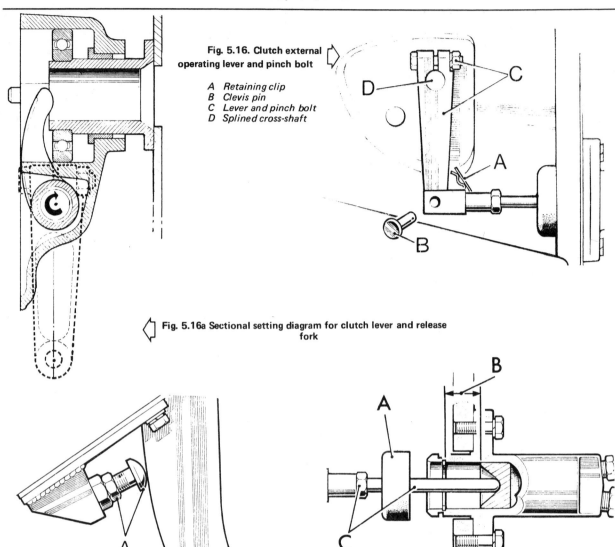

Fig. 5.16. Clutch external operating lever and pinch bolt

A   Retaining clip
B   Clevis pin
C   Lever and pinch bolt
D   Splined cross-shaft

Fig. 5.16a Sectional setting diagram for clutch lever and release fork

Fig. 5.17. Clutch pedal stop and locknut (A)

Fig. 5.18. Slave cylinder push-rod setting diagram

A   Dust excluder   C   Push-rod and locknut
B   Specified dimension 0.790 in
     (20.0 mm)

The clutch pedal is depressed until the piston is almost touching the circlip. At this point the pedal is held in position until the stop is adjusted up to the pedal. The pedal is now released and the stop screwed out another full turn. This operation is quite obviously a two handed job requiring some assistance.

21 Secure the pedal stop by tightening up the locknut. Make a final check of the operation, ensuring that the piston does in fact stop before hitting the circlip and at the end of the pedal travel.

22 Replace the floor carpet and carry out a check of the fluid level in the reservoir.

9   Bleeding the hydraulic system

1   Whenever the clutch hydraulic system has been overhauled, a part renewed, or the level in the reservoir is too low, air will have entered the system, necessitating the system to be bled. During this operation the level of hydraulic fluid in the reservoir should not be allowed to fall below half full, otherwise air will be drawn in again.

2   Obtain a clean and dry glass jam jar; plastic tubing at least 12 inches long and able to fit tightly over the bleed nipple of the slave cylinder; a supply of Castrol Girling Brake and Clutch Fluid; and someone to help.

3   Check that the master cylinder reservoir is full, and if it is not, fill it, and cover the bottom inch of the jar with hydraulic fluid.

4   Wipe the bleed nipple on the slave cylinder free of dust and dirt and open the bleed nipple one turn, preferably using a ring spanner, which should be kept in place on the bleed nipple (Fig. 5.19).

5   Place one end of the tube squarely over the nipple and insert the other end in the jam jar so that the tube orifice is below the level of the fluid.

6   The assistant should now pump the clutch pedal up and down in a succession of long and short strokes with the pedal at the top of the stroke. The pedal should be pushed down through its full stroke to the stop and at this point the bleed nipple tightened. Allow the pedal to return to the clutch engaged position and slacken the bleed screw again. Depress the clutch

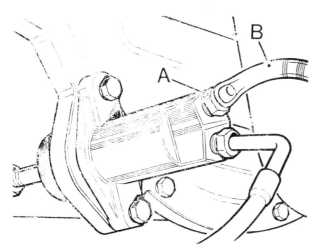

Fig. 5.19. Slave cylinder ready for bleeding

A *Bleed nipple*   B *Bleed tube*

pedal three rapid short strokes followed by a full downward
stroke. Retighten the bleed screw. Continue this sequence until
all air is eliminated from the system, this being indicated by the
flow of air bubbles into the glass jar ceasing.
7 Should any difficulty be experienced in removing all air from
the hydraulic system, it is recommended that the slave cylinder
be removed and held in the vertical position with the bleed
nipple at the top.
8 NEVER use the fluid bled from the hydraulic system
immediately for topping up the master cylinder, but allow to
stand for at least 24 hours in a sealed airtight container, so
allowing the minute air bubbles held in suspension to escape.

10 Clutch - removal, inspection and refitment

1 Remove the gearbox as described in Chapter 6.
2 The clutch cover is secured to the flywheel by a peripheral
ring of bolts. Mark the position of the clutch cover in relation to
the flywheel.
3 Unscrew the securing bolts evenly, a turn at a time in
diametrically opposite sequence, to avoid distortion. The three
bolts located in the deep recesses of the cover should not be
disturbed.
4 When the bolts are finally removed, withdraw the pressure
plate assembly from the flywheel and catch the driven plate as it
is released from the face of the flywheel (Fig. 5.20).
5 The pressure plate assembly should not be dismantled but if
worn, cracked or distorted, it should be renewed on an exchange
basis.
6 Examine the driven plate for wear. If the linings are worn
almost down to the rivets then a factory reconditioned unit
should be obtained on an exchange basis - do not waste your
time trying to reline the plate, it seldom proves satisfactory.
7 If there is evidence of oil staining, find the cause which will
probably be a faulty gearbox input shaft oil seal or a crankshaft
rear oil seal.
8 Check the machined surfaces of the flywheel and pressure
plate; if grooved or scored then the flywheel should be machined
(within the specified limits - see Chapter 1), and the pressure
plate assembly renewed.
9 Check the release bearing for smooth operation. There should
be no harshness or slackness in it and it should spin reasonably
freely bearing in mind that it is grease sealed. (Refer to next
Section).
10 It is important that no oil or grease gets on the clutch plate
friction linings or the pressure plate and flywheel faces. It is
advisable to replace the clutch with clean hands and to wipe
down the pressure plate and flywheel faces with a clean rag

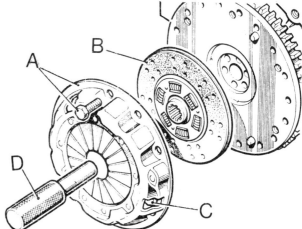

Fig. 5.20. Major clutch components

A *Clutch cover and bolt*   C *Recessed bolts*
B *Driven plate*   *(not to be unscrewed)*
                                                   D *Centralising tool*

before assembly begins.
11 Place the clutch plate against the flywheel, ensuring that it is
the correct way round. The flywheel side of the driven plate has
the shorter hub boss. If the plate is fitted the wrong way round,
it will be quite impossible to operate the clutch.
12 Replace the clutch cover assembly loosely on the dowels.
Replace the six bolts and spring washers and tighten them finger
tight so that the clutch plate is gripped but can still be moved.
    The clutch disc must now be centralised so that when the
engine and gearbox are mated, the gearbox first motion shaft
splines will pass through the splines in the centre of the driven
plate.
13 Centralisation can be carried out quite easily by inserting a
roundbar or long screwdriver through the hole in the centre of
the clutch, so that the end of the bar rests in the small hole in
the end of the crankshaft containing the spigot bush. Ideally an
old first motion shaft should be used.
14 Using the first motion shaft spigot bush as a fulcrum, moving
the bar sideways or up and down will move the clutch disc in
whichever direction is necessary to achieve centralisation.
15 Centralisation is easily judged by removing the bar and
viewing the driven plate hub in relation to the hole in the centre
of the clutch cover plate diaphragm spring. When the hub
appears exactly in the centre of the hole all is correct. Alternatively the first motion shaft will fit the bush and centre of the
clutch hub exactly, obviating the need for visual alignment.
16 Tighten the clutch bolts firmly in a diagonal sequence to
ensure that the cover plate is pulled down evenly and without
distortion of the flange. Finally tighten the bolts down to a
torque wrench setting of 20 lb/ft (2.8 kg/m).

11 Clutch withdrawal mechanism - removal, inspection, overhaul and refitment

1 Remove the gearbox as described in Chapter 6.
2 The oil should be drained from the gearbox.
3 Slacken the pinch bolt securing the external clutch lever to
the splined cross shaft. Withdraw the lever from the shaft using a
suitable withdrawal tool.
4 Remove the securing bolts from the withdrawal unit housing,
and remove the housing. Note the jointing washer which will
have to be renewed on reassembly (Fig. 5.21).
5 **Inspection and overhaul:** Fig. 5.22 shows the components of
the clutch withdrawal unit. The parts should be examined for
wear and renewed as necessary. In any event, a new oil seal for
the cross shaft is a must. Likewise a new jointing washer for the
cross shaft end cover.

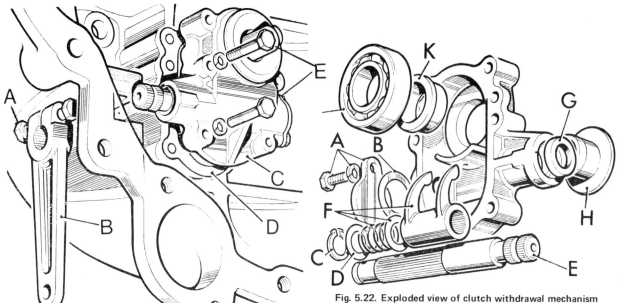

Fig. 5.21. Removing the clutch withdrawal unit

A Pinch bolt   C Housing
B Clutch external lever   D Gasket
                                       E Securing bolts

6 The unit must be dismantled observing the following procedures:

7 Remove the end cover from the cross shaft, and remove the circlip within. Following the circlip is the thrust washer.

8 The cross shaft may now be withdrawn which will in turn release the operating fork, the spring and a second thrust washer. Note the order of removal to facilitate reassembly.

9 Remove the oil seal from its recess in the housing. It will have to be renewed.

10 Push out the sleeve from the withdrawal race and remove the race.

11 Finally remove the bush.

12 Thoroughly clean all the parts and carry out examination for wear. Fit new parts as required.

13 To reassemble the withdrawal unit reverse the dismantling procedure. The following points should be noted: Make sure that the withdrawal race fits against the shoulder of the sleeve. The bolts securing the cross shaft end cover should be tightened to a torque figure of 8 lb ft (1 kg/m).

14 Refer to Sections 3 and 8 for checking and adjustment procedure.

12 Clutch faults

There are four main faults to which the clutch and release mechanism are prone. They may occur by themselves or in conjunction with any of the other faults. They are clutch squeal, slip, spin and judder.

13 Clutch squeal - diagnosis and cure

1 If on taking up the drive or when changing gear, the clutch squeals, this is sure indication of a badly worn clutch release bearing. As well as regular wear due to normal use, wear of the clutch release bearing is much accentuated if the clutch is ridden or held down for long periods in gear, with the engine running. To minimise wear of this component the car should always be taken out of gear at traffic lights or for similar hold ups.

2 It may be found that if the clutch release bearing is very

Fig. 5.22. Exploded view of clutch withdrawal mechanism

A Cross-shaft end cover and   F Spring, thrust washer
   bolts   and fork
B Joint washer   G Oil seal
C Circlip   H Sleeve
D Thrust washer   J Release bearing
E Cross-shaft   K Bush

badly worn due to lack of lubrication or overheating; a different type of noise, being of a more harsh or grinding nature, may be experienced.

3 The clutch release bearing is not an expensive item and it is recommended that it always be renewed during a major clutch overhaul.

14 Clutch slip - diagnosis and cure

1 Clutch slip is a self-evident condition which occurs when the clutch friction plate is badly worn; the release arm free travel is insufficient; oil or grease have got onto the flywheel or pressure plate faces; or the pressure plate itself is faulty.

2 The reason for clutch slip is that, due to one of the faults listed above, there is either insufficient pressure from the pressure plate, or insufficient friction from the friction plate to ensure solid drive.

3 If small amounts of oil get onto the clutch, they will be burnt off under the heat of clutch engagement, in the process gradually darkening the linings. Excessive oil on the clutch will burn off leaving a carbon deposit which can cause bad slip, or fierceness, spin and judder.

4 If clutch slip is suspected, and confirmation of the condition is required, there are several tests which can be made:-

a) With the engine in 2nd or 3rd gear and pulling lightly up a moderate incline, sudden depression of the accelerator pedal may cause the engine to increase its speed without any increase in road speed. Easing off on the accelerator will then give a definite drop in engine speed without the car slowing.

b) Drive the car at a steady speed in top gear and braking with the left leg, try to maintain the same speed by depressing the accelerator. Providing the same speed is maintained a change in the speed of the engine confirms that slip is taking place.

c) In extreme cases of clutch slip the engine will race under normal acceleration conditions. If slip is due to oil or grease on the linings, a temporary cure can sometimes be effected by squirting carbon tetrachloride into the clutch housing. The permanent cure, of course, is to renew the clutch driven plate, and trace and rectify the oil leak.

15 Clutch spin - diagnosis and cure

1 Clutch spin is a condition which occurs when there is a leak in the clutch hydraulic actuating mechanism; the release arm free travel is excessive; there is an obstruction in the clutch, either on the primary gear splines or in the operating lever itself; or oil may have partially burnt off the clutch linings and left a resinous deposit, which is causing the clutch disc to stick to the pressure plate or flywheel.

2 The reason for clutch spin is that due to any or a combination of, the faults just listed, the clutch pressure plate is not completely freeing from the centre plate, even when the clutch pedal is fully depressed.

3 If clutch spin is suspected, the condition can be confirmed by extreme difficulty in engaging first gear from rest, difficulty in changing gear, and very sudden take-up of the clutch drive at the fully depressed end of the clutch pedal travel as the clutch is released.

4 Check the operating lever free travel. If this is correct, examine the clutch master cylinder and slave cylinders and the interconnecting hydraulic pipe for leaks. Fluid in one of the rubber boots fitted over the end of either the master or slave cylinder is a sure sign of a leaking piston seal.

5 If these points are checked and found to be in order, then the fault lies internally in the clutch, and it will be necessary to remove the clutch for examination.

16 Clutch judder - diagnosis and cure

1 Clutch judder is a self-evident condition which occurs when the gearbox or engine mountings are loose or too flexible; when there is oil on the faces of the clutch friction plate; or when the clutch pressure plate has been incorrectly adjusted.

2 The reason for clutch judder is that due to one of the faults just listed, the clutch pressure plate is not freeing smoothly from the friction disc, and is snatching.

3 Clutch judder normally occurs when the clutch pedal is released in 1st or reverse gears, and the whole car shudders as it moves backwards or forwards.

Chapter 6
Manual gearbox and automatic transmission

Contents

Specifications

MANUAL GEARBOX

Type ... ... Four forward speeds and reverse. Synchromesh on all forward speeds. Single helical constant mesh

Ratios (gear):

1st	3.625 : 1
2nd	2.133 : 1
3rd	1.391 : 1
4th	1.00 : 1
Reverse	3.430 : 1

Ratios (final drive):

1st	11.165 : 1
2nd	6.57 : 1
3rd	4.284 : 1
4th	3.08 : 1
Reverse	10.564 : 1

Oil capacity ... ... 3.25 pints (1.75 litres)

AUTOMATIC TRANSMISSION

Type (early)	Borg Warner type 35
(later)	Borg Warner type 65

Ratios (gear): ... ... Torque converter stall ratio

Direct (top)	1 : 1	2.16
Intermediate (2nd)	1.45 : 1	2.16
Low (1st)	2.39 : 1	2.16
Reverse	2.09 : 1	—

Ratios (final drive):

1st	7.36
2nd	4.47
3rd	3.08
Reverse	6.45

Upshift speeds (using 'kick-down') - maximum
    1st to 2nd ... ...   36 to 45 mph (58 to 72 kph)
    2nd to 3rd ... ...   68 to 78 mph (109 to 125 kph)

Fluid capacity ... ...   12 pints (6.8 litres)

Fluid temperature ... ...   80 to 100° C (176 to 212° F)

Engine stall speed ... ...   1950 to 2250 rev/min.

Torque wrench settings:

	lb ft	kg m
MANUAL GEARBOX		
Bell housing to engine bolts	25	3.5
Bell housing to gearbox bolts	50	7.0
Gearchange shaft housing nuts	8	1.0
Rear output driving flange nut	75	10.5
Selector fork pinch bolt (1st/2nd, 3rd/4th)	20	2.8
Selector fork pinch bolt (reverse)	12	1.6
Speedometer drive housing bolts (small)	8	1.0
Speedometer drive housing bolts (large)	25	3.5
Top cover bolts	15	2.0
Bell housing cover plate bolts	8	1.0
Reverse gearshaft retaining plate bolt	8	1.0
Selector fork stop bolt locknuts	8	1.0
Selector shaft detent ball plate bolts	8	1.0
Selector shaft seal plate bolts	8	1.0
AUTOMATIC TRANSMISSION		
Torque converter to drive plate bolts	25/30	3.5/4.0
Driveplate to crankshaft flange bolts	50	7.0
Transmission case to bellhousing bolts	8/13	1.0/1.7
Extension housing to transmission case	13	1.7
Oil pan bolts	13	1.7
Coupling flange to driven shaft	25	3.5
Torque converter housing to driveplate housing	30	4.0

1 General description

The gearbox has four forward speeds and reverse controlled by a short remote gearchange lever. Synchromesh action is applied to all forward gears.

The gearbox is mounted at the rear of the engine in the conventional manner and the casing is made of a light alloy casting. The constant mesh gears are of helical cut profile to ensure quiet operation and the synchromesh is of the baulk-ring design. The remote gearchange lever operates three selector shafts, two of which are for the forward speeds and the remaining one for the reverse gear.

The primary shaft and mainshaft run in single track ball races, whilst the layshaft gear cluster has the rather unusual feature of being supported by roller bearings at front and rear.

2 Gearbox - operations with unit in car

1 Dismantling or servicing which can be carried out to the gearbox without removing it from the car is limited to the speedometer drive housing and the oil pump.
2 These components are accessible if the gearbox rear mounting is removed and the rear of the gearbox carefully lowered to provide adequate working clearance.
3 Dismantling procedure for the speedometer drive housing and the oil pump is given in Section 4.

3 Gearbox - removal and refitment

1 Disconnect the lead from the battery negative terminal. Jack up the rear of the car and support adequately.

2 Mark the position of the bonnet hinge plates and then unscrew the retaining bolts and with the help of an assistant, remove the bonnet.
3 Remove the air cleaner and the fan blade assembly.
4 Within the car, remove the screws which secure the moulded cover "5" to the gearbox tunnel (Fig. 6.1).
5 Remove the gearchange lever assembly "6" and then peel back the carpet on the left-hand side of the gearbox and remove the cover plate "7".
6 Through this aperture, disconnect the speedometer drive cable "8".
7 Peel back the carpet on the right-hand side of the gearbox and remove the large rubber grommet "9".
8 Disconnect the leads from the reverse lamp switch "10". (photo)
9 Unscrew and remove the three bolts "11" which are accessible from within the engine compartment and secure the clutch bellhousing to the engine (Fig. 6.2).
10 Drain the gearbox oil and remove the front section of the exhaust pipe.
11 Remove the propeller shaft as described in the next Chapter.
12 Disconnect the clevis pin from the clutch slave cylinder operating rod and then unbolt the cylinder from the bellhousing and tie it up out of the way. There is no need to disconnect the hydraulic line.
13 Remove the cover plate from the clutch bellhousing.
14 Support the gearbox with a jack, preferably of the trolley type and then detach the gearbox rear mounting.
15 Lower the jack and remove the remaining bolts which secure the clutch bellhousing to the engine.
16 Continue to lower the jack until the gearbox can be withdrawn from beneath and to the rear of the car.
17 Refitting is a reversal of removal but observe the following points:

a) Centralise the clutch driven plate (Chapter 5).
b) Check the clutch linkage adjustment (Chapter 5).
c) Refill the gearbox.

4 Gearbox - dismantling

1 Remove the gearbox as described in the preceding Section.

2 Remove the output drive flange "17" (Fig. 6.5). The flange securing nut is very tight and in the absence of a special tool, a length of flat steel bar should be drilled to engage with two of the flange studs and used as a retaining lever while the nut is unscrewed. If this operation is being carried out with the gearbox in position in the car, then top gear should be selected and the flywheel starter ring gear jammed with a cold chisel to prevent the output drive flange turning.

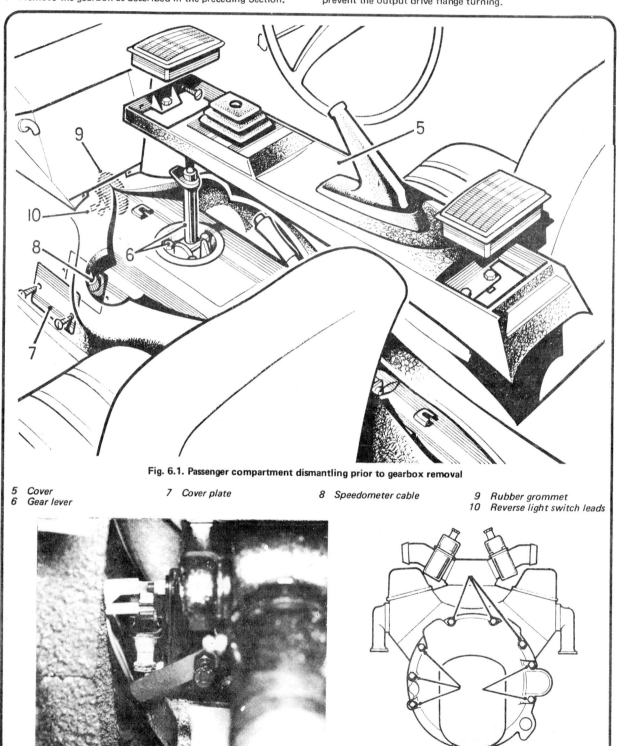

Fig. 6.1. Passenger compartment dismantling prior to gearbox removal

5	Cover	7	Cover plate	8	Speedometer cable	9	Rubber grommet
6	Gear lever					10	Reverse light switch leads

3.8 Reversing lamp connections

Fig. 6.2. Bellhousing to engine bolts

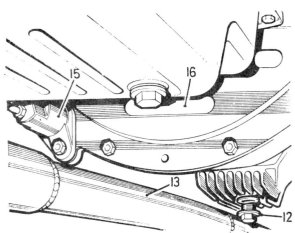

Fig. 6.3. View of underside of gearbox

12 Drain plug	15 Clutch slave cylinder
13 Exhaust pipe	16 Bellhousing cover plate

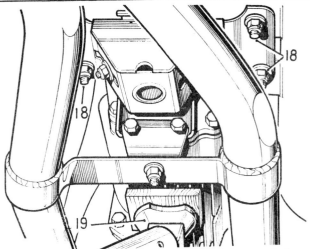

Fig. 6.4. Gearbox rear mounting bolts (18) and support jack insulated with block of wood (19)

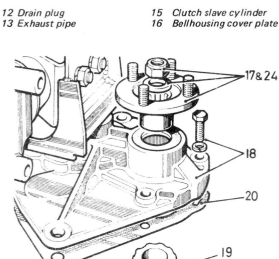

Fig. 6.5. Speedometer drive housing and output drive flange

17 Drive flange	20 Gasket
18 Speedometer drive housing and bolt	23 Mainshaft
19 Worm gear	24 Drive flange nut and washer

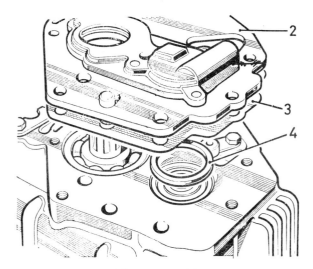

Fig. 6.6. Oil pump (2) joint gasket (3) and layshaft bearing shim (4)

3 Remove the speedometer drive housing, the gasket and the worm gear.

4 The oil pump may now be withdrawn together with its gasket followed by the shim for the layshaft bearing.

5 Unbolt and remove the gearchange shaft housing "5" (Fig. 6.7). Remove the reverse light switch "6" and bracket.

6 Remove the seal retaining plates "7".

7 From the top of the gearbox remove the retaining plate, joint washer and detent springs "8" (Fig. 6.8).

8 Withdraw the rubber plug "9".

9 Pack the selector ball locations "10" with heavy grease to retain the balls.

10 Remove the gearbox top cover "11" complete with the grease retained selector balls and then pick out the balls and clean the grease from the holes.

11 Withdraw the interlock plungers "13".

12 Refer to Fig. 6.9 and screw a bolt "14" threaded 10 UNF into the end of the reverse selector guide rod "21" and withdraw the rod.

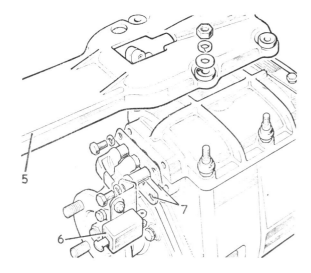

Fig. 6.7. Gearchange shaft housing (5) reverse light switch (6) and seal retaining plates (7)

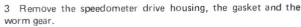

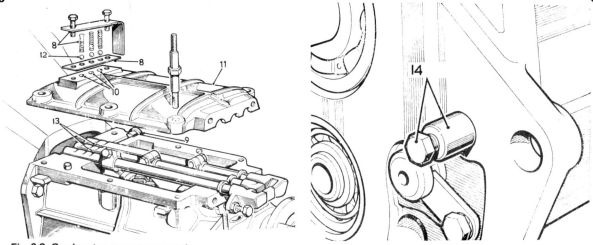

Fig. 6.8. Gearbox top cover components

8	Retaining plate and joint washer	11	Top cover
10	Selector spring holes	12	Detent balls
		13	Interlock plungers

Fig. 6.9. Reverse selector guide rod and withdrawal bolt (14)

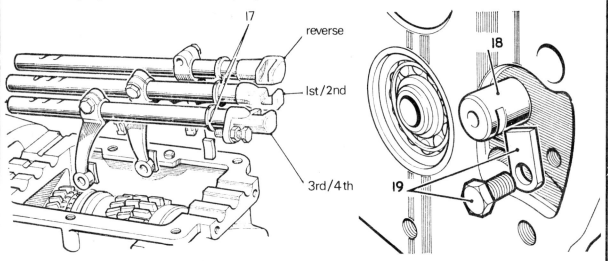

Fig. 6.10. Selector shafts and forks (17) shaft seals

reverse

1st/2nd

3rd/4th

Fig. 6.11. Reverse gear idler shaft retaining plate and bolt (19) idler shaft (18)

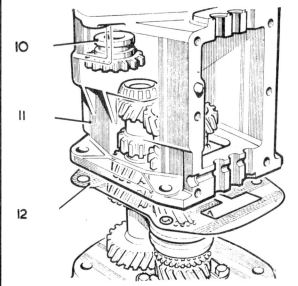

Fig. 6.12. Withdrawing gearbox main casing

10	Reverse gear	12	Joint gasket
11	Gearbox casing		

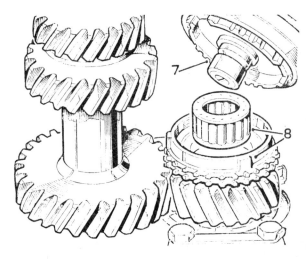

Fig. 6.13. Mainshaft (7) synchromesh cone and needle roller bearing (8)

13 Lift out the reverse gear selector fork and shaft (Fig. 6.10).
14 Lift out the two remaining selector forks and shafts together, taking care that the shoes located in each selector fork do not fall into the gearbox during the operation.
15 If essential, the forks and seals may be removed from the selector shafts.
16 Remove the bolt and retaining plate from the reverse gear idler shaft and withdraw the shaft.
17 Unscrew and remove the bolts within the clutch bellhousing which retain the bellhousing to the gearbox casing. Remove the clutch withdrawal mechanism (Chapter 5).
18 Stand the gearbox upright on the mouth of the bellhousing.
19 Refer to Fig. 6.12 and push reverse gear to one side to clear first gear on the mainshaft and then withdraw the gearbox casing. Peel off the casing to bellhousing gasket.
20 Withdraw the mainshaft complete with gears from the primary pinion.
21 Remove the cynchromesh cone with needle roller bearing "9" from the primary pinion (Fig. 6.14).
22 Remove the bearing retaining plates "10" from the rear of the bellhousing.
23 Refer to Fig. 6.15, hold the layshaft and tap the primary pinion shaft rearwards until the layshaft can be withdrawn. Withdraw the primary pinion and the bearing baffle plate.
24 The gearbox is now dismantled into major components.

5 Gearbox - examination and renovation

1 Carefully clean and then examine all component parts for general wear, distortion, slackness of fit and damage to machined faces and threads.
2 Examine the gearwheels for excessive wear and chipping of teeth. Renew them as necessary. If a gear on the mainshaft needs replacement, check that the corresponding layshaft gear is not equally damaged. If it is, the whole laygear cluster may need replacing also.
3 All gears should be a running fit on the mainshaft, with no signs of rocking. The hubs should not be a sloppy fit on the splines.
4 As one of the main causes of most gearbox ailments is the failure of ball or roller bearings on the primary drive gear, mainshaft or laygear cluster, carefully inspect the bearings for wear or roughness, as wear may not readily be apparent. If there is any doubt always obtain and fit new bearings.
5 Inspect the four synchroniser rings, although for renewal of these the mainshaft has to be completely dismantled.
6 Selector forks and shafts should be examined for signs of

wear or ridging on the faces which run in the hub grooves. Also inspect the two phosphor bronze shoes on the selector forks.
7 Before finally deciding to dismantle the mainshaft and replace parts, it is advisable to make enquiries regarding parts availability and cost and also to consider the acquisition of a new or used complete gearbox. There is a lot to be said for getting a unit from a breaker in the first place and fitting it to the car. The gearbox removed from the car can then be overhauled at leisure if necessary.
8 If the gearbox is to be completely reconditioned, a matched set of gears is required comprising first speed mainshaft gear, second speed mainshaft gear, third speed mainshaft gear, primary pinion, reverse gear, inner and outer members for low gear and layshaft gear cluster.
9 To carry out a detailed check of gear tolerances, the mainshaft will have to be dismantled, details of which are given in Section 7.

6 Gearbox bearings - renewal

1 Remove the circlip from the primary pinion shaft. Withdraw the shim and extract the bearing with a suitable puller.
2 The new bearing must be fitted the same way round as the original and in the absence of a press, use a tubular drift **located on the inner bearing track**.
3 Fit the original shim and circlip and check the clearance between the shim and circlip using feeler gauges. The clearance must not exceed 0.002 in. (0.05 mm). If necessary fit a thicker shim, available in 0.002 in. (0.05 mm) steps between 0.088 in. (2.23 mm) and 0.094 in. (2.38 mm).
4 When the clearance is correct, fit a new circlip.
5 Refer to Fig. 6.17 and pull the two taper roller bearings "13" from the layshaft.
6 Drift the bearing outer tracks from the gearbox casing and bellhousing.
7 Press the mainshaft bearing "16" from the casing.
8 Press new taper roller bearings onto each end of the layshaft. Do not mix the roller bearings and their tracks as they are produced as matched sets.
9 Press the new outer tracks into the bellhousing and gearbox casing.
10 The layshaft bearing preload must now be checked and adjusted.
11 Lay a new bellhousing to gear casing joint washer in position.
12 Locate the layshaft in position on the bellhousing and then fit the gear casing to the bellhousing, tightening the securing bolts to 50 lb/ft (7.0 kg/m).

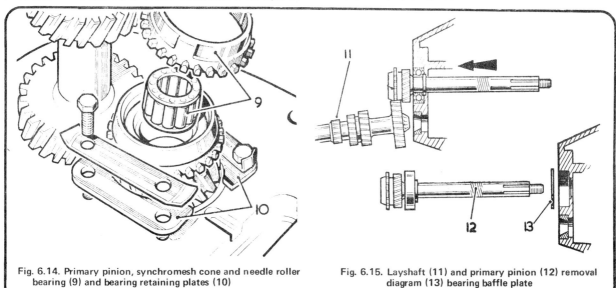

Fig. 6.14. Primary pinion, synchromesh cone and needle roller bearing (9) and bearing retaining plates (10)

Fig. 6.15. Layshaft (11) and primary pinion (12) removal diagram (13) bearing baffle plate

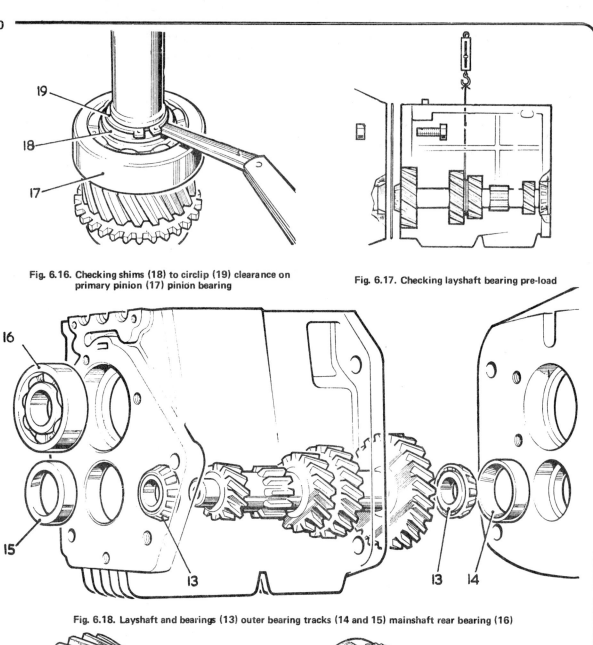

Fig. 6.16. Checking shims (18) to circlip (19) clearance on primary pinion (17) pinion bearing

Fig. 6.17. Checking layshaft bearing pre-load

Fig. 6.18. Layshaft and bearings (13) outer bearing tracks (14 and 15) mainshaft rear bearing (16)

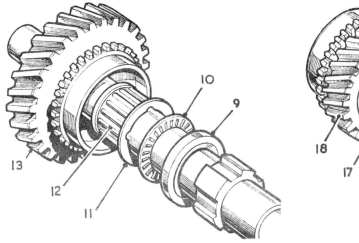

Fig. 6.19. Mainshaft front end detail

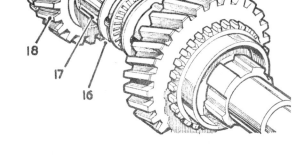

Fig. 6.20. Mainshaft 3rd speed gear (18) needle roller bearing (15 and 17) scalloped thrust washers (16) needle roller type thrust washer

9	Thrust washer	11	Scalloped thrust washer
10	Needle roller type thrust washer	12	Needle roller bearing
		13	Second gear

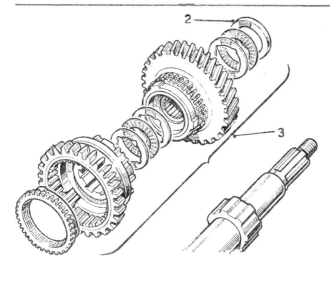

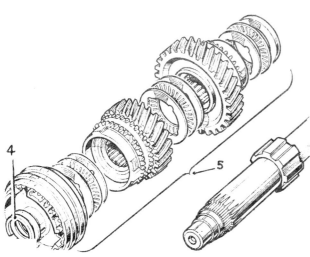

Fig. 6.21. Mainshaft assembly detail (needle roller thrust washers)

2   Thick thrust washer   4   Spring ring
3   Rear end components   5   Front end components

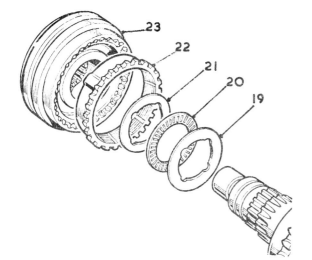

Fig. 6.22. 3rd/4th synchromesh unit (23) synchromesh cone (22) scalloped thrust washers (19 and 21) (20) needle roller thrust washer

13 Oil the layshaft bearings; place the original shim on the layshaft rear bearing.

14 Fit the oil pump to the gearbox, using a new joint washer and aligning the drive.

15 Lay a new joint washer on the oil pump and fit the speedometer drive housing tightening the bolts (small) to 8 lb/ft (1.0 kg/m), large 25 lb/ft (3.5 kg/m).

16 Using a spring balance and cord wrapped round the layshaft larger diameter groove (Fig. 6.17), check the turning resistance (bearing pre-load) which should be between 2 and 6 lb (0.9 to 2.7 kg). Where this is not the case, substitute a shim of different thickness for the original one which is located between the oil pump and the layshaft bearing outer race. Shims are available in 0.001 in. (0.02 mm) steps between 0.093 in. (2.36 mm) and 0.123 in. (3.12 mm).

17 When the correct bearing preload has been established, remove the speedometer housing, the oil pump, the gearbox casing and layshaft. Remember to retain carefully the selected shim.

18 Smear the outside diameter of the mainshaft rear bearing with Loctite and press it into the gearbox casing.

19 The mainshaft front bearing is located inside the primary pinion and should be fitted during reassembly of the gearbox (see Section 10).

7   Mainshaft - dismantling, inspection and re-assembly

1   Two types of mainshaft thrust washers may be encountered, needle roller and bronze type.

(A) Needle roller thrust washers
2   Support the first speed gear "3" (Fig. 6.21) and drift the mainshaft to free the thick thrust washer "2".

3   Withdraw the other components from the rear end of the mainshaft.

4   Remove the spring ring "4" from the front end of the mainshaft and then draw off the remaining components.

5   Wash all components in paraffin and examine for wear. Obtain a new spring ring. If new needle roller thrust bearings and washers are being installed, do not degrease them but fit them as supplied.

6   To the front of the mainshaft fit the thrust washer "9" (Fig. 6.19) chamfer facing rear of mainshaft), the needle roller thrust bearing "10", the scalloped thrust washer "11" and the needle roller bearing "12".

7   Fit the second speed gear (cone to rear of mainshaft) "13".

8   Fit the scalloped thrust washer "16" (Fig. 6.20), the needle roller thrust bearing "15" another scalloped thrust washer "16" and the needle roller bearing "17".

9   Fit the third speed gear with its synchromesh cone toward the front end of the mainshaft.

10 Refer to Fig. 6.22 and fit the components in the sequence shown. Temporarily refit the original shim washer "24" and spring ring "25" (Fig. 6.23).

11 A pressure of approximately 60 lb (28 kg) must now be applied to the end face of the inner member of the 3rd/4th synchromesh unit to ensure that all clearance is taken up between the mainshaft components. With the pressure applied, check the clearance between the spring ring and the shim washer using feeler gauges. The clearance must not exceed 0.003 in. (0.07 mm). If it does, substitute a shim washer of different thickness; they are available in 0.003 in. (0.07 mm) steps between 0.095 in. (2.41 mm) and 0.113 in. (2.87 mm).

12 When the correct clearance is established, fit a new spring ring.

13 To the rear end of the mainshaft fit the synchro. cone "30" 1st/2nd synchro. unit "31", plain thrust washer '32", needle roller thrust washer "33", scalloped thrust washer "34" (Fig. 6.24).

14 Refer to Fig. 6.25 and fit the components in the order shown but note that the thrust washer "40" must be pressed onto the mainshaft (chamfer facing gearwheels), so that its rear face is

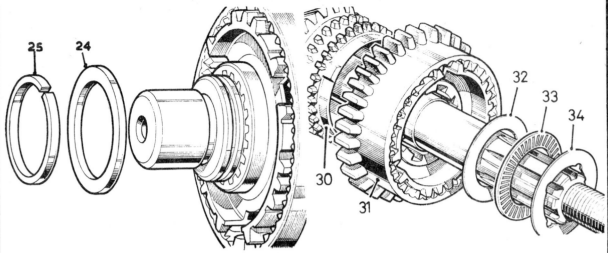

Fig. 6.23. Mainshaft spring ring (25) and thick thrust washer (24)

Fig. 6.24. Mainshaft rear end components

30 Synchro cone	33 Needle roller type thrust
31 1st/2nd synchro unit	washer
32 Plain thrust washer	34 Scalloped thrust washer

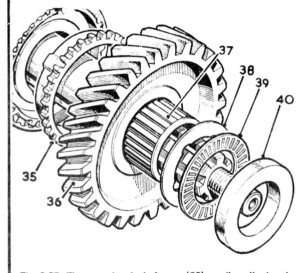

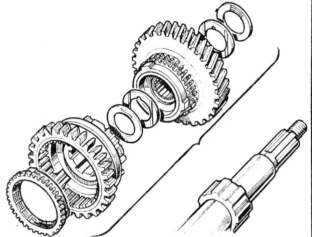

Fig. 6.25. First speed mainshaft gear (36) needle roller bearing (37) scalloped thrust washer (38) needle roller thrust washer (39) first speed thrust washer (40)

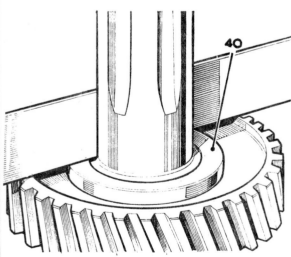

Fig. 6.26. Checking mainshaft thrust washer (40) face is flush with mainshaft shoulder

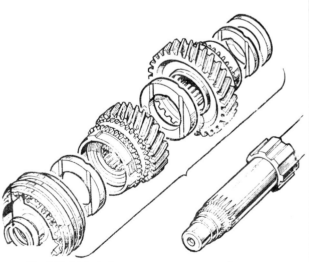

Fig. 6.27. Mainshaft assembly fitted with bronze type thrust washers

flush with the shoulder on the mainshaft (Fig. 6.26).

(B) Bronze thrust washers
15 Dismantling and reassembly of mainshafts using bronze type of thrust washers is similar to the procedure just described for those fitted with needle roller type thrust washers and the location and fitting sequence of components is shown in Fig. 6.27. The following differences in clearances however must be observed: Spring ring to shim washer clearance 0.004 to 0.008 in. (0.1 to 0.2 mm). First speed gear endfloat 0.004 to 0.008 in. (0.1 to 0.2 mm). If necessary adjust the endfloat by substituting a shim washer of different thickness.

---

8   Synchromesh units - servicing

---

1   Remove the synchromesh units from the mainshaft as described in the preceding Section.
2   Cover the unit with a piece of cloth to prevent the springs and balls flying out when it is dismantled.
3   Push the sleeve from the hub and then collect the springs, balls and blocks and retain them safely.
4   Wash the components in paraffin and examine carefully for wear or damage. If this is evident, the unit must be renewed as an assembly as the inner and outer components are matched in production.
5   To reassemble 1st/2nd unit lay the sleeve (gear side downward) on a clean surface. Fit the hub (internal splined side leading) so that the alignment marks "7" (Fig. 6.30) correspond.
6   Fit the blocks (radiused faces outwards) the springs and the balls and lift the sleeve to retain the balls and then lift it further until the balls locate in the sleeve grooves.
7   To reassemble 3rd/4th unit the procedure is similar to that just described but the sleeve may be fitted either way round.

---

9   Speedometer drive housing - servicing

---

1   Remove the speedometer drive housing as described in Section 4.
2   Withdraw the nylon housing, thrust washer and drive spindle "2" (Fig. 6.31).
3   Pick out the spindle oil seal "3".
4   Prise out the oil seal "4".
5   Refit new oil seals and renew any other worn components.
6   Refitment is a reversal of dismantling but smear the outer diameter of the large oil seal with jointing compound.

---

10 Gearbox - reassembly

---

1   Immerse the clutch bellhousing in boiling water for a few minutes to expand it slightly so that the bearing baffle plate can be fitted into the primary pinion bore in the bellhousing.
2   Fit the primary pinion and the layshaft together and fit them to the bellhousing.
3   Install the bearing retaining plates at the rear of the bellhousing.
4   Fit the synchromesh cone and needle roller bearing to the primary pinion.
5   Insert the mainshaft complete with gear assemblies to the primary pinion.
6   Smear the mating faces of the bellhousing and the gearbox casing with jointing compound and fit a new joint gasket.
7   Place reverse gear in position in the gearbox casing (lead on teeth towards front of gearbox).
8   Lower the gearbox casing onto the bellhousing at the same time pushing reverse gear to one side.
9   Secure the gearbox casing to the bellhousing by inserting two bolts but do not fit the nuts at this stage.
10 Install the reverse idler shaft and fit the retaining plate, engaging the slot in the shaft and secure with a bolt (no washer) to a torque of 8 lb/ft (1.0 kg/m).

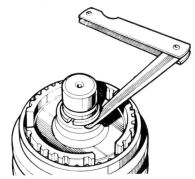

Fig. 6.28. Checking spring ring to thrust washer clearance on mainshaft fitted with bronze type thrust washers

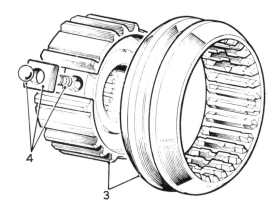

Fig. 6.29. Components of a synchromesh unit

3   Hub and sleeve   4   Balls, springs and
                                          sliding blocks

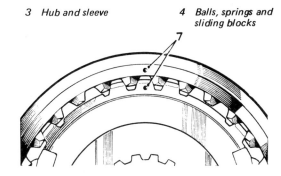

Fig. 6.30. Synchromesh unit inner and outer alignment marks (7)

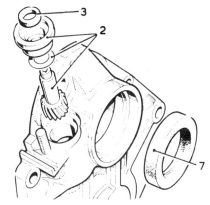

Fig. 6.31. Speedometer drive components

2   Drive spindle assembly   3 & 7 Oil seals

11 Fit the remaining gearbox to bellhousing bolts, screw on all the nuts and tighten to a torque of 50 lb/ft (7.0 kg/m).

12 Refit the selector shafts. If the forks and seals have been removed, refit the seals with the smaller diameter of the seals towards the forks.

13 Install the 1st/2nd and 3rd/4th selector fork/shaft assemblies, ensuring that the shoes engage correctly with their respective synchromesh units.

14 Fit the reverse fork and shaft, locating correctly the reverse gear.

15 Fit the reverse selector guide rod.

16 Push the seals along the selector shafts to clear the detent grooves and then insert the interlock plungers.

17 Locate the top cover on its dowels taking care not to damage the new bellhousing gasket edge which projects and then secure the cover with the two centre studs (Fig. 6.32).

18 Move selector shaft "25" rearwards, to select third gear.

19 Mount a dial gauge as shown and then insert the 3rd/4th detent ball and its spring. Hold the spring compressed to locate the selector shaft in its correct position (which is achieved by the action of the detent ball in its groove) and zero the dial gauge.

20 Release the pressure on the detent spring and pull the 3rd/4th selector shaft fully to the rear and note the reading on the dial gauge. This should be between 0.025 and 0.030 in. (0.63 and 0.76 mm). If adjustment is required then this is carried out by moving the position of the fork on the shaft. When adjustment is correct, tighten the pinch bolt to a torque of 20 lb/ft (2.8 kg/m).

21 Repeat the foregoing procedure with the 1st/2nd selector shaft but the shaft must be pushed fully forward and the dial gauge reading should be between 0.045 and 0.050 in. (1.14 and 1.27 mm).

22 Remove the top cover, detent springs and balls and then fit the reverse stop bolt "36" but without the distance piece and switch striker arm (Fig. 6.33).

23 Using a feeler gauge, adjust the stop bolt to provide a clearance of 0.035 in. (0.9 mm) between the end of the bolt and the gearbox case.

24 Select first gear and hold it fully rearward.

25 Push reverse shaft forward until the stop bolt just contacts the gearbox casing. At this stage, the reverse idler gear should just contact the gear teeth on the outer sleeve of the low gear synchromesh unit, but should not rotate when it is turned. If this is not the case, adjust the position of the fork on the reverse selector shaft then tighten the pinch bolt to a torque of 12 lb/ft (1.6 kg/m).

26 When adjustment is satisfactory, fit the top cover, detent balls and springs and tighten the securing studs to a torque of 15 lb/ft (2.0 kg/m).

27 Replace the rubber plug, the retaining plate, joint washer and detent springs together with the seal retaining plates.

28 Replace the reverse light switch and bracket and the gearchange shaft housing.

29 Prime the gearbox oil pump with fresh oil and smear a new joint gasket with gasket cement. Install the layshaft bearing shim and install the oil pump to the gearbox casing.

30 Locate a new joint gasket smeared with gasket cement and fit the speedometer drive housing, tightening the smaller bolts to 8 lb/ft (1.0 kg/m) and the larger ones to 25 lb/ft (3.5 kg/m).

31 Coat the mainshaft splines with Loctite and then push on the output driving flange and secure it with the special washer and self-locking nut (torque 75 lb/ft (10.5 kg/m).

32 Select reverse gear and fit the switch striker arm and distance piece to the reverse stop bolt. Adjust the stop bolt to give an end clearance of 0.015 in. (0.4 mm) between its end face and the gearbox case. Tighten the stop bolt locknut ensuring that the reverse light switch is in the correct attitude.

33 Move the reverse selector to the neutral position.

34 Slacken the 3rd/4th selector shaft stop bolt and its locknut. Select fourth gear and adjust the stop bolt clearance in a similar manner to that described in paragraph 32.

35 Secure the locknut and move the selector to the neutral position.

11 Gearchange lever - removal and refitment

1 Slacken the gearchange lever knob locknut and unscrew the knob.

2 Unscrew and remove the locknut and withdraw the sleeve and spring.

3 Remove the front and rear ashtrays from the gearbox tunnel moulded cover.

4 Locate and remove the two nuts to be found under the rear ashtray location and the single nut under the front ashtray location.

5 Undo and remove the two Phillips head screws at the front of the moulded cover.

6 Lift up the flap at the forward edge of the rubber grommet base and remove the self-tapping screw.

7 Undo and remove the two crosshead screws securing the radio speaker grille to the console unit. These screws are to be found between the petrol reserve control and choke control. Lift away the speaker grille.

8 Remove the gearchange lever sleeve.

9 Slide both front seats as far back as they will go and keep the locking levers in their raised position.

10 Carefully roll back the handbrake rubber grommet and to assist removal of the grommet smear the handbrake handle and the grommet with a little silicone grease.

11 Lift the forward edge of the cover over and off the gearchange lever.

12 Apply the handbrake and slide the cover forward and upwards so as to enable the leading edge to protrude into the aperture at the console. At the same time carefully push the handbrake grommet off the handbrake handle.

13 Release the handbrake fully and lift away the cover assembly.

14 Undo and remove the three bolts that secure the retaining cap assembly and then lift away the gear lever and retaining cap from the inside of the car.

15 The gearchange lever may now be separated from the support plate once the four bolts and self-locking nuts have been removed.

16 Refitting the gearchange lever is the reverse sequence to removal. It will, however, be necessary to check the alignment of the gearchange lever. Details of this operation are given in Section 12.

17 It is important that the reverse stop sleeve clears the shoulder on the reverse stop when pulled upwards, so as to enable reverse gear to be selected. Adjustment may be made by unscrewing the spring retaining sleeve until the stop sleeve clears the reverse stop shoulder.

12 Gearchange shaft - removal, refitment and adjustment

1 Jack up the rear of the car and position on firmly based axle stands located at the body jacking points or, alternatively, position the rear of the car over a pit or on a ramp.

2 If the rear of the car is jacked up always supplement the jack with supporting axle stands or blocks so that danger is minimised should the jack collapse.

3 If the rear wheels are off the ground, place the car in gear, or put the handbrake on to ensure that the propeller shaft does not turn when an attempt is made to loosen the nuts securing the propeller shaft universal joint flanges to the rear of the gearbox and to the final drive extension shaft flange.

4 The propeller shaft is carefully balanced to fine limits and it is important that it is replaced in exactly the same position as it was in prior to its removal. Scratch a mark on the propeller shaft and mating flanges to ensure accurate refitting when the time comes for reassembly.

5 Undo and remove the four nuts and bolts which hold the flange of the propeller shaft to the flange on the final drive extension shaft.

6 Push the propeller shaft forwards, lower the rear end and place on the floor.

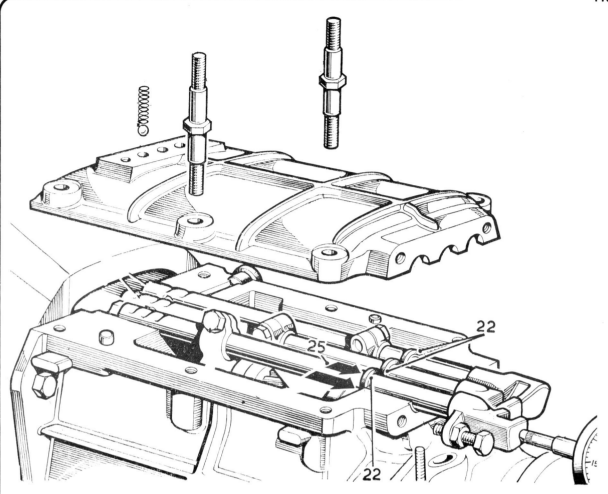

Fig. 6.32. Top cover assembly

25   3rd/4th selector shaft   22   Shaft oil seals

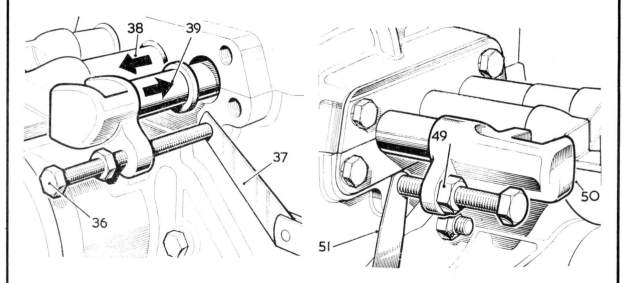

Fig. 6.33. Adjusting reverse stop bolt clearance   **Fig. 6.34. Checking 3rd/4th selector shaft stop bolt clearance**

36   Stop bolt   38   1st/2nd selector shaft   49   Locknut   51   Feeler gauge
37   Feeler gauge   39   Reverse selector shaft   50   3rd/4th selector shaft

7 Undo and remove the four nuts which hold the flange of the propeller shaft to the flange on the rear of the gearbox.

8 Push the propeller shaft rearwards and lift it away from the underside of the car.

9 Undo and remove the two nuts and bolts that secure the gearchange shaft and selector lever retainer cap, bush and plate to the support plate.

10 Carefully push the reverse selector shaft forward so as to engage gear. Rotate the selector shaft through 90° in an anti-clockwise direction so as to clear the selector gate.

11 Lower the selector shaft to clear the gearchange lever and then withdraw the shaft rearwards.

12 If it is necessary to remove the selector lever from the shaft, it will be necessary to reset the adjustment as detailed later in this Section.

13 To remove the support plate, undo and remove the four bolts that secure the bottom plate, and lift away the plate and rubber block, working underneath the car.

14 Refitment is the reverse sequence to removal. It is important that the gearchange lever ball and spherical seating are not lubricated.

15 If the selector lever setting relative to the selector rod has been disturbed, it will be necessary to adjust the position of the selector lever.

16 Refer to Fig. 6.35 and make sure that there is a clearance between the gearchange lever and tunnel finisher when first and reverse gears are selected.

17 Should it be noticed that dimensions A and B are not equal the gearchange lever support plate must be moved until equidistant movement is obtained.

18 Move the gearchange lever to the central position of neutral and very gently push it forwards until the detent is felt. Do not move the lever forwards any further.

19 Note the position of the gearchange lever relative to the vertical and this should be 10° as shown in Fig. 6.36.

20 Should the angle be incorrect, remove the reverse switch access hole rubber grommet and with a socket or 'T' spanner slacken the selector lever clamp bolt.

21 Place the gearchange lever in the vertical position and then move it forwards in the same plane until it is at 10° to the vertical. Tighten the clamp bolt on the selector lever. Make sure that the selector lever is in a vertical position relative to the gearchange shaft.

22 Move the gearchange lever to the first gear position.

23 Slacken the selector lever clamp bolt again and move the gearchange lever to the left until it contacts the reverse stop. Then lift the reverse stop and move the gearchange lever approximately 1/8 inch to the left.

24 Tighten the selector lever clamp bolt and check for correct selection of all gears by road testing.

13 Manual gearbox - fault diagnosis

Faults in the gearbox can range from small noises and minor deficiencies in engagement of gears and operation of synchro-mesh, to serious faults consisting of loud whines, serious vibrations or inability to engage or remain in one or more gears. For serious faults there is no alternative to removing the gearbox and either overhauling it completely or fitting another. For minor faults, other than those which can be detected in the change mechanism rather than the gearbox, it is more a question of how long can the fault be tolerated before taking action. Once something starts to wear to a degree which is noticeable, things usually start to deteriorate rapidly.

Unfortunately, the amount of trouble to rectify a minor fault will be the same as for a major one - removal and dismantling of the gearbox. One may save something on spare parts but even this is problematical as it is not until the gearbox is stripped that many faults can be diagnosed accurately. Some faults can go on for thousands of miles without further deterioration to the whole unit - a worn synchro. cone for example. Failure of the mainshaft bearing could, however, completely ruin the whole assembly in a few hundred miles.

The following list is intended as a guide to aid decisions on WHEN to take action:-

Fault	Cause
Ineffective synchromesh on one or more gears. Jumps out of one or more gears.	Worn synchro cones. Worn blocker bars. Worn selector forks. Weak detent springs. Worn gear engagement dogs. Worn selector hub fork groove. Selector fork loose on rail (rare).
Noisy - rough - whining, vibration.	Worn bearings and/or laygear thrust washers (initially) resulting in extended wear generally due to play and backlash.
Noisy and difficult engagement of gear. Difficult selecting forward or reverse gears and moving change lever out of gear.	Clutch not disengaging properly. Worn change lever linkage, particularly on steering column controls. General wear on remote control. General wear on remote control.

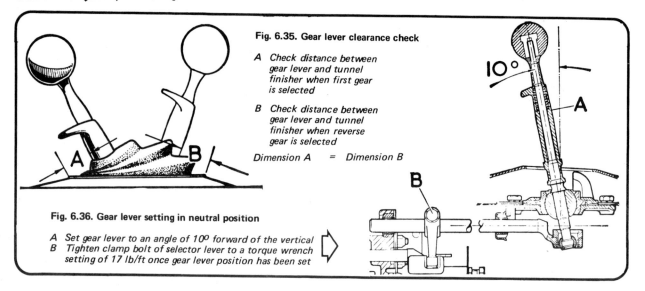

Fig. 6.35. Gear lever clearance check

A *Check distance between gear lever and tunnel finisher when first gear is selected*

B *Check distance between gear lever and tunnel finisher when reverse gear is selected*

Dimension A   =   Dimension B

Fig. 6.36. Gear lever setting in neutral position

A *Set gear lever to an angle of 10° forward of the vertical*
B *Tighten clamp bolt of selector lever to a torque wrench setting of 17 lb/ft once gear lever position has been set*

14 General description

The automatic transmission unit fitted originally to the Rover 3500 and early 3500 S models was the Borg Warner type 35.

Later 3500 model vehicles are equipped with a type 65 unit of the same manufacture. This later transmission provides smoother changes and incorporates a new starter inhibitor switch. The speed selector is cable operated compared with the rod type linkage of the earlier units.

The system comprises two main components:-

1 A three element hydrokinetic torque converter coupling capable of torque multiplication at an infinitely variable ratio between 2 : 1 and 1 : 1.

2 A torque/speed responsive and hydraulic epicyclic gearbox, comprising a planetary gearset providing three forward ratios and one reverse ratio.

Due to the complexity of the automatic transmission unit, if performance is not up to standard or overhaul is necessary, it is imperative that rectification be left to the local main agents who will have the special equipment and knowledge for fault diagnosis and rectification.

The content of this Chapter is therefore confined to supplying general information and any service information and instruction that can be used by the owner.

15 Identification of types

1 Each unit has a serial number plate attached to it and the following information provides a guide to vehicle production date and differences between the units.

2 **Series 3 FU** fitted to earliest models - six position quadrant P - R - N - D2 - D1 - L.

3 **Series 7 FU** superseded type 3 FU and incorporated new speed selector quadrant P - R - N - D - 2 - 1, also shorter downshift cable and self-adjusting front servo (brake band).

4 **Series 9 FU** fitted to special export models and then later to all 3500 S versions. Identified by flexible fluid filler tube.

5 **Series 267**, modified to provide interchangeability between Rover 3500 and 3½ litre models. Serial number commences 04-35-000-387.

6 **Series 303** incorporates modified torque converter, bell-housing, downshift cam and cable and fluid filter. Components not interchangeable with earlier units but complete transmission is.

7 The appropriate downshift cable type may be identified by reference to the type number stamped on the cable entry locknut (Fig. 6.37A).

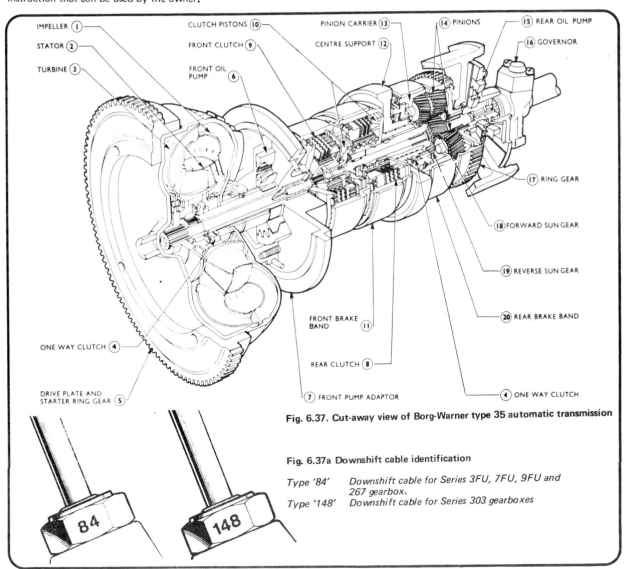

Fig. 6.37. Cut-away view of Borg-Warner type 35 automatic transmission

Fig. 6.37a Downshift cable identification

Type '84'   Downshift cable for Series 3FU, 7FU, 9FU and 267 gearbox.

Type '148'   Downshift cable for Series 303 gearboxes

16 Maintenance

1   Keep the exterior of the transmission unit and the air intake grilles clear of mud or dirt otherwise overheating may occur.
2   Check the fluid level regularly as described in Routine Maintenance Section at the front of this manual.
3   If the unit has been drained, it is recommended that only new fluid is used. Fill up to the correct level on the dipstick by gradually refilling the unit, the exact amount will depend on how much was left in the converter after draining.

17 Downshift cable (gearbox types 3 FU, 7 FY, 9 FU and 267) - checking and adjustment

1   Run the car for a minimum of 3 miles (4 km) to ensure that the engine and transmission are at normal operating temperature.
2   Chock the front wheels of the car and apply the handbrake fully.
3   A pressure gauge will be required for connection to the take off point at the rear of the transmission housing "3" (Fig. 6.38), also a tachometer which should be connected between the "CB" terminal on the coil and earth, (Fig. 6.39). Where a tachometer designed for four cylinder engines is utilised it must be remembered that the indication on the dial will be double the actual engine revs and the figure must therefore be halved.
4   Check that the downshift cable is correctly attached and that the transmission fluid level is satisfactory.
5   Check the pressures in accordance with the following chart which should be progressive as the accelerator pedal is depressed.
6   Where the pressure readings are incorrect, screw the downshift cable adjuster in or out as required (Fig. 6.40).

DOWNSHIFT CABLE ADJUSTMENT CHART:

Pressure check speeds:
Engine speed must be increased by the use of the accelerator pedal, not by manual manipulation of the carburettor linkage.
There must be a progressive rise in pressure between engine idle speed and 1,200 rev/min corresponding to accelerator pedal movement.

Model	Engine temperature	Gear to be selected	Engine idle speed	Pressure engine idle speed	Increase engine speed to:	Pressure at 800 rev/min	Further increase engine speed to:	Pressure at 1200 rev/min
Rover 3500	Run car for a minimum of 4 km (3 miles) to ensure engine and gearbox are at normal running temperatures	D1 or D according to selector pattern	600-650 rev/min	3,8-5,6 kgf/cm^2 (55-80 lbf/in^2)	800 rev/min	4,9-7,7 kgf/cm^2 (70-110 lbf/in^2)	1,200 rev/min	7,0 kgf/cm^2 (100 lbf/in^2) minimum
Rover 3500 with emission control		D	700-750 rev/min	3,8-5,6 kgf/cm^2 (55-80 lbf/in^2)	800 rev/min	4,9-7,7 kgf/cm^2 (70-110 lbf/in^2)	1,200 rev/min	7,0 kgf/cm^2 (100 lbf/in^2) minimum

Fig. 6.38. Line pressure take off point (3) and pressure gauge/tachometer

Fig. 6.39. Connection diagram for tachometer leads (5)

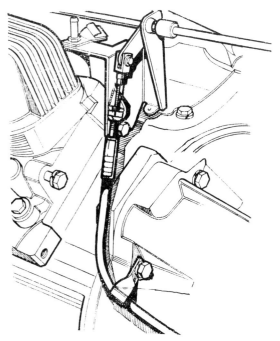

Fig. 6.40. Downshift cable adjuster (gearbox types 3FU, 7FU, 9FU and 267

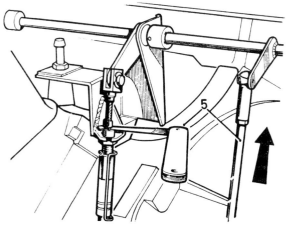

Fig. 6.41. Checking downshift cable stop clearance (type 303 gearbox) (5) accelerator coupling shaft

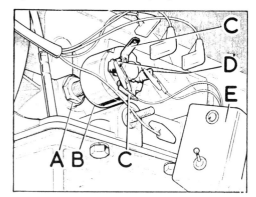

Fig. 6.42. Adjusting early type starter inhibitor switch

A *Switch locknut*   D *Starter inhibitor terminals*
B *Switch*   E *Test lamp*
C *Reverse light terminals*

18 Downshift cable (gearbox type 303) - checking and adjustment

1   Operate the car for a minimum of 3 miles (4 km) until the engine and transmission reach normal working temperature.
2   Check the ignition timing and dwell angle (Chapter 4).
3   Connect an independent tachometer and check the engine idling speed which should be from 600 to 650 rev/min. (emission control fitted - 700 to 750 rev/min.). Adjust the carburettors if necessary.
4   With the engine idling, operate the accelerator coupling shaft until the idling speed just starts to rise, then maintaining this setting, check the gap between the crimped stop on the inner cable and the end of the adjuster which should be between 0.010 and 0.020 in. (0.25 and 0.50 mm) (Fig. 6.41).
5   If the gap is incorrect, connect a pressure gauge as described in Section 16, start the engine and move the speed selector lever to 'D'.
6   Check the pressure readings in accordance with the following specifications:
At specified idling speed 55 to 80 lb/in^2 (3.86 to 5.62 kg/cm^2)
At 1200 rev/min. 80 lb/in^2 minimum (5.62 kg/cm^2).
7   Where the pressure readings are incorrect, adjust the downshift cable gap as previously specified and then recheck the pressures. If the readings are still wrong, suspect an internal fault in the transmission unit or a downshift cable of incorrect type.

19 Torque converter - balancing

1   The engine and transmission unit are finally balanced by selective fitting of special balance bolts in the front face of the starter ring gear. Occasionally due to the power train having settled down or worn slightly, vibration can be felt at the rear of the engine at certain engine speeds and this will indicate the need for rebalancing.
2   Obtain a selection of balance bolts from your Rover dealer.
3   Remove the cover plate from the lower front face of the converter housing.
4   Remove the balance bolts from their original location and move them round 180° and refit them.
5   Sit in the car and hold the engine at a steady 2000 rev/min. and feel any improvement through the steering wheel. If there is an improvement, substitute heavier or lighter bolts to see if any remaining vibration can be eliminated. If having moved the bolts, the vibration is worse, substitute heavier or lighter ones in the original locations.
6   It will be obvious that this balancing operation is very much a 'trial-and-error' procedure until the best possible balance bolt arrangement can be achieved.

20 Starter inhibitor switch (early type) - removal, refitment and adjustment

1   The following procedure will normally only be required where the switch has been removed for renewal or the switch locknut has become loose.
2   Make a note of the electrical cable connections on the switch and then disconnect the terminals from the switch (larger terminals for reverse light).
3   Using a small open-ended spanner slacken the switch locknut and unscrew the switch from the transmission case.
4   Refitting is the reverse sequence to removal. It will, however, be necessary to adjust the switch as detailed in the subsequent paragraphs.
5   Select D2, D1 or L or D, 2, 1 according to model.
6   Slacken the switch locknut and undo but do not remove the switch.
7   Connect a 12-volt test lamp and battery circuit across the two reverse light terminals "C" (Fig. 6.42). Gradually screw in the switch until the light goes out. Make a pencil mark on the

switch and casing.

8 Disconnect the test lamp circuit from the reverse terminals and reconnect them to the starter inhibitor terminal "D". The test lamp bulb should now be off.

9 Screw the switch in approximately one turn until the test lamp bulb ignites. Make a new mark on the transmission case opposite to the pencil mark on the switch.

10 Disconnect the test lamp circuit. Unscrew the switch until the switch pencil mark is in the mid-way position between the two previously made marks on the casing.

11 Tighten the locknut and connect all four cables to the switch cable.

12 Check that the starter will only operate in positions N and P.

21 Starter inhibitor switch (later self-adjusting type) - removal and refitment

1 This type of switch is fully interchangeable with the earlier non-adjustable type.

2 Disconnect the battery earth (negative) terminal.

3 Remove the front exhaust pipe section.

4 Disconnect the leads from the inhibitor switch.

5 Apply a spanner to the squared section of the switch and then unscrew it by hand.

6 Check that the dimension "7" (Fig. 6.43) is 0.375 in. (9 mm). If necessary, flick the plunger with the thumb to enable it to extend under spring pressure.

7 Move the speed selector to "P" and then fit the sealing washer to the switch.

8 Screw the switch into the transmission casing and tighten it to a torque of not more than 8 lb/ft (1.10 kg/m).

9 Connect the starter leads to the straight switch terminals and the reverse light leads to the angled ones.

10 Connect the battery lead and refit the exhaust pipe then check that the starter will only operate with the speed selector in the "N" or "P" positions.

22 Speed selector linkage - adjustment

1 It is important that the selector linkage is adjusted if it has been disturbed or has become worn.

2 The components of the linkage together with setting dimensions are shown in Fig. 6.44.

3 Check and adjust the length of each rod taking the measurements from the ball joint centres.

4 Place the selector lever in "N" and adjust the lower control rod so that its ball joint stud will drop into the eye of the lever without having to strain the rod in either direction (Figs. 6.45 and 6.46).

5 Check the operation of the selector lever, making sure that the linkage does not over ride the operating lever detent positions.

6 When adjustment is correct, tighten all nuts and check that the balljoints are set in the centre of their arcs of travel.

7 On later models having cable operated speed selector gear, adjustment is carried out by setting both the hand control lever and the selector lever on the transmission casing to "P". Adjust the cable adjuster until the connecting clevis pin will slide into the cable and selector lever connector without any movement of the cable being required.

23 Front servo brake band (early models) - adjustment

1 Later models have a self-adjusting type unit and this operation is not therefore required.

2 Drain the transmission fluid and remove the oil pan (Fig. 6.47).

3 Slacken the locknut and unscrew the brake band adjuster bolt.

4 Locate a metal block (¼ in. - 6.35 mm) thick between the

end of the adjuster bolt and the servo piston pin. Tighten the adjuster bolt to 10 lb in only.

5 Tighten the locknut to between 15 and 20 lb/ft (2 to 2.8 kg/m) and then remove the metal block.

6 Refit the oil pan using a new gasket and fill the unit with fresh fluid of the specified grade.

24 Rear brake band - adjustment

1 The adjuster for the rear servo brake band is accessible from inside the car after removing the carpet on the transmission tunnel and withdrawing the rubber plug.

2 Slacken the adjuster screw locknut and then tighten the adjuster screw to a torque of 10 lb/ft (1.4 kg/m). Now turn the adjuster screw back one complete turn and tighten the locknut to between 25 and 30 lb/ft (3.5 to 4.0 kg/m).

25 Automatic transmission - removal and refitment

1 Disconnect the lead from the battery negative terminal.

2 Remove the air cleaner.

3 Disconnect the downshift cable at the carburettor and from its retaining clips.

4 Disconnect the throttle linkage at the rear of the engine below the heater box.

5 Remove the fan guard and top mounting bracket from the top of the radiator.

6 Disconnect the pipe between the radiator header tank and the inlet manifold.

7 Detach the transmission filler tube and breather pipe.

8 Drain the radiator and disconnect the heater hoses.

9 Remove the front section of the exhaust pipe.

10 Remove the propeller shaft (Chapter 7) and then jack up the rear of the car sufficiently high to permit withdrawal of the transmission and bellhousing from underneath and to the rear of the car.

11 Drain the fluid from the transmission unit and then remove the fluid filler tube.

12 Disconnect the speedometer cable from the transmission unit.

13 Disconnect the leads from the starter inhibitor switch.

14 Disconnect the speed selector control rods or cable according to type.

15 Support the engine sump using a jack and a block of wood to insulate it.

16 Remove the transmission rear mounting and then very carefully lower the jack so that the oil cooler pipe unions can be disconnected.

17 Remove the selector control rod connections at the bellhousing and then withdraw the ring of bolts which secure the transmission casing to the torque converter bellhousing. As these bolts are withdrawn the weight of the transmission unit must be adequately supported and not allowed to hang upon the input shaft.

18 Withdraw the gearbox to the rear which will leave the torque converter attached to the drive plate and the bellhousing attached to the engine.

19 Refitment is a reversal of removal but before offering up the transmission casing to the bellhousing, align the two drive plate dogs horizontally, also the front pump engagement slots.

20 Support the transmission until the bellhousing securing bolts are inserted and tightened to a torque of between 8 and 10 lb/ft (1 to 1.4 kg/m).

21 Refill with fluid of the approved type and check the speed selector linkage adjustment, also the operation of the starter inhibitor switch and downshift cable.

26 Torque converter and bellhousing - removal and refitment

1 Remove the transmission unit as described in the preceding

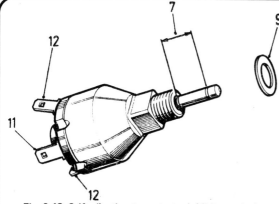

Fig. 6.43. Self adjusting type starter inhibitor switch

7 Setting dimension 0.375 in   11 Starter terminals
   (9 mm)   12 Reverse light terminals
9 Seal

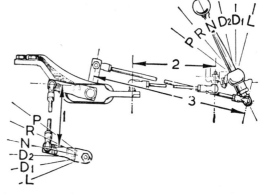

Fig. 6.44. Selector rod adjustment diagram

1 Vertical rod 7¾ in   (401.6 mm)
   (197 mm)   3 Control rod 20 13/16 in
2 Tie rod 15 13/16 in   (528.6 mm)

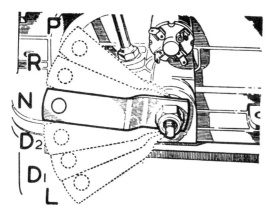

Fig. 6.45. Selector lever positions (early type 35 transmission)

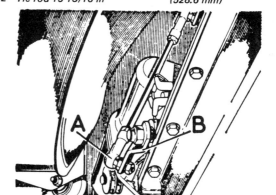

Fig. 6.46. Speed selector lower control rod

A Lower control rod   B Selector lever

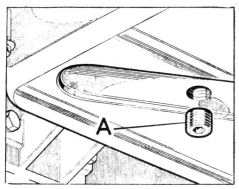

Fig. 6.47. Automatic transmission drain plug (A)

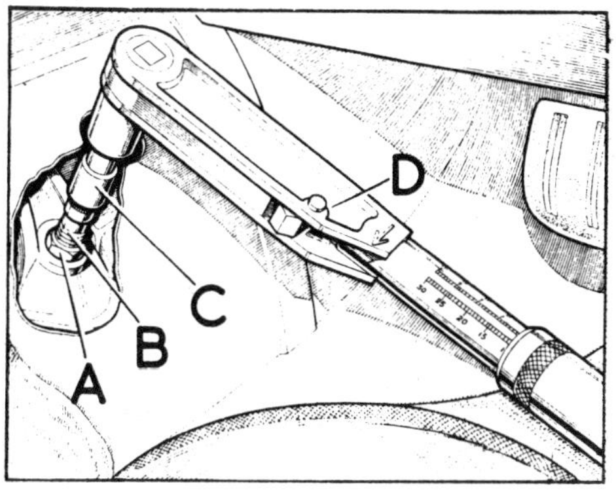

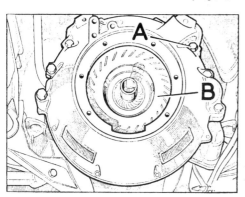

Fig. 6.48. Adjusting rear brake band

A Locknut   C Socket
B Adjusting screw   D Torque wrench

Fig. 6.49. Bellhousing and torque converter (transmission unit removed)

A Bellhousing securing bolts   B Torque converter

Section.

2   Remove the cover plate from the front of the bellhousing.

3   Remove the eight bolts which secure the bellhousing to the engine.

4   Mark the relative position of the torque converter to the drive plate and then remove the four bolts which secure the torque converter to the drive plate. These are accessible two at a time through the cover plate aperture by rotating the engine.

5   Support the torque converter during removal of the securing bolts and then withdraw it catching the residue of oil which has been retained within the converter.

6   Refitment is a reversal of removal but tighten all bolts to the torque settings specified.

7   Where a new torque converter is to be installed then the positioning of it on the drive plate without alignment marks (as is the case with an original component) may cause out of balance running and reference should be made to Section 19 of this Chapter.

8   Where the combined weight is acceptable then the transmission unit together with the torque converter bellhousing and torque converter may be removed as an assembly by carrying out operations 1 to 16 of Section 24, and operations 2, 3 and 4 of this Section.

27 Fault diagnosis - automatic transmission

Stall test procedure:

The function of a stall test is to determine that the torque converter and gearbox are operating satisfactorily.

1   Check the condition of the engine. An engine which is not developing full power will affect the stall test readings.

2   Allow the engine and transmission to reach correct working temperatures.

3   Connect a tachometer to the vehicle.

4   Chock the wheels and apply the handbrake and footbrake.

5   Select 'I' or 'R' and depress the throttle to the 'kickdown' position. Note the reading on the tachometer which should be 1,800 rev/min. If the reading is below 1,000 rev/min. suspect the converter for stator slip. If the reading is down to 1,200 rev/min. the engine is not developing full power. If the reading is in excess of 2,000 rev/min. suspect the gearbox for brake bind or clutch slip. **Note:** Do not carry out a stall test for a longer period than 10 seconds, otherwise the transmission will become overheated.

Converter diagnosis

Inability to start on steep gradients, combined with poor acceleration from rest and low stall speed (1,000 rev/min.) indicates that the converter stator uni-directional clutch is slipping. This condition permits the stator to rotate in an opposite direction to the impeller and turbine, and torque multiplication cannot occur.

Poor acceleration in third gear above 30 mph and reduced maximum speed indicates that the stator unidirectional clutch, has seized. The stator will not rotate with the turbine and impeller and the 'fluid flywheel' phase cannot occur. This condition will also be indicated by excessive overheating of the transmission although the stall speed will be correct.

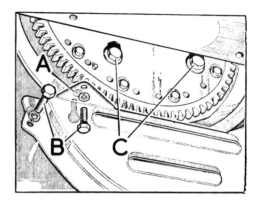

Fig. 6.50. Torque converter to drive plate securing bolts (C)

A, *Bellhousing cover plate*   B *Cover plate bolts*

Road test procedure:

1   Check that the engine will only start with the selector lever in 'P' or 'N' and that the reverse light operates only in 'R'.

2   Apply the handbrake and with the engine idling select 'N' - 'D', 'N' - 'R' and 'N' - 'I'. Engagement should be positive.

3   With the transmission at normal running temperature select 'D', release the brakes and accelerate with minimum throttle. Check 1 - 2 and 2 - 3 shift speeds and quality of change.

4   At a minimum road speed of 30 mph select 'N' and switch off ignition. Allow the road speed to drop to approximately 28 mph, switch on the ignition, select 'D' and the engine should start.

5   Stop the vehicle, select 'D' and re-start, using 'full throttle'. Check 1 - 2 and 2 - 3 shift speeds and quality of change.

6   At 25 mph apply 'full throttle'. The vehicle should accelerate in third gear and should not downshift to second.

7   At a maximum of 45 mph, 'kickdown' fully, the transmission should downshift to second.

8   At a maximum of 31 mph in third gear 'kickdown' fully. The transmission should downshift to first gear.

9   Stop the vehicle, select 'D' and re-start using 'kickdown'. Check the 1 - 2 and 2 - 3 shift speeds.

10 At 40 mph in third gear, select 'I' and release the throttle. Check 2 - 3 downshift and engine braking.

11 With 'I' still engaged stop the vehicle and accelerate to over 25 mph using 'kickdown'. Check for slip, 'squawk' and absence of upshifts.

12 Stop the vehicle and select 'R'. Reverse using 'full throttle' if possible. Check for slip and clutch 'squawk'.

13 Stop the vehicle on a gradient. Apply the handbrake and select 'P'. Check the parking pawl holds when the handbrake is released. Turn the vehicle around and repeat the procedure. Check that the selector lever is held firmly in the gate in 'P'.

Chapter 7 Propeller shaft and universal joints

Contents

Specifications

Type	Open shaft with sliding sleeve (Hardy-Spicer - needle bearing)
Shaft diameter	2.5 in. (63.5 mm)
Overall length (face to face):	
Manual gearbox	44.750 in. (1136.65 mm)
Automatic transmission	39.5 in. (1003.3 mm)

Torque wrench setting:	lb ft	kg m
Flange nuts	30	4

1 General description

Drive is transmitted from the gearbox to the final drive extension housing flange by means of a finely balanced tubular propeller shaft. Fitted at each end of the shaft is a universal joint, which allows for vertical movement of the rear axle. Each universal joint comprises a four-legged centre spider, four-needle roller bearings and two yokes. Fore and aft movement of the rear axle is absorbed by a sliding spline at the front of the propeller shaft which slides over a mating spline on the rear of the front universal joint splined sleeve.

All models are fitted with sealed type universal joint yoke bearings, but the splined sleeve has a grease nipple which must be lubricated every 5,000 miles.

2 Propeller shaft - removal and refitment

1 Jack up the rear of the car and position on firmly based axle stands located at the body jacking points. Alternatively, position the rear of the car over a pit or on a ramp.

2 If the rear of the car is jacked up always supplement the jack with supporting axle stands or blocks so that danger is minimised should the jack collapse.

3 If the rear wheels are off the ground, place the car in gear, or put the handbrake on to ensure that the propeller shaft does not turn when an attempt is made to loosen the nuts securing the propeller shaft universal joint flanges to the rear of the gearbox and to the final drive extension shaft flange.

4 The propeller shaft is carefully balanced to fine limits and it is important that it is replaced in exactly the same position it was in prior to its removal. Paint a mark on the edges of the propeller shaft flanges and corresponding ones on the edges of the front and rear driving flanges.

5 Undo and remove the four nuts and bolts which hold the flange of the propeller shaft to the flange on the final drive extension shaft.

6 Push the propeller shaft forwards and lower the rear end of the propeller shaft and place on the floor.

7 Undo and remove the four nuts which hold the flange of the propeller shaft to the flange on the rear of the gearbox. The

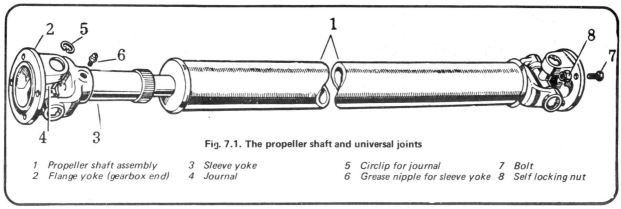

Fig. 7.1. The propeller shaft and universal joints

1 Propeller shaft assembly   3 Sleeve yoke   5 Circlip for journal   7 Bolt
2 Flange yoke (gearbox end)   4 Journal   6 Grease nipple for sleeve yoke   8 Self locking nut

bolts are a press fit into the gearbox mainshaft flange so they should be left in place.

8   Push the propeller shaft rearwards and lift the propeller shaft away from the underside of the car.

9   Replacement of the propeller shaft is a reversal of the above procedure. Ensure that the mating mark scratched on the mating flanges line up correctly.

3   Universal joints - inspection and repair

1   Wear in the needle roller bearings is characterised by vibration in the transmission, clonks on taking up the drive, and in extreme cases of lack of lubrication, metallic squeaking and ultimately grating and shrieking sounds as the bearings break up.

2   It is easy to check if the needle roller bearings are worn with the propeller shaft in position, by trying to turn the shaft with one hand, the other hand holding the flange on the final drive extension shaft when the rear universal joint is being checked, and the front half coupling when the front universal joint is being checked. Any movement between the propeller shaft and the front and rear half couplings is indicative of considerable wear. If worn, the old bearings and spiders will have to be discarded and a repair kit, comprising new universal joint spiders, bearings, oil seals, and retainers purchased. Check also by trying

to lift the shaft and noticing any movement in the joints.

3   Examine the propeller shaft splined sleeve and propeller shaft splines for wear. Also check if the yokes are badly worn. If wear is evident, an exchange propeller shaft must be fitted. It is not possible to fit oversize bearings and journals to the trunnion bearing holes.

4   Universal joints - dismantling

1   Clean away all traces of dirt and grease from the circlips located on the ends of the bearing cups, and remove the clips by pressing their open ends together with a pair of pointed pliers or circlip pliers (photo), and lever them out with a screwdriver. If they are difficult to remove, tap the bearing cup face resting on top of the spider with a mallet which will ease the pressure on the circlip.

2   Take off the bearing cups on the propeller shaft yoke. To do this select two sockets from a socket spanner set, one large enough to fit completely over the bearing cup and the other smaller than the bearing cup.

3   Open the jaws of the vice and with the sockets opposite each other and the universal joint in between, tighten the vice and so force the narrower socket to move the opposite cup partially out of the yoke into the larger socket (photo).

4.1 Extraction a universal joint circlip

4.3 Pressing out a joint bearing cup using a vice

4.4 Twisting out a bearing cup

4.5 Using a socket to tap home a bearing cup

4 Remove the cup with a pair of pliers. Remove the opposite cup, and then free the yoke from the propeller shaft (photo).

5 To remove the remaining two cups, now repeat the instructions given in paragraph 3, or use a socket and hammer as illustrated (photo).

6 To separate the splined sleeve from the propeller shaft, undo the knurled collar and withdraw the splined sleeve from the propeller shaft.

7 An alternative method of removing the bearing cups is to strike the propeller shaft with a wooden or soft faced mallet until the cup emerges (Fig.7.2). The bearing cup can then be screwed out of the yoke by gripping it in a vice.

5 Universal joints - reassembly

1 Thoroughly clean out the yokes and journals.

2 Fit new oil seals and retainers onto the spider journals, place the spider onto the propeller shaft yoke, and assemble the needle rollers in the bearing races with the assistance of some thick grease. Fill each bearing about a third full with Castrolease LM or similar, and fill the grease holes in the journal spider making sure all air bubbles are eliminated.

3 Refit the bearing cups onto the spider and tap the bearings home or press them in using a vice, so they lie squarely in position. Replace the circlips.

4 Check the felt seal within the knurled collar and if it shows signs of leaking or damage fit a new seal.

5 Align the arrow on the propeller shaft with the arrow on the sliding yoke as shown in Fig.7.3, and fit the two parts together. Screw the knurled collar onto the sliding yoke and lubricate the splines by applying a grease gun to the grease nipple in the sliding yoke.

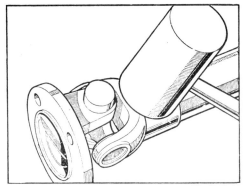
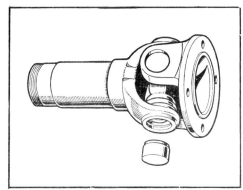

Fig. 7.2. Universal bearing cup removal

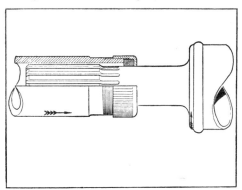

Fig. 7.3. Alignment arrows on sliding joint

6 Fault diagnosis - Propeller shaft and universal joints

Symptom	Reason/s	Remedy
Vibration	Misalignment	Check arrows align.
	Worn splines or journals	Recondition.
Noisy operation	Worn or dry joints	Renew.
	Loose flange nuts	Tighten.
	Worn sleeve splines	Renew.

Chapter 8 Rear axle

Contents

Specifications

Type	Hypoid (crownwheel and bevel pinion)	
Ratio	3.08 : 1	
Hub bearing preload	5 to 10 lb (2.2 to 4.5 kg)	
Pinion housing and pinion housing cover clearance	0.003 to 0.005 in. (0.07 to 0.12 mm)	

Torque wrench settings:	lb ft	kg m
Drive shaft flange to disc bolts	85	11.9
Bearing housing to pinion housing bolts	30	4.0
Cover to pinion housing bolts (small)	15	2.0
Cover to pinion housing bolts (large)	30	4.0
Extension to pinion housing bolts	30	4.0
Brake caliper hinge pin (nut)	35	4.9
(plug)	25 to 35	3.5 to 4.9
Coupling flange to extension shaft bolts	35	4.9
Hub to de Dion tube bolts	25	3.5
Stabiliser (Panhard) rod to final drive unit	30	4.0
Extension housing to flexible mounting	35	4.8
Flexible mounting to front bracket	17	2.3
Final drive rear mounting bracket to flexible mounting ...	45	6.2

1 General description

The hypoid final drive and differential unit is rubber mounted to the underside of the car body by means of a crosswise mounting bracket which is part of the De Dion rear suspension.

The final drive casing comprises two parts which are bolted together. Each half casing has a detachable bearing retainer which also acts as an end cover. Located on the right-hand casing is an extension in which is placed the final drive pinion running in two taper roller bearings. Attached to the front end of the final drive pinion housing is an extension shaft which transmits the drive of the relatively short propeller shaft to the drive pinion. The extension shaft is located at its rear end by means of a splined female which engages with the externally splined drive pinion shaft. At the front end it is supported in a single ball bearing located in the forward end of the extension housing. A flange is splined to the forward end of the shaft and this acts as a coupling to the rear universal joint of the propeller shaft.

Fitted to the front end of the pinion extension housing is a special harmonic damper which keeps transmission noise to a minimum.

The front end of the extension housing is attached to the underside of the car by a special rubber cushioned mounting bracket.

Attached to each differential side gear by means of splines is a two flanged half shaft, each being supported by a single ball bearing which is situated in the detachable bearing retainer. The latter also acts as an anchor for the caliper units of the inboard disc brakes which are fitted to either side of the final drive unit.

The main advantage of mounting the final drive unit to the underside of the body is to reduce the unsprung weight, therefore contributing to the road holding and general comfort of the driver and passengers.

2 Maintenance

Every 5,000 miles (8,000 km) clean the area around the combined filler and level plug located at the rear of the unit housing. Undo and remove the plug. Top up with Castrol Hypoy until the oil is level with the bottom of the filler plug hole when the car is standing on level ground. It is important that the unit is not overfilled.

Every 20,000 miles (32,000 km) undo and remove the combined filler and level plug and also the drain plug and allow the oil to drain out. Preferably this should be done when the oil is warm. Refit the drain plug and refill with 2½ pints of Castrol Hypoy oil.

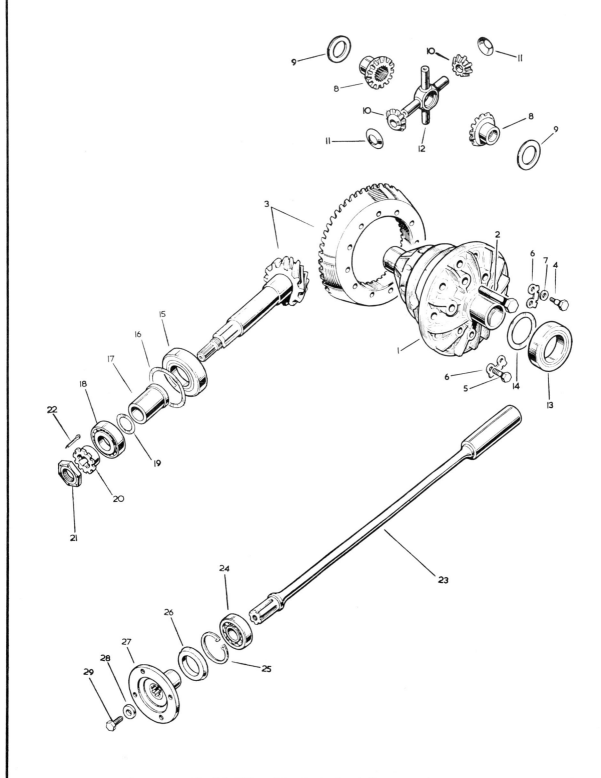

Fig. 8.1. Differential and extension shaft components

1	Differential case	8	Differential side wheel	15	Pinion bearing	22	Split pin
2	Bolt	9	Thrust washer	16	Shim	23	Extension shaft
3	Crownwheel and pinion	10	Differential pinion	17	Spacer	24	Extension shaft bearing
4	Crownwheel bolt	11	Thrust washer	18	Pinion bearing	25	Circlip
5	Crownwheel bolt	12	Pinion cross-pin	19	Shim	26	Oil seal
6	Lock plate	13	Bearing	20	Locking collar	27	Coupling flange
7	Plain washer	14	Shim	21	Pinion locknut	28	Plain washer
						29	'Wedglock' bolt

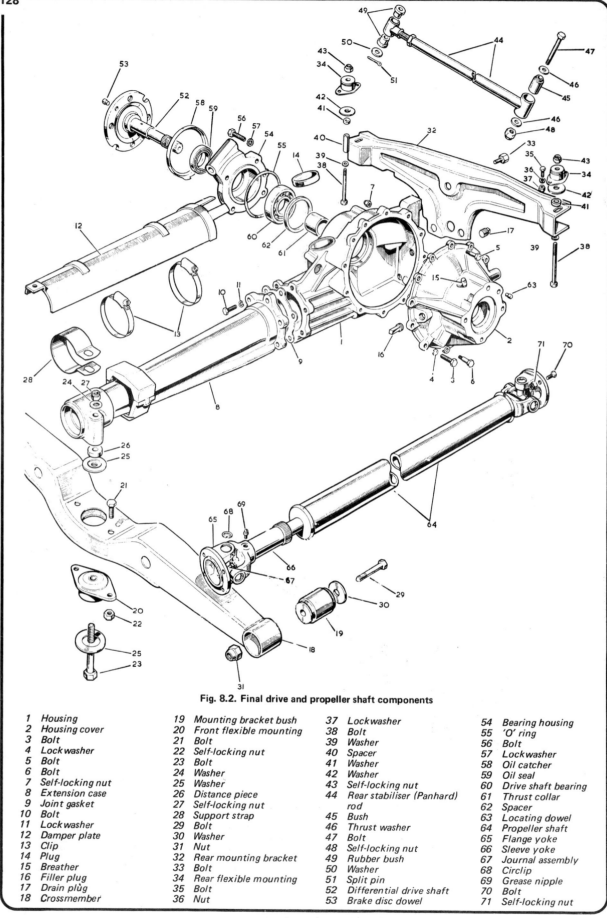

Fig. 8.2. Final drive and propeller shaft components

1	Housing	19	Mounting bracket bush	37	Lockwasher	54	Bearing housing
2	Housing cover	20	Front flexible mounting	38	Bolt	55	'O' ring
3	Bolt	21	Bolt	39	Washer	56	Bolt
4	Lockwasher	22	Self-locking nut	40	Spacer	57	Lockwasher
5	Bolt	23	Bolt	41	Washer	58	Oil catcher
6	Bolt	24	Washer	42	Washer	59	Oil seal
7	Self-locking nut	25	Washer	43	Self-locking nut	60	Drive shaft bearing
8	Extension case	26	Distance piece	44	Rear stabiliser (Panhard) rod	61	Thrust collar
9	Joint gasket	27	Self-locking nut			62	Spacer
10	Bolt	28	Support strap	45	Bush	63	Locating dowel
11	Lockwasher	29	Bolt	46	Thrust washer	64	Propeller shaft
12	Damper plate	30	Washer	47	Bolt	65	Flange yoke
13	Clip	31	Nut	48	Self-locking nut	66	Sleeve yoke
14	Plug	32	Rear mounting bracket	49	Rubber bush	67	Journal assembly
15	Breather	33	Bolt	50	Washer	68	Circlip
16	Filler plug	34	Rear flexible mounting	51	Split pin	69	Grease nipple
17	Drain plug	35	Bolt	52	Differential drive shaft	70	Bolt
18	Crossmember	36	Nut	53	Brake disc dowel	71	Self-locking nut

The oil level of the De Dion tube of the rear suspension should be checked every 10,000 miles (16,000 km) and topped up with Castrol GTX oil until the level of oil is at the bottom of the combined filler/level plug hole. This plug is located at the top centre of the De Dion tube.

It is recommended that every 10,000 miles (16,000 km) the rubber boots be inspected for damage or signs of perishing and if evident, new ones fitted.

Never jack up the car by locating the jack under the De Dion tube, always use the rear jacking point or tube (Fig.8.3).

3 Rear hub and external drive shaft - removal, overhaul and refitment

If it is required to overhaul the rear hub it will be necessary to have the use of a press or a large engineer's vice and a selection of suitable packing pieces. Make sure that these are available before commencing work.

2 Remove the wheel trim and slacken the road wheel nuts. Chock the front wheels, jack up the rear of the car and support on axle stands as shown. Remove the road wheel nuts and lift away the road wheel.

3 Undo and remove the six bolts and self locking nuts that secure the rear hub bearing housing to the De Dion assembly.

4 Undo and remove the four bolts and lock plates that secure the drive shaft flange yoke to the differential drive shaft.

5 The hub and drive shaft assembly may now be lifted away from the underside of the car.

6 Should it be necessary to overhaul the drive shaft journals this is similar to the overhaul of the propeller shaft universal joints and full information will be found in Chapter 7. Note, however, that the journals on the drive shafts are fitted with lip seals which are designed to prevent dirt ingress. Care must be taken in removing and refitting these seals.

7 To overhaul the rear hub, first release the lock washer from the yoke shaft nut and then undo and remove the yoke retaining nut and lock washer. A cross sectional view of the hub is shown in Fig.8.4, and an exploded view in Fig.8.5.

8 Withdraw the external drive shaft from the hub assembly.

9 Using either the table of a press or the open jaws of an engineer's vice support the rear hub as shown in Fig.8.6 and with a brass drift and hammer, carefully drift the driving flange from the bearing housing.

10 Lift away the collapsible spacer.

11 The inner bearing must next be removed and for this a medium size two leg puller with long flat feet will be required. Locate the feet behind the bearing and with a thrust block in the end of the screw thread, carefully remove the inner bearing.

12 The two oil seals may now be removed from the bearing housing by carefully using a copper drift.

13 Using a suitable sized drift, carefully remove the two roller races from the bearing housing noting which way round they are fitted.

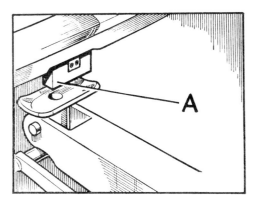
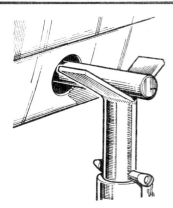

Fig. 8.3. Rear jacking point A and correct method of supporting bodyframe with 7/8 in diameter (22 mm) rod inserted in jacking tube

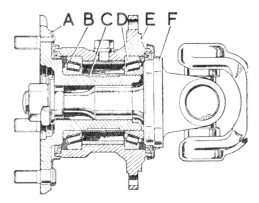

Fig. 8.4. Cross sectional view of hub

A Driving flange for road wheel
B Outer bearing
C Collapsible tube
D Inner bearing
E Bearing housing
F Drive shaft

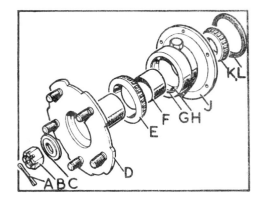

Fig. 8.5. Rear hub components

A Split pin
B Castellated nut
C Washer
D Driving flange
E Outer bearing
F Collapsible tube
G Oil seal
H Bearing outer track
J Bearing housing
K Inner bearing
L Oil seal

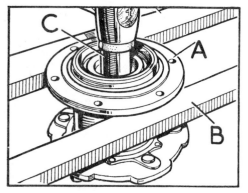

Fig. 8.6. Dismantling rear hub

A   Rear hub
B   Support blocks
C   Brass drift

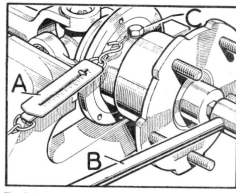

Fig. 8.7. Measuring rear hub pre-load

A   Spring balance
B   Socket wrench
C   Cord attached
to plug

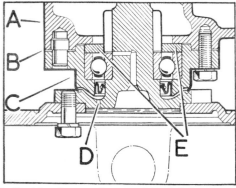

Fig. 8.8. Checking clearance between drive shaft housing and pinion housing

A   Pinion clearance
B   Correct clearance 0.003 to
0.010 in (0.07 to 0.25
mm)
C   Drive shaft bearing housing
D   Breather passages
E   Spacer 0.261 in (6.6 mm)
thick

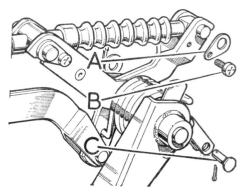

Fig. 8.9. Handbrake cable, rear connections

A   Retaining plate
B   Crosshead screw
C   Clevis pin

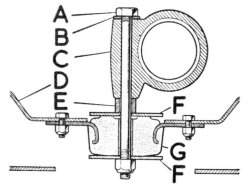

Fig. 8.10. Final drive front flexible mounting (early 3500 models)

A   Bolt
B   Washer
C   Final drive unit
D   Mounting bracket
E   Distance piece
F   Large washer
G   Flexible mounting

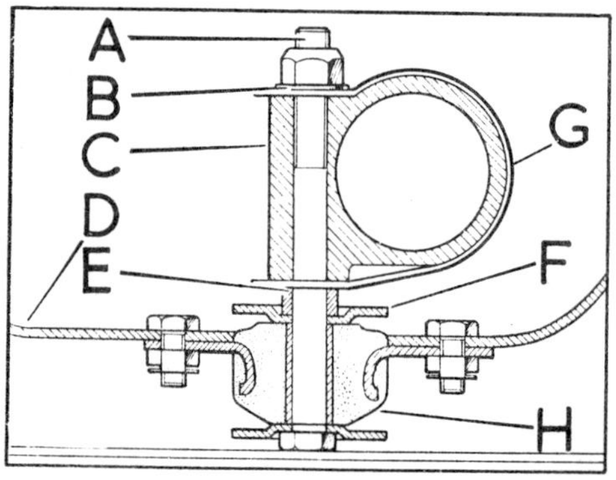

Fig. 8.11. Final drive front flexible mounting (later 3500 and 3500 S models)

A   Bolt
B   Washer
C   Final drive unit
D   Mounting bracket
E   Distance piece
F   Dished washer
G   Support bracket
H   Flexible mounting

14 Using a sharp knife and a little wet or dry paper clean all traces of 'Loctite' from the splines.

15 Inspect the bearings for signs of overheating as indicated by discolouration, and the rollers and tracks for signs of wear or pitting and if suspect obtain new parts. A new collapsible spacer will be required also new oil seals.

16 Using suitably sized drifts carefully press the new roller bearing races into the bearing housing. Make sure that they are the correct way round and that they are pressed fully home.

17 Insert a new oil seal to the outer side of the outer hub with the lip facing inwards and pack with a little grease.

18 Carefully press the outer roller bearing onto the drive flange making sure that it is the correct way round and that it is pressed fully home.

19 Slide a new collapsible spacer over the driving flange and position the driving flange onto the bearing housing.

20 Place the roller bearing onto the driving flange and with a suitable sized drift drive it on as far as possible.

21 Carefully fit a new oil seal to the inner side of the bearing housing with the lip facing inwards.

22 Thoroughly clean the splines of the yoke shaft using methylated spirits to remove any trace of grease and then sparingly apply Loctite sealant grade AVV.

23 Fit the yoke shaft into the hub assembly.

24 Refit the lock washer and lightly tighten the nut.

25 If the existing bearings are being re-used mount the hub assembly in a vice as shown in Fig.8.7, and tighten the nut until the new collapsible spacer is just trapped. There should be approximately 0.060 inch endfloat in the assembly.

26 Using a spring balance as will be found in many kitchens note the torque required to rotate the hub by pulling on a piece of string attached to the hub as shown.

27 Slowly tighten the nut until the torque required to rotate the hub is between 3 and 8 lbs above the seal friction reading as taken in the previous paragraph. It is important that care is taken in tightening the nut as the required reading must not be exceeded.

28 When new bearings are being fitted hold the hub assembly in a vice and tighten the nut until the load on the bearings is such that a pull of between 5 and 10 lbs is required to rotate the hub.

29 When the required pre-load has been obtained lock the nut by bending over the lock washer tab.

30 To refit the hub and external drive shaft assembly, position the assembly onto the De Dion tube whilst at the same time locating the drive shaft flange onto the brake disc and differential drive shaft.

31 Refit the six nuts and bolts that secure the hub bearing housing to the De Dion tube and tighten to a torque wrench setting of 20 lb/ft.

32 Secure the drive shaft flange to the brake disc and differential drive shaft with the four bolts and new locking washers and tighten to a torque wrench setting of 85 lb/ft. Make sure that there is a minimum clearance of 0.010 inch between the ends of the bolts and the oil catcher.

33 Lock the bolts by bending over the locking washers.

34 Refit the road wheel and replace the road wheel nuts.

35 Raise the rear of the car, remove the stands and lower the car. Tighten the road wheel nuts and refit the wheel trim.

36 Do not use the car for a period of 12 hours so that the 'Loctite' can fully cure.

4 Differential drive shaft - removal and refitment

1 Jack up the car and secure on stands.

2 Remove the road wheels.

3 Remove the rear brake pads as described in the next Chapter.

4 Remove the four bolts and lock plates which secure the drive shaft flange to the final drive output flange, expand the De Dion tube and allow the shaft to fall clear.

5 Rotate the brake disc until the dowel holes are parallel with the calipers and then ease the disc from the dowels and withdraw it.

6 Disconnect the brake pipe which runs between the calipers and plug the line to prevent fluid leakage.

7 Disconnect the handbrake linkage at the caliper lever and on left-hand calipers remove the bellcrank bracket from the differential casing.

8 Remove the caliper unit as described in Chapter 8.

9 Place a container underneath the final drive assembly.

10 Remove the four bolts and spring washers which secure the bearing housing to the pinion housing, rotating the flange to gain access to the bolt heads.

11 Withdraw the differential drive shaft and bearing housing, complete with spacer and if fitted, the 'O' ring.

12 Due to the need for special tools and press, any reconditioning of the drive shafts is best left to your Rover dealer.

13 Commence refitting by placing the original bearing spacer over the bearing and then offer the drive shaft assembly to the pinion housing or cover.

14 Before fitting the securing bolts check that the clearance between the face of the drive shaft/pinion housing is between 0.003 and 0.010 in (0.07 and 0.25 mm) (Fig. 8.08). This is the correct bearing preload and any deviation from the clearance specified will be due to damage or incorrect assembly.

15 Now remove the drive shaft housing and fit the brake caliper (Chapter 9) using the original shims. Secure with two bolts and spring washers and tighten them to 60 lb/ft (8.5 kg/m).

16 Refit the assembly to the pinion housing and the 'O' ring (if fitted). Smear gasket cement on the housing joint faces and tighten the securing bolts to 30 lb/ft (4 kg/m).

17 Refit the brake disc for an alignment check and secure it with four bolts and packing washers. Rotate the disc and drive shaft until the dowel holes are parallel with the caliper and then ease the disc between the caliper pads and onto the dowels.

18 Refit the outer footbrake and handbrake pads (Chapter 9).

19 Reconnect all brake hydraulic pipes and the handbrake linkage.

20 Remove the four temporary bolts and packing washers from the brake disc and position the external drive shaft onto the brake disc.

21 Secure the drive shaft flange yoke to the disc and differential drive assembly with four bolts and new lock plates and tighten them to 85 lb/ft (11.5 kg/m). Ensure that when finally fitted there is a clearance between the set bolts and the oil catcher of 0.010 in (0.2 mm).

22 Bleed the brakes (Chapter 9) and fit the road wheel.

23 Adjust the handbrake (Chapter 9).

24 Lower the car and check the final drive oil level topping up if necessary to the bottom of the filler plug hole.

5 Final drive unit - removal and refitment

1 Slacken the rear road wheel nuts, jack up the rear of the car using the jacking points provided and then remove the road wheels.

2 Unscrew and remove the four special bolts and lockwashers which secure the hub drive shafts to the brake discs.

3 Disconnect the handbrake cable from the rear brake calipers by slackening the two crosshead screws "B" and retaining plates "A". Remove the lower clevis pin from the left-hand side caliper and detach the cable from the two levers (Fig.8.9).

4 Disconnect the propeller shaft at its rear driving flange first having marked the flange edges for exact replacement.

5 On early models (3500) remove the self-locking nut which secures the front of the final drive unit to its mounting bracket. Jack up the front of the final drive unit so that the flexible mounting bolts are accessible. Release the flexible mounting retaining the washer and distance piece.

6 On later 3500 models and all 3500 S cars, disconnect the final drive unit front mounting bracket and then disconnect the flexible and rigid brake lines at the right-hand side of the final drive unit. Plug the fluid pipes to prevent loss of fluid.

7 With 3500S models, disconnect the brake pad wear indicator light leads at the plug connectors.

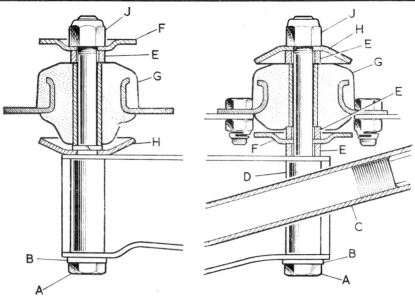

Fig. 8.12. Sectional view of final drive rear flexible mountings (early 3500 models)

A Bolt
B Washer

C Stabiliser rod
D Distance piece

E Distance washer
F Dished washer

G Flexible mounting
H Cone washer
J Self-locking nut

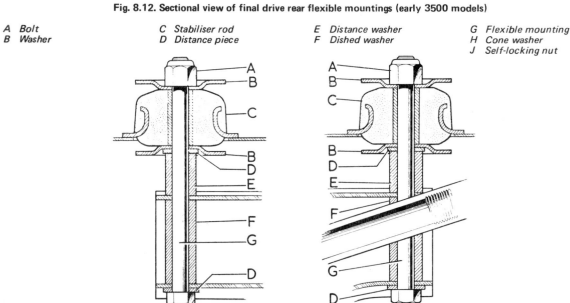

Fig. 8.13. Final drive rear flexible mountings (later 3500 and 3500 S models)

A Self-locking nut
B Dished washer

C Flexible mounting
D Plain washer

E Short distance piece
F Long distance piece

G Bolt

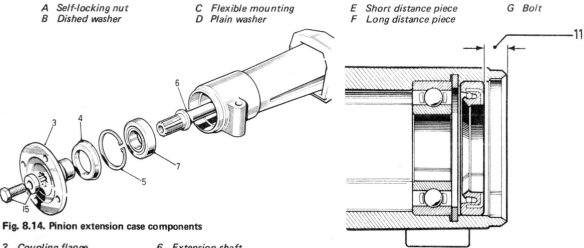

Fig. 8.14. Pinion extension case components

3 Coupling flange
4 Oil seal
5 Circlip

6 Extension shaft
7 Bearing
15 Coupling flange bolt and
    special washer

**Fig. 8.15. Cross-sectional view of pinion extension case bearing
and oil seal (11) 0.355 to
0.375 in (9.0 to 9.5 mm)**

8 Support the rear end of the final drive unit with a jack and remove the three bolts which secure it to the rear mounting bracket.

9 Refitting is a reversal of removal but the following points must be noted.

The front flexible mounting should be secured to its bracket by tightening the nuts to a torque of 17 lb/ft (2.3 kg/m) when the car is standing on the ground. Tighten the final drive unit extension case to flexible mounting bolts to a torque of 35 lb/ft (4.8 kg/m). Check the oil level in the final drive unit and bleed the brakes (Chapter 9).

6 Final drive unit - servicing

Due to the need for special tools and equipment it is not recommended that this work should be undertaken by the home mechanic but entrusted to a Rover dealer.

7 Pinion extension case assembly - removal, servicing and refitment

1 Jack up the car and support on stands.

2 Drain the oil from the final drive unit.

3 Disconnect the rear propeller shaft flange.

4 Jack up the front of the final drive casing but ensure that the jack is kept clear of the pinion extension case.

5 On early 3500 models jack up one end of the extension case front mounting bracket to relieve the load on the mounting bracket securing bolt. Remove the bolt and then release the bracket by gently lowering the jack.

6 Remove the six bolts which secure the pinion extension case to the final drive unit and then lift the extension case clear of the front mounting bracket.

7 If it is necessary to overhaul the extension casing, first undo and remove the bolt and special shaped washer securing the extension shaft drive coupling. For this it will be necessary to hold the flange securely. Remove the flange using a three leg puller and thrust block.

8 With a screwdriver withdraw the oil seal noting which way round it is fitted.

9 Remove the circlip that retains the special self aligning bearing, with a pair of circlip pliers.

10 Using a soft faced hammer or soft metal drift carefully drive the extension shaft and bearing from the rear of the extension housing.

11 With a soft metal drift or three leg puller and thrust block remove the bearing from the shaft.

12 All parts should be cleaned and inspected for signs of damage or wear. Remove all traces of Loctite from the splines on the extension shaft and threads of the coupling flange bolt.

13 It should be noted that the harmonic damper positioned at the forward end of the extension case must not be disturbed as it is specially adjusted to match the extension housing.

14 To reassemble fit the bearing onto the extension shaft using a tubular drift of suitable size.

15 Insert the extension shaft into the extension casing and drift into position with a soft faced hammer and soft metal drift.

16 Refit the bearing retaining circlip making sure that it is seating correctly.

17 Carefully fit a new oil seal with the lip facing inwards. Tap into position using a tubular drift of suitable diameter (Fig. 8.15).

18 Apply a little Loctite sealant grade AVV to the splines of the extension shaft and thread of the coupling flange fixing bolt. Assemble the coupling flange to the extension shaft and secure with the bolt and plain washer. Tighten the bolt to a torque wrench setting of 35 lb/ft (4.8 kg/m) and leave for 12 hours to cure.

19 To refit the extension case assembly is the reverse sequence to removal. The following two additional points should be noted.

20 The extension casing bolts should be tightened to a torque wrench setting of 30 lb/ft (4 kg/m).

21 Do not forget to refill the final drive unit with oil. It has a capacity of 2½ pints.

8 Rear stabiliser rod - removal and refitment

1 To remove the rear stabiliser rod, undo and remove the bolt and self locking nut that secures the stabiliser to the final drive unit.

2 With a pair of pliers straighten and extract the split pin and then lift away the plain washer that secures the stabiliser bar to the underside of the body. The stabiliser may then be lifted away.

3 Should it be necessary the rubber bushes may be removed and new ones pressed into position. The best way to do this is to use a piece of tubing of the same diameter as the outside of the bush and a large bench vice.

4 To refit the stabiliser rod settle the rear of the car by rocking it up and down several times and then refit the rod to the underside of the body. It will be necessary to compress the rubber but this is not too difficult to do.

5 Adjust the length of rod so that the bolt just fits easily at the final drive unit and insert the bolt. Refit the self locking nut and tighten securely.

9 Modifications

The rear suspension fitted to late model 3500 and all 3500S cars differs from that fitted to earlier 3500 models. In conjunction with the modified suspension, the final drive unit, the rear drive flanges, the drive shafts and the propeller shafts are all balanced to closer limits. The final drive mountings are re-designed and the static laden car height is reduced by ¼ in (6 mm).

10 Fault diagnosis - Rear axle

Symptom	Reason/s	Remedy
Oil leaks	Loose drain or filler plugs	Tighten.
	Worn oil seals	Renew.
	Damaged joint washers	Renew.
Noisy operation	Worn bearings	Renew.
	Incorrect tolerances	Adjust.
	Worn universal joints	Recondition.

Chapter 9 Braking system

Contents

Specifications

3500 models

Type	Girling hydraulic four wheel disc with servo
Master cylinder pushrod free movement	0.020 in. (0.50 mm)
Disc diameter:	
Front	10.82 in. (274 mm)
Rear	10.690 in. (272 mm)
Disc thickness:	
Front	0.505 in. (12.83 mm)
Rear	0.380 in. (9.65 mm)
Minimum thickness after refacing:	
Front	0.450 in. (11.43 mm)
Rear	0.330 in. (8.38 mm)
Friction pad area:	
Front (each pad)	6.735 in.^{2} (43.45 cm^2)
Total area	27.0 in.^{2} (174.0 cm^2)
Rear (each pad)	5.765 in.^{2} (37.25 cm^2)
Total area	23.0 in.^{2} (148.0 cm^2)
Caliper cylinder internal diameter:	
Front	1 x 2.25 in. (57 mm) 2 x 1.59 in. (40.3 mm)
Rear	0.75 in. (19.05 mm)
Vacuum servo unit:	
Model	Girling Type 8
Effective vacuum cylinder diameter	8 in. (203.2 mm)
Vacuum cylinder stroke	2.18 in. (55.37 mm)
Slave cylinder diameter	0.7 in. (17.8 mm)
Hydraulic reaction piston diameter	5/16 in. (7.9 mm)

3500S models

Type	Lockheed dual hydraulic circuit. The system is Girling based with the exception of the following components and reference should be made to model 3500 specifications for Girling component details

Master cylinder and vacuum servo unit: ... ... Lockheed — Dualine

Master cylinder rod free movement ... ... 1/16 in. (1.5 mm)

Torque wrench settings (both):

	lb ft	kg m
Front caliper to suspension	60	8.5
Rear caliper to final drive housing	60	8.5
Disc to front hub	44	6.0
Disc to final drive flange	68 (early models)	9.3
	35 (later models)	11.9
Rear hub to de Dion tube	20	2.8

1 General description

Three thousand five and 3500 models are equipped with a braking system of Girling manufacture (hydraulic servo-assisted type) having outboard discs at the front and inboard discs at the rear. The handbrake operates the rear calipers through an independent mechanical linkage.

The front caliper units are fitted to the suspension swivel columns and are operated by single pistons within the inner section of the caliper body and two pistons within the outer section.

Swivel type calipers are fitted at the rear. In the event of failure of the servo unit, the hydraulic system is unaffected except that higher pedal pressures will be required to provide the same degree of retardation previously experienced.

3500S models are equipped with a dual circuit hydraulic system to provide completely independent front and rear braking circuits. The caliper units in this system remain Girling type but the master cylinder and vacuum servo unit are of Lockheed manufacture. A number of safety features are incorporated in both systems and include a fluid level warning light in conjunction with a handbrake "ON" indicator. The 3500S is fitted with disc pads which have built-in electrical wear indicators. A pressure failure warning switch is also fitted to the dual circuit system.

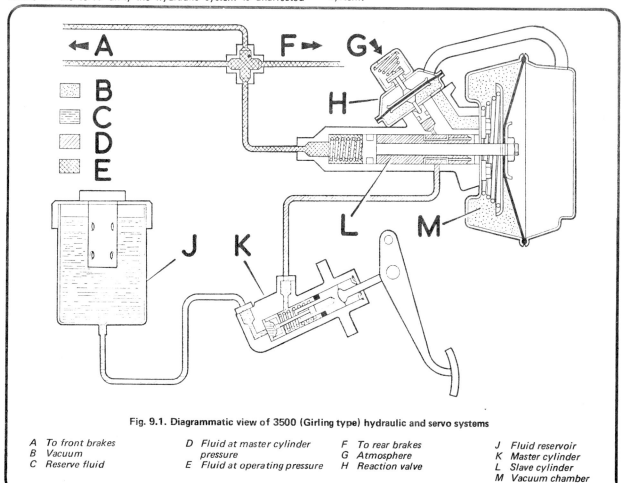

Fig. 9.1. Diagrammatic view of 3500 (Girling type) hydraulic and servo systems

A To front brakes	D Fluid at master cylinder	F To rear brakes	J Fluid reservoir
B Vacuum	pressure	G Atmosphere	K Master cylinder
C Reserve fluid	E Fluid at operating pressure	H Reaction valve	L Slave cylinder
			M Vacuum chamber

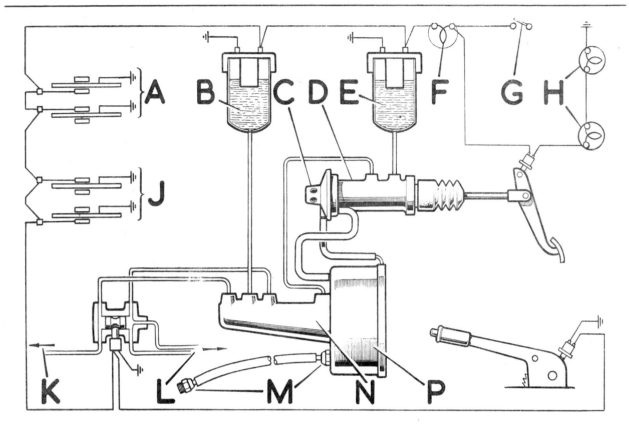

Fig. 9.2. Layout of dual circuit (3500 S) braking system

A   Front brake pads
B   Fluid reservoir for front
    brakes
C   Reaction valve
D   Master cylinder

E   Fluid reservoir for
    rear brakes
F   Brake warning light
G   Ignition switch

H   Stop lamps
J   Rear brake pads
K   To rear brakes
L   To front brakes

M   Non-return valve in
    manifold pipe
N   Slave cylinder (tandem)
P   Servo unit

2 Maintenance

Refer to the Routine Maintenance Section at the front of this manual.

3 Brake pads (front) (3500 models) - inspection, removal and refitment

1   Jack up the front of the car and support adequately on stands or blocks.
2   Remove the road wheels.
3   Inspect the thickness of the friction lining. If it has worn to 1/8 in (3 mm) or less then the pads must be renewed.
4   Remove the clip "B" from the retaining pin "A" (Fig. 9.3).
5   Withdraw the pads complete with anti-rattle springs and damping shims.
6   Using a flat piece of wood or a tyre lever, press the caliper pistons into the bottom of the cylinder bores. Do not lever against the periphery of the disc.
7   Fit the new friction pads and damping shims. The shim with the larger surface area fits behind the pad on the single piston side of the caliper. Check that the arrow cut-out points in the direction of forward rotation.
8   Refit the anti-rattle springs, the pad retaining pins and their clips.
9   Give several applications of the brake pedal to position the pad against the discs.
10 Refit the road wheels and lower the car.

4 Brake pads (front) (3500S models) - inspection, removal and refitment

1   The procedure is similar to that described in the preceding section but the following additional points must be noted.
2   Disconnect the pad thickness wear indicator lead at its plug connector (photo).
3   When refitting the pads, the one with the electrical lead fits on the single piston side of the caliper unit (photo).

5 Brake pads (rear) (3500 models) - inspection, removal and refitment

1   Slacken the rear road wheel nuts, jack up the rear of the car and support on stands or blocks at the jacking points. Remove the road wheels.
2   Inspect the thickness of the friction material of the pad, if it has worn down to 1/16 in (1.5 mm) or less than the pad must be renewed (photo).
3   Knock back the tabs on the lock plate at the front of the caliper body, unscrew the bolt and withdraw the retainer plate "A" and the anti-rattle spring "B" (Fig.9.4).
4   Swing the top of the inner disc pad forward and then withdraw the pad towards the rear of the vehicle.
5   Knock back the tabs on the lockplate which secure the bolt at the rear of the caliper, slacken the bolt to release the tension of the anti-rattle spring on the outer disc pad.
6   Pull the caliper outwards and remove the outer pad from the

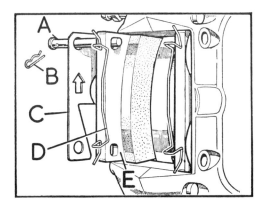

Fig. 9.3. Front brake pad removal

A Pin retaining pads
B Special clip for pin
C Damping shim
D Anti-rattle spring
E Brake pad

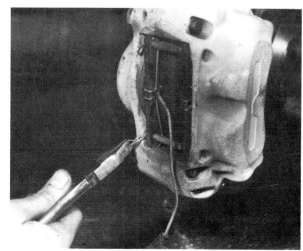

4.2 Removing disc pad retaining pin clip from 3500 S front caliper. Note wear indicator lead disconnected at plug

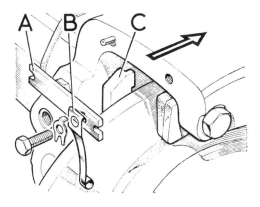

Fig. 9.4. Rear inner brake pad removal

A Retainer plate
B Anti-rattle spring
C Withdraw inner pad in direction arrowed

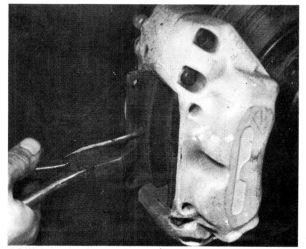

4.3 Withdrawing front brake pad (fitted with wear indicator) from single piston side of 3500 S caliper

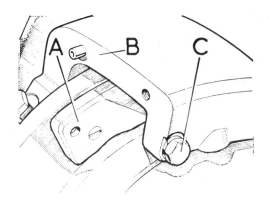

Fig. 9.5. Rear outer brake pad removal

A Outer brake pad
B Caliper pulled outwards
C Drag pin

5.2 Rear brake calipers and discs

drag pins "C" (Fig.9.5).

7 Disconnect the caliper handbrake lever at both the link plate and link lever.

8 Unscrew and remove the bolts which secure the handbrake bellcrank lever to the finel drive pinion housing. Withdraw the handbrake mechanism and allow it to hang clear of the calipers. This work is required to provide enough clearance for the piston setting tool which will be required when refitting the pads.

9 Commence refitting by pushing the caliper towards the final drive housing. From the end of the caliper nearest the front of the car fit the piston setting tool over the projecting caliper piston. The setting tool is available from Rover dealers (Part No. 601962) and is recommended for this work but a substitute tool or even a screwdriver may be used to engage with the projecting cam if care is taken (photo).

10 Turn the piston anticlockwise one complete turn, remove the tool, wipe the dirt from the projecting nose of the piston and apply a smear of brake grease. Now turn the piston clockwise until it is right home and the clicking of the adjuster ratchet can be heard. Check that the piston lever is vertical otherwise unscrew it until it is.

11 Examine the ends of the drag pins for the outer disc pad. If they are distorted renew them.

12 Fitting the pads is a reversal of removal but ensure that the inner anti-rattle spring is fitted at the forward position with the domed part outwards.

13 Tighten the pad retaining plates to a torque of 9 lb/ft (1.2 kg/m). Refit the road wheels and lower the car.

6 Brake pads (rear) (3500S models) - inspection, removal and refitment

1 The procedure is similar to that described in the preceding section but observe the following additional points.

2 Disconnect the lead from the battery negative terminal.

3 Disconnect the pad wear electrical lead (photo).

4 On late models, remove the bias spring as well as the handbrake connections (Fig. 9.7) and withdraw the outer pads in either direction. Swing the rear end of the inner pads downwards and withdraw them towards the front of the car.

5 When refitting the inner pad retaining plate note that the offset cut out must be uppermost (Fig. 9.8).

7 Caliper (front) - removal, servicing and refitment

1 Jack up the front of the car and support at the jacking points on stands or blocks. Remove the road wheels.

2 Unscrew the fluid reservoir cap and place a piece of thin polythene sheeting over the top of the reservoir and refit the cap. This will help to create a vacuum and prevent loss of fluid when the fluid lines are disconnected.

3 Brush the exterior of the caliper free from dust also the fluid pipe union. Remove the pipe clip at the swivel pillar.

4 Disconnect the hydraulic pipe at the caliper union and seal the pipe end with a bleed nipple cap to prevent loss of fluid or dirt entering.

5 Remove the disc pads (Section 3 or 4).

6 Remove the shield strap bolts "D" (Fig. 9.9) and then bend back the locking tabs and remove the caliper securing bolts "B". Lift the caliper away. **On no account loosen the bolts which hold the two halves of the caliper together.**

7 Remove the rubber boots from the inner and outer pistons (Fig. 9.10).

8 Place a pad of clean rag between the pistons and then apply pressure from a tyre pump at the fluid inlet union of the caliper and eject the pistons. Mark the two smaller pistons with a piece of masking tape so that they will be returned to their respective cylinders.

9 Pick out the rubber sealing rings from the cylinder bores making sure that you do not scratch the bore surfaces.

10 Unscrew and remove the bleed screw.

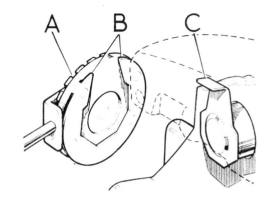

Fig. 9.6. Piston setting tool (rear caliper,

A Piston setting tool
B Slots in tool for lever on piston
C Lever on piston

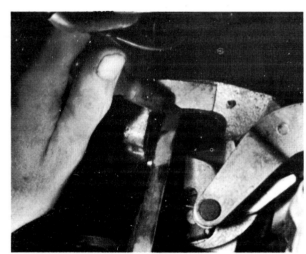

5.9 Moving rear caliper piston lever

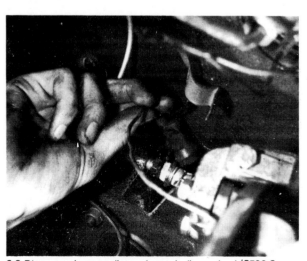

6.3 Disconnecting rear disc pad wear indicator lead (3500 S models)

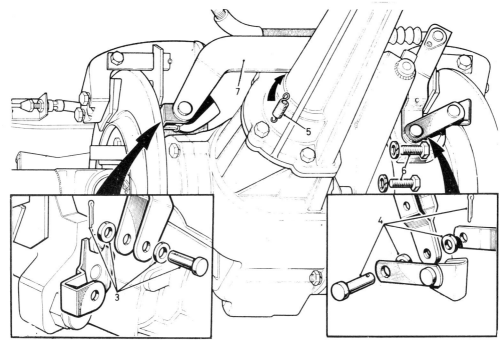

Fig. 9.7. Handbrake connections (late models)

3	RH clevis connection	5	Bias spring	bolts
4	LH clevis connection	6	Bellcrank lever bracket	7 Link

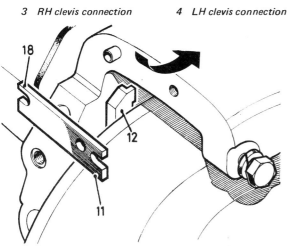

Fig. 9.8. Rear caliper inner pad retaining plate (cut-outs uppermost)

12   Pad   18   Retaining plate

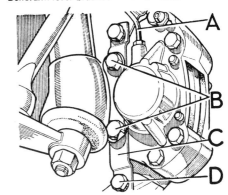

Fig. 9.9. Front caliper fixings

A   Fluid feed pipe   C   Strap, shield to caliper
B   Bolts fixing caliper   D   Bolts fixing strap to shield

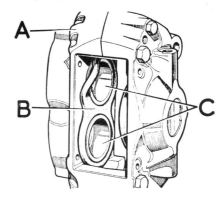

Fig. 9.10. Front caliper dust excluding boot (B) caliper body (A) pistons (C)

11 Wash all components in methylated spirit or clean brake fluid and examine the piston and cylinder surfaces for scoring or 'bright' wear areas. If these are evident, renew the complete caliper on an exchange basis.

12 Discard all rubber seals and obtain a repair kit.

13 Dip the new seals in clean brake fluid and locate them in the cylinder grooves using the fingers only to manipulate them.

14 Fit new dust excluding boots and then insert the pistons (lubricated with clean brake fluid) squarely into their respective bores. Check that the lips are correctly located in the piston grooves.

15 Screw in the bleed nipple.

16 Refitting the caliper is a reversal of removal but use new securing bolt locking plates and tighten the bolts to a torque of 60 lb/ft (8.5 kg/m).

17 Bleed the system, according to type, Sections 16 or 17.

8 Caliper (rear) - removal and refitment

1 Jack up the rear of the car and support on stands or blocks. Remove the road wheel.

2 Disconnect the handbrake linkage as described in Sections 5 or 6.

3 If the right-hand caliper is being removed, disconnect the hydraulic pipe at the supporting bracket on the underside of the body shell also the bridge pipe which connects the two calipers. Cap the open ends of the pipe with bleed nipple caps and use a piece of polythene sheeting under the reservoir cap to prevent loss of fluid.

4 If the left-hand caliper only is being removed then the bridge pipe only need be disconnected.

5 On early models, before removing the handbrake lever stop pin "F" (Fig. 9.11) rotate the lever as far as it will go and retain it with a rubber band or piece of string to prevent its withdrawal and displacement of the tappet (Fig. 9.12).

6 On later models having an extended, spring loaded plug "E" (Fig.9.13) the handbrake lever "F" must be withdrawn before a spanner can be engaged with the hexagon of the plug.

7 Using a socket spanner, unscrew and the spring loaded plug according to type.

8 Using an Allen key, rotate the pivot pin until it is unscrewed from the bearing at the other end.

9 Remove the bearing at the rear of the caliper and push the pivot pin out towards the front of the car. Remove the caliper unit.

10 Temporarily replace the lever stop screw and remove the rubber band or string.

11 Refitting is a reversal of removal but always fit new 'O' rings to the bearing and pull it into position by screwing in the pivot pin with the Allen key and tightening it to a torque of 35 lb/ft (4,9 kg/m).

12 Tighten the spring loaded plug to a torque of between 28 and 35 lb/ft (3.8 to 4.9 kg/m).

13 When installation is complete, bleed the brakes.

9 Rear caliper - servicing

1 Remove the self locking nuts which retain the cover (Fig. 9.14).

2 Lift off the cover, large and small seals and the piece of anti-corrosive paper.

3 Mark the strut "B" (Fig. 9.15) to ensure correct refitment and then withdraw it by lifting lever "C".

4 Press the lever down and withdraw it complete with its pawl.

5 Push the piston upwards and prise off the main spring over the two studs. Lift off the beam (Fig. 9.16).

6 Mark the sleeves in relation to their studs and then remove both sleeves and detach the "S"'spring.

7 Unscrew the knurled pushrod and withdraw the piston from below.

8 Unscrew the Allen screw and remove the location plate and stop washer.

9 Rotate the handbrake lever and eject the tappet.

10 Place a pad of rag over the hydraulic piston and then apply pressure from a tyre pump at the fluid entry port and eject the piston.

11 Unscrew the stop pin and withdraw the handbrake lever and shaft.

12 Remove all remaining 'O' rings, retainers, bleed screw and drag pins.

13 The caliper is now completely dismantled and the two cover nuts, the two drag pins and all rubber components should be discarded.

14 Clean all components in methylated spirit or clean hydraulic fluid. Examine the piston and cylinder bore surfaces for scoring or 'bright' wear areas. If evident, renew the complete caliper assembly on an exchange basis.

15 Obtain the correct caliper repair kit.

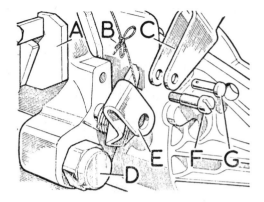

Fig. 9.11. Handbrake linkage (early models)

A   *Inner brake pad*
B   *String retaining handbrake lever*
C   *Link lever*
D   *Spring-loaded plug*
E   *Handbrake lever*
F   *Stop pin for handbrake lever*
G   *Clevis pin for handbrake lever*

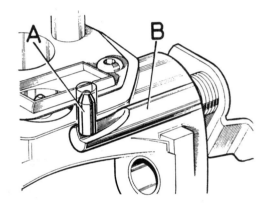

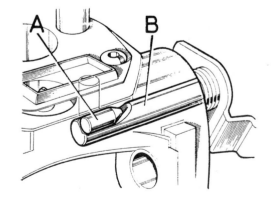

Fig. 9.12. Correct and incorrect location of handbrake tappet

A Tappet   *B Lever*

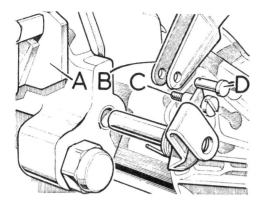

Fig. 9.13. Withdrawal of handbrake lever (late models)

A Inner brake pad
B Link lever
C Stop pin for handbrake lever
D Clevis pin for handbrake lever

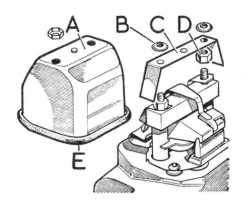

Fig. 9.14. Rear caliper cover components

A Cover
B Rubber seal, small
C Anti-corrosive paper
D Nut for beam
E Rubber seal, large

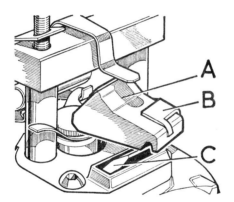

Fig. 9.15. Rear caliper strut (A) pawl (B) and lever (C)

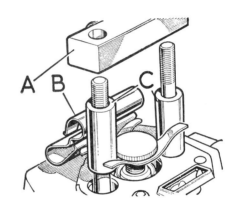

Fig. 9.16. Rear caliper beam (A) 'S' spring (B) and sleeves (C)

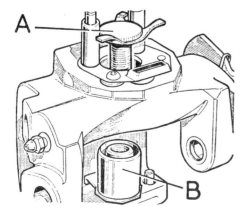

Fig. 9.17. Rear caliper push rod (A) and piston (B)

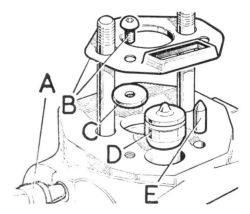

Fig. 9.18. Rear caliper location plate (B) stop washer for piston (C) piston (D) handbrake tappet (E). (A) is air pressure line to eject piston

142

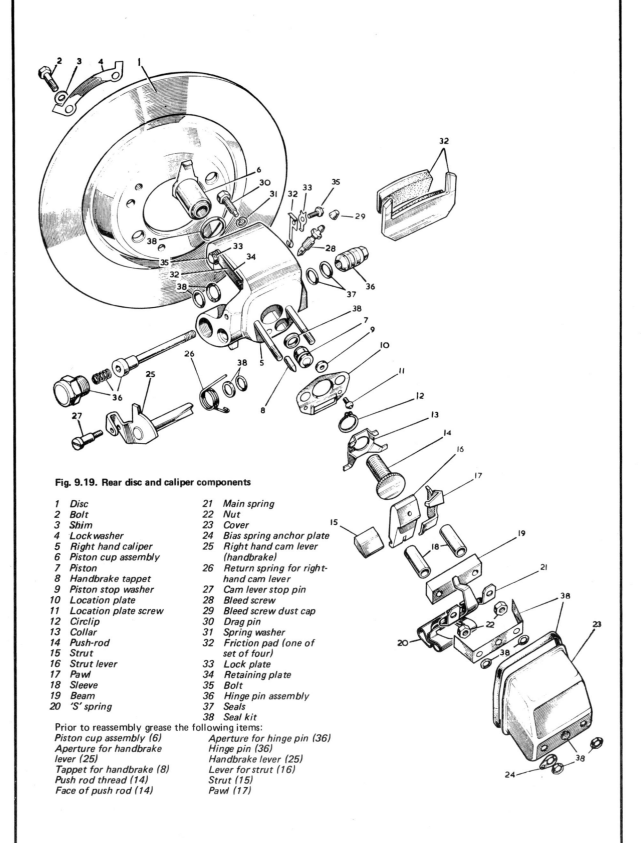

Fig. 9.19. Rear disc and caliper components

1	Disc	21	Main spring
2	Bolt	22	Nut
3	Shim	23	Cover
4	Lockwasher	24	Bias spring anchor plate
5	Right hand caliper	25	Right hand cam lever (handbrake)
6	Piston cup assembly	26	Return spring for right-hand cam lever
7	Piston	27	Cam lever stop pin
8	Handbrake tappet	28	Bleed screw
9	Piston stop washer	29	Bleed screw dust cap
10	Location plate	30	Drag pin
11	Location plate screw	31	Spring washer
12	Circlip	32	Friction pad (one of set of four)
13	Collar	33	Lock plate
14	Push-rod	34	Retaining plate
15	Strut	35	Bolt
16	Strut lever	36	Hinge pin assembly
17	Pawl	37	Seals
18	Sleeve	38	Seal kit
19	Beam		
20	'S' spring		

Prior to reassembly grease the following items:
Piston cup assembly (6)
Aperture for handbrake lever (25)
Tappet for handbrake (8)
Push rod thread (14)
Face of push rod (14)
Aperture for hinge pin (36)
Hinge pin (36)
Handbrake lever (25)
Lever for strut (16)
Strut (15)
Pawl (17)

16 Observe scrupulous cleanliness during reassembly.

17 Fit the new seal to the piston so that the smaller diameter of the seal is nearer to the pointed end of the piston.

18 Apply approved brake grease (Rover part no 514577) during reassembly of the components annotated in Fig. 9.19 and commence by inserting the handbrake tappet, pointed end uppermost.

19 Screw in the knurled headed pushrod, three turns only.

20 Locate the studs, sleeves, beam and "S" spring.

21 Fit the pawl to the lever and insert the assembly at an angle between the beam and head of the pushrod, pulling the piston down at the same time. Align the lever squarely and press into position.

22 Tighten the nuts which secure the main spring and beam to a figure of 28 lb/ft (3.8 kg/m).

23 Check the operation of the caliper unit by operating the handbrake lever. The pawl should click as the lever moves and the knurled head of the pushrod should rotate one tooth as it returns.

24 Screw the piston fully in and turn the lever to the position indicated in Fig. 9.21.

25 Refit the cover using new 'O' rings.

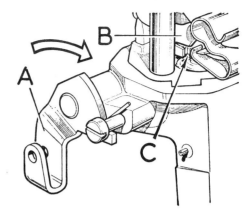

Fig. 9.20. Testing rear caliper handbrake mechanism

A *Handbrake lever*
B *Pawl*
C *Knurled head of pushrod*

10 Disc (front) - removal and refitment

1 Jack up the front of the car and remove the road wheel.

2 Remove the front hub as described in Chapter 11.

3 Remove the five bolts which secure the disc to the hub flange. Use a hide or plastic faced mallet to separate the two components.

4 If the disc is deeply scored it should be renewed or reground within the specified tolerances (see Specifications).

5 Refitting is a reversal of removal but tighten the securing bolts to 44 lb/ft (6 kg/m).

11 Disc (rear) - removal and refitment

1 Jack up the rear of the car and remove the road wheels.

2 Remove the rear brake pads (Section 5 or 6).

3 Remove the four bolts and their lockplates which secure the drive shaft flange to the final drive output flange, expand the De Dion tube so that the shaft falls clear.

4 Rotate the disc until the dowel holes are parallel to the caliper units.

5 Ease the disc from the dowels and withdraw it.

6 Check the disc for deep grooves or scores and renew or regrind if these are evident.

7 Refitting is a reversal of removal.

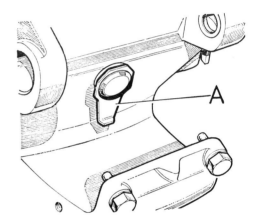

Fig. 9.21. Position of piston lever (A) in rear caliper after reassembly

12 Master cylinder /Girling - 3500 model) - removal and refitment

1 Clean the external surfaces and union connections by brushing away dust and mud and then wiping with a rag soaked in methylated spirit.

2 Disconnect the fluid feed pipe which runs between the hydraulic reservoir and the master cylinder. Drain the fluid from the reservoir into a suitable container; remove the reservoir.

3 Disconnect the fluid feed pipe at the master cylinder which supplies the servo unit.

4 Plug or blank off all open pipes and ports to prevent loss of fluid or entry of dirt.

5 Unscrew and remove the three nuts and one bolt which secure the heat shield, spacer plate and master cylinder to the body shell. Detach only the heat shield at this stage.

6 Unscrew the locknut from the foot pedal operating rod and unscrew the rod through the trunnion, at the same time withdraw the master cylinder complete with its spacer plate. Unscrew the retaining bolt and remove the master cylinder from the spacer plate.

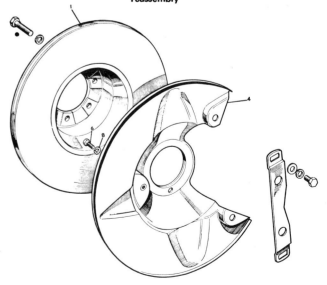

Fig. 9.22. Front disc (1) shield (4) and securing bolts and strap

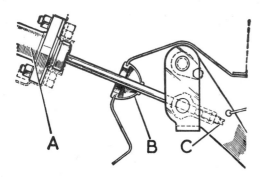

Fig. 9.23. Sectional view of Girling type master cylinder to pedal trunnion

A Master cylinder
B Grommet
C Pushrod

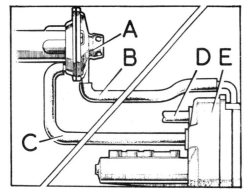

Fig. 9.24. Air and vacuum pipe connections (Lockheed tandem master cylinder)

A Air control valve
B Vacuum and air inlet pipe
C Cacuum pipe, air control valve to vacuum chamber
D Vacuum pipe, vacuum chamber to inlet manifold
E Servo vacuum chamber

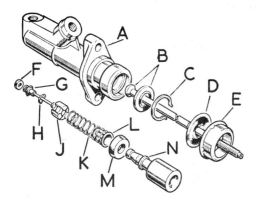

Fig. 9.25. Exploded view of Girling type master cylinder

A Master cylinder body	G Valve stem
B Push rod and retaining washer	H Spring washer
	J Valve spacer
C Circlip	K Return spring
D Dust seal	L Spacer retainer
E Cap for dust seal	M Piston seal
F Valve seal	N Piston

7 Commence refitment by connecting the master cylinder to the spacer plate by using the top bolt only.

8 Locate the master cylinder by screwing its pushrod into the foot pedal trunnion until the pushrod projects by about 1 in (25.4 mm). Position the heat shield and tighten the master cylinder bolts.

9 Adjust the pushrod length so that the lower edge of the brake pedal pad is 6½ in (165 mm) from the body interior floor pan (not carpet surface). Tighten the locknut.

10 Connect the fluid pipes and then fill the fluid reservoir and bleed the brakes (Section 16).

13 Master cylinder (Lockheed - 3500S models) - removal and refitment

1 Clean all external dirt from the master cylinder and the fluid unions.

2 Remove the dipstick from the engine and the left-hand elbow from the air cleaner.

3 Disconnect the fluid reservoir and disconnect the fluid inlet pipe at the master cylinder, allowing the fluid to drain into a suitable container.

4 Disconnect the servo fluid feed line at the master cylinder, also the air and vacuum pipes.

5 Unscrew the two bolts which secure the master cylinder and withdraw the unit leaving the operating pushrod in position.

6 Refitting is a reversal of removal but check and adjust if necessary the brake pedal (Section 26).

7 Bleed the hydraulic system (Section 17).

14 Master cylinder (Girling type) - servicing

1 The internal parts of the master cylinder are shown in Fig. 9.25.

2 Carefully ease the dust seal cap "E" and seal "D" from the body of the master cylinder.

3 With a pair of circlip pliers remove the circlip "C" and withdraw the operating pushrod "B" complete with the dished washer.

4 The piston assembly "N" may now be removed by applying a low pressure air jet to the master cylinder body inlet port. Take great care as the piston may fly out.

5 With a small screwdriver ease the locking lip of the spring retainer "L" clear of the shoulder on the piston and separate the piston.

6 Compress the return spring "K" and position the valve stem so as to align with the larger hole in the spring retainer "L". Remove the spring "K" and retainer "L".

7 Slide the valve spacer "J" over the valve stem "G".

8 Remove the spring washer "H" noting which way round it is fitted, and then the valve seal "F" from the valve stem.

9 Carefully remove the piston seal "M" from the piston noting which way round it is fitted.

10 Examine the bore of the cylinder carefully for any signs of scores or ridges, and if this is found to be smooth all over new seals can be fitted. If there is any doubt of the condition of the bore then a new cylinder must be fitted.

11 If examination of the seals shows them to be apparently oversize, swollen, or very loose on the plunger, suspect oil contamination in the system. Oil will swell these rubber seals, and if one is found to be swollen it is reasonable to assume that all seals in the braking system will need attention.

12 Thoroughly clean all parts in either clean hydraulic fluid or methylated spirit. Ensure that the ports are clean.

13 All components should be assembled wet by dipping in clean brake fluid.

14 Fit a new valve seal "F" the correct way round so that the flat side is correctly seating on the valve head "G". Fig. 9.26 shows this in detail.

15 Place the dished washer "H" with the dome against the underside of the valve head. Hold it in position with the valve

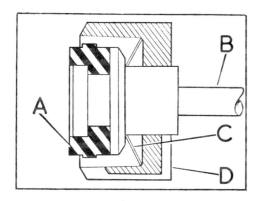

Fig. 9.26. Sectional view of Girling master cylinder valve

A *Valve stem*   C *Spring washer*
B *Valve stem*   D *Valve spacer*

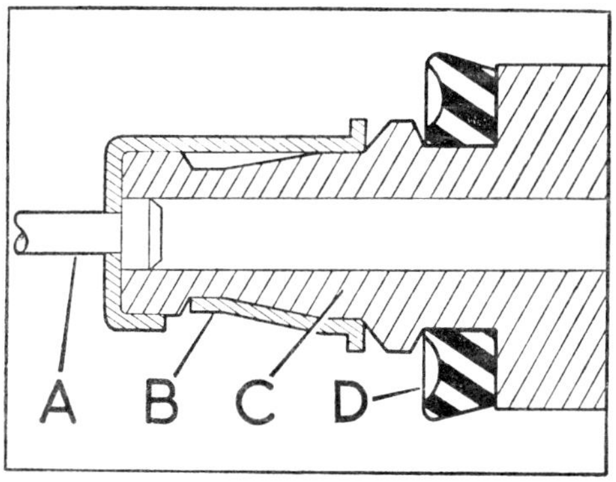

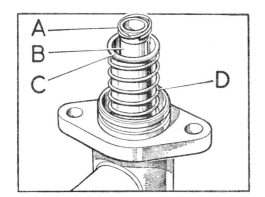

Fig. 9.27. Sectional view of Girling master cylinder piston and spring retainer

A *Valve stem*   C *Piston*
B *Prong in locked position* D *Seal*

Fig. 9.28. Retaining ring for piston spring (Lockheed master cylinder)

A *Retaining ring*   C *Retainer for spring*
B *Piston*   D *Spring*

spacer "J" ensuring that the legs face towards the valve seal "F".
16 Replace the plunger return spring "K" centrally on the spacer "J", insert the spacer retainer "L" into the spring "K" and depress until the valve stem "G" engages in the keyhole of the spacer retainer "L".
17 Ensure that the spring is central on the spacer before fitting a new piston seal "M" onto the piston "N" with the flat face against the face of the plunger.
18 Insert the reduced end of the piston into the spring retainer "L" until the lip engages under the shoulder of the piston and press home the lip.
19 Check that the master cylinder bore is clean and smear with clean brake fluid. With the piston suitably wetted with brake fluid insert the assembly into the bore with the valve end first. Ease the lip of the piston seal carefully into the bore.
20 Replace the pushrod "B" and refit the circlip "C" into the groove in the cylinder body. Smear the sealing into the areas of the dust seal "D" and "E" and pack the interior of the seal with rubber grease. Refit the seal to the master cylinder body.
21 The master cylinder is now ready for refitting to the car. If a replacement master cylinder is to be fitted it will be necessary to lubricate the seals before fitting to the car as they have a protective coating when originally assembled. Remove the blanking plug from the hydraulic pipe union seating. Ease back and remove the pushrod dust cover so that the clean brake fluid can be injected at these points. Operate the piston several times so that the fluid will spread over all internal working surfaces.

15 Master cylinder (Lockheed tandem type) - servicing

1 Support the master cylinder in a vice fitted with jaw protectors so that the air control valve is uppermost.
2 Unscrew the five screws which secure the cover to the air control valve housing. Lift off the cover complete with air valve sub assembly. If necessary, the filter can be renewed by detaching the snap-on cap but do not dismantle beyond this. If the valve is faulty, renew it as an assembly.
3 Refer to Fig. 9.29 and remove the rubber diaphragm "11" and support "12". Remove the two bolts "13" now exposed, and lift away the housing "15" and gasket "25".
4 Reposition the master cylinder in the vice so that the boot "45" and pushrod "46" can be removed.
5 Depress the spring retainer "C" (Fig. 9.28) so that the retaining ring "A" can be removed from its groove. Do not distort the ring during removal or scratch the piston surface. Remove the spring and spring retainer.
6 Depress the piston and remove the circlip which retains the plastic bearings. Withdraw the piston assembly.
7 Remove the inlet and outlet adaptors, copper washers and trap valve and spring from the outlet adaptor.
8 Remove the master cylinder from the vice and tip out the lever which is located in its nose.
9 Remove the valve piston by gently pushing it with a blunt rod inserted through the fluid outlet port. Pull the piston out with the fingers **not pliers**.
10 To strip the main piston assembly, first remove the plastic bearings "C" complete with 'O' ring "B" (Fig. 9.30).
11 Prise off the plastic spring retainer complete with spring from the nose of the piston. Remove the main seal and piston washer.
12 Clean all components in methylated spirit or clean hydraulic fluid. Discard all rubber components.
13 Examine the piston and cylinder bore surfaces. If there is evidence of scoring or 'bright' wear areas, renew the master cylinder complete.
14 Check that all ports and drillings are clear, do not enlarge them by probing but apply air pressure from a tyre pump. Check that the curved spring insert in the trap valve body is intact and undamaged.
15 Observe absolute cleanliness during reassembly.
16 Lubricate the cylinder bores with clean brake fluid and holding the master cylinder with the mouth of its bore uppermost at an inclined angle, drop the valve piston operating lever

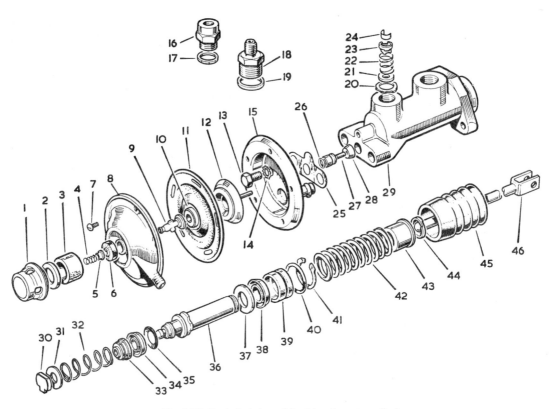

Fig. 9.29. Exploded view of Lockheed master cylinder

1	Cap	13	Screw	25	Gasket	37	Bearing
2	Washer	14	Washer	26	Seal	38	Secondary seal
3	Filter	15	Valve housing	27	Piston	39	Bearing
4	Spring	16	Outlet adaptor	28	Seal	40	'O' ring
5	Valve cap	17	Washer	29	Body	41	Circlip
6	Valve rubber	18	Inlet adaptor	30	Lever	42	Spring
7	Screw	19	Washer	31	Retainer	43	Retainer
8	Valve cover	20	Washer	32	Spring	44	Retaining ring
9	Valve stem	21	Washer	33	Retainer	45	Boot
10	Valve rubber	22	Spring	34	Main seal	46	Pushrod
11	Diaphragm	23	Valve body	35	Piston washer		
12	Diaphragm support	24	Spring	36	Piston		

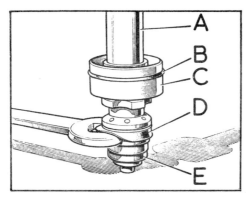

Fig. 9.30. Main piston (Lockheed master cylinder)

A Piston
B 'O' ring
C Bearing
D Main seal
E Retainer for spring

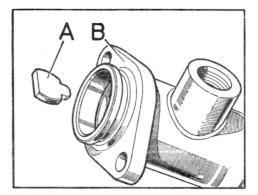

Fig. 9.31. Valve piston operating lever (A) and Lockheed master cylinder (B)

into it so that its tab locates in the recess.

17 Secure the master cylinder in the vice so that its mouth is uppermost.

18 Assemble the components to the main piston using only the fingers to locate the new seals.

19 Dip the piston assembly in clean hydraulic fluid and enter it into the cylinder ensuring that the seal lip or 'O' ring are not trapped or displaced. Fit the circlip and operate the piston to ensure correct operation.

20 Locate the return spring and its retainer over the exposed portion of the piston and compress the spring to uncover the groove for the retaining ring which should now be fitted.

21 Smear the inside of the rubber boot with rubber grease and slide the pushrod into it. Insert the pushrod into the end of the piston and secure the boot in the groove in the master cylinder body.

9 Insert the trap valve body and spring into the outlet port (spring leading). Fit a new copper washer onto the adaptor and tighten to a torque of 33 lb/ft (4.6 kg/m).

10 Fit a new copper washer to the inlet adaptor and tighten to a similar torque.

11 Reposition the master cylinder body in the vice so that the air valve housing is uppermost.

12 With the fingers, fit a new seal to the air valve piston (lip facing away from recessed head) dip in clean hydraulic fluid and insert the assembly into the cylinder bore ensuring that the seal lip is not trapped or bent back.

13 Fit a new gasket, the valve housing (bolts to a torque of 14 lb/ft (1.9 kg/m) and the diaphragm support (spigot leading)

14 Locate the valve cover so that its projections engage with the slots in the diaphragm. Insert and tighten the securing screws in diametrically opposite sequence.

16 Bleeding the hydraulic system (3500 model -single circuit type)

1 Check the fluid level in the brake reservoir and top up if necessary with fluid which has been stored in an airtight container and has remained unshaken for 24 hours.

2 Connect a bleed tube to the bleed nipple on the left-hand rear caliper after removing the dust cap.

3 Pour some hydraulic fluid into a jar and submerge the end of the bleed tube in the fluid.

4 During the whole of the bleeding operation, the level in the fluid reservoir must be maintained to prevent air being drawn into the system through an exposed reservoir to master cylinder feed pipe. The end of the bleed tube must also always be kept covered by the fluid in the jar.

5 Using a small spanner, preferably ring, slacken the bleed nipple about ½ a turn.

6 Have an assistant depress the brake pedal fully and then allow the pedal to return with the foot removed from it. Repeat the process until air bubbles cease to emerge from the end of the submerged bleed tube. Allow a five second interval between pedal strokes to ensure full recuperation of the master cylinder.

7 With the pedal held in the fully depressed position tighten the bleed screw (do not overtighten). Remove the bleed tube and refit the nipple dust cap.

8 On cars fitted with the new style radiator grille treatment, it is possible that due to the thickness of the front carpet and insulation material the brake pedal cannot be fully depressed to the extent of its travel. It is recommended therefore that the carpet be removed for the bleeding operation.

9 Remember to top up the fluid reservoir and then as there is only one nipple for the rear brakes, repeat the process on the front caliper furthest from the brake pedal and then finally the one nearest the brake pedal (photo).

10 Top up the fluid reservoir to the correct level.

11 Check the brakes, any sponginess or excessive travel will be due to air still being trapped in the system and the cycle of operations will have to be repeated. Continued failure to obtain the correct braking action may be due to a faulty master

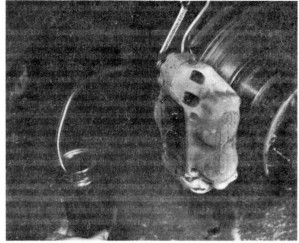

16.9 Bleeding a front caliper unit

cylinder.

17 Bleeding the hydraulic system (3500S model - dual circuit type)

1 Check that the fluid level is correct in both reservoirs.

2 The most effective way of bleeding this type of system is to bleed one front and the single rear caliper units simultaneously Obtain the help of two assistants and acquire two bleed tubes and jars.

3 Fit the bleed tubes to the single rear and the front driver's side bleed nipples. Open both nipples.

4 Carry out the bleeding procedure as described in the preceding section and when air bubbles cease to emerge from the front nipple, close it.

5 Transfer the front bleed tube to the opposite front caliper and repeat the process. Tighten front and rear bleed nipples and remove the bleed tubes. Refit all three dust caps.

6 Top up the fluid reservoir to the correct level.

18 Hoses (flexible) - inspection, removal and refitment

Inspect the condition of the flexible hydraulic hoses leading from the chassis mounted metal pipes to the brake backplates. If any are swollen, damaged, cut, or chafed they must be renewed.

1 Unscrew the metal pipe union nut from its connection to the hose, and then holding the hexagon on the base with a spanner, unscrew the attachment nut and washer.

2 The chassis end of the hose can now be pulled from the chassis mounting brackets and be quite free.

3 Disconnect the flexible hydraulic hose from the caliper unit. **Note:** When releasing the hose from the caliper unit the chassis end must be freed first.

4 Replacement is a straightforward reversal of the above procedure.

19 Handbrake lever - removal, overhaul and refitment

1 Chock the rear wheels securely to prevent car movement during removal of the console cover.

2 Remove the front and rear ashtrays and undo the two nuts located under the rear ashtray and the nut under the front ashtray.

3 Remove the two crosshead screws at the front of the cover.

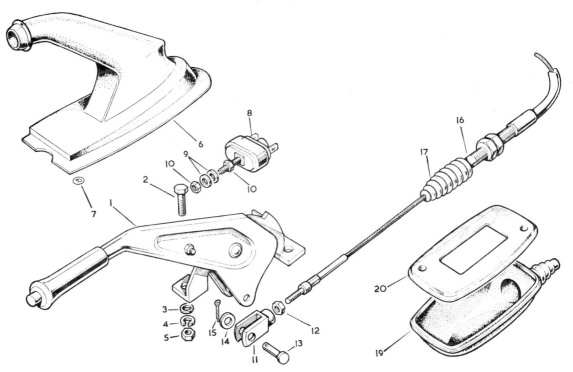

Fig. 9.32. Handbrake lever, cable and switch

1 Handbrake lever	7 'Starlock' washer, fixing grommet to tunnel finisher	12 Nut, fork end to cable	17 Grommet, front end
2 Bolt	8 Switch for warning light	13 Clevis pin	18 Grommet, rear end
3 Packing washer	9 Plain washer	14 Plain washer	19 Grommet for handbrake linkage (under tunnel)
4 Spring washer	10 Nut	15 Split pin	20 Retaining plate for handbrake linkage grommet
5 Nut	11 Fork end for brake cable	16 Handbrake cable	
6 Grommet for handbrake lever			

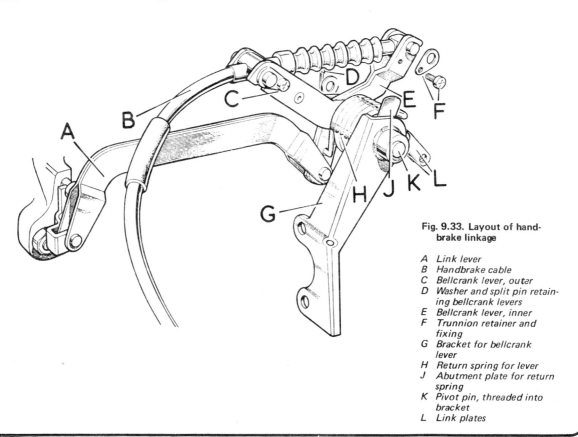

Fig. 9.33. Layout of handbrake linkage

A Link lever
B Handbrake cable
C Bellcrank lever, outer
D Washer and split pin retaining bellcrank levers
E Bellcrank lever, inner
F Trunnion retainer and fixing
G Bracket for bellcrank lever
H Return spring for lever
J Abutment plate for return spring
K Pivot pin, threaded into bracket
L Link plates

4 Carefully raise the flat on the forward edge of the handbrake grommet base and remove the drive screw.

5 Locate the two crosshead screws securing the speaker grille to the console unit and remove these two screws. Lift away the speaker grille. If a radio set is installed it will be necessary to disconnect the two speaker cables.

6 Release the gearchange lever knob locknut and remove the knob spring retaining sleeve and the gearchange lever sleeve.

7 Move the front seats as far to the rear as possible by sliding on their runners. Raise the seat locking levers.

8 Carefully roll back the handbrake grommet and apply a smear of MS4 Silicone grease to both the grommet and the handbrake handle.

9 Gently lift the forward edge of the cover over and off from the gearchange lever.

10 Pull the handbrake lever until it is in the fully 'on' position. Do not, however, force for extra movement.

11 Slide the cover forwards and upwards to enable the forward edge to protrude into the aperture at the top of the console and at the same time, push the handbrake grommet off the handbrake handle.

12 Release the handbrake and withdraw the cover assembly.

13 Extract the split pin and remove the clevis pin for the handbrake rod at the relay linkage.

14 Undo and remove the two bolts that secure the handbrake lever assembly to the propeller shaft tunnel.

15 Note which way round the handbrake switch cables are fitted to the rear of the switch and disconnect the cables.

16 The handbrake lever and operating rod may now be removed.

17 To overhaul the handbrake lever, first extract the split pin and remove the clevis pin that secures the brake rod to the handbrake lever.

18 Extract the split pin and withdraw the clevis pin from the ratchet pawl. Also remove the special plain steel washer.

19 Hold the handbrake lever in the normal 'off' position and depress the plunger so that the pawl may be drawn away in a downwards direction.

20 Examine all moving parts for wear, especially the pawl, and obtain new parts as required.

21 To reassemble place the handbrake lever on its side and depress the release plunger.

22 Insert the pawl into position and align the clevis pin holes with a small screwdriver.

23 Fit the clevis pin, plain steel washer and secure with a new split pin. Bend over the legs to lock.

24 Fit the handbrake rod to the lever and secure with the clevis pin. Lock the clevis pin with a new split pin and bend over the legs to lock it.

25 To refit the handbrake lever and the console cover is the reverse sequence to removal. Check the operation of the handbrake 'on' position warning light to ensure that it operates correctly.

20 Handbrake linkage - removal and refitment

1 The linkage is shown in Fig. 9.33. Undo and remove the two crosshead screws and remove together with the trunnion retainers "F" from the inner and outer bellcrank levers.

2 Remove the handbrake cable from the inner and outer bellcrank levers "c" and "E".

3 Extract the split pin and withdraw the clevis pins so that the link lever "A" and the link plates "L" may be disconnected from the bellcrank levers "C" and "E".

4 Extract the split pin "D" and withdraw the clevis pin that secures the bellcrank lever and return spring to the pivot pin. The parts may be lifted away as an assembly.

5 If considered necessary remove the pivot pin and abutment plate from the bracket and then the bracket from the final drive unit.

6 Detach the handbrake cable at the handbrake lever. Ease back the inner cable rubber sleeve and remove the nut, now exposed. The handbrake cable may now be withdrawn.

7 To refit the handbrake linkage is the reverse sequence to removal. It is important, however, that the inner cable clevis must fit to the handbrake lever without any tension in the cable. The outer cable nuts should be in the midway position on the thread.

21 Servo unit (Girling - 3500 type) - removal and refitment

1 Clean the external surfaces of the unit and the fluid pipe unions by first brushing and then wiping with a rag soaked in methylated spirit.

2 Disconnect the servo feed pipe at the five way junction and blank off the union at the junction.

3 Disconnect the vacuum pipe at the non-return valve on the servo.

4 Disconnect the pipe from the master cylinder at the servo unit. Plug all open pipes and ports.

5 From under the front wing, unscrew the servo unit securing nuts.

6 Remove the nut and bolt from the bracket which supports the slave cylinder to the bodyframe.

7 The servo can now be withdrawn.

8 Refitting is a reversal of removal but bleed the hydraulic system when installation is complete.

22 Servo unit (Lockheed - 3500S type) - removal and refitment

1 Clean the external surfaces of the unit and the fluid pipe unions by first brushing and then wiping with a rag soaked in methylated spirit.

2 Disconnect the three air and vacuum pipes from the servo vacuum chamber and move them to one side.

3 Disconnect the electrical leads from the right-hand brake fluid reservoir and from the pressure failure switch (Section 29). Drain the reservoir and discard the fluid and remove the reservoir.

4 Disconnect, at the servo unit end, the master cylinder to servo pipe and the two feed pipes to the pressure failure switch.

5 Slacken the servo rear mounting bolt and remove the servo securing nuts from under the front right-hand wing valance.

6 Withdraw the servo unit and plug all open pipes and ports.

7 Refitting is a reversal of the removal procedure.

23 Servo unit (Girling) - dismantling, servicing and reassembly

1 Secure the servo unit in an engineer's bench vice with soft faces between the jaws at the slave cylinder. Do not overtighten otherwise the slave cylinder can be distorted.

2 Carefully insert the blade of a screwdriver in one of the cover

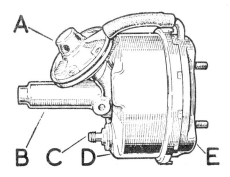

Fig. 9.34. Girling type vacuum servo unit

A *Air valve assembly*   D *Vacuum chamber*
B *Slave cylinder*   E *Vacuum chamber cover*
C *Non-return valve*

holes of the air filter and prise the cover off. Lift away the sorbo rubber washer, filter and spring. These parts are shown in Fig. 9.37.

3 Undo and remove the five screws that secure the valve cover to the housing and withdraw the cover from the rubber hose, lift off the reaction valve diaphragm "A", (Fig. 9.38) and support "B" and separate from the housing "C".

4 Undo and remove the three countersunk head screws "A", (Fig. 9.39) and separate the valve housing "B" together with the gasket "C" from the slave cylinder body "D".

5 Lift away the cup seal "B" (Fig. 9.40) from the valve piston "A".

6 Carefully prise the vacuum non-return valve "E", from the vacuum shell "D". Lift away the seal "F".

7 Reposition the servo unit in the vice so that the vacuum shell is placed uppermost.

8 It will now be necessary to make up a special tool so that the end cover can be removed. The best method is to obtain a piece of flat metal bar and drill two holes to match the stud locations. Fit the tool and secure with two 5/16 inch UNF nuts and turn the tool in an anticlockwise direction. It will be necessary to apply considerable pressure to complete this operation.

9 Release the rubber diaphragm "A", (Fig. 9.41) from the diaphragm support "C" by peeling it from the rim of the vacuum shell, and then lifting off the groove "B" of the support.

10 Press the diaphragm support "A" (Fig. 9.42) downwards and shake the key "B" from the diaphragm support "A". Once the key is free remove the support "A" and the large return spring "C".

11 With a screwdriver bend back the tabs on the locking plate "A" (Fig. 9.43) and remove the three set bolts. Lift away the locking plate "A" and abutment plate "E". Separate the vacuum chamber "B", together with the gasket "C" from the slave cylinder body "F".

12 Withdraw the pushrod and internal parts from the slave cylinder as shown in Fig. 9.44.

13 Remove the guide "F" (Fig. 9.45) large gland seal "E" and spacer "D" from the pushrod "C". Also remove the small piston seal "A" from the piston "B".

14 Should it be necessary to remove the piston from the rod hold the pushrod between soft faces in a vice and with a small screwdriver expand the spring clip "D" (Fig. 9.46) on the piston "B" and carefully ease the clip off the piston. It is important that the piston is not scratched.

15 The piston "B" may now be separated from the pushrod "A" by pressing out the small pin "C".

should be carefully inspected for signs of wear, damage or rusting and if any parts are suspect new ones should be obtained.

17 An overhaul repair kit is available and will include all rubber parts as well as new piston.

18 To refit the slave cylinder piston to the pushrod first secure the pushrod "D" (Fig. 9.47) in between soft faces in a vice and then slide the slave cylinder piston over the tapered end of the pushrod.

19 Hold the small spring within the piston back towards the diaphragm end of the pushrod and insert the small pin into the hole in the pushrod, making sure that the end of the spring rests against the pin and that it does not pass through the coil of the spring.

20 Once the pin has been refitted satisfactorily, expand the spring clip and pass it over the piston to secure the pin. Again care must be taken not to scratch the piston.

21 Remove the pushrod from the vice. Soak a small 'U' section seal onto the end of the slave cylinder piston so that the groove in the seal is facing towards the head of the piston.

22 Reassemble the spacer with the larger diameter against the head of the piston, and follow up with the larger gland seal suitably wetted, with the grooved face leading onto the pushrod.

23 Mount the slave cylinder body between soft faces in a vice, and then fit the pushrod assembly into the bore of the slave cylinder taking care not to nip or damage the seals in any way.

24 Next refit the pushrod guide into the slave cylinder so that its flat face is innermost in the bore.

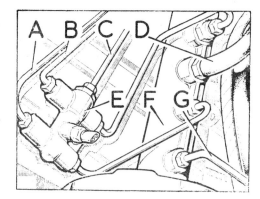

Fig. 9.35. Hydraulic pipe connections (Girling servo unit)

A To rear brakes
B To right-hand front brake
C To left-hand front brake
D From fluid reservoir
E Five-way junction and pressure failure switch
F Tandem slave cylinder
G From master cylinder.

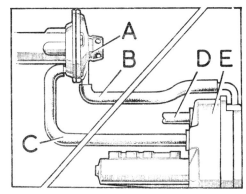

Fig. 9.36. Air and vacuum pipe connections (Girling servo unit)

A Air control valve at master cylinder
B Vacuum and air inlet pipe
C Vacuum pipe, air control valve to vacuum chamber
D Vacuum pipe, vacuum chamber to inlet manifold
E Servo vacuum chamber

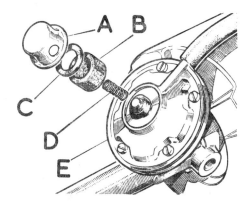

Fig. 9.37. Withdrawing filter and cover (Girling servo unit)

A Air filter cover
B Filter
C Sorbo washer
D Valve spring
E Valve cover

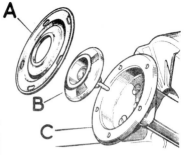

Fig. 9.38. Separating reaction valve
diaphragm from support (Girling
servo unit)

A   Reaction valve diaphragm
B   Diaphragm support
C   Valve housing

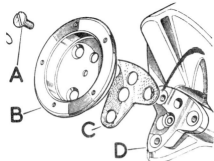

Fig. 9.39. Removing air valve body
(Girling servo unit)

A   Screw fixing body
B   Body for air valve
C   Gasket
D   Slave cylinder body

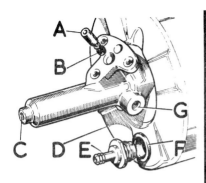

Fig. 9.40. Removal of air valve piston
and non-return valve (Girling servo unit)

A   Air valve piston
B   Seal
C   Outlet connection
D   Vacuum chamber
E   Non-return valve
F   Seal
G   Inlet connection

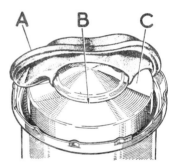

Fig. 9.41. Diaphragm removal (Girling
servo unit)

A   Diaphragm
B   Groove
C   Diaphragm support

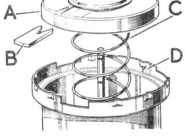

Fig. 9.42. Removing diaphragm support
and spring (Girling servo unit)

A   Diaphragm support
B   Key
C   Return spring
D   Vacuum chamber

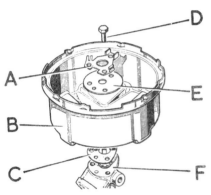

Fig. 9.43. Vacuum chamber removal
(Girling servo unit)

A   Lockplate
B   Vacuum chamber
C   Gasket
D   Securing bolt
E   Abutment plate
F   Slave cylinder

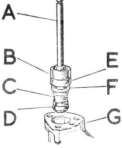
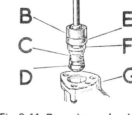

Fig. 9.44. Removing pushrod assembly
(Girling servo unit)

A   Pushrod
B   Pushrod guide
C   Piston
D   Piston seal
E   Gland seal
F   Spacer
G   Slave cylinder body

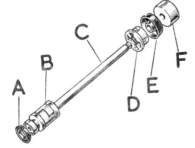

Fig. 9.45. Pushrod components
(Girling servo unit)

A   Piston seal
B   Piston
C   Pushrod
D   Spacer
E   Gland seal
F   Pushrod guide

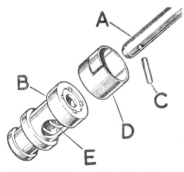

Fig. 9.46. Disconnecting piston from
pushrod (Girling servo unit)

A   Pushrod
B   Piston
C   Pin
D   Spring clip
E   Piston spring

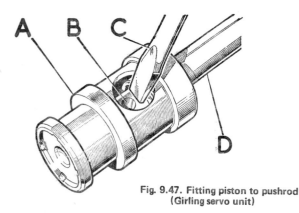

Fig. 9.47. Fitting piston to pushrod
(Girling servo unit)

A Piston
B Hole for pin
C Screwdriver
D Pushrod

25 Position a new gasket over the pushrod guide and then refit the vacuum shell with the abutment plate and the locking plates. With a small screwdriver line up the holes with the tapered holes in the slave cylinder and insert the three securing bolts. Tighten these bolts to a torque wrench setting of between 12 to 14 lb/ft (1.7 to 2.0 kg/m) and lock by bending up the locking tabs.
26 Make sure that the pushrod is in the fully withdrawn position and place the return spring over the pushrod and locate the diaphragm support on the end of the pushrod. Compress the support and secure by fitting the key into the slot in the side of the diaphragm support. Ensure that the key engages with the groove in the pushrod and that it is pushed right in.
27 The smaller diameter of the diaphragm should now be stretched into position on the diaphragm support making sure that it is correctly fitted into its groove. Next locate the outer edge of the diaphragm in the vacuum shell.
28 If the flat face of the diaphragm should have a buckled attitude it is an indication that the diaphragm has not been assembled correctly. Recheck that the inner and outer edge of the diaphragm are seating correctly.
29 The end cover may now be refitted. With the special tool fitted, press down and turn in a clockwise direction until it is

locked. It will be necessary to initially place the end cover so that when it is locked the air pipe is in the correct position relative to the face of the air valve.
30 Undo the two nuts securing the tool to the end cover and lift away the tool.
31 Release the slave cylinder from the grip of the vice and reposition it so that the air valve face is uppermost.
32 Next ease the cup into the groove in the air valve piston so that the lip of the cup faces the shouldered end of the piston. Insert the piston into the valve bore of the slave cylinder.
33 Place a new gasket into the slave cylinder and then position the valve housing in the gasket carefully aligning three holes with a small screwdriver. Refit the three countersunk headed screws and tighten them to a torque wrench setting of between 5 and 7 lb/ft (0.7 and 1.0 kg/m).
34 Stretch the reaction valve diaphragm onto the diaphragm support and insert the pushrod of the diaphragm support through the hole in the valve housing.
35 The valve rubber may now be stretched and fitted with the groove around its inside diameter onto the valve stem flange using the fingers only. Do not use any metal or wooden tools to do this.
36 Insert the valve stem through the hole in the valve cover and fit the second valve rubber over the valve stem. Secure by fitting on the snap-on cap. If this is difficult it is permissible to warm up the cup in hot water.
37 Inspect the original hose and if necessary fit a new rubber hose. Insert the valve cover end into the hose and then position the cover onto the valve housing. Secure the cover with the five self tapping screws. It is important that the reaction valve diaphragm is not trapped between the valve cover bosses and the valve housing.
38 It is recommended that the air filter cover valve and seals be renewed as a new assembly, as the valve stem and seals are a selective assembly.
39 If the air filter is dirty it should be either washed out with methylated spirits and blown dry with an air line, or alternatively, a new filter fitted.
40 Place the air filter over the air valve and then position the metal spring over the snap-on cap.
41 Refit the sorbo rubber washer in the air filter cover and snap the assembly into the air valve cover.
42 Inspect the non-return valve assembly sealing rubber, and if necessary renew. Place the sealing rubber into the valve and push the valve into its location in the end cover.

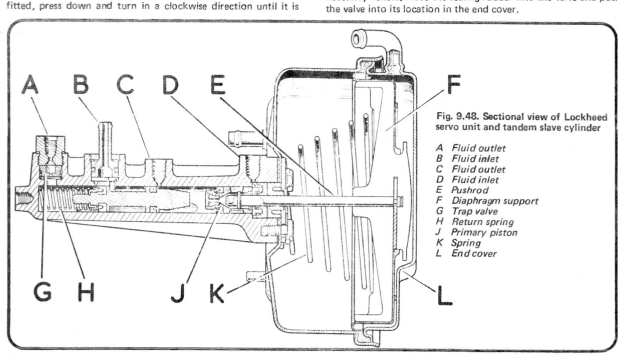

Fig. 9.48. Sectional view of Lockheed servo unit and tandem slave cylinder

A Fluid outlet
B Fluid inlet
C Fluid outlet
D Fluid inlet
E Pushrod
F Diaphragm support
G Trap valve
H Return spring
J Primary piston
K Spring
L End cover

24 Servo unit (Lockheed) - dismantling, servicing and reassembly

1 Secure the servo slave cylinder in a vice fitted with jaw protectors. Incline the cylinder at an angle of 45° with the fluid ports uppermost.

2 Using a tool similar to that described in the preceding Section, turn the servo unit end cover in an anticlockwise direction as far as the cover stops will permit and lift off the cover.

3 Detach the rubber diaphragm now exposed and then turn the diaphragm support so that the pushrod retaining key slot faces downwards.

4 Vibrate the support with the hands to release the key and then extract the pushrod which will be ejected by pressure of the main return spring. Extract the spring.

5 Bend back the lockplate tabs and remove the bolts and lockplate, abutment plate and the servo shell.

6 Withdraw the pushrod/piston assembly from the servo slave cylinder and then slide off the plastic bearing, rubber cup and plastic spacer. If necessary, the pushrod can be detached from the piston by opening the retaining clip to expose the connecting pin which can then be driven out (Fig. 9.52).

7 Unscrew the fluid inlet adaptor or if a circlip is used remove it and remove the secondary piston stop from the base of the port (Fig 9.53).

8 Remove the secondary piston and spring. If the piston is difficult to eject, tap the cylinder body gently with a rubber or hide mallet.

9 Remove the seals, washer, spring and retainer from the piston.

10 Unscrew the adaptor in the outlet port at the end of the slave cylinder and remove the trap valve and spring.

11 Discard all rubber components and check that the surfaces of the piston and cylinder bore are not scored and that 'bright' wear areas are not evident. If they are, renew the assembly complete.

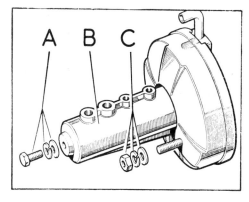

Fig. 9.49. Lockheed servo unit attachment bolts

A Bolt, servo rear mounting
B Servo unit
C Fixings, servo front mounting

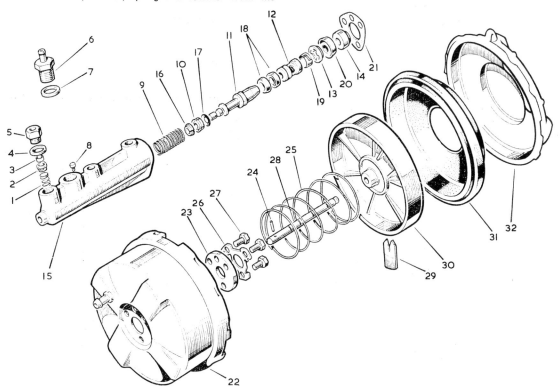

Fig. 9.50. Exploded view of Lockheed servo unit and tandem slave cylinder

1 Spring	9 Spring	17 Piston washer	25 Spring
2 Valve body	10 Seal	18 Seals	26 Lockplate
3 Spring	11 Secondary piston	19 Clip	27 Screw
4 Washer	12 Primary piston	20 Rubber cup	28 Pushrod
5 Outlet adaptor	13 Spacer	21 Gasket	29 Key
6 Inlet adaptor	14 Bearing	22 Vacuum shell	30 Diaphragm support plate
7 Washer	15 Body	23 Abutment plate	31 Diaphragm
8 Stop pin	16 Retainer	24 Pin	32 End cover

154

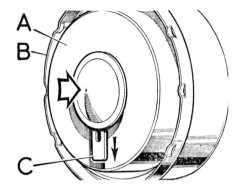

Fig. 9.51. Retaining key (C) for pushrod (Lockheed servo unit)

B   Vacuum chamber shell   A   Diaphragm support

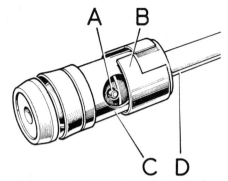

Fig. 9.52. Primary piston and pushrod assembly (Lockheed servo unit)

A Pin
B Retaining clip
C Primary piston
D Pushrod

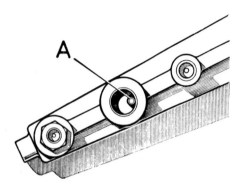

Fig. 9.53. Location of secondary piston stop pin (A) (Lockheed servo unit)

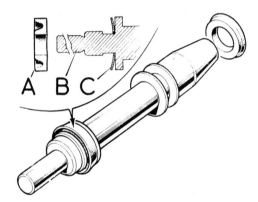

Fig. 9.54. Secondary piston assembly (Lockheed servo unit)

A Seal
B Piston
C Piston washer

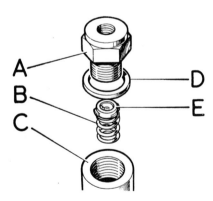

Fig. 9.55. Trap valve components (Lockheed servo unit)

A Outlet adaptor
B Spring
C Outlet port
D Washer
E Trap valve

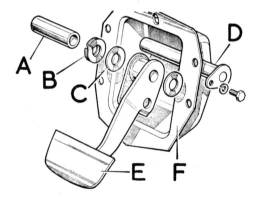

Fig. 9.56. Brake pedal components (3500 models)

A Distance piece   D Pivot spindle
B Double spring washer   E Pedal
C Shim washer   F Pedal bracket

12 Blow out all ports and drillings with compressed air and check that the curved spring insert in the trap valve body is intact and undamaged. Obtain new copper washers for the slave cylinder adaptors.

13 Observe absolute cleanliness during reassembly and wash all components in methylated spirit or clean hydraulic fluid and lay them out on a clean sheet of paper.

14 Lubricate the cylinder bore with hydraulic fluid and then locate the washer over the secondary piston head extension (convex face to piston). Fit the two seals to the piston so that their lips are as shown in Fig. 9.54.

15 Fit the spring retainer and the spring.

16 Apply brake fluid to the piston seals and insert the secondary piston assembly into the cylinder bore so that the spring enters first. Ensure that the seal lips are not trapped or bent back.

17 Depress the piston against the spring pressure until the piston head passes the piston stop hole in the inlet port. Fit the stop pin and secure it by fitting the inlet adaptor and tightening it to a torque of 33 lb/ft (4.6 kg/m).

18 Fit the trap valve to the outlet port and tighten to a similar torque.

19 Insert the pushrod into the primary piston and then using a small screwdriver, compress the piston spring to expose the hole in the rod. Fit the retaining pin and release the tension of the spring so that it bears on the protruding ends of the pin.

20 Slide on the pin retaining clip, checking its fit and ensuring that it does not extend beyond the diameter of the piston.

21 Fit the piston seal, using the fingers only to manipulate it. Dip the piston in clean hydraulic fluid and insert it into the cylinder bore, follow with the spacer, pushrod seal and bearing, fitting them one at a time to the pushrod.

22 Locate a new gasket and position the servo shell on the mounting face of the cylinder. Fit the abutment and lockplate and tighten the three securing bolts to a torque of 13 lb/ft (1.8 kg/m). Bend over the lockplate tabs.

23 Insert the main return spring with its first coil spaced round the abutment plate followed by the diaphragm support (key slot uppermost).

24 Depress the support until the pushrod groove is visible through the slot and insert the key.

25 Ensure that the rubber servo diaphragm is completely dry and free from brake fluid or rubber grease and fit it to the support.

26 Lightly smear the outer rim of the diaphragm with hydraulic fluid and engage it round the rim of the servo shell.

27 Refit the end cover using the special tool. Check that the end

cover does not trap or distort the diaphragm. Make sure that the vacuum pipe nozzle on the end cover will be correctly located on completion.

25 Brake pedal (3500 models) - removal and refitment

1 From beneath the front wing, remove the two bolts which secure the accelerator pedal to the body shell.

2 Unhook the brake pedal return spring.

3 Remove the four bolts which secure the brake pedal bracket to the bodyshell.

4 Slacken the locknut on the brake pedal pushrod.

5 Using a screwdriver engaged in its end slot, screw the pushrod through the pedal trunnion at the same time withdrawing the pedal/bracket assembly.

6 Remove the trunnion and the bolt which secures brake pedal pivot spindle to the bracket. Withdraw the brake pedal pivot spindle.

7 Withdraw the pedal, distance piece and double coil lockwasher.

8 Refitting is a reversal of removal but grease the crossshaft spindle and bush and seal the flanges of the pedal bracket box with sealant.

9 Screw the pushrod into the pedal trunnion so that it projects about 1 in (25.4 mm).

10 Adjust the height of the brake pedal by screwing the pushrod in or out until the measurement between the underside of the pedal rubber and the car interior floor (carpet removed) is between 6½ and 6¾ in (165 to 171 mm).

11 Finally, fit the pushrod locknut and attach the pedal return spring.

26 Brake pedal (3500S models) - removal and refitment

1 The procedure is much the same as described in the preceding Section although the individual components differ (Fig. 9.57).

2 The method of resetting the pedal is entirely different and the specified brake pedal height as given for 3500 types applies, but is obtained by adjusting the length of the brake pedal arm stop pin.

3 With the brake pedal dimension correctly set, check that there is a clearance between the end of the pushrod and the master cylinder piston (pedal in fully released position) of 1/16 in (1.5 mm). Adjust if necessary by screwing the pushrod in or out.

4 After brake pedal removal, refitment or adjustment, the stop lamp switch will almost certainly need checking and adjustment. To do this connect a torch battery and test lamp between the two switch terminals. With the brake pedal fully released, screw in the switch until the test lamp lights and then turn the switch back five flats. Tighten the locknut and remove the test lamp. Switch on the ignition and check the operation of the stop lamps.

27 Fluid reservoir (3500 models) - removal and refitment

1 Undo and remove the bolts that secure the support bracket to the wing valance.

2 Make a note of the electrical cable connections at the switch on the reservoir cap and disconnect the cables.

3 Disconnect the main feed cap to the master cylinder and blank off the master cylinder union to stop any dirt ingress. Also plug the end of the flexible pipe with a sharpened pencil or other means so that hydraulic fluid does not spill onto the bodywork.

4 Refitting the hydraulic fluid reservoir is the reverse sequence to removal. It will however, be necessary to bleed the hydraulic system, details of which will be found in Section 16 of this Chapter.

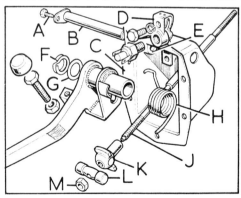

Fig. 9.57. Brake pedal components (3500 S models)

A   Retaining bolt, pivot
    spindle
B   Pivot spindle
C   Box bracket for
    brake pedal
D   Stop lamp switch
E   Distance piece
F   Double spring washer

G   Shim washer
H   Return spring,
    brake pedal
J   Pushrod
K   Adjusting sleeve,
    pushrod
L   Trunnion
M   Locknut

28 Fluid reservoir (3500S models) - removal and refitment

1 The procedure is similar to that described in the preceding Section except that individual reservoirs are fitted - one for each braking circuit.

2 On some early 3500S models with single circuit hydraulic systems, the under bonnet fluid reservoir was of combined type supplying the brake and clutch master cylinders. If this is removed then the brake and clutch hydraulic systems must both be bled on refitment.

29 Hydraulic pressure failure switch (3500S) - removal and refitment

1 This switch is fitted to dual hydraulic systems and is essentially a 'floating' piston which is kept in balance by the equal pressures within the two independent circuits. In the event of pressure failure in one circuit the piston is displaced by the pressure in the other and closes an electrical circuit to illuminate a warning lamp on the instrument panel.

2 To remove, disconnect the electrical leads.

3 Disconnect the five fluid pipes from the five way union and blank off all pipes and ports.

4 Remove the securing bolt and withdraw the five way union/switch assembly.

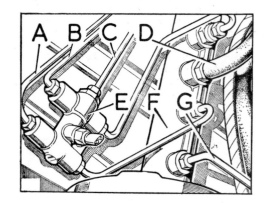

Fig. 9.58. Hydraulic pressure failure switch and pipes (3500 S models)

5 Refitting is a reversal of removal, then bleed the braking circuits as described in Section 17.

30 Fault diagnosis - Braking system (all models)

Symptom	Reason/s	Remedy
Spongy pedal action	Air in system	Bleed.
	Defective seals	Renew.
	Scored discs	Renew or re-grind.
	Excessive front hub end-float	Adjust.
	Low fluid level in reservoir	Top-up and bleed.
Juddering brakes	Loose front wheel bearings	Adjust.
	Excessive disc run-out	Renew.
Loss of pressure	Leak in hydraulic system	Rectify and bleed.
Hard brake pedal	Faulty master cylinder	Service.
Hard brake pedal and less effective braking	Defective servo slave cylinder	Overhaul.
	Vacuum valve not seating	Renew.
	Vacuum pipe leaking	Renew.
	Servo filter choked	Renew.
Low braking efficiency	Worn or incorrect type pads	Renew.
	Defective master cylinder	Overhaul.
	Defective servo unit	Overhaul.
	Low fluid level	Top up and bleed system.
	Leak in system	Rectify and bleed system.
Brakes grab or application fierce	Oil soaked friction pads	Renew.
	Servo end cover seal defective	Renew.
	Damaged end cover or balance pipe	Renew.
	Valve cover not seating	Adjust.
	Balance pipe restriction washer missing	Clear.
	Defective master cylinder piston return spring	Renew.
	Atmospheric valve not seating	Renew.
	Valve spring broken	Renew.
	Scored disc	Renew or re-grind.
	Corroded disc	Renew.
Brakes pull car to one side	Oil soaked friction pads	Renew.
	Defective flexible hose	Renew.
	Glazed pads	Renew.
	Incorrect tyre pressures	Inflate.

Symptom	Reason/s	Remedy
Applicable to 3500S models when brake warning light illuminates (ignition switched on).		
Light on continuously	Handbrake applied	Release.
Light on when brakes applied	Friction pads worn	Renew.
Light on when brakes applied — pedal has excessive travel	Pressure failure in one hydraulic circuit	Check system for leaks or overhaul master cylinder
Brakes squeal	Seized caliper pistons	Overhaul or renew.
	Worn pads	Renew.
	Handbrake pads not retracting	Overhaul.
	Stones imbedded in pads	Remove or renew pads.
Brakes overheating	Defective master cylinder	Overhaul.
	Incorrect pedal adjustment	Adjust.
Brakes drag	Loose front wheel bearings	Adjust.
	Brake line restricted	Renew section affected.
	Restriction in master cylinder	Overhaul.
	Servo piston sticking	Overhaul.
	Vacuum cylinder end cover seal defective	Renew.
Brakes lock	Oil soaked pads	Renew.
	Defective system seals	Renew in master cylinder, slave cylinder or caliper.
Lack of servo assistance	Servo vacuum piston seal worn	Renew.
	Damaged vacuum cylinder	Renew.
	Worn slave cylinder seal	Renew.
	Master cylinder seal worn	Renew.
	Valve spring broken	Renew.
	Vacuum seal not seating	Renew.
	Vacuum pipe damaged or loosely connected	Renew or tighten clips.
	Vacuum piston return spring broken	Renew.
	Low fluid level in reservoir	Top up and bleed.

Chapter 10 Electrical system

Contents

Specifications

System type	12 volt negative earth
Battery	60 amp/hr at 20 hr. rate

Alternator:

Type	Lucas 11AC
Rating	45 amps
Nominal voltage	12
Nominal direct current output	43 amps
Field coil resistance at 20° C (68° F)	3.8 ohms
Maximum rotor speed	12500 rev/min.
Stator phases	3
Rotor poles	8
Field coils	1

Brush length:
New ... ...   5/8 in. (15.9 mm)
Minimum ... ...   5/32 in. (4.0 mm)

Alternator control box ... ...   Lucas type 4TR

Alternator field isolating relay (Three thousand five models only)
Nominal voltage ... ...   12 volts
Cut-in voltage ... ...   6.0 to 7.5 volts
Drop off voltage ... ...   4.0 volts minimum
Resistance of operating winding ... ...   76 ohms
Alternator warning light control ... ...
Resistance of actuator wire and internal ballast resistor
(Terminals AL and E) ... ...   14/16 ohms

Starter motor:
Type ... ...   Lucas M45G (pre-engaged)
Cranking speed ... ...   100 - 150 engine rev/min.
Starter pinion teeth   9

Windscreen wiper ... ...   Lucas electric variable speed

Windscreen washer:
Early three thousand five ... ...   Lucas electric
All later models ... ...   Trico electric

Bulbs and headlamp units (12 volt)
Headlamp (sealed beam) inner ... ...   Lucas 75W
Headlamp (sealed beam) outer ... ...   Lucas 37½/50W
Headlamp (bulb) inner SP410 45W
Headlamp (bulb) outer SP411 40/45W
Side ... ...   Lucas No. 989   6W
Stop/tail ... ...   Lucas No. 380   21/6W
Direction indicator ... ...   Lucas No. 382   21W
Rear number plate ... ...   Lucas No. 989   6W
Reverse ... ...   Lucas No. 382   21W
Instrument panel ... ...   2.2W capless
Warning ... ...   3W capless
Interior ... ...   Lucas No. 272   10W
Rotary map ... ...   Lucas No. 989   6W
Rear luggage boot ... ...   Lucas No. 209   5W
Selector illumination, automatic transmission ... ...   Lucas No. 256   3W
Switch panel ... ...   Lucas No. 254   6W
Hazard warning switch ... ...   Lucas No. 281   2W

1 General description

The electrical system is of 12 volt negative earth type. The battery is charged by a belt driven alternator with separate electronic voltage regulator.

Four headlamps are fitted, the outer pair providing main and dipped beams and the inner pair main beam only.

A wide selection of electrical accessories are fitted including reversing and luggage boot lamps, an electric clock, cigar lighter, variable speed windscreen wipers and electric washers.

The coolant temperature and fuel gauges are of the bimetal, electrically operated type.

3500S models (up to October 1971) had additional equipment which included electrically operated windows, variable delay type wipers, a buzzer type anti-theft system (North America and certain other territories), a map reading lamp, hazard warning lamps, and brake warning lamps to cover low fluid level and disc pad wear.

2 Battery - removal and refitment

1 The battery is located in the right-hand side of the luggage boot.
2 Remove the two wing nuts or on 3500S models the two plastic knobs and remove the battery cover.
3 Remove the screws or pinch bolts which secure the leads to the battery terminals.
4 Remove the nuts and washers from the battery securing studs and lift out the battery.
5 Refitment is a reversal of removal but smear the terminals with petroleum jelly to prevent corrosion.

3 Battery - maintenance and inspection

1 Normal weekly battery maintenance consists of checking the electrolyte level in each cell to ensure that the separators are covered by ¼ inch of electrolyte. If the level has fallen, top up the battery using distilled water only. Do not overfill. If a battery is overfilled or any electrolyte spilled, immediately wipe away the excess as electrolyte attacks and corrodes any metal it comes into contact with very rapidly.
2 As well as keeping the terminals clean and covered with petroleum jelly, the top of the battery, and especially the tops of the cells, should be kept clean and dry. This helps prevent corrosion and ensures that the battery does not become partially discharged by leakage through dampness and dirt.
3 Once every three months, remove the battery and inspect the battery securing wing nuts, the battery clamp plate, tray and battery leads for corrosion (white fluffy deposits on the metal which are brittle to touch). If any corrosion is found, clean off the deposit with ammonia and paint over the clean metal with an anti-rust, anti-acid paint.
4 At the same time inspect the battery case for cracks. If a

crack is found, clean and plug it with one of the proprietary compounds marketed by firms such as Holts, for this purpose. If leakage through the crack has been excessive, then it will be necessary to refill the appropriate cell with fresh electrolyte as detailed later. Cracks are frequently caused to the top of the battery cases by pouring in distilled water in the middle of winter **after** instead of **before** a run. This gives the water no chance to mix with the electrolyte and so the former freezes and splits the battery case.

5 If topping up the battery becomes excessive and the case has been inspected for cracks that could cause leakage, but none are found, the battery is being overcharged and the voltage regulator will have to be checked and reset.

6 With the battery on the bench at the three month interval check, measure the specific gravity with a hydrometer to determine the state of charge and condition of the electrolyte. There should be very little variation between the different cells and if a variation in excess of 0.025 is present it will be due to either:-

a) Loss of electrolyte from the battery at some time caused by spillage or a leak, resulting in a drop in the specific gravity of the electrolyte when the deficiency was replaced with distilled water instead of fresh electrolyte.

b) An internal short circuit caused by buckling of the plates or a similar malady pointing to the likelihood of total battery failure in the near future.

7 The specific gravity of the electrolyte for fully charged conditions at the electrolyte temperature indicated, is listed in Table A. The specific gravity of a fully discharged battery at different temperatures of the electrolyte is given in Table B.

Table A

Specific gravity - battery fully charged
1.268 at 100°F or 38°C electrolyte temperature
1.276 at 80°F or 27°C electrolyte temperature
1.280 at 70°F or 21°C electrolyte temperature
1.284 at 60°F or 16°C electrolyte temperature
1.288 at 50°F or 10°C electrolyte temperature
1.292 at 40°F or 4°C electrolyte temperature
1.296 at 30°F or -1.5°C electrolyte temperature

Table B

Specific gravity - battery fully discharged
1.098 at 100°F or 38°C electrolyte temperature
1.102 at 90°F or 32°C electrolyte temperature
1.106 at 80°F or 27°C electrolyte temperature
1.110 at 70°F or 21°C electrolyte temperature
1.114 at 60°F or 16°C electrolyte temperature
1.118 at 50°F or 10°C electrolyte temperature
1.122 at 40°F or 4°C electrolyte temperature
1.126 at 30°F or -1.5°C electrolyte temperature

4 Battery - electrolyte replenishment

1 If the battery is in a fully charged state and one of the cells maintains a specific gravity reading which is 0.025 or more lower than the others, and the check of each cell has been made with a voltage meter to check for short circuits (a four to seven second test should give a steady reading of between 1.2 and 1.8 volts), then it is likely that the electrolyte has been lost at some time from the cell with the low reading.

2 Top the cell up with a solution of 1 part sulphuric acid to 2.5 parts of water. If the cell is already fully topped up draw some electrolyte out of it with a pipette. The total capacity of each cell is ¾ pint.

3 When mixing the sulphuric acid and water NEVER ADD WATER TO SULPHURIC ACID - always pour the acid slowly onto the water in a glass container. IF WATER IS ADDED TO SULPHURIC ACID IT WILL EXPLODE.

4 Continue to top up the cell with the freshly made electrolyte

and then recharge the battery and check the hydrometer readings.

5 Battery - charging

1 In winter time when heavy demand is placed upon the battery, such as when starting from cold and much electrical equipment is continually in use, it is a good idea to occasionally have the battery fully charged from an external source at the rate of 3.5 to 4 amps.

2 Continue to charge the battery at this rate until no further rise in specific gravity is noted over a four-hour period.

3 Alternatively, a trickle charger, charging at the rate of 1.5 amps can be safely used overnight.

4 Specially rapid 'boost' charges which are claimed to restore the power of the battery in 1 to 2 hours are most dangerous as they can cause serious damage to the battery plates through overheating.

5 While charging the battery note that the temperature of the electrolyte should never exceed 100°F.

6 Always disconnect both battery cables before the external charger is connected otherwise serious damage to the alternator may occur.

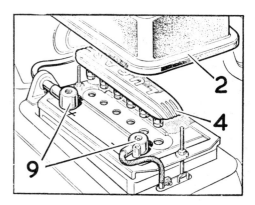

Fig. 10.1. Lucas type battery

2 Battery cover
4 Vent cover
9 Terminals

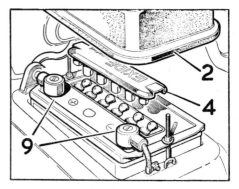

Fig. 10.2. Exide type battery

2 Battery cover
4 Vent cover
9 Terminals

6 Alternator - general description

The main advantage of the alternator lies in its ability to provide a high charge at low revolutions. This is especially welcome to city dwellers as driving slowly in heavy traffic with a dynamo invariably leads to little or no charge reaching the battery. In similar conditions, even with the wiper, lights, heater and perhaps radio switched on, the Lucas 11AC alternator will ensure a charge reaching the battery.

An important feature of the alternator system is its output control, this being based on thick film hybrid integrated micro-circuit techniques.

The alternator is of the rotating field, ventilated design. It comprises, principally a laminated stator on which is wound a star connected three-phase output and an eight-pole rotor carrying the field winding. The front end of the rotor shaft runs in a ball race bearing and the rear in a needle roller race, each of which is lubricated for life, and natural finish aluminium diecast end brackets incorporating the mounting lugs.

The rotor is belt driven from the engine through a pulley keyed to the rotor shaft and a pressed steel fan adjacent to the pulley draws cooling air through the machine. This fan forms an integral part of the alternator specifications. It has been designed to provide adequate air flow with a minimum of noise and to withstand the high stresses associated with maximum speeds.

The brush gear for the field system is mounted on the slip ring end bracket. Two carbon brushes bear against a pair of concentric brass slip rings carried on a moulded disc attached to the end of the rotor. Also attached to the slip ring end brackets are six silicon diodes connected in a three-phase bridge to rectify the generated alternating current to direct current for use in charging the battery and supplying power to the electrical system.

The alternator output is controlled by an electrical voltage regulator unit and a warning light control unit to indicate to the driver when all is not well.

7 Alternator - maintenance

1 The equipment has been designed for the minimum amount of maintenance in service, the only items subject to wear being the brushes and bearings.
2 Brushes should be examined after about 75,000 miles, (120,000 km) and renewed if necessary. The bearings are pre-packed with grease for life, and should not require further attention.
3 Check the fan belt every 5,000 miles (8000 km) for correct adjustment as described in 'Routine Maintenance'.

8 Alternator - special procedures

Whenever the electrical system of the car is being attended to or external means of starting the engine are used, there are certain precautions that must be taken otherwise serious and expensive damage can result.
1 Always make sure that the negative terminal of the battery is earthed. If the terminal connections are accidentally reversed, or if the battery has been reverse charged, the alternator diodes will burn out.
2 The output terminal on the alternator marked 'BAT' must never be earthed, but should always be connected directly to the positive terminal of the battery.
3 Whenever the alternator is to be removed or when disconnecting the terminals of the alternator circuit, always disconnect the battery earth terminal first.
4 The alternator must never be operated without the battery to alternator cable connected.
5 Should it be necessary to use a booster charger or booster battery to start the engine always double check that the negative cables are connected to negative terminals and positive cables to positive terminals.

9 Alternator - removal and refitment

1 Disconnect the leads from the battery terminals.
2 Slacken but do not remove the pivot mounting bolts and the adjuster strap bolt.
3 Push the alternator in towards the engine and disconnect the driving belt from the alternator pulley.
4 Disconnect the 35 amp Lucar terminal and the two field cables from the terminal block at the rear of the alternator. Remove the Lucar connection from the 'AL' connector on the alternator rear cover (photo).
5 Remove the mounting bolts and the adjuster strap bolts. Lift the alternator from its mountings.
6 Refitment is a reversal of removal. Adjust the driving belt as described in 'Routine Maintenance'.

10 Alternator - fault finding and servicing

Due to the specialist knowledge and equipment required to test or service an alternator it is recommended that if the performance is suspect, the car be taken to an automobile electrician, who will have the facilities for such work. Because of this recommendation no further details of service information are given other than the renewal of brushes and the checking and adjustment of the output control unit.

11 Alternator - brush renewal

1 Remove the single screw and withdraw the plastic cover from the slip-ring end bracket "J" (Fig. 10.3).
2 Unscrew the nut "A" (Fig. 10.4), the spring washer, 35 amp Lucar blade and plastic strip from the output terminal.
3 Remove the locknut and washer, the two brush box securing screws and their washers and withdraw the brush box.
4 Measure the length of the brushes. If they are worn to 5/32 in (4 mm) or less, renew them.
5 Check that the brushes move freely in their holders, if not, clean the holders in fuel and smooth the brushes with a fine file.
6 Refitment is a reversal of removal.

12 Alternator output control - testing and adjustment

1 Disconnect the main output lead from the alternator or

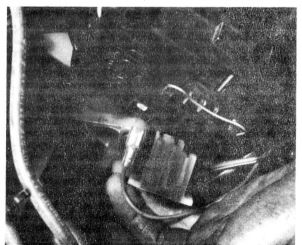

9.4 Alternator plug and lead removal

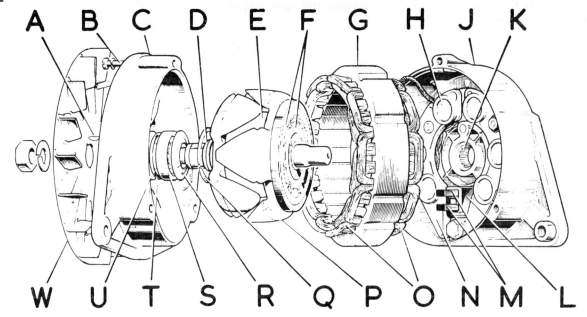

Fig. 10.3. Exploded view of the alternator

A Woodruff key	F Slip rings	L Brush box	Q Circlip
B Tie bolt	G Stator	M Brushes	R Retaining plate
C Drive end bracket	H Diodes	N Diode heat sink	S Bearing
D Jump ring shroud	J Slip ring end bracket	O Stator winding	T 'O' ring
E Rotor field winding	K Needle roller bearing	P Rotor	U 'O' ring retainer
			W Fan

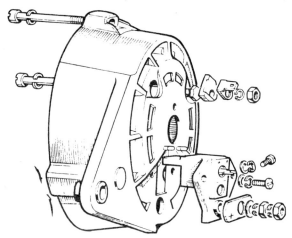

Fig. 10.4. Alternator brush holder

Fig. 10.5. Alternator control unit - testing diagram

A Ammeter	switch
B Relay	D Side and tail lamp
C Side and tail lamp	V Voltmeter

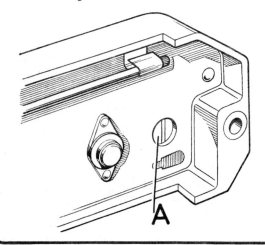

Fig. 10.6. Adjuster screw (A) on alternator control unit

starter solenoid and connect a 0-50 ammeter in series with the lead and its connection (Fig. 10.5).

2 Connect an accurate voltmeter between the battery terminals and note the reading with all electrical equipment switched off.

3 Switch on the side and tail lamps to provide an electrical discharge of 2 amps.

4 Start the engine and run the alternator at 3000 rev/min for at least eight minutes to stabilise the system voltage. If the charging current is greater than ten amps continue to run the engine until the current drops to ten amps. The voltmeter should then indicate between 13.9 and 14.3 volts.

5 If the voltage remains stable but outside the specified limits, adjust the control unit in the following way. If the voltage increases uncontrollably, then the unit is faulty and must be renewed.

6 Switch off the engine and remove the control unit securing screws. Invert the unit and scrape away the sealing plug which covers the potentiometer to adjuster screw "A" (Fig. 10.6).

7 Restart the engine and operate at the previously specified speed. Turn the adjuster screw until the indicated voltage is within the stipulated range. A fractional movement of the screw will cause a marked alteration to the voltage reading.

8 Stop and restart the engine and recheck the adjustment.

9 Refit the control unit, connect the alternator output lead and disconnect the ammeter and voltmeter.

13 Alternator warning light control

A warning light is fitted on the instrument panel to indicate a 'no charge' condition in the event of non-operation of the alternator.

The warning light is illuminated when the car is stationary or is being driven slowly. The light is extinguished when the output voltage begins to rise. It is connected through the alternator terminal AL to the centre point of one pair of the six alternator control diodes and to earth.

Should the warning light indicates lack of charge, check this unit before the alternator. If it is suspect it must be replaced with a similar new unit. Although similar in design to the direction indicator flasher unit, it is not interchangeable.

14 Starter motor - general description

The starter motor is of the pre-engaged type. When the starter switch is actuated, the solenoid mounted on the top of the starter motor pushes the drive gear into engagement with the flywheel or driveplate ring gear, through the medium of a pivoted fork. It is only when the drive is fully engaged that the main starter motor contacts close and the engine is rotated. When the engine fires, any possibility of the engine attempting to drive the starter motor is removed by a clutch unit within the drive gear assembly.

15 Starter motor - testing on engine

1 If the starter motor fails to operate then check the condition of the battery, by turning on the headlamps. If they glow brightly for several seconds and then gradually dim, the battery is in an uncharged condition.

2 If the headlamps glow brightly and continue to glow, and it is obvious that the battery is in good condition, then check the tightness of the battery wiring connections (and in particular the earth lead from the battery terminal to its connection on the bodyframe). If the positive terminal on the battery becomes hot when an attempt is made to operate the starter, this is a sure sign of a poor connection on the battery terminal. To rectify remove the terminal, clean the inside of the cap and the terminal post thoroughly and reconnect. Check the tightness of the connections at the relay switch and at the starter motor.

16 Starter motor - removal and refitment

1 Disconnect the battery earth lead from the battery terminal post.

2 Make a special note of the starter motor cable connections at the rear of the solenoid and disconnect the cables.

3 Remove the upper starter motor securing nut and bolt.

4 Working under the car, loosen and then remove the one lower starter motor securing nut and bolt taking care to support the motor so as to prevent damage to the drive component.

5 Lift the starter motor out of engagement with the flywheel ring gear and lower it from the car.

6 Replacement is a straightforward reversal of the removal procedure. Take extreme care to ensure that the cables on the back of the solenoid are reconnected correctly.

17 Starter motor - dismantling and reassembly

1 With the starter motor on the bench, loosen the screw on the cover band and slip the cover band off. An exploded view of this starter motor is shown in Fig. 10.7.

2 Disconnect the cable link between the lower solenoid terminal and the starter motor casing by undoing and removing the terminal nut and spring washer at the rear of the solenoid.

3 Undo and remove the two solenoid securing nuts and spring washers and withdraw the solenoid from the drive end bracket.

4 Move the starter pinion away from the armature to the end of its travel, then disengage the solenoid plunger from its engagement lever and withdraw the plunger and spring.

5 With a piece of wire bent into the shape of a hook lift back each of the brushes in their holders by pulling on the flexible connectors (Fig. 10.8). If the brushes are so worn that their faces do not rest against the commutator, or if the ends of the brush leads are exposed on their working faces, they must be renewed.

6 If any of the brushes tend to stick in their holders, then wash them with a petrol moistened rag and if necessary lightly polish the sides of the brushes with a very fine file until the brushes move quite freely in their holders.

7 If the surface of the commutator is dirty or blackened, clean it with a petrol moistened rag. Secure the starter motor in a vice and check it by connecting a heavy gauge cable between the starter motor cable and a 12 volt battery.

8 Connect the cable from the other battery terminal to earth on the starter motor body. If the motor turns at high speed it is in good order.

9 If the starter motor still fails to function, or if it is wished to renew the brushes, it is necessary to further dismantle the motor.

10 Lift the brush spring with the wire hook, and lift all four brushes out of their holders one at a time.

11 Undo and remove the two long tie bolts from the commutator end of the starter motor body, and pull off the commutator end bracket.

12 Remove the drive end bracket from the starter motor body.

13 Carefully push out the moving pole shoe pivot pin and lift away the pole shoe.

14 Undo and remove the two screws that secure the earth leads to the starter motor body. One lead is also soldered to one side of the contact points and must be cut as near to the connection as possible using a pair of side cutters.

15 Remove the brushes from the starter motor body.

16 Using the pair of side cutters, cut the insulated field coil brush leads as near to the field coil connections as possible and remove the brushes.

17 If new brushes are to be fitted, check that the new brushes move freely in their holders, as detailed previously. If cleaning the commutator with petrol fails to remove all the burnt areas and spots, then work a piece of glass paper round the commutator. If the commutator is very badly worn, remove the drive gear as detailed in the following Section. Then mount the armature in a lathe and with the lathe turning at high speed, take a very fine cut out of the commutator and finish the surfaces by polishing

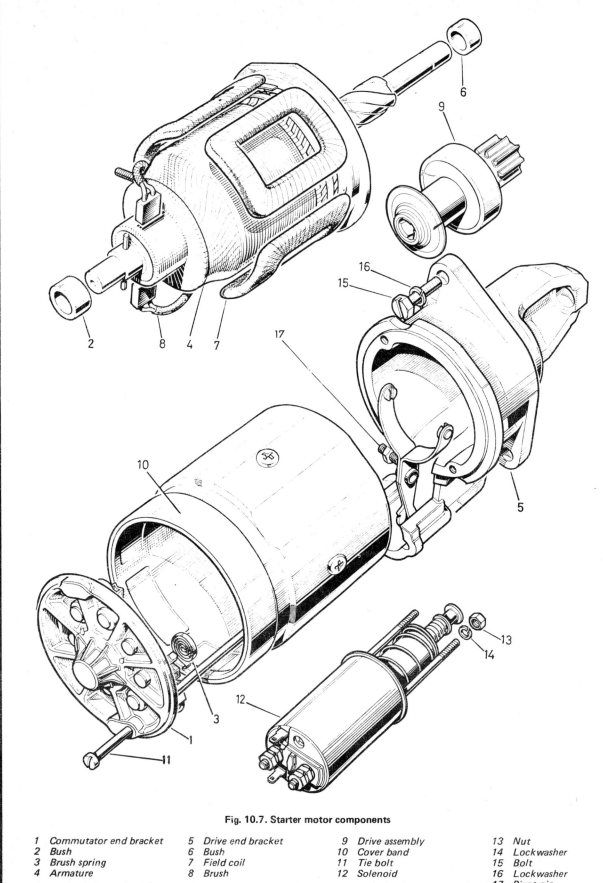

Fig. 10.7. Starter motor components

1 Commutator end bracket	5 Drive end bracket	9 Drive assembly	13 Nut
2 Bush	6 Bush	10 Cover band	14 Lockwasher
3 Brush spring	7 Field coil	11 Tie bolt	15 Bolt
4 Armature	8 Brush	12 Solenoid	16 Lockwasher
			17 Pivot pin

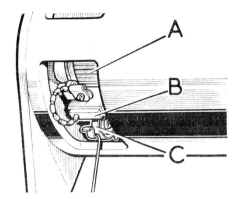

Fig. 10.8. Starter motor brush removal

A Commutator
B Brush
C Spring

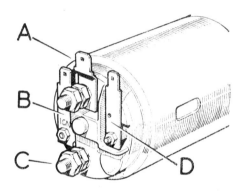

Fig. 10.9. Starter solenoid terminals

A Battery   C Starter
B Ignition   D Starter switch

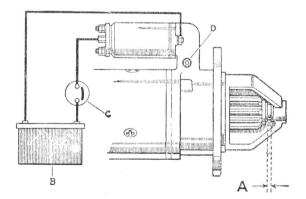

Fig. 10.10. Starter pinion clearance setting diagram (solenoid energised)

A Gap 0.005 to 0.015 in   C Switch
   (0.12 to 0.40 mm)   D Pivot pin
B Battery

with glass paper. **Do not undercut the mica insulators between the commutator segments.**

18 With the starter motor dismantled, test the four field coils for an open circuit. Connect a 12 volt battery with a 12 volt bulb in one of the leads between the two ends of each field coil. An open circuit is proved by the bulb not lighting.

19 If the bulb lights, it does not necessarily mean that the field coils are in order, as there is a possibility that one of the coils will be earthing at the yoke or pole shoes.

20 To check this, remove the lead from the brush connector and place it against a clean portion of the starter motor body. If the bulb lights, the field coils are earthing. Replacement of the field coils calls for the use of a wheel operated screwdriver, a soldering iron, caulking and riveting operations and is considered beyond the scope of the majority of owners. The starter motor body should be taken to a reputable electrical engineering works for new field coils to be fitted. Alternatively purchase an exchange starter motor.

21 If the armature is damaged, it will be evident after visual inspection. Look for signs of burning, discolouration and for conductors that have lifted from the commutator.

22 Reassembly is a straightforward reversal of the dismantling procedure.

18 Starter motor drive gear - removal and refitment

1 Dismantle the starter motor as described in the preceding Section.

2 Using a small screwdriver or a pair of circlip pliers, remove the circlip that retains the drive pinion assembly onto the armature shaft. In order to do this, the shaft collar will first have to be driven back with a piece of tubing to expose the circlip. Slide the drive assembly from the armature shaft.

3 Carefully hold the drive pinion assembly, but not by holding the one-way clutch, in a vice, and remove the circlip behind the spring retainer plate.

4 It should be noted that the drive pinion and one-way clutch assembly is serviceable as a complete unit and individual parts are not available.

5 To refit, first place the spring and retainer plate onto the drive pinion and one-way clutch unit and secure in position with the circlip.

6 Refit the drive pinion assembly onto the armature shaft with the spring retainer placed nearest to the starter motor body. Secure in position with the circlip.

7 Check that the retaining ring is fitted over the circlip before refitting the drive end housing to the starter motor. Refer to Fig. 10.10, and reset the pinion clearance using feeler gauges and rotating the eccentric pivot pin "D".

19 Fuses - three thousand five and 3500 models

The fuse box is located within the engine compartment on the left-hand wing valance.

Position:
1—2   35 amp   Horns, cigar lighter illumination and interior lights.
3—4   35 amp   Windscreen washer, stop lights and flasher lights.
5—6   2 amp   Cigar lighter, clock and panel illumination.
7—8   15 amp   Heater and wiper motor.

20 Fuses - 3500S models

The fuse box is located within the right-hand glove compartment.

Position:

1—2	35 amp	Battery control
3—4	35 amp	Ignition control
5—6	5 amp	Parking lights
7—8	5 amp	Side and tail lights
9—10	5 amp	Panel lights
11—12	25 amp	Headlamp, main, inner
13—14	15 amp	Headlamp, main, outer
15—16	10 amp	Headlamp, RH dip
17—18	10 amp	Headlamp, LH dip
19—20	25 amp	Wiper and heater
21—22	25 amp	Hazard warning and flasher
23—24	35 amp	Air conditioning

21 Flasher (direction indicator) - fault finding and rectification

1   The flasher unit is located in its carrier within the driver's side glove compartment.

2   If the flasher unit fails to operate, or works very slowly or rapidly, check the flasher indicator circuit as detailed below before assuming there is a fault in the unit itself.

a) Examine the direction indicator bulbs, front and rear for broken filament.

b) If the external flashers are working, but the internal flasher warning light has ceased to function, check the filament in the warning light bulb and replace with a new bulb if necessary.

c) If a flasher bulb is sound, but does not work, check all the flasher circuit connections with the aid of the wiring diagram.

d) In the event of total indicator failure, check the fuse applicable, see Sections 19 or 20. It will be fairly obvious if this fuse has blown, as it also protects the stop lamps and electric screen washer.

e) With the ignition switched on, check that the current is reaching the flasher unit by connecting a voltmeter between the '+' or 'B' terminal and earth. If it is found that current is reaching the unit, connect the two terminals '+' or 'B' and 'L' and operate the flasher switch. If the warning light comes on, this proves that the flasher unit itself is at fault and must be replaced, as it is not possible to dismantle and repair it. Before removing make a special note of the electrical connections to ensure correct refitting to the unit.

22 Hazard warning flasher unit - removal and refitment

1   Where hazard warning lamps are fitted, the controlling unit is located within the driver's side glove compartment.

2   Remove the unit by withdrawing it from its socket, noting carefully the location of the electrical leads.

3   Refitment is a reversal of removal and disconnection.

23 Windscreen wiper mechanism - maintenance

1   Renew the wiper blades at intervals of 12,000 miles (19000 km) or more frequently if they fail to wipe cleanly.

2   Lubricate the link type drive pivots (3500 models) occasionally with engine oil.

3   Smear the rubber washers surrounding the wiper arm spindles with glycerine to preserve them.

24 Wiper blades - removal and refitment

1   Lift the wiper arm away from the windscreen and remove the old blade by turning it slowly towards the arm and then disengage the arm from the slot in the blade (Fig. 10.13).

2   To fit a new blade, slide the end of the wiper arm into the slotted spring fastening in the centre of the blade. Push the blade firmly onto the arm, until the raised portion of the arm is fully home in the hole in the blade.

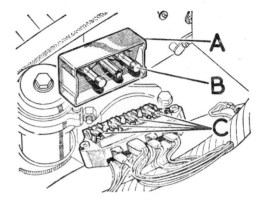

Fig. 10.11. Fuse box (Three thousand five and 3500)

A   Cover
B   Spare fuse
C   Fuses in circuit

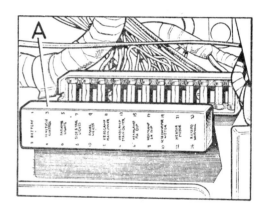

Fig. 10.12. Fuse box (3500 S type)

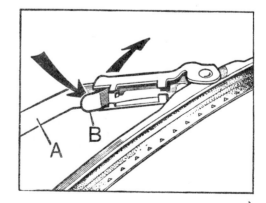

Fig. 10.13. Windscreen wiper blade removal

A   Arm
B   Spring tag

25.2 Removing wiper arm

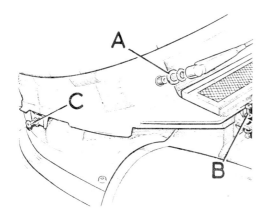

Fig. 10.14. Air intake securing bolts

A *Wiper spindle nut and washer*
B *Air intake to heater bolts*
C *Air intake to bodyshell bolts*

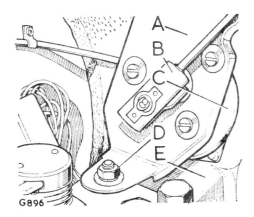

Fig. 10.15. Wiper motor location (RHD)

A *Bracket*
B *Link*
C *Motor*
D *Locknut to steering box bracket*
E *Steering box*

25 Wiper arms - removal and refitment

1 Before removing a wiper arm, turn the windscreen wiper switch on and off to ensure the arms are in their normal parked position, parallel to the bottom of the windscreen.
2 To remove an arm, pivot the arm back and pull the wiper arm head off the splined sleeve. If the arm proves difficult to remove, a screwdriver with a wide blade can be used to lever the wiper arm head off the splined sleeve. Care must be taken not to damage the spline (photo).
3 When replacing an arm, position it so that it is in the correct relative parked position and then press the arm head onto the splined drive until it is fully home on the splines.

26 Wiper motor and linkage (three thousand five and 3500 models) - removal, refitment and adjustment

1 Disconnect the battery negative lead.
2 Remove the wiper blades and arms.
3 Open the bonnet and remove the crosshead screws and washers and nuts which secure the air intake valance.
4 Remove the valance to wheel box screws and withdraw the air intake valance.
5 Slacken the locknut which clamps the link drive and spacer to the bodyshell.
6 Remove the locknut from the motor bracket which is mounted on the steering box cover plate.
7 Disconnect the electrical leads from the wiper motor.
8 Lift the motor complete with linkage from between the heater and bodyshell.
9 Remove the circlip from the motor end of link "E" (Fig. 10.16) and lift the link from its bush.
10 Remove the three screws which secure the wiper motor to the support bracket and remove the motor.
11 Refitment is a reversal of removal but ensure that the wiper motor is in the self-parked position before fitting the wiper arms to the spindles so that they lie parallel to the lower screen frame. Check that the wiper arm retaining clip is fully engaged with the groove in the spindle.
12 Should the windscreen wipers fail, or work very slowly, then check the terminals of the motor for loose connections and make sure the insulation of all the wiring is not cracked or broken, thus causing a short circuit. If this is in order, then check the current the motor is taking by connecting an ohmmeter in the circuit and turning on the wiper switch. Consumption should be between 2.3 and 3.1 amps.
13 If no current is passing through the motor, check that the switch is operating correctly. If the wiper motor takes a very high current, check the wiper blades for freedom of movement. If this is satisfactory, check the gearbox cover and gear assembly for damage (see following Section 29 which applies).
14 If the motor takes a very low current ensure that the battery is fully charged. Check the brush gear and ensure the brushes are bearing on the commutator. If not, check the brushes for freedom of movement and, if necessary, renew the tension springs. If the brushes are very worn they should be replaced with new ones. Check the armature by substitution if this unit is suspect.

27 Wiper motor and rack and pinion drive (3500S models) - testing and adjustment

1 When operating correctly, the wiper blades should operate at between 40 and 50 cycles per minute when the wiper switch is set to the slow speed position and between 60 and 70 cycles per minute in the fast speed position.
2 If the required speeds are not reached, the cause will probably be found in the rack cable or wheel boxes.
3 When the rack cable is disconnected from the motor and the wiper blades are away from the windscreen glass, the maximum

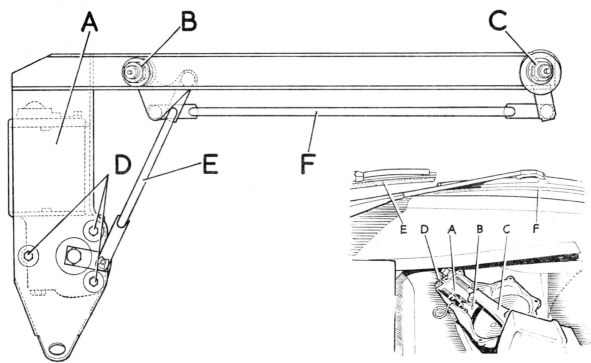

Fig. 10.16. Link type wiper layout

A	Wiper motor	D	Securing bolts
B	Link	E	Link
C	Link	F	Link

Fig. 10.17. Rack and pinion type wiper motor adjustment

A	Contacts	D	Adjuster
B	Cam	E	Wiper blade
C	Crank	F	Wiper blade

permissible force required to move the cable rack should not exceed 6 lb. If this force is greater, further investigation will be necessary, probably requiring removal of the system, thoroughly cleaning, and re-packing with approved grease.

4 It is recommended that before the end cover is refitted after completion of the previous test the limit switch contacts ('A', Fig. 10.17) be inspected for signs of burning which would be the reason for inconsistent self parking.

5 Should signs of burning be evident at the limit switch contacts and no other visible sign of trouble be apparent, the limit switch should be adjusted. Clean the contact points with a very fine contact file or glass paper. Reconnect the rack and reset the limit switch by turning the knurled nut 'D' positioned near to the wiper motor gearbox cable outlet, half a turn at a time until the wiper blades just reach the correct parking position.

28 Wiper motor and cable drive (3500S models) - removal and refitment

1 Disconnect the lead from the battery negative terminal.
2 Remove the wiper arms from their spindles.
3 Slacken (right off) the wheelbox locknuts.
4 Open the bonnet and unscrew and remove the air intake panel.
5 If air conditioning is fitted, remove the section of the insulator cover nearest to the wiper motor.
6 Disconnect the vacuum pipe from the delay governor on the wiper motor (photo).
7 Mark the electrical leads attached to the delay governor and disconnect them.
8 Unscrew the union nut on the drive cable guide tube at the wiper motor end.
9 Remove the two motor to mounting bracket screws.

10 Lift the wiper motor from its location so that the connector plug for the electrical leads can be detached.
11 Remove the wiper motor/gearbox assembly complete with attached drive cable from the engine compartment by drawing the cable through the guide tube and out of engagement with the wheelboxes.
12 Unbolt the delay governor and cover from the gearbox section of the wiper assembly.
13 Detach the circlip and plain washer from the now exposed cross-shaft pivot pin.

28.6 Wiper arm location (rack and pinion type)

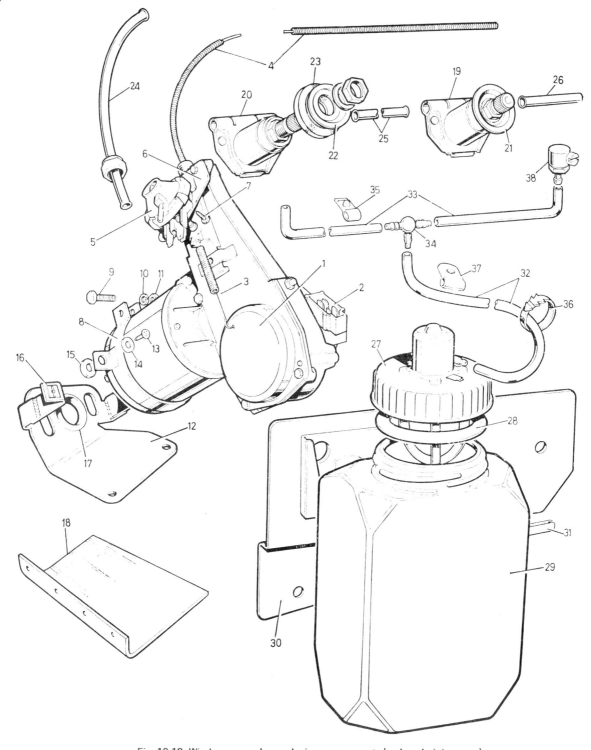

Fig. 10.18. Windscreen washer and wiper components (rack and pinion type)

1 Wiper motor assembly	10 Spring washer	20 Wheelbox assembly	30 Mounting bracket
2 Park switch	11 Nut	21 Cover washer	31 Protection strip
3 Return spring for breech block	12 Mounting bracket	22 Cover washer	32 Plastic tubing
4 Drive cable	13 Screw	23 Grommet	33 Plastic tubing
5 Governor	14 Plain washer	24 Outer casing	34 'T' piece connector
6 Bracket	15 Grommet	25 Outer casing	35 Clip
7 Screw	16 Locknut	26 Outer casing	36 Cleat for tubing
8 Clamp bracket	17 Grommet	27 Motor, pump and cap assembly	37 Clip for tubing
9 Screw	18 Shield	28 Seal for cap	38 Windscreen washer nozzle
	19 Wheelbox assembly	29 Reservoir	

14 Lift off the cross-shaft from the cable and pivot pin.

15 Ease out the threaded ferrule and withdraw the drive cable.

16 The wheelboxes may be removed after withdrawing their rubber grommets and distance tubes. Withdraw the wheelboxes complete with drive cable guide tube.

29 Wiper motor (3500S models) - servicing

1 Undo the screws that hold the gearbox cover in place and lift away the cover.

2 Undo and remove the two through bolts from the commutator end bracket. Pull out the connector and free the end bracket from the yoke.

3 Carefully remove the brush gear as a unit from the commutator and then withdraw the yoke.

4 Clean the commutator and brush gear and if worn fit new brushes. The resistance between adjacent commutator segments should be 0.34 to 0.41 ohm.

5 Carefully examine the internal wiring for signs of chafing, breaks or charring which would lead to a short circuit. Insulate or replace any damaged wires.

6 Measure the value of the field resistance which should be between 12,8 to 14 ohms. If a lower reading than this is obtained it is likely that there is a short circuit and a new field coil should be fitted.

7 Renew the gearbox gear if the teeth are damaged, chipped or worn.

8 Reassembly is a straightforward reversal of the dismantling sequence, but ensure the following items are lubricated:-

a) Immerse the self-aligning armature bearing in SAE 20 engine oil for 24 hours before assembly.

b) Oil the armature bearings in SAE 20 engine oil.

c) Soak the felt lubricator in the gearbox with SAE 20 engine oil.

d) Grease generously the worm wheel bearings, crosshead, guide channel, connecting rod, crankpin, worm, cable rack and wheel boxes and the final gear shaft.

30 Headlamp sealed beam unit - removal and refitment

1 Remove the three crossheaded screws which retain the half of the radiator grille nearest the lamp unit. Remove the grille half section (photo).

2 Slacken the three screws "A" (Fig. 10.19), turn the lamp unit anticlockwise and disengage it from the screws.

3 Remove the adaptor plug at the rear of the unit as the unit is withdrawn (photo).

4 Refitment is a reversal of removal and headlamp re-alignment is not normally required provided other rim screws have not been altered.

5 When refitting the grille, ensure that the rubber mounting pads engage correctly in the slots (photo).

31 Headlamp - alignment

1 Due to the special equipment, the pair of twin beam headlamps should be adjusted by your Rover dealer. The alignment procedure for twin beam headlamps is not the same as that for single beam systems and if adjustment is attempted it will give unsatisfactory results. In an emergency, the headlamp units can be adjusted individually by means of the two screws shown in Fig. 10.20.

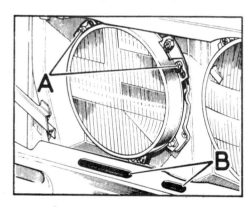

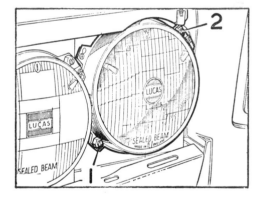

Fig. 10.19. Headlamp sealed beam unit securing screws (A) and rubber grille pad slots (B)

Fig. 10.20. Headlamp adjustment screws (1) horizontal (2) vertical

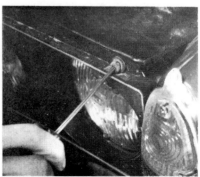

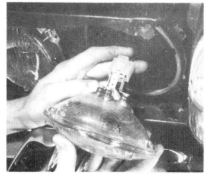

30.1 Radiator grille removal

30.3 Disconnecting sealed beam headlamp plug

30.5 Refitting radiator grille

32 Flasher lamp (front) - early 3500S models - bulb renewal and lamp removal

1   Refer to Fig. 10.21 and remove the two retaining screws "D" which retain the chrome bezel "C".
2   Withdraw the lens "B" and withdraw the bulb "A".
3   If the complete lamp unit is to be removed, disconnect the lead from the battery negative terminal and then remove the lamp to bumper securing bolt and disconnect the leads.
4   Refitment is a reversal of removal.

33 Side and flasher lamps (front) - all later models - bulb renewal and lamp removal

1   Undo and remove the four crosshead screws that secure the light lens to the light body.
2   Lift away the light lens and the foam rubber seal (photo).
3   The bulbs may be renewed at this stage (photo).
4   Undo and remove the three screws that secure the light body to the front wing.
5   The light body may now be withdrawn until the three-way wiring connector is visible. Make a note of the cable connections and disconnect the three cables. Finally lift away the light body.
6   Refitment is the reverse sequence to removal.

34 Tail lamp unit (early 3500 models) - bulb renewal and lamp removal

1   Undo and remove the crosshead screws that secure the light lens to the light body.
2   Lift away the light lens and the foam rubber seal. The bulb may be renewed at this stage.
3   Undo and remove the screws that secures the light body to the rear wing.
4   Make a note of the light unit cable connections at the main wiring harness and disconnect the cable. Attach a piece of string or wire to the tail light wiring when withdrawing it from the body, as it will facilitate the refitting of the wiring through the grommet in the side panel.
5   Carefully withdraw the light unit body and at the same time ease the cables through the grommet.
6   Refitment is a reversal of removal.

35 Tail/flasher/reversing lamps (all later models) - bulb renewal and lamp removal

1   Remove the lens retaining screws as appropriate. It should be noted that the upper lenses overlap the lower ones and access to the lower bulbs can only be obtained after removal of the upper

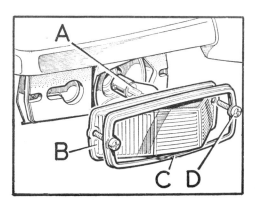

Fig. 10.21. Front flasher (early 3500 S)

A   Bulb   C   Bezel
B   Lens   D   Retaining screw

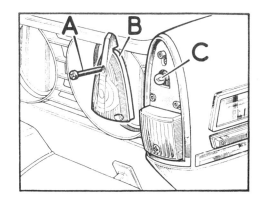

Fig. 10.22. Side lamp (early 3500 S)

A   Screw   C   Bulb lower lens
B   Lens   is decorative

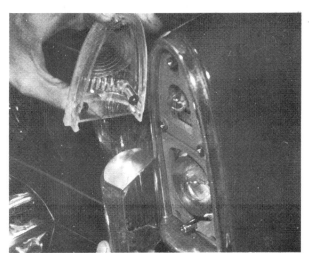

33.2 Front side/flasher lens removal

33.3 Front flasher bulb renewal

lenses (photo).

2 The bulbs are now accessible for removal or replacement (photo).

3 Disconnect the head from the battery negative terminal.

4 Remove the rear wing trim panel from inside the luggage boot.

5 Disconnect the electrical leads at their snap connectors but first note their colour coding. Feed the leads through the grommet in the wing.

6 From outside the car, peel off the foam rubber gasket and withdraw the three screws which hold the lamp unit to the wing. Withdraw the lamp unit complete with electrical leads.

36 Number plate lamp - bulb renewal and lamp removal

1 Refer to the photograph and remove the two cover securing screws "C".

2 Lift off the cover and renew the bulbs as appropriate (photo).

3 If the lamp unit is to be removed, disconnect the lead from the battery negative terminal and then disconnect the lead at the lamp terminal.

4 From inside the rear bumper, remove the two lamp securing screws, detaching the earth lead at the same time.

5 Refitment is a reversal of removal.

37 Reflectors (rear) - after Sept 1970 - removal and refitment

1 Remove the two screws at the base of the reflector and lift the reflector shroud outwards and upwards.

2 Remove the rubber pad and two screws and washers which secure the retainer to the wing. Withdraw the reflector.

3 Refitment is a reversal of removal.

38 Side marker/flasher repeater reflector (3500S - North America) - removal and refitment

1 Insert a hard, thin plastic strip between the reflector chrome rim and its sealing gasket.

2 Prise the reflector away from its wing fixings and peel off the rubber gasket.

3 Refit by banging home with the heel of the hand making sure that the pins and dowel engage correctly.

35.1 Removing rear lamp cluster lens

35.2 Renewing reversing lamp bulb

36.1 Removing number plate lamp cover

36.2 Renewing number plate lamp bulb

39 Front wing side/side marker repeater lamps (3500S - North America) - bulb renewal and lamp removal

1 To renew the bulb in either lamp, remove the lens securing screws and withdraw the lens.
2 To remove the side lamp, disconnect the lead from the battery negative terminal.
3 Remove the lens and bulb and peel back the foam rubber pad to expose the three retaining screws.
4 Remove the screws, disconnect the electrical leads and withdraw the lamp unit.
5 To remove the side marker/repeater lamp, withdraw the lens and bulb.
6 Prise the lamp base and fixings from engagement with the wing. Disconnect the electrical leads.
7 Refitment in both cases is a reversal of removal.

40 Courtesy lamp (interior) - bulb removal

1 The courtesy lamp is operated by a plunger switch located in each of the four door pillars. It is also controlled independently from a switch mounted on the facia panel.
2 To renew the bulb, press the lens upwards, and rotate it in an anticlockwise direction and then withdraw it. Refitment is a reversal of removal (photo).

41 Map reading lamp - bulb renewal

1 Open the glove compartment lid and pull the bulb holder, against the tension of its spring retainers, out of engagement with the lamp unit.
2 Refitment is a reversal of removal.

42 Luggage boot and under bonnet lamps (3500S models) - bulb removal

1 The boot bulb is accessible after removal of the glass cover (two screws).
2 The under bonnet lamp bulb is accessible after rotating the lamp lens in an anticlockwise direction and removing it.

43 Speed selector indicator (auto transmission) - bulb renewal

1 Spring out the indicator plate "A" from the selector lever housing (Fig. 10.26).
2 Slide the indicator plate upwards and detach the festoon type bulb from its carrier.
3 Refitment is a reversal of removal.

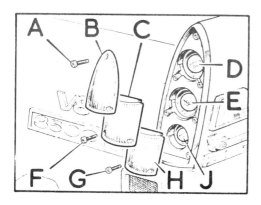

Fig. 10.23. Rear lamp cluster (all late models)

40.2 Removing courtesy lamp cover

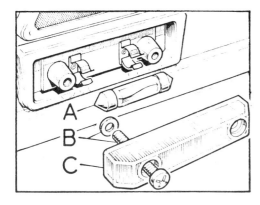

Fig. 10.24. Side marker lamps (U. America) or flasher repeaters

A Festoon bulb   C Lens
B Screw and sealing washer

Fig. 10.25. Map reading lamp

A Bulb   B Holder

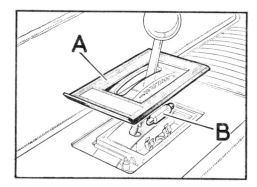

Fig. 10.26. Speed selector (auto. transmission) bulb renewal

A   *Indicator plate*
B   *Festoon bulb*

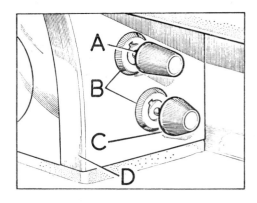

Fig. 10.27. Instrument panel control knobs

A   *Speedometer trip*
B   *Lock ring*
C   *Panel light*
D   *Finisher*

44.2 Detaching instrument panel finisher

44.3 Withdrawing instrument panel casing

44.4 Renewing instrument panel bulb

45.2 Removing instrument securing screw

44 Warning lamp and panel bulbs - renewal

1 Pull off the speedometer trip control and panel light switch knobs (Fig. 10.27). Unscrew the locking rings.
2 Spring off finishers at either end of instrument panel (photo).
3 Remove the retaining screws at each end of the instrument panel and ease the front panel forward away from the instrument (photo).
4 Withdraw the faulty bulb by pulling it straight from its holder (photo). The bulbs used are of the capless type.

45 Instruments - removal and refitment

1 Individual instruments may be removed from their mounting panel after access to them has been gained as described in the preceding Section.
2 Remove the securing screws from the individual instrument (photo) ease it forward and detach the electrical leads from the back.
3 The clock has a fast/slow regulator on its rear face.
4 Removal of the speedometer head will necessitate disconnecting the drive cable (see Sections 48 or 49).
5 Refitting an instrument is a reversal of the removal procedure.

46 Instrument panel (three thousand five) - removal and re-fitment

1 Disconnect the lead from the battery negative terminal.
2 Lift the two securing clips which are located above the warning lights and remove the cover.

3 Remove the top facia rail. To do this, the clock and tachometer will first have to be removed (Figs. 10.28 or 10.29).
4 Disconnect the speedometer cable (Section 48) remove the two panel securing screws and pull the panel forward. Disconnect the instrument wiring but identify the leads and their respective terminals before doing so.
5 Refitment is a reversal of removal.

47 Instrument panel (all later models) - removal and refitment

1 Carry out operations 1, 2 and 3, Section 44.
2 Disconnect the lead from the battery negative terminal.
3 Remove the two panel securing bolts located at each end of the panel.
4 Pull the panel forward and disconnect the speedometer cable (Section 49) leaving the angular drive attached to the rear of the panel.
5 Identify the connecting leads and multi-pin plugs before withdrawing them. Remove the instrument panel.

48 Speedometer cable (three thousand five) - removal and refitment

1 Raise the carpet on the left-hand side of the transmission tunnel and remove the plug which covers the speedometer drive entry to the transmission unit.
2 Remove the exposed nut and retainer which hold the cable to the transmission.
3 From the rear of the speedometer head unscrew the knurled cable securing ring and withdraw the cable assembly.
4 Withdraw the cable complete with sealing grommet through the floor pan.

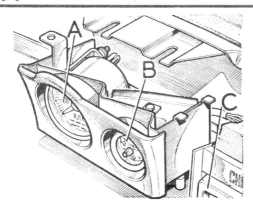

Fig. 10.28. Clock and tachometer (Three thousand five models)

A Tachometer   C Speedometer
B Clock

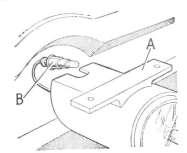

Fig. 10.29. Clock location (without tachometer) (Three thousand five models)

A Casing bracket   B Bulb holder

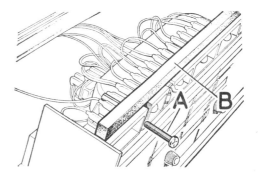

Fig. 10.30. Instrument panel (Three thousand five models)

A Securing screw   B Insulation

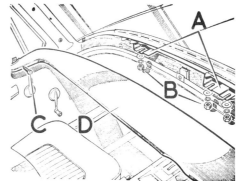

Fig. 10.31. Facia top moulding

A Securing clips   C Screws
B Nuts   D Facia moulding

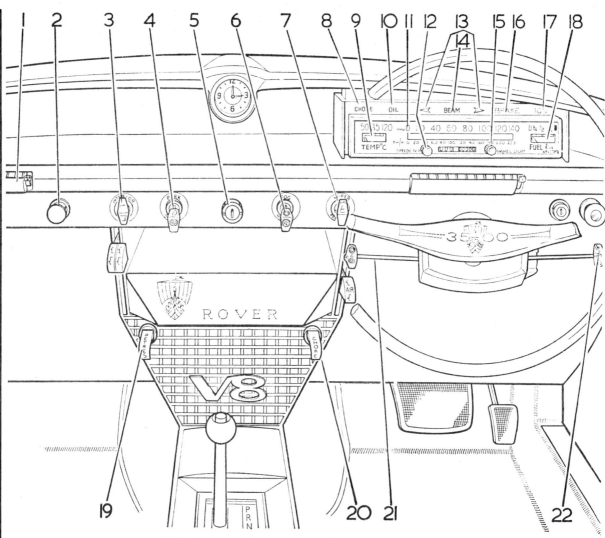

Fig. 10.32. Controls and instrumentation (Three thousand five models)

1 Fresh air vent	7 Wiper switch	13 Direction indicator arrows	18 Fuel gauge
2 Cigar lighter	8 Choke warning lamp	14 Main beam warning	19 Fuel reserve control
3 Interior light switch	9 Temperature gauge	lamp	20 Choke
4 Side lamp switch	10 Oil warning lamp	15 Panel lamp switch	21 Dipper/flasher switch
5 Ignition switch	11 Speedometer	16 Brake warning lamp	22 Direction indicator/horn
6 Headlamp switch	12 Speedometer trip	17 Ignition lamp	switch

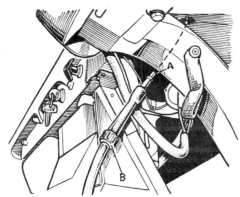

Fig. 10.33. Connection of the speedometer cable to the speedometer head (Three thousand five models)

A Drive cable   B Extension sleeve

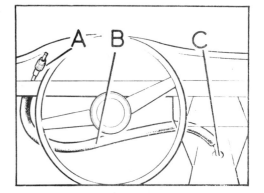

Fig. 10.34. Connection of the speedometer cable to the speedometer head (3500 S models)

A Cable   C Grommet
B Insulating tube

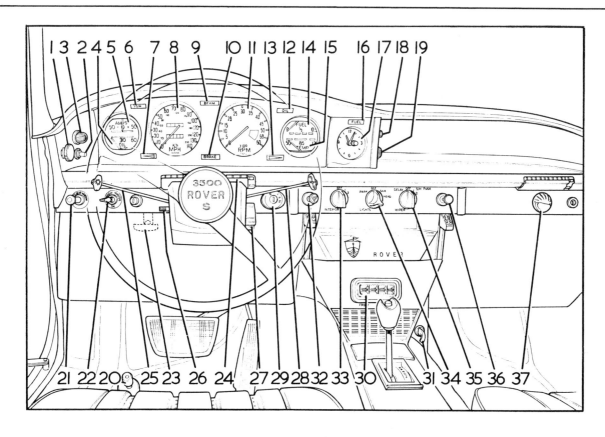

Fig. 10.35. Controls and instrumentation (3500 S up to October 1971)
Layout is similar after this date for both 3500 and 3500 S but latter model fitted with
manual gearbox

1 'Icelert' warning lamp	10 Brake warning lamp	20 Dipper switch
rheostat	11 Tachometer	21 Heated rear window switch
2 'Icelert' lamp test button	12 Oil pressure warning lamp	22 Window lift master switch
3 'Icelert' warning lamp	13 Direction indicator arrow	23 Bonnet release
4 Oil pressure gauge	14 Fuel gauge	24 Fresh air vent
5 Ammeter	15 Water temperature gauge	25 Headlamp flasher
6 Ignition warning lamp	16 Fuel reserve warning lamp	26 Delay control for wipers
7 Direction indicator arrow	17 Clock	27 Steering column rake adjuster
8 Speedometer	18 Speedometer trip knob	28 Direction indicator and horn
9 Main beam warning lamp	19 Panel lamp rheostat	29 Combined ignition, starter

switch and steering column
lock
30 Side window raise and
lower switches
31 Fuel reserve switch
32 Hazard warning switch
33 Interior light switch
34 Side, head and fog lamp
switches
35 Wiper switch
36 Cigar lighter
37 Map reading lamp

5 Refitment is a reversal of removal. If any difficulty is experienced in connecting the cable to the speedometer head then withdraw the instrument as described in Sections 44 and 45.

49 Speedometer cable (3500S models) - removal and refitment

1 Remove the instrument panel (Section 47) and disconnect the speedometer cable from the head by unscrewing the knurled ring.
2 Remove the radio speaker (self-tapping screws).
3 Remove the screws which secure the window lift switch panel, draw the panel forward and disconnect the plugs from the window lift switches.
4 Disconnect the lower end of the cable assembly from the gearbox by following the procedure described in the preceding Section.

50 Steering column stalk switch - removal and refitment

1 The switch controls the following operations according to

model:

    3500 - Headlamp main beam, flasher and dipper
            Direction indicator and horn
    3500S - Headlamp flasher, direction indicator, horn
2 Remove the steering wheel (Chapter 11).
3 Spring off the plastic cover from the steering column nacelle.
4 Disconnect the switch wiring making sure to identify and mark the leads.
5 Remove the switch by unscrewing the securing screws.
6 Refitment is a reversal of removal.

51 Headlamp dipper switch (early 3500S) - removal and re-fitment

1 This is of floor mounted type and is accessible after removal of the driver's side carpet.
2 Mark the electrical leads, remove the securing screws and withdraw the switch.
3 When the switch has been refitted, seal its mounting bracket against the entry of water with a suitable sealant.

52 Switch panel (three thousand five) - removal and refitment

1   Disconnect the lead from the battery negative terminal.
2   Unscrew the locking rings from the glove box locks.
3   Remove the cigar lighter.
4   Slacken the steering column clamp nut, lower the column
and remove the securing nuts and washers which hold the panel
to the bodyshell. These are accessible from behind the panel.
5   Withdraw the panel in two sections and then disconnect the
wiring and switches as required.
6   Refitment is a reversal of removal.

53 Switch panels (all later models) - removal and refitment

1   Disconnect the battery earth lead.
2   To remove the centre panel, pull back the rubber finisher at
each end of the panel and remove the four securing screws.
3   Pull the panel forward and mark the electrical leads before
disconnecting them.
4   Individual switches may be removed after depressing the
knob retaining plunger and removing the knob and then
unscrewing the locking ring.
5   To remove the driver's side switch panel, remove all the
individual switches with the exception of the ignition switch.
6   Unscrew the glove compartment lock locking ring.
7   Slacken the steering column clamp nut and lower the
column.
8   Remove the screw from the bottom edge of the panel nearest
the driver's door.
9   Peel back the rubber finisher on the centre switch panel and
remove the two securing screws.
10 Prise the right-hand side of the ignition switch finisher from
the panel and remove the nut from the rear of the ignition
switch panel. Remove the panel as two halves (flexibly joined).
11 Removal of the switch panel from the passenger side is
similar but the map reading lamp bulb holder must be removed
first.
12 Installation of all three switch panels is a reversal of the
removal procedure.

54 Window winder mechanism (electric) - early 3500S models - removal and refitment

1   The electric motor may be removed from the door cavity in
the following way.
2   Disconnect the lead from the battery negative terminal.
3   Remove the door interior trim panel (Chapter 12).
4   Disconnect the lead plugs at the door switch (rear doors only,
front door switches are facia mounted).
5   Remove the three motor securing screws and withdraw the
motor assembly from the door.
6   Access to the window lift relay and thermal cut-out is
obtained by removing the right-hand glove compartment and
withdrawing the two screws which hold the mounting bracket to
the right-hand side of the console unit.
7   Lift out the bracket and after noting their positions disconnect the electrical leads.
8   Remove the four screws which secure the lift relay and the
thermal cut-out to their mounting brackets.

55 Heated rear screen - general

1   The heater element is of printed circuit type fused to the
glass interior surface.
2   Abrasives must not be used to clean the glass nor must labels
or stickers be removed by scraping.
3   Do not store hard objects on the rear shelf which might
scratch or damage the heater filament material.

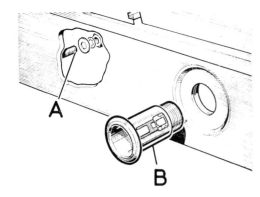

**Fig. 10.36. Switch panel removal (first stage) (Three thousand
five models)**

A   Bolt
B   Cigar lighter

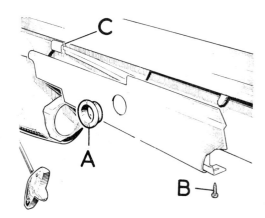

**Fig. 10.37. Switch panel removal (second stage) (Three
thousand five models)**

A   Glove compartment lock locking ring
B   Screw
C   Joint

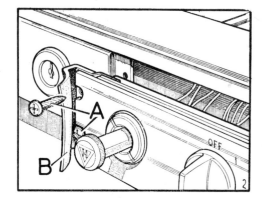

Fig. 10.38. Switch panel securing screws (3500 S models)

A   Securing screws
B   Rubber finisher

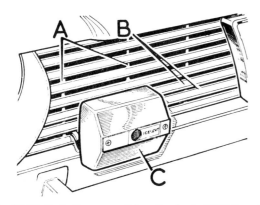

Fig. 10.39. 'Icelert' sensor unit location (early 3500 S models)

A   Radiator grille   *B   Sensor unit*

56 Horn - removal and refitment

1   Twin horns are fitted, one mounted below each of the pairs of headlamps and attached to the bodyframe.
2   Mark the electrical leads and disconnect them from the horn terminals.
3   Unscrew and remove the horn securing bolts.
4   Refitment is a reversal of removal.

57 'Icelert' - description and operation

This device was fitted to the front of early 3500S models. It is essentially a temperature sensing unit which indicates by means of a warning lamp on the facia panel when the road surface temperature is at freezing point. Greater driving care can then be taken particularly in 'black ice' conditions.

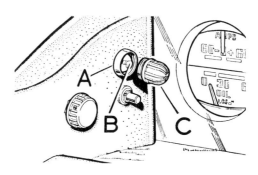

Fig. 10.40. Method of bulb renewal ('Icelert' warning lamp)

A   Bezel   *C   Lens*
B   Bulb

Occasionally depress the test button to check the working of the warning lamp (ignition switched on) if the lamp does not illuminate, renew the bulb.

58 Supplementary lamps - installation

1   Where it is decided to fit fog or pass lights, the following conditions must be observed.
2   The lamp centres must be not less than 2 ft (0.6096 m) from the ground otherwise the lamp can only be used in conditions of fog or falling snow.
3   Two lamps must be installed and operated as a pair. It is wise therefore, to wire them through one switch.
4   Remember to check the depth of the lamps before purchasing them as there is a restricted amount of space only between the bumper or over-riders and the radiator grille.

For 'Fault diagnosis' see next page.

59 Fault diagnosis - Electrical system

Symptom	Reason/s	Remedy
STARTER MOTOR FAILS TO TURN ENGINE		
No electricity at starter motor	Battery discharged	Charge battery.
	Battery defective internally	Fit new battery.
	Battery terminal leads loose or earth lead not securely attached to body	Check and tighten leads.
	Loose or broken connections in starter motor circuit	Check all connections and tighten any that are loose.
	Starter motor switch or solenoid faulty	Test and replace faulty components with new.
Electricity at starter motor: faulty motor	Starter brushes badly worn, sticking, or brush wires loose	Examine brushes, replace as necessary, tighten down brush wires.
	Commutator dirty, worn, or burnt	Clean commutator, recut if badly burnt.
	Starter motor armature faulty	Overhaul starter motor, fit new armature.
	Field coils earthed	Overhaul starter motor.
STARTER MOTOR TURNS ENGINE VERY SLOWLY		
Electrical defects	Battery in discharged condition	Charge battery.
	Starter brushes badly worn, sticking, or brush wires loose	Examine brushes, replace as necessary, tighten down brush wires.
	Loose wires in starter motor circuit	Check wiring and tighten as necessary.
STARTER MOTOR OPERATES WITHOUT TURNING ENGINE		
Mechanical damage	Pinion or flywheel gear teeth broken or worn	Fit new gear ring to flywheel, and new pinion to starter motor drive.
Starter motor noisy or excessively rough engagement	Pinion or flywheel gear teeth broken or worn	Fit new gear teeth to flywheel, or new pinion to starter motor drive.
Lack of attention or mechanical damage	Starter motor retaining bolts loose	Tighten starter motor securing bolts. Fit new spring washer if necessary.
BATTERY WILL NOT HOLD CHARGE		
Wear or damage	Battery defective internally	Remove and fit new battery.
	Electrolyte level too low or electrolyte too weak due to leakage	Top up electrolyte level to just above plates.
	Plate separators no longer fully effective	Remove and fit new battery.
	Battery plates severely sulphated	Remove and fit new battery.
Insufficient current flow to keep battery charged	Fan/alternator belt slipping	Check belt for wear, renew if necessary, and tighten.
	Battery terminal connections loose or corroded	Check terminals for tightness, and remove all corrosion.
	Alternator not charging properly	Remove and overhaul.
	Short in lighting circuit causing continual battery drain	Trace and rectify.
	Regulator unit not working correctly	Check setting, adjust or renew if defective.
IGNITION LIGHT FAILS TO GO OUT, BATTERY RUNS FLAT		
Alternator not charging	Fan belt loose and slipping, or broken	Check, replace, and tighten as necessary.
	Brushes worn, sticking, broken or dirty.	Examine, clean, or replace brushes as necessary.
	Brush springs weak or broken	Examine and test. Replace as necessary.
	Internal fault in alternator or control circuit	Seek specialists advice.

Failure of individual electrical equipment to function correctly is dealt with alphabetically, item by item, under the headings listed below.

Fuel gauge gives no reading	Fuel tank empty!	Fill fuel tank.
	Electric cable between tank sender unit and gauge earthed or loose	Check cable for earthing and joints for tightness.
	Fuel gauge case not earthed	Ensure case is well earthed.
	Fuel gauge supply cable interrupted	Check and replace cable if necessary.
	Fuel gauge unit broken	Replace fuel gauge.

Symptom	Reason/s	Remedy
Fuel gauge registers full all the time	Electric cable between tank unit and gauge broken or disconnected	Check over cable and repair as necessary.
Horn operates all the time	Horn push either earthed or stuck down	Disconnect battery earth. Check and rectify source of trouble.
	Horn cable to horn push earthed	Disconnect battery earth. Check and rectify source of trouble.
Horn fails to operate	Blown fuse	Check and renew if broken. Ascertain cause.
	Cable or cable connection loose, broken or disconnected	Check all connections for tightness and cables for breaks.
	Horn has an internal fault	Remove and overhaul horn.
Horn emits intermittent or unsatisfactory noise	Cable connections loose	Check and tighten all connections.
	Horn incorrectly adjusted	Adjust horn until best note obtained.
Lights do not come on	If engine not running, battery discharged	Push-start car (manual gearbox) and charge battery.
	Light bulb filament burnt out or bulbs broken	
	Wire connections loose, disconnected or broken	Check all connections for tightness and wire cable for breaks.
	Light switch shorting or otherwise faulty	By-pass light switch to ascertain if fault is in switch and fit new switch as appropriate.
Lights come on but fade out	If engine not running battery discharged	Push-start car (manual gearbox) and charge battery.
Lights give very poor illumination	Lamp glasses dirty	Clean glasses.
	Reflector tarnished or dirty	Fit new reflectors.
	Lamps badly out of adjustment	Adjust lamps correctly.
	Incorrect bulb with too low wattage fitted	Remove bulb and replace with correct grade.
	Existing bulbs old and badly discoloured	Renew bulb units.
	Electrical wiring too thin not allowing full current to pass	Re-wire lighting system.
Lights work erratically - flashing on and off especially over bumps	Battery terminals or earth connection loose	Tighten battery terminals and earth connection.
	Lights not earthing properly	Examine and rectify.
	Contacts in light switch faulty	By-pass light switch to ascertain if fault is in switch and fit new switch as appropriate.
Wiper motor fails to work	Blown fuse	Check and replace fuse if necessary.
	Wire connections loose, disconnected, or broken	Check wiper wiring. Tighten loose connections.
	Brushes badly worn	Purchase reconditioned wiper motor.
	Armature worn or faulty	Purchase reconditioned wiper motor.
	Field coils faulty	Purchase reconditioned wiper motor.
Wiper motor works very slowly and takes excessive current	Commutator dirty, greasy, or burnt	Examine drive and straighten out severe curvature. Lubricate.
	Drive to wheelboxes too bent or unlubricated.	
	Wheelbox spindle binding or damaged	Remove, overhaul, or fit replacement.
	Armature bearings dry or unaligned	Remove, overhaul, or fit replacement.
	Armature badly worn or faulty	Remove, overhaul, or fit replacement.
Wiper motor works slowly and takes little current	Brushes badly worn	Fit replacement unit.
	Commutator dirty, greasy, or burnt	Fit replacement unit
	Armature badly worn or faulty	Fit replacement unit.
Wiper motor works but wiper blades remain static	Driving cable rack disengaged or faulty	Examine and if faulty, renew.
	Wheelbox gear and spindle damaged or worn	Overhaul or fit new gearbox.
	Wiper motor gearbox parts badly worn	

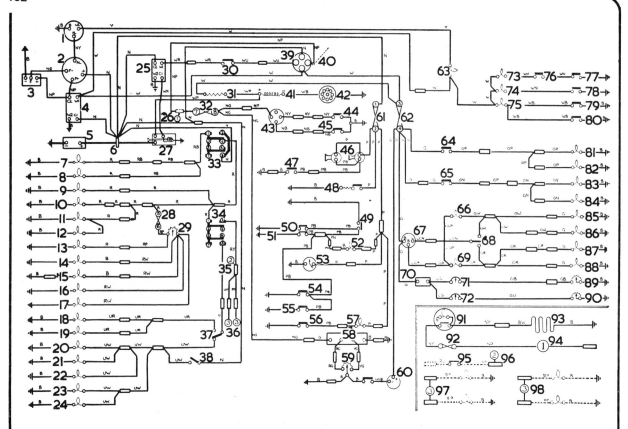

Key to circuit diagram, Three thousand five RHD models

1 Relay for ignition warning light	34 Switch for headlamps	66 Warning light indicator, LH
2 Alternator	35 Pick-up point for long-range	67 Direction indicator unit
3 Control box, 4TR	driving lamp switch	68 Switch for direction indicator
4 Relay for alternator	36 Pick-up points for long-range	69 Warning light, indicator, RH
5 Battery, 60 AH	driving lamps	70 Bi-metal voltage regulator
6 Terminal post	37 Switch for headlamp, dip	71 Fuel gauge
7 Side and park lamp, RH	38 Switch for headlamp, flash	72 Temperature gauge
8 Tail and park lamp, RH	39 Switch for ignition and starter	73 Warning light for choke
9 Side lamp, LH	40 Pick-up point for radio feed and	74 Warning light for oil pressure
10 Tail lamp, LH	illumination	75 Warning light for brake fluid level and
11 Number plate illumination	41 Ignition coil	handbrake
12 Number plate illumination	42 Distributor	76 Switch for choke control
13 Cigar lighter illumination	43 Heater blower unit, 2-speed	77 Thermostat switch for choke control
14 Clock illumination	44 Switch, fast speed, heater blower	78 Switch for oil pressure warning light
15 Automatic transmission gear selector	45 Switch, slow speed, into blower	79 Switch for handbrake
illumination	46 Twin horns	80 Switch for brake fluid level
16 Panel illumination	47 Switch for horns	81 Stop lamp, RH
17 Panel illumination	48 Cigar lighter and switch	82 Stop lamp, LH
18 Headlamp dip beam , LH	49 Switch for interior light	83 Reverse lamp, RH
19 Headlamp dip beam, RH	50 Switch for front door, LH	84 Reverse lamp, LH
20 Headlamp main beam, RH	51 Switch for front door, RH	85 Direction indicator lamp, front RH
21 Headlamp main beam, RH	52 Interior light	86 Direction indicator lamp, rear RH
22 Warning light for headlamp main beam	53 Clock	87 Direction indicator lamp, rear LH
23 Headlamp main beam, LH	54 Switch for rear door, RH	88 Direction indicator lamp, front LH
24 Headlamp main beam, LH	55 Switch for rear door, LH	89 Fuel level indicator in fuel tank
25 Relay for starter motor	56 Switch for boot light	90 Transmitter for water temperature
26 Pick-up point for heated backlight	57 Boot lamp	91 Illuminated switch for heated backlight
27 Starter motor, pre-engaged type	58 Screen wiper motor	92 In-line fuse for heated backlight
28 Fuse, 5 - 6, 2 amp	59 Switch for wiper and screen washer	93 Heated backlight
29 Rheostat switch for panel illum-	60 Screen washer	94 Pick-up point for heated backlight
ination	61 Fuse, 1 - 2, 35 amp	95 Switch for long-range driving lamp
30 Inhibitor switch for automatic	62 Fuse, 3 - 4, 35 amp	switch
transmission	63 Warning light for ignition	96 Pick-up point for long-range driving
31 Ballast resistor	64 Switch for stop lamp	lamp switch
32 Fuse, 7 - 8, 15 amp	65 Switch for reverse lamps	97 Pick-up point and long-range driving lamps
33 Switch, for side and park lamps		98 Pick-up point and long-range driving lamps

Key to cable colours

B — Black   G — Green   LG — Light green   N — Brown   R — Red   W — White   U — Blue

Y — Yellow   P — Purple

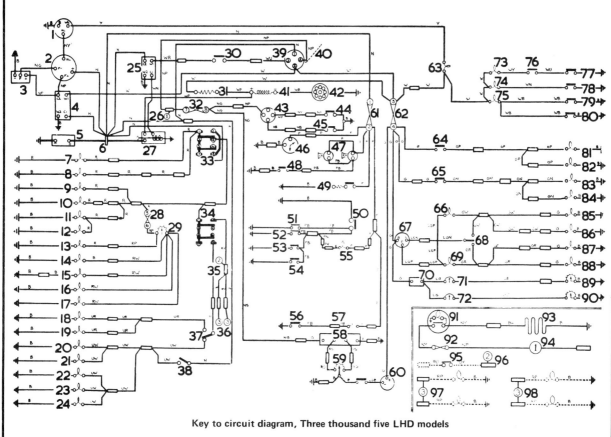

Key to circuit diagram, Three thousand five LHD models

1	Relay for ignition warning light
2	Alternator
3	Control box, 4TR
4	Relay for alternator
5	Battery, 60 AH
6	Terminal post
7	Side and park lamp, LH
8	Tail and park lamp, LH
9	Side lamp, RH
10	Tail lamp, RH
11	Number plate illumination
12	Number plate illumination
13	Cigar lighter illumination
14	Clock illumination
15	Automatic transmission gear selector illumination
16	Panel illumination
17	Panel illumination
18	Headlamp dip beam, LH
19	Headlamp dip beam, RH
20	Headlamp main beam, RH
21	Headlamp main beam, RH
22	Warning light for headlamp main beam
23	Headlamp main beam, LH
24	Headlamp main beam, LH
25	Relay for starter motor
26	Pick-up point for heated backlight
27	Starter motor, pre-engaged type
28	Fuse, 5 - 6, 2 amp
29	Rheostat switch for panel illumination
30	Inhibitor switch for automatic transmission
31	Ballast resistor
32	Fuse, 7 - 8, 15 amp
33	Switch for side and park lamp
34	Switch for headlamps
35	Pick-up point for long-range driving lamp switch
36	Pick-up point for long-range driving lamps
37	Switch for headlamp, dip
38	Switch for headlamp, flash
39	Switch for ignition and starter
40	Pick-up point for radio feed and illumination
41	Ignition coil
42	Distributor
43	Heater, blower unit, 2-speed
44	Switch, fast speed, heater blower
45	Switch, slow speed, heater blower
46	Clock
47	Twin horns
48	Switch for horns
49	Cigar lighter and switch
50	Switch for interior light
51	Switch for front door, LH
52	Switch for front door, RH
53	Switch for rear door, RH
54	Switch for rear door, LH
55	Interior light
56	Switch for boot light
57	Boot lamp
58	Screen wiper motor
59	Switch for screen wiper and screen washer
60	Screen washer
61	Fuse, 1 - 2, 35 amp
62	Fuse, 3 - 4, 35 amp
63	Warning light for ignition
64	Switch for reverse lamp
65	Switch for reverse lamp
66	Warning light for direction indicator, LH
67	Direction indicator unit
68	Switch for direction indicator
69	Warning light for direction indicator, RH
70	Bi-metal voltage regulator
71	Fuel gauge
72	Temperature gauge
73	Warning light for choke
74	Warning light for oil pressure
75	Warning light for brake fluid level and handbrake
76	Switch for choke control
77	Thermostatic switch for choke control
78	Switch for oil pressure warning light
79	Switch for handbrake
80	Switch for brake fluid level
81	Stop lamp, RH
82	Stop lamp, LH
83	Reverse lamp, RH
84	Reverse lamp, LH
85	Direction indicator lamp, front RH
86	Direction indicator lamp, rear RH
87	Direction indicator lamp, rear LH
88	Direction indicator lamp, front LH
89	Fuel level indicator in fuel tank
90	Transmitter for water temperature
91	Illuminated switch for heated backlight
92	In-line fuse for heated backlight
93	Heated backlight
94	Pick-up point for heated backlight
95	Switch for long-range driving lamp
96	Pick-up point for long-range driving lamp
97	Pick-up point for long-range driving lamp
98	Pick-up point for long-range driving lamp

Key to cable colours

B — Black G — Green LG — Light green N — Brown R — Red W — White U — Blue
Y — Yellow P — Purple

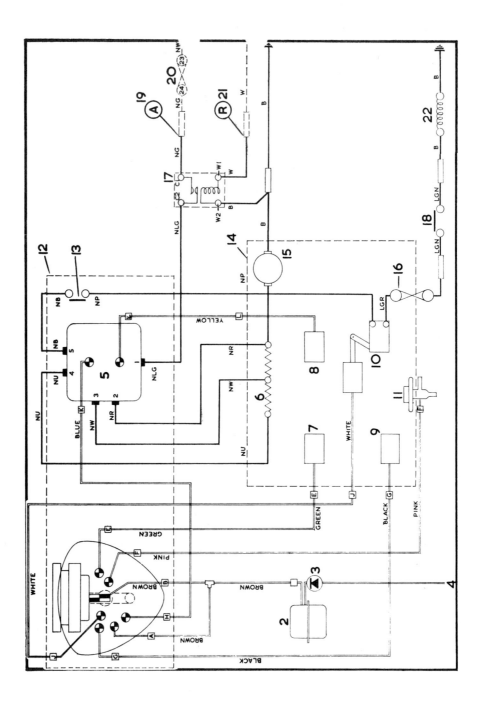

Circuit diagram, 3500 S air conditioning system

185

Key to circuit diagram, 3500 S air conditioning system

Encircled letters are pick-up points and relate to the main circuit diagrams, Part one and Part two
Double light lines represent vacuum pipe connections
Single heavy lines represent electrical circuit

1 Diverter-modulator
2 Vacuum reserve tank
3 Non-return valve
4 To inlet manifold
5 Diverter-switch
6 Resistor for blower motor
7 Mode valve
8 Fresh air circulation
9 Defrost circulation
10 Variable thermostat
11 Water valve

12 Dotted lines indicate switch box on console unit
13 Switch, air conditioning isolation
14 Dotted lines indicate heater-cooler unit
15 Blower motor
16 In-line fuse, 10 amp
17 Relay, 6RA
18 Switch, high pressure cut-out
19 Pick-up point at fuse box
20 Fuse 23 - 24, 35 amp
21 Pick-up point at 'A' post body connections
22 Electro-magnetic clutch

Key to cable colours

B — Black
G — Green
NG — Brown/green
Y — Yellow
BW — Black/white
P — Purple
PN — Purple/brown

PW — Purple/white
PY — Purple/yellow
RP — Red/purple
RY — Red/yellow
UB — Blue/black
UY — Blue/yellow
W — White

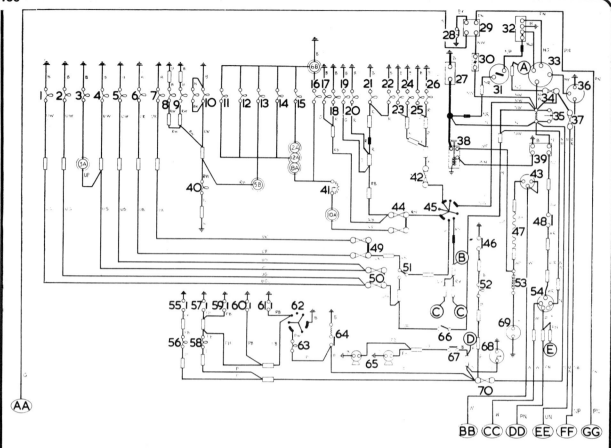

Key to circuit diagram, 3500 S models, Part one

Encircled letters "AA" to 'GG' relate to Part two of the circuit diagram
Encircled figures and letters denote printed circuit and plug pick-up points on printed circuit board. Figure for pin number, letter for plug

1	Headlamp, main beam, LH outer	25	Side marker lamp, front LH
2	Headlamp main beam, RH outer	26	Side-park lamp LH. RH on RH stg. Colour code RB
3	Warning light, main beam. RH stg. models. Connected to headlamp main beam RH inner	27	Battery
4	Headlamp main beam, LH inner	28	Switch, window lift isolation
5	Headlamp main beam, RH inner	29	Relay 6RA, window lift
6	Headlamp dip beam, RH	30	Thermal cut-out, window lift
7	Headlamp dip beam, LH	31	Switch, alternator, isolation
8	Window lift switch	32	
9	Illumination	33	Alternator
10		34	Fuse 23 - 24, 35 amp
11		35	Ammeter
12		36	Relay, 3AW ignition warning light
13	Instrument panel illumination	37	Fuse 21 - 22, 25 amps
14		38	Starter motor, pre-engaged
15		39	Relay, 6RA, starter motor
16		40	Gear selector illumination
17	Side marker lamp, front RH	41	Switch, panel lights
18	Side lamp, RH, LH on RH stg. Colour code R	42	Fuse 5 - 6, 5 amp
19	Side marker lamp, rear RH	43	Tachometer
20	Tail lamp, RH. LH on RH stg. Colour code R	44	Fuse 7 - 8 and 9 - 10, 5 amp
21	Number plate	45	Switch, main lights
22	Illumination	46	Switch, hood light
23	Side marker lamp, rear LH	47	Resistive cable
24	Tail-park lamp, LH. RH on RH stg. Colour code RB	48	Switch, inhibitor, automatic transmission

49	Fuse 15 - 16 and 17 - 18, 10 amp
50	Fuse 11 - 12, 25 amp and 13 - 14 15 amps
51	Switch, headlamps dip
52	Under hood lamp
53	Ignition coil
54	Switch, ignition and steering column lock
55	Switch, trunk light
56	Trunk light
57	Switch, rear door RH
58	Interior light in roof
59	Switch, rear door LH
60	Switch, front door RH
61	Switch, front door LH
62	Switch, interior and map light
63	Map light, above glove box
64	Cigar lighter and switch
65	Electric horns
66	Switch, headlamp flash
67	Switch, horns
68	Clock
69	Distributor
70	Fuse 1 - 2, 35 amp

Key to cable colours

B	Black	NY	Brown/Yellow	RN	Red/Brown	UN	Blue/Brown	WB	White/Black
G	Green	P	Purple	RP	Red/Purple	UP	Blue/Purple	WK	White/Pink
N	Brown	PB	Purple/Black	RW	Red/White	UR	Blue/Red	WN	White/Brown
NB	Brown/Black	PN	Purple/Brown	RY	Red/Yellow	UW	Blue/Yellow	WP	White/Purple
NG	Brown/Green	PW	Purple/White	U	Blue	UW	Blue/Yellow	WR	White/Red
NR	Brown/Red	R	Red	UB	Blue/Black	UY	Blue/Yellow	WU	White/Blue
NW	Brown/White	RB	Red/Black	UG	Blue/Green	W	White	WY	White/Yellow
								UK	Blue/Pink

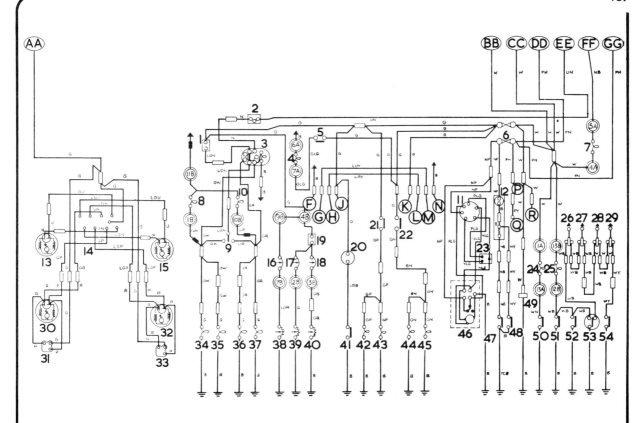

Key to circuit diagram, 3500 S models, Part two

Encircled letters 'AA' to 'GG' relate to Part one of the circuit diagram
Encircled figures and letters denote printed circuit and plug pick-up points on printed circuit board. Figure for pin number, letter for plug

1   Flasher unit, 8FL
2   Hazard flasher unit
3   Switch and warning light, hazard flasher
4   Warning light, fuel reserve
5   Switch, fuel reserve
6   Fuses 3 - 4, 35 amp and 19 - 20, 25 amp
7   Warning light, ignition
8   Warning light, indicator arrow RH
9   Switch, flasher lights
10 Warning light, indicator arrow LH
11 Switch, windshield wiper
12 Heater motor
13 Motor, window lift, RH front
14 Switch, 4-way, window lift
15 Motor, window lift, RH front
16 Oil pressure gauge
17 Water temperature gauge
18 Fuel gauge
19 Regulator, 10 volt
20 Windshield washer

21 Switch, stop light
22 Switch, reverse light
23 Delay governor, windshield wiper
24 Warning light, oil pressure
25 Warning light, brake fluid reservoirs, shuttle valve and pad wear indicators
26 Brake pad wear warning electrode, front RH
27 Brake pad wear warning electrode, front LH
28 Brake pad wear warning electrode, rear RH
29 Brake pad wear warning electrode, rear LH
30 Motor, window lift, LH rear
31 Switch, window lift, LH rear door
32 Motor, window lift, RH rear
33 Switch, window lift, RH rear door
34 Direction indicator lamp, rear RH
35 Direction indicator lamp, rear LH

36 Direction indicator lamp, rear LH
37 Direction indicator lamp, front LH
38 Transmitter, oil pressure
39 Transmitter, water temperature
40 Fuel level indicator in tank
41 Switch, windshield washer
42 Stop lamp, LH
43 Stop lamp, RH
44 Reverse lamp, LH
45 Reverse lamp, RH
46 Motor, windshield wiper
47 Switch, heater motor, slow speed
48 Switch, heater motor, fast speed
49 Fuel pump
50 Switch, oil pressure
51 Switch, brake fluid reservoir, master cylinder
52 Switch, brake fluid reservoir, servo unit
53 Switch, brake shuttle valve
54 Switch, handbrake

Key to cable colours

B — Black	GW — Green/White	NLG — Brown/Light Green	U — Blue
G — Green	LGN — Light Green/Brown	NB — Brown/Black	LGU — Light Green/Blue
GB — Green/Black	LGP — Light Green/Purple	NP — Brown/Purple	RLG — Red/Light Green
GLG — Green/Light Green	LGR — Light Green/Red	NY — Brown/Yellow	W — White
GP — Green/Purple	LRY — Light Red/Yellow	P — Purple	WB — White/Black
GR — Green/Red	LUY — Light Blue/Yellow	PN — Purple/Brown	WY — White/Yellow
GU — Green/Blue	N — Brown	R — Red	

Key to circuit diagram Rover 3500 Automatic 'New Look' models Chassis Suffix 'B' and 3500 S manual Chassis Suffix 'A'

Encircled figures and letters denote printed circuit and plug pick-up points on printed circuit board. Figure for pin number, letter for plug

1　Alternator 11 AC
2　Control box, 4TR for alternator
3　Battery, 12 volt
4　Terminal post
5　Starter motor
6　Relay for starter motor
7　Side lamp LH
8　Tail lamp LH　　　　　　　　　7 - 8 and,
9　Pick-up point for trailer socket　13 - 14—
10　Number plate illumination.　　reversed on
11　Number plate illumination　　LH stg.
12　Pick-up point for trailer socket　models
13　Tail lamp and park RH
14　Side lamp and park RH
15　Instrument panel illumination
16　Switch
17　Automatic transmission, indicator plate illumination
18　Headlamp dip beam LH
19　Headlamp dip beam RH
20　Headlamp main beam, outer LH
21　Headlamp main beam, outer RH
22　Warning light, main beam
23　Headlamp main beam, inner LH
24　Headlamp main beam, inner RH
25　Switch, heater, slow speed
26　Switch, heater, fast speed
27　Heater motor
28　Relay for ignition warning light
29　Warning light, ignition
30　Tachometer
31　Ballast resistor (cable)
32　Ignition coil
33　Distributor
34　Switch, automatic transmission inhibitor
35　Switch, ignition (steering column lock)
36　Pick-up point for radio
37　Ammeter
38　Pick-up point for auxiliary lamps
39　Switch, main lighting
40　Pick-up points for heater or air conditioning (connect as required)
41　Switch, headlamp, dip
42　Switch, headlamp, flash

43　Fuse 5 - 6, 5 amp for side light and tail light RH　　　　Reversed on LH
44　Fuse 7 - 8, 5 amp side light and tail light LH, number plate illumination　stg. models
45　Fuse 9 - 10, 8 amp, instrument panel, switch panel and gear change selection illumination
46　Fuse 17 - 18, 10 amp, headlamp LH dip
47　Fuse 15 - 16, 10 amp headlamp RH dip
48　Fuse 13 - 14, 15 amp, headlamp main outer
49　Fuse 11 - 12, 25 amp, headlamp main inner and main beam warning light
50　Fuse 23 - 24, 15 amp heater
51　Fuse 3 - 4, 25 amp, hazard warning
52　Fuse 1 - 2, 25 amp, horns, clock, cigar lighter, interior lights
53　Switch, instrument panel illumination
54　Electric horns
55　Switch for horns
56　Clock
57　Cigar lighter
58　Switch, interior lights
59　Switch, front door LH
60　Map light
61　Switch, front door RH
62　Switch, rear door LH
63　Switch, rear door RH
64　Interior light centre
65　Pick-up point for trailer socket
66　Switch, boot light
67　Boot light
68　Flasher unit, hazard warning
69　Pick-up point for air conditioning
70　Pick-up point for air conditioning
71　Heated backlight
72　Brake pad wear warning electrodes, rear
73　Brake pad wear warning electrodes, front
74　Pick-up point for dual-line brakes (where fitted)
75　In-line fuse 25 amp for heated backlight
76　Switch for heated backlight
77　Relay for heater and heated backlight
78　Switch, screen wiper
79　Delay governor, screen wiper
80　Screen wiper motor

81　Fuse 21 - 22, 25 amp, screen washer, stop lamps, reverse lamps, gauges and flashers
82　Fuse 19 - 20, 25 amp, screen wiper switch, delay governor and screen wiper
83　Switch, stop lamp
84　Pick-up point for mechanical stop lamp switch (when fitted)
85　Switch, reverse light or automatic transmission inhibitor
86　Regulator, 10 volt, fuel and water temperature gauge
87　Flasher unit 8 FL
88　Pick-up point for trailer socket
89　Hazard switch and warning light
90　Warning light, choke
91　Switch, choke warning light
92　Switch, choke warning light in cylinder head
93　Warning light, oil pressure
94　Switch, oil pressure warning light
95　Warning light, brake
96　Switch, brake fluid reservoir
97　Switch, handbrake
98　Screen washer reservoir motor
99　Switch, screen washer
100　Pick-up point for trailer socket
101　Stop lamp RH
102　Stop lamp LH
103　Reverse lamp RH
104　Reverse lamp LH
105　Fuel gauge
106　Tank unit for fuel gauge
107　Water temperature gauge
108　Transmitter for water temperature gauge
109　Oil pressure gauge
110　Transmitter, oil pressure gauge
111　Indicator, front LH
112　Indicator, rear LH
113　Warning light indicator LH
114　Switch indicators
115　Warning light indicators RH
116　Indicator, rear RH
117　Indicator, front RH

189

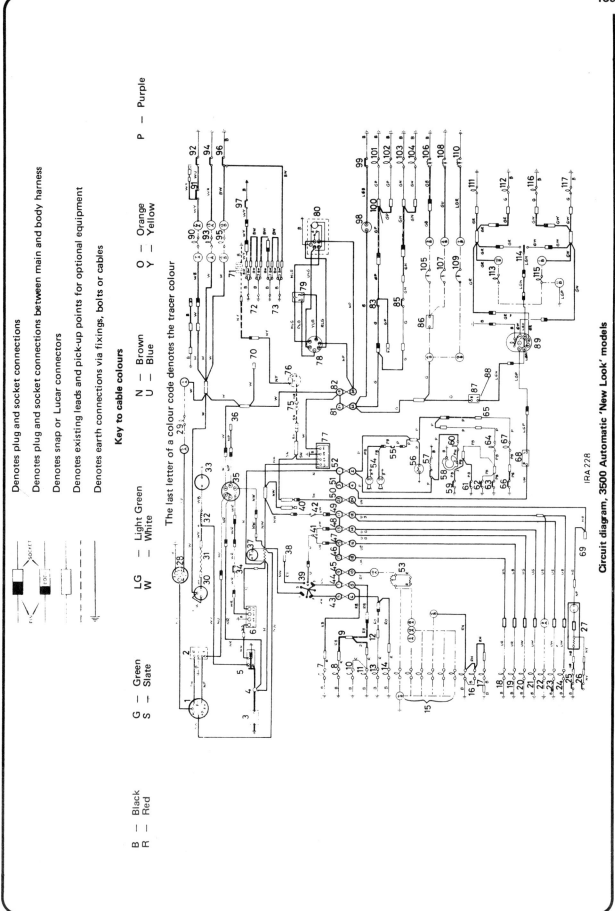

Circuit diagram, 3500 Automatic 'New Look' models

Key to cable colours

The last letter of a colour code denotes the tracer colour

Denotes plug and socket connections

Denotes plug and socket connections between main and body harness

Denotes snap or Lucar connectors

Denotes existing leads and pick-up points for optional equipment

Denotes earth connections via fixings, bolts or cables

B — Black
R — Red

G — Green
S — Slate

LG — Light Green
W — White

N — Brown
U — Blue

O — Orange
Y — Yellow

P — Purple

IRA 228

Key to circuit diagram Rover 3500 Automatic 'New Look' models Chassis Suffix 'A' (September 1970 onwards)

Encircled figures denote pick-up points for optional extra equipment
Encircled letters and figures denote printed circuit and plug pick-up points on printed circuit board. Figure denotes pin number, letter denotes plug

1 Relay for ignition warning light, type 3AW
2 Alternator, Lucas, type 11AC
3 Control box, Lucas, type 4TR
4 Relay for starter motor
5 Alternator contacts, ignition switch
6 Battery
7 Side and park lamp
8 Tail and park lamp
9 Side lamp
10 Tail lamp
11 Number plate illumination
12 Number plate illumination
13 Instrument panel illumination
14 Switch panel illumination
15 Headlamp dip beam, LH
16 Headlamp dip beam, RH
17 Headlamp main beam, RH
18 Headlamp main beam, RH
19 Warning light for headlamp main beam
20 Headlamp main beam, LH
21 Headlamp main beam, LH
22 Steering column lock switch
23 Ammeter shunt
24 Starter motor, pre-engaged
25 Pick-up point for auxiliary lamps
26 Fuses 5 and 6, 2 amp
27 Pick-up point for air conditioning circuit
28 Fuses 7 and 8, 35 amp
29 Main lighting switch
30 Rheostat for panel lights
31 Ballast resistor
32 Illumination for gear selector
33 Switch for headlamp dip

34 Pick-up point for headlamp flash, special markets
35 Switch for headlamp flash
36 Screen wiper motor
37 Pick-up point for heated backlight
38 Pick-up point for radio
39 Pick-up point for air conditioning circuit
40 Heater blower unit, two-speed
41 Fuses, 1, 2, 3 and 4, 35 amp
42 Twin horns
43 Switch for horns
44 Cigar lighter and switch
45 Hazard warning flasher unit
46 In-line fuse
47 Rotary map light
48 Switch for front door, LH
49 Switch for front door, RH
50 Switch for interior light
51 Interior light
52 Clock
53 Switch for rear door, RH
54 Switch for rear door, LH
55 Boot lamp
56 Switch for windscreen wiper
57 Delay switch for windscreen wiper
58 Warning light for ignition
59 Warning light for choke
60 Warning light for oil pressure
61 Warning light for brake fluid reservoir, hand brake and pad wear indicators
62 Ballast resistor cable
63 Tachometer
64 Switch for reverse lamps
65 Switch and warning light for hazard warning

66 Flasher unit, type 8FL
67 Warning light, indicator, LH
68 Warning light, indicator, RH
69 Bi-metal voltage regulator for instruments
70 Fuel contents gauge
71 Coolant temperature gauge
72 Oil pressure gauge
73 Screen washer motor
74 Switch for stop lights, hydraulic
75 Pick-up point, stop light switch, mechanical
76 Switch for choke control
77 Thermostat switch for choke control
78 Switch for oil pressure warning light
79 Brake pad wear warning electrode, rear LH
80 Brake pad wear warning electrode, rear RH
81 Switch for handbrake warning light
82 Brake pad wear warning electrode, front RH
83 Brake pad wear warning electrode, front LH
84 Pick-up point for dual braking system
85 Ignition coil
86 Distributor
87 Reverse lamp, RH
88 Reverse lamp, LH
89 Direction indicator lamp, front LH
90 Direction indicator lamp, rear LH
91 Direction indicator switch
92 Direction indicator lamp, rear RH
93 Direction indicator lamp, front RH
94 Tank unit, fuel contents gauge
95 Transmitter, coolant temperature
96 Transmitter, oil pressure
97 Switch for screen washer
98 Stop lamp, RH
99 Stop lamp, LH

Key to cable colours

B – Black
G – Green
LG – Light Green
N – Brown
P – Purple
R – Red
W – White
U – Blue
Y – Yellow

The last letter of a colour code denotes the tracer colour

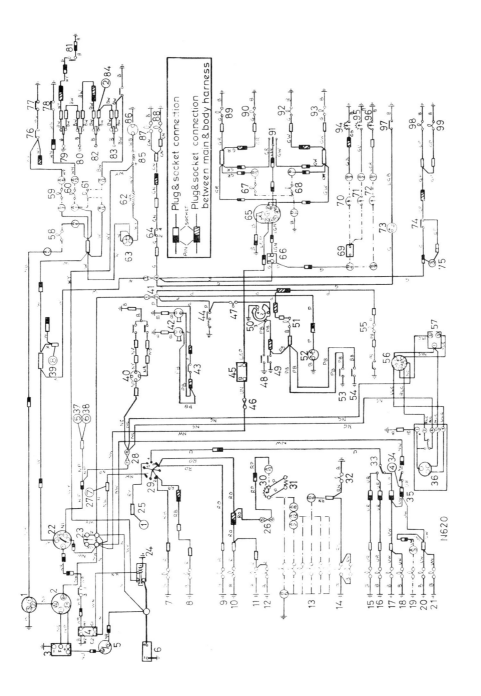

Circuit diagram, 3500 Automatic 'New Look' models
Chassis Suffix 'A'

Plug & socket connection

Plug & socket connection
between main & body harness

Chapter 11 Suspension and steering

Contents

Specifications

Front suspension:

Type ... ...   Independent with horizontal coil springs and hydraulic shock absorbers and anti-roll bar

Coil springs (Three thousand five and 3500):
Number of working coils 6 3/8
Free length ... ...   16.281 in. (413.5 mm)

Coil springs (3500S):
Number of working coils 7 1/3
Free length ... ...   17.12 in. (434.8 mm)

Shock absorbers:
Type ... ...   Telescopic, double acting, hydraulic

Rear suspension:

Type ... ...   Semi-independent, de Dion tube, coil springs, telescopic shock absorbers and stabiliser rod

Coil springs	Three thousand five up to chassis suffix A	Three thousand five from suffix B. All other models
Number of working coils	5½	5.4
Free length	13.312 in. (338.0 mm)	13.218 in. (335.7 mm)

de Dion tube:
Capacity ... ...   1/3 pint (0.2 litre) SAE 20W

Manual steering:

Type ... ...   Burman F3, recirculating ball, variable ratio

Ratio	Variable 25.1 : 1 (straight ahead) 26.0 : 1 (on lock)	
Steering wheel turns (lock-to-lock)	4¼	
Turning circle (between kerbs)	31.5 ft. (9.6 m)	

Power steering:

Type	Adwest - Varamatic	
Ratio	Variable 19.3 : 1 (straight ahead) 15.4 : 1 (on lock)	
Steering wheel turns (lock-to-lock)	3¼	
Turning circle (between kerbs)	31.5 ft. (9.6 m)	
Fluid capacity	4 pints (2 litres)	

Wheels and tyres:

Wheels:

Type	5½ JSL x 14 in.	
Nuts	7/16 in. U.N.F.	

Tyres:	185 x HR 14	
Pressures (cold)	FRONT	REAR
Two passengers and luggage	28	30
Four passengers and luggage	30	34

Steering geometry*:

Camber	$0^o \pm 1^o$
Castor angle	$1\frac{1}{2}^o$ positive $\pm \frac{1}{2}^o$
Steering axis inclination	8°
Toe-in	1/8 in. (3.0 mm) $\pm$ 1/16 in. (1.5 mm)

checked with car unladen and five gallons of fuel in tank.

Torque wrench settings:	lb/ft	kg m
Front suspension:		
Caliper to suspension member	60	8.5
Top ball joint nut	55 to 85	7.5 to 11.5
Bottom ball joint nut	60 to 75	8.5 to 10.0
Bottom link strut to ball joint	60 to 75	8.5 to 10.0
Bottom link to bodyshell	54	7.5
Bottom link strut to bodyshell	54	7.5
Bottom link to swivel pillar	60 to 75	8.5 to 10.0
Top link securing bolts	30	4.0
Anti-roll bar cap bolts	30	4.0
Rear suspension:		
Bottom link bolts	54	7.5
de Dion tube/elbows	8	1.0
Top link bolts	54	7.5
Wheel hub housing to de Dion tube	20	2.7
Axle flange to disc	85	11.5
Steering:		
Drop arm nut	130	17.9
Power steering valve cap (pump)	35	4.9
Power steering box cover bolts	42	6.0

1 General description

Upon inspection of the front suspension system as shown in Fig. 11.1 it will be seen that it is of a rather unusual design whereby coil springs are mounted horizontally in the wheel arch and are assisted by double acting telescopic shock absorbers.

The long front wheel swivels carry the disc brake assemblies and at their lower ends are located by transverse wishbone type suspension arms which are rubber mounted to the underbody at their inner ends. The upper ends of the front wheel swivels are attached to bellcrank shaped leading upper suspension arms

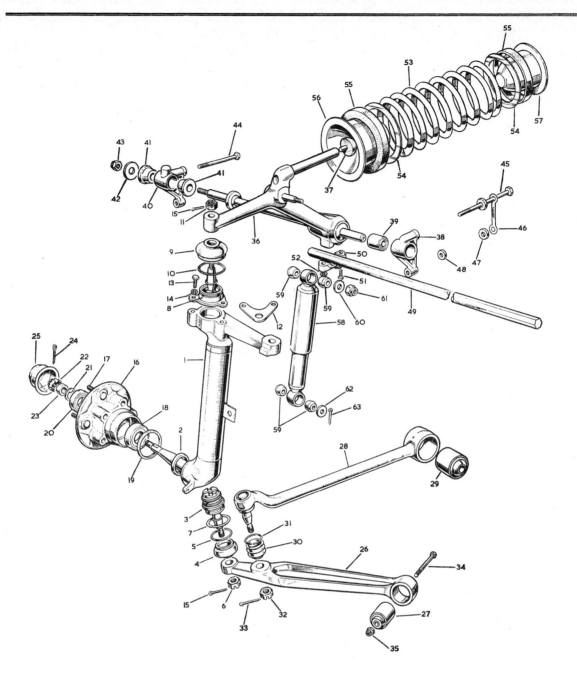

Fig. 11.1. Layout of front suspension

1	Swivel pillar	16	Hub assembly	32	Castellated nut	48	Washer
2	Distance piece	17	Road wheel stud	33	Split pin	49	Anti-roll bar
3	Ball joint	18	Inner bearing	34	Bolt	50	Anti-roll bar mounting
4	Flexible boot	19	Oil seal	35	Self-locking nut	51	Set screw
5	Boot retainer	20	Outer bearing	36	Top link	52	Lock washer
6	Castellated nut	21	Thrust washer	37	Rebound stop	53	Coil spring
7	Balljoint retaining ring	22	Locking cap	38	Top link bracket	54	Shim
8	Top balljoint	23	Hub nut	39	Bush	55	Insulator
9	Flexible boot	24	Split pin	40	Top link	56	Support cup
10	Boot retainer	25	Hub cap	41	Bush	57	Bump rubber
11	Castellated nut	26	Bottom link	42	Washer	58	Shock absorber
12	Brake hose mounting plate	27	Bottom link bush	43	Self-locking nut	59	Mounting bushes
13	Setscrew	28	Bottom link strut	44	Setscrew	60	Washer
14	Lockwasher	29	Bottom link	45	Setscrew	61	Self-locking nut
15	Split pins	30	Rubber boot	46	Lockplate	62	Washer
		31	Boot retainer	47	Washer	63	Split pin

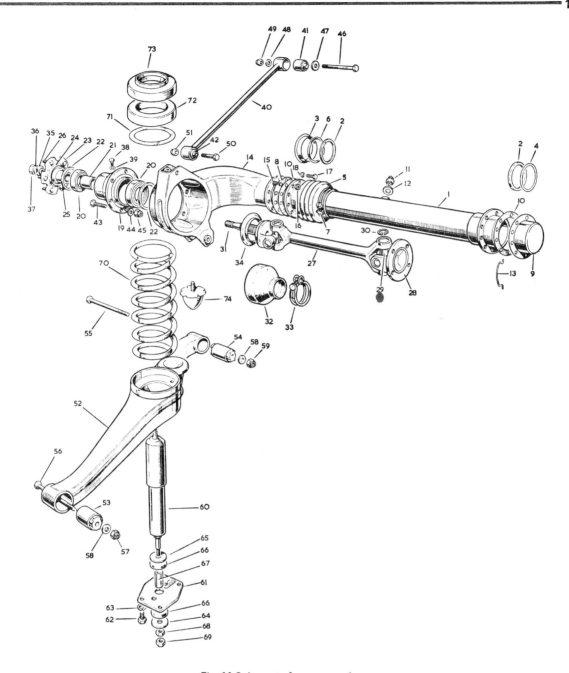

Fig. 11.2. Layout of rear suspension

1	De Dion tube	19	Hub bearing housing	37	Nut	56	Bolt
2	Oil seal	20	Hub bearing	38	Plug	57	Self-locking nut
3	Oil seal retainer	21	Collapsible spacer	39	Plug washer	58	Washer
4	Oil seal retaining ring	22	Oil seal	40	Top link	59	Self-locking nut
5	Dust excluder	23	Driving flange	41	Top link bush	60	Shock absorber
6	Dust excluder retainer	24	Outer dust excluder	42	Top link bush	61	Shock absorber lower mounting
7	Dust excluder clip	25	Screw	43	Bolt	62	Setscrew
8	Blanking plate	26	Road wheel stud	44	Washer	63	Lock washer
9	Blanking plate	27	Drive shaft	45	Self-locking nut	64	Washer
10	Joint washer	28	Flange yoke	46	Bolt	65	Washer
11	Filler plug	29	Journal	47	Plain washer	66	Rubber cushion
12	Joint washer	30	Journal circlip	48	Dished washer	67	Sleeve
13	Spring clip	31	Yoke shaft	49	Self-locking nut	68	Nut
14	Elbow	32	PVC shield	50	Bolt	69	Locknut
15	Elbow stud	33	Shield clip	51	Self locking nut	70	Road spring
16	Nut	34	Inner dust excluder	52	Bottom link	71	Shim
17	Setscrew	35	Washer	53	Bottom link bush	72	Insulators
18	Lockwasher	36	Lockwasher	54	Bottom link bush	73	Support cup
				55	Bolt	74	Bump rubber

which pivot on very long transverse bearings on the bulkhead.

The coil springs are anchored in the bulkhead at their outer ends and located at the front end of the bellcrank pushrods of the upper suspension arms.

The shock absorbers are fitted between the centre of the upper arms and at their lower ends to the body. They are so mounted that their main working parts and oil recuperation chambers remain stationary. This positioning eliminates any possibility of aeration and frothing.

The bearing bosses of the upper suspension arms are joined across the car by means of a single hectagonal bar which serves as an anti-roll bar.

The rear suspension is of the semi-independent de Dion design with stabiliser rods and double acting shock absorbers. From Fig. 11.2 it will be seen that the de Dion tube is of a fixed length and locates the rear wheels laterally and that the drive shafts have specially designed sliding members.

The de Dion tube itself is located by a Watts linkage which has long trailing links fitted at the front and short leading links at the rear. The transverse location for the suspension is provided by the solid hub drive shafts on early produced models and the tubular shafts on later models, in conjunction with a Panhard stabiliser rod fitted laterally between the final drive and underside of the body.

Because of its design the rear suspension system gives the advantages of both the beam axle and also independent rear suspension systems. The unsprung weight is reduced and the alteration of road wheel angle and track variation minimised.

Manual steering is of Burman, recirculating ball, variable ratio type. Power steering (early 3500S as standard and then optionally available on all models) is of Adwest - Varamatic type. A steering relay/damper of hydraulic type is fitted to all models.

A universal joint is placed between the steering box inner column and the steering column shaft on the end of which is a 17 in (431.8 mm) diameter steering wheel. The steering box is located close to the bulkhead and positioned such that it cannot be easily damaged if the front of the car is subjected to a collision.

The swivel pillars are anchored to the top link assemblies and the bottom link strut assembly by means of ball joints which do not require any maintenance.

Note: The rear suspension fitted to early three thousand five models differed from that installed on later cars which have no modified final drive mountings, also the final drive, flanges, driveshafts and propeller shaft are balanced to closer limits and the suspension height reduced by fitting shorter springs.

2 Hubs (front) - servicing and adjustment

1 Jack up the car and remove the road wheel (photo).
2 Remove the brake caliper as described in Chapter 9.
3 Remove the hub cap using a cold chisel (photo).
4 Withdraw the split pin (photo).
5 Withdraw the special nut locking cap, the nut and the thrust washer.
6 Withdraw the hub assembly, catching the outer taper roller bearing in the process.
7 Wipe and then wash out all trace of old grease from the bearings and hub interior with paraffin. Dry with a non-fluffy rag and then examine the inner and outer bearing tracks. The inner oil seal will have to be prised out of its location before the inner bearing can be extracted. Inspect the bearing for signs of wear by holding the inner track and rotating the outer track, checking for roughness of movement. Again hold the inner track and rock the outer track to check for sideways movement.
8 Look at the inner diameter of the inner track and the outer diameter of the outer track for signs of movement on its location. If the bearing is suspect always fit a new one.
9 Bearing tracks should be removed by drifting them out using a brass or copper rod. If both front hubs are being fitted with bearings at the same time, do not mix the tracks and races of the

new bearings, but keep them in their respective cartons until required as the bearings are manufactured as matched sets.

If the oil seal has been disturbed it must be renewed as most likely it will have been distorted upon removal.

10 To reassemble the front hub bearing, first carefully replace the bearing distance piece and oil seal using a tubular drift of a suitable diameter to contact the outer track.
11 Pack the space between the bearings half full with Castrol LM grease and then fit the hub assembly to the stub axle taking care not to damage the oil seal.
12 Fit the outer bearing, the thrust washer (engaging its tongue correctly) and the nut (photo).
13 Adjust the nut so as to give a zero endfloat. Do not overtighten the nut. The best method of determining endfloat is to use a dial indicator gauge mounted as shown in Fig. 11.3.
14 Reposition the dial indicator gauge as shown in Fig. 11.4 and position the probe on the outer diameter of the disc. Slowly rotate the disc and check that the run-out does not exceed 0.003 in (0.07 mm). If the run-out exceeds this limit, the disc should be repositioned on the hub and the run-out rechecked. Should this still not produce a satisfactory result, a distorted disc should be suspected and a new disc obtained and fitted.
15 Re-adjust the hub nut to give an endfloat of between 0.003 and 0.005 in (0.07 and 0.12 mm). Fit the locking cap in such a position that the split pin can be inserted without having to move the nut (photo).
16 Lock the special hub nut with a new split pin and bend over the legs to secure it. Repack the hub cap with Castrol LM grease and gently tap the cap into position with a soft faced hammer (photo).
17 Refit the caliper, the roadwheel and lower the jack.

3 Swivel pillar and bottom ball joint (front suspension) - removal and refitment

1 Refer to Section 2 of this Chapter amd remove the front hub assembly.
2 Extract the split pin and slacken the slotted nut to be found at the bottom of the ball joint of the swivel pillar at the bottom link.
3 Disconnect the ball joint taper by using wedges or an extractor.
4 Remove the nut and separate the swivel pillar from the bottom link.
5 Extract the split pin from the slotted nut of the swivel pillar top ball joint at the top link. Also extract the split pin from the slotted nut of the steering side rod ball joint at the swivel pillar end. The two nuts should now be slackened but not yet removed.
6 Refer to paragraph 3 above and break the taper of both the ball joints. Remove the two nuts once the joints have been broken.
7 The swivel pillar may now be completely removed.
8 Using a small screwdriver carefully remove the flexible rubber boot on the swivel pillar bottom ball joint. Take care not to jab the screwdriver through the rubber boot.
9 Extract the retaining ring from the bottom ball joint.
10 A special ball joint extracter, part number 600962 will now be required to remove the ball joint from the swivel pillar. An illustration of this is shown in Fig. 11.5, and if the tool is not available, one can be made from a piece of tube. 'U' shaped angle iron and a piece of plain steel bar, suitably drilled and welded to the tube as shown.
11 If it is necessary to remove the top ball joint from the swivel pillar, full information will be found in Section 8 of this Chapter.
12 To refit the bottom ball joint using a suitable sized tubular drift, drive the ball joint into the swivel pillar housing.
13 Refit the bottom ball joint retaining ring.
14 Ease the flexible boot into position with the screwdriver, again taking care not to puncture the rubber boot. Obviously if the original one was damaged a new one must be fitted.

2.1 Road wheel removal

2.3 Hub cap removal

2.4 Withdrawing hub nut split pin

2.12 Fitting front hub thrust washer and nut

2.15 Fitting front hub locking cap

2.16 Fitting hub cap

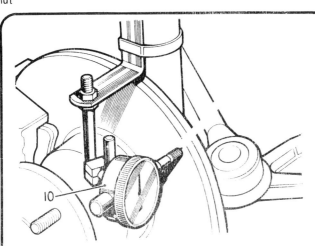

Fig. 11.3. Checking front disc run-out with a dial gauge (10)

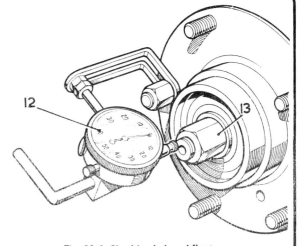

Fig. 11.4. Checking hub end-float

12 Dial gauge   13 Hub nut

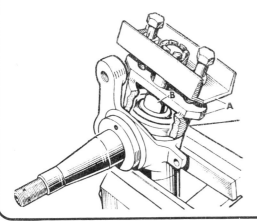

Fig. 11.5. Using an extractor (A) to disconnect a front suspension bottom balljoint (B)

15 Refitting the swivel pillar is the reverse sequence to removal. The ball joint nuts must be tightened to a torque wrench setting of 55 to 85 lb/ft (7.6 to 11.8 kg/m) (Top ball joint) and 60 to 75 lb/ft (8.3 to 10.4 kg/m) (Bottom ball joint).
16 Refit the hub as detailed in Section 2 of this Chapter.

4 Shock absorber (front) - removal and refitment

1 Remove the wheel trim and slacken the wheel nuts. Chock the rear wheels, apply the handbrake, jack up the front of the car and support the body on axle stands. Remove the road wheels.
2 Place a jack under the suspension making sure that it will not slip off and carefully raise it so as to take the weight off the shock absorber.
   On 3500S models the brake pipe and the pad wear warning light lead must be released from the swivel pillar.
3 Extract the split pin from the bottom mounting with a suitable pin punch.
4 Lift away the plain washer and prise out the outer rubber bush with a wide bladed screwdriver.
5 Undo and remove the nut from the top shock absorber fixing and lift away the washer and outer rubber bush.
6 The shock absorber may now be lifted away from the underside of the wing.
7 Remove the inner bushes and inspect the bushes for signs of oil contamination or perishing. Obtain new bushes if the original ones are suspect.
8 Refitting the shock absorber is the reverse sequence to removal. If the bushes are a little tight and difficult to insert into the shock absorber they may be lubricated with a little rubber grease.
   Always use a new split pin.

5 Front road spring and top link assembly - removal, servicing and refitment

1 Before commencing work it will be necessary to obtain three special spring retaining rods. These have a part number of 600304 and are shown in Fig. 11.6. These can be made up of high tensile steel rod but difficulty may be experienced in forming the ends if forging facilities are not available. Do not try to compromise as serious damage or injury can result in the spring running wild.
2 Some owners have found it beneficial to remove the front wing. This is an easy operation and full details will be found in Chapter 12.
3 With the assistance of three heavy persons press down on the front of the car so as to compress the spring as much as possible so that the three spring retaining rods can be inserted. The rods should be inserted through the road spring front support cup and into the slots in the bump rubber rear support (Fig. 11.7).
4 Important The retainers must be turned through exactly 90° so as to prevent the spring from expanding. Rotate the spring through one complete turn so as to ensure that the retainer rods have seated correctly.
5 Remove the wheel trim and slacken the wheel nuts. Chock the rear wheels, apply the handbrake, jack up the front of the car and support on axle stands. Remove the road wheel.
6 Undo and remove the upper shock absorber securing nut. Lift away the washer and outer rubber bush.
7 The top swivel pillar ball joint should next be removed from the top link. To do this extract the split pin and slacken the slotted nut that secures the top ball joint to the top link.
8 Remove the three bolts that secure the brake hose mounting plate and top ball joint to swivel pillar.
9 Using a suitable lever on the bottom link, hold the bottom link downwards and then, using a drift carefully tap the top ball joint from the swivel column.
10 It will now be necessary to use a two legged puller and suitable metal thrust block to break the taper of the ball joint.

Remove the nut and ball joint.
11 Remove the bolts and lock plates that secure the anti-roll bar cap to the top link and lift away the cap.
12 Remove the locker lid and cut and bend the bulkhead insulation panel as illustrated in Fig. 11.8 working from inside the right-hand side of the car. Note: If the left-hand suspension assembly is being worked upon, the insulation of the left-hand side will have to be cut.
13 Release the lock plate tabs and remove the two bolts that secure the top link inner mounting bracket. This is readily accessible when the door is fully opened.
14 Release the lock plate tabs and remove the two bolts that secure the top link outer mounting bracket. Like the inner mounting bracket, this is readily accessible when the door is fully opened.
15 Remove the top link assembly stiffener, spacing washers and coil spring.
16 To check and overhaul the spring, compress the spring, making sure it is firmly supported and will not fly out of a press, and remove the three spring retainer rods. Release the pressure on the spring.
17 The spring coils should be checked for signs of excessive rusting, fractures or splitting, and, if evident a new pair of springs must be fitted. If only one spring is fitted the car may be slightly higher on one side than the other.
18 Inspect the rubber cushions and bump rubber for signs of oil contamination or deterioration and obtain new parts as necessary.
19 Compare the length of the spring with the spring data in the Specifications at the beginning of this Chapter. If it has settled unduly, new springs must be fitted.
20 Reassemble the shims, rubber cushions, bump rubber and support cap to the spring. Turn the support cap until the slots in the cap and bump rubber are in line ready to accept the retainer rods.
21 Compress the spring and insert the three retainer rods and turn through just 90°. Release the spring from the press once you are satisfied that the three retainer rods are correctly located.
22 To overhaul the top link assembly, undo and remove the self locking nut and plain washer that secures the top link to the outer mounting bracket. Then undo and remove the bolt that secures the stiffener to the bracket.
23 Withdraw the mounting bracket together with the two rubber bushes and press off the inner mounting bracket and bush.
24 Inspect all parts for wear and fit new parts as necessary.
25 When pressing the inner mounting bracket complete with bush back onto the top link, make sure the bracket mounting face is correctly aligned at 90° to the anti-roll bar cap mounting face as shown in Fig. 11.9.
26 Refit the outer mounting bracket together with the rubber bushes making sure that the mounting face lines up with the corresponding face on the inner mounting bracket.
27 Refit the plain washer and self locking nut.
28 To refit the spring and top link assembly is the reverse sequence to removal. The following additional points should however be noted.
29 Before the retainer rods are removed, make sure that the road spring is correctly seating against the bulkhead location.
30 Before refitting the top link brackets to the body slightly bend the tabs of new lock plates so that they can be easily bent to their locked positions when required.
31 The anti-roll bar cap should be refitted once the spring retainer rods have been removed.
32 Tighten the top link and anti-roll bar fixing bolts to a torque wrench setting of 30 lb/ft (4.1 kg/m).
33 Always fit a new split pin to the top of the swivel pillar ball joint slotted nut.

6 Front suspension bottom link strut - removal and refitment

1 Remove the wheel trim and slacken the wheel nuts. Chock

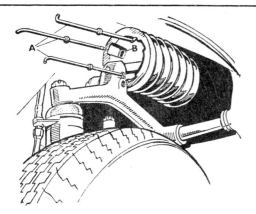

Fig. 11.6. Fitting front road spring retainers (A) slots in spring end cap (B)

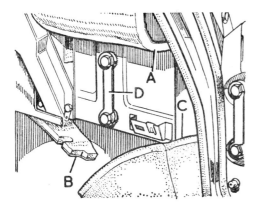

Fig. 11.8. Front suspension top link bolts

A, B & C Cut-away insulation   D Bracket, bolts and lockplate

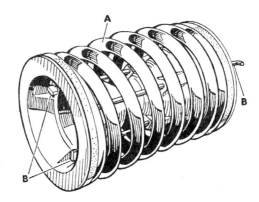

Fig. 11.7. Front road spring (A) removed and held by retainers (B) in compressed state

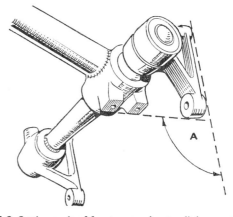

Fig. 11.9. Setting angle of front suspension top link mounting bracket A is 90°

the rear wheels, apply the handbrake, jack up the front of the car and support the body on axle stands. Remove the road wheel.

2 Extract the split pin and remove the slotted nut that secures the bottom link strut to the bottom link.

3 Undo and remove the nut and bolt that secures the bottom link strut to the body. Lift away the strut.

4 Inspect the ball joint for wear and if worn it will be necessary to renew the complete strut.

5 Check the bush for signs of ovality or wear. This may be drifted out and a new one fitted using a drift of suitable size.

6 Refitting the bottom link strut is the reverse sequence to removal. Always fit new split pins.

7 It is important that the bolts securing the strut to the body and the bottom link are tightened once the road wheel has been refitted and the car is on the ground in the normal unladen condition.

8 The bottom link strut to bottom link (ball joint) should be tightened to a torque wrench setting of 60 to 75 lb/ft (8.3 to 10.4 kg/m) and the bottom link strut to body 54 lb/ft (7.5 kg/m).

7 Front suspension bottom link - removal and refitment

1 Remove the wheel trim and slacken the wheel nuts, chock the rear wheels, jack up the front of the car and place on axle stands. Remove the road wheel.

2 Extract the split pin and then slacken the two slotted nuts that secure the bottom link to the swivel pillar and strut to the bottom link.

3 It will now be necessary to use a two legged puller and suitable metal thrust block to break the taper of the ball joints. Remove the nut once the joint has been broken.

4 Undo and remove the self locking nut and bolt that secures the bottom link to the body. The link may now be lifted away.

5 Inspect the bottom link bush for wear and renew if necessary by drifting out the old one and fitting a new bush.

6 Refitting the bottom link is the reverse sequence of removal. It is however necessary to tighten up the bolt that fixes the bottom link to the body once the car has been lowered to the ground and is in its normal static unladen condition. This bolt should be tightened to a torque wrench setting of 54 lb/ft (7.5 kg/m).

8 Front suspension top ball joint - removal and refitment

1 Remove the wheel trim and slacken the wheel nut. Chock the rear wheels, apply the handbrake, jack up the front of the car and support the body on axle stands. Remove the road wheel.

2 Extract the split pin and slacken the slotted nut that secures the top ball joint to the top link.

3 Undo and remove the three bolts that secure the brake hose mounting plate and top ball joint to the swivel pillar.

4 With a suitable lever on the bottom link, hold the bottom link downwards and with a drift of suitable size drive the top ball joint from the swivel column.

5 It will be necessary to use a two legged puller and suitable metal thrust block to break the taper of the ball joint. Remove the nut once the joint has been broken and then lift away the ball joint.

6 To refit the top ball joint, first make sure that the bolt holes
are correctly lined up and then fit the top ball joint mounting
for the top brake hose and the three set bolts onto the swivel
pillar.
7 Whilst the bolts are being tightened lightly tap the ball joint.
8 Inspect the flexible rubber boot for signs of perishing or
damage and obtain a new one if suspect. Fit the rubber boot
easing it into position with a small screwdriver.
9 Refitting is the reverse sequence to removal. The top ball
joint slotted nut must be tightened to a torque wrench setting of
55 to 85 lb/ft (7.6 to 11.8 kg/m). Fit a new split pin to the
slotted nut.

9 Anti-roll bar - removal and refitment

1 Remove both front wheel trims and slacken the wheel nuts.
Chock the rear wheels, apply the handbrake, jack up the front of
the car and support the body on axle stands.
2 Undo and remove the four bolts and lock plates that secure
the anti-roll bar caps to the top links. Lift away the anti-roll bar
caps.
3 The anti-roll bar may now be lifted away from the underside
of the car wing.
4 To refit the anti-roll bar, first make sure that the contact
surfaces of the anti-roll bar and also those of the locating
housing and cap, are clean.
5 Refit the caps and secure in position with the lock plate and
bolts.
6 Tighten the bolts to a torque wrench setting of 30 lb/ft (4.0
kg/m) and lock by bending up the locking tabs.

10 Rear coil spring - removal and refitment

1 Remove the wheel trim and slacken the road wheel nuts.
2 Chock the front wheels and jack up the rear of the car until
the rear wheels are approximately 12 in (304.8 mm) from the
ground. Support the rear of the body on axle stands at the rear
jacking points.
3 Remove the wheel nuts and lift away the road wheel.
4 Position a jack under the bottom link as shown in Fig. 11.10.
For this it is preferable that a garage hydraulic jack be used.
5 Raise the bottom link just sufficiently to allow the lower end
of the shock absorber fixing to be released by undoing and
removing the nuts and rubber cushions.
6 Remove the nut and bolt that secures the bottom link to the
de Dion tube.
7 Gradually lower the jack, so lowering the bottom link, and
lift away the coil spring and its support plate.
8 Inspect the spring coils for signs of excessive rusting,
fractures or splitting and if evident a new pair of springs must be
fitted. If only one spring is fitted the car may be slightly higher
on one side than the other.
9 Compare the length of the spring with the spring data in the
Specifications at the beginning of this Chapter. If it has settled
unduly, new springs must be fitted.
10 Refitting the rear spring is the reverse sequence to removal
with the exception that the bottom link must not be tightened
until the car is on the ground and in the normal unladen
condition. The bolt should then be tightened to a torque wrench
setting of 54 lb/ft (7.5 kg/m).
11 Make quite sure that the spring is correctly seated at its top
and bottom positions so that there is no possibility of it moving.

11 Rear shock absorber - removal and refitment

1 Lift out rear seat cushion. Undo and remove the two self
tapping screws that secure the bottom of the rear seat squab to
the body, and lift away the squab from inside the car.
2 Undo and remove the two nuts that secure the retainer for
the rubber cushion, the rubber cushion and the top of the shock

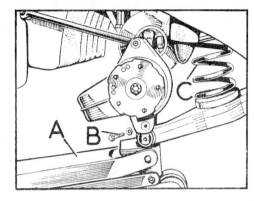

Fig. 11.10. Removing a rear road spring (A) jack (B) bottom link
bolt (C) road spring

absorber to the body panel.
3 Chock the front wheels, remove the rear wheel trim and
slacken the wheel nuts. Jack up the rear of the car and support
on axle stands placed at the rear body jacking points. Remove
the wheel nuts and lift away the road wheel.
4 Unscrew and remove the four bolts and spring washers that
secure the lower shock absorber mounting to the bottom link.
The shock absorber may now be lifted away from the rear
suspension.
5 If necessary remove the shock absorber lower mounting.
6 Inspect the shock absorber for leaks and, if evident, a new
unit must be fitted.
7 To check the operation of the shock absorber, secure one end
in a vice and then push and pull the free end throughout its
complete operating stroke ten or twelve times. It should be
observed that greater resistance is felt when the shock absorber is
being pulled outwards. Should this condition not be felt a new
shock absorber must be fitted.
8 To refit the shock absorber first assemble it to the lower
mounting.
9 Carefully jack up the bottom link and guide the shock
absorber into its location in the body panel mounting. Secure
the lower mounting to the bottom link.
10 Refit the rubber cushion and nuts to the top of the shock
absorber and lock in position.
11 Refit the road wheel and replace the wheel nuts. Lower the
car to the ground and tighten the wheel nuts securely.
12 Replace the squab and secure with the two self tapping
screws. Refit the rear seat cushion.

12 Rear suspension top link - removal and refitment

1 Remove the wheel trim and slacken the wheel nuts. Chock
the rear wheels, apply the handbrake, jack up the front of the
car and support the body on axle stands. Remove the road
wheel.
2 Position a jack under the rear end of the bottom link and
raise a few inches so as to relieve the load on the top link.
3 Undo and remove the two nuts and bolts that secure the top
link to the de Dion tube and the body. The link may be lifted
away.
4 If the left-hand link is being removed, it will be necessary to
lift away the spare wheel and rear luggage compartment trim so
as to expose the link rear bolts.
5 If the bushes are worn they may be drifted out and new ones
fitted using a suitable sized metal drift.
6 To refit the top link is the reverse sequence to removal. The
securing bolts must however, be tightened to a torque wrench
setting of 54 lb/ft (7.5 kg/m) once the car has been lowered to
the ground and is in the normal static unladen condition.

13 Rear suspension lower link - removal and refitment

1 Refer to Section 10 and remove the rear coil spring.
2 Undo and remove the nut, bolt and two plain washers from the front end of the lower link. Lift away the link.
3 If the bushes are worn the link should be exchanged complete as the bushes are not serviced separately.
4 Refitment of the lower link is the reverse sequence to removal. The securing bolts must be tightened to a torque wrench setting of 54 lb/ft (7.5 kg/m) once the car has been lowered to the ground and is in the normal static unladen condition.

14 de Dion tube - removal, overhaul and refitment

1 Remove the rear wheel trims and slacken the rear wheel nuts. Chock the front wheels and jack up the rear of the car and support on axle stands located under each of the bottom links below the coil springs. Remove the road wheels.
2 Undo and remove the eight bolts and lock plates that secure the hub drive shaft flange yokes to the differential drive shafts. Mark the respective flanges so that they are correctly refitted upon reassembly.
3 Undo and remove the twelve bolts and self locking nuts that retain the bearing housings for the rear hubs to the de Dion tube. Remove the hub and drive shaft as a complete assembly.
4 Undo and remove the bolts that secure the top links to the de Dion tube and disconnect the links from the elbow.
5 Slacken the bolts that secure the lower links to the de Dion tube and allow the de Dion tube to pivot downwards. When this position has been reached the bolt may then be completely removed.
6 Lift away the de Dion tube from the underside of the car.
7 Undo and remove the brass drain plug and allow the oil to drain out into a container having a capacity of approximately 1/3rd pint.
8 With a scriber or file mark the de Dion tube and elbow at the connecting flanges to ensure correct reassembly.
9 Undo and remove the four nuts and twelve set bolts with spring washers and detach the right-hand and left-hand de Dion tube elbows.
10 The blanking plates and packing washer (if fitted) may now be removed.
11 Extract the retaining clip "A" (Fig. 11.11) from the left-hand end of the inner tube.
12 Slacken the dust excluder clip and ease out the dust excluder and garter spring from its location. The inner tube assembly may now be removed from the outer tube assembly.
the outer tube assembly.
13 Lift away the dust excluder, garter spring and clip.
14 If further dismantling is necessary the left-hand seal, packing washer (when fitted) and retainer may next be removed by carefully prising it out of its housing.
15 The right-hand seal and retainer may be removed by carefully drifting out with a long soft metal drift.
16 All parts should be thoroughly washed and dried on a non-fluffy rag. Any part showing signs of wear or damage should be renewed.
17 To reassemble the de Dion tube first slide the gaiter, garter spring and clip onto the right-hand side of the outer tube.
18 Carefully fit a new seal and flexible packing washer (if originally fitted) into the retainer and smear with MS4 Silicone grease. Fit the seal and retainer to the right-hand end.
19 Fit the seal and retainer to the left-hand end of the outer tube in a similar manner.
20 Replace the respective cup using a suitable oil resisting jointing compound on the mating faces.
21 Refit the inner tube assembly into the outer tube assembly.
22 Refit the retaining clip to the left-hand end of the inner tube.
23 Replace the de Dion tube elbows, locating the four studs correctly and tightening the bolts to a torque wrench setting of 8 lb/ft (1.1 kg/m). Make sure that when the right-hand elbow is

being fitted, the dust excluder is located before the bolts are fitted. Tighten the dust excluder clip.
24 Refill the de Dion tube with 1/3rd pint of oil and refit the brass drain plug.
25 To refit the de Dion tube assembly is the reverse sequence to removal. It is however, important that the top and bottom link bolts are tightened to the required torque wrench setting once the car has been lowered to the ground and is in the normal static unladen condition.
26 The recommended torque wrench setting for the bottom link to de Dion tube, bottom link to body, top link to de Dion tube and top link to body is 54 lb/ft (7.5 kg/m). The wheel bearing housing bolts should be tightened to a torque wrench setting of 20 lb/ft (2.7 kg/m) and the drive shaft flange yoke to differential drive shaft 85 lb/ft (11.5 kg/m).

15 Suspension height - (Three thousand five models) checking

1 If the car is lower at one side than the other, the suspension height setting should be checked in the following manner.
2 Set the car on level ground (unladen) with approximately 5 gallons (22.73 litres) of fuel in the tank.
3 Check that the tyres are correctly inflated to the specified pressures.
4 The dimensions given in Figs. 11.12 or 11.13 are based upon a hub centre to tyre tread surface dimension (wheel radius) of 11.593 in (294.0 mm). This should be the case when the tyre is in good condition.
5 If the height "B" differs then an appropriate allowance must be made when measuring dimension "D".
6 Where the results of the dimensional check are not in

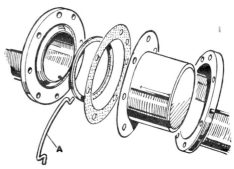

Fig. 11.11. Retaining clip (A) for de Dion tube

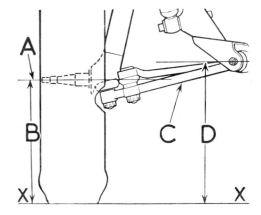

Fig. 11.12. Front suspension height setting diagram (Three thousand five)

A Wheel centre
B 11 19/32 in. (294.0 mm)
C Bottom link

D 13 27/32 in. ± ¼ in. (352.0 mm ± 6.0 mm)
x – x floor level

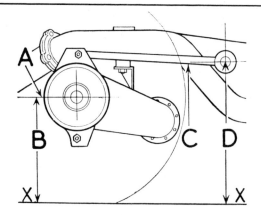

Fig. 11.13. Rear suspension height setting diagram (Three thousand five)

A   Wheel centre line
B   11 19/32 in. (294.0 mm)
C   Top link
D   Up to final drive suffix A inclusive 17 1/32 in. ± ¼ in. (434.0 mm ± 6.0 mm). From final drive suffix B onwards 16 25/32 in. ± 1/8 in. (426.0 mm ± 3.0 mm) x − x level floor surface

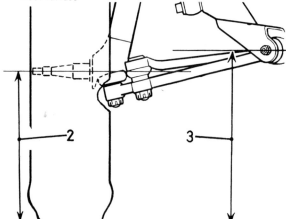

Fig. 11.14. Front suspension height setting diagram (3500 and 3500 S)

For key see text

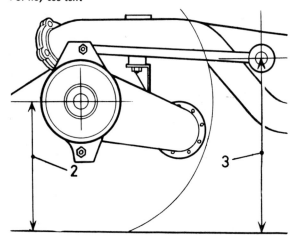

Fig. 11.15. Rear suspension height setting diagram (3500 and 3500 S)

For key see text

accordance with the diagram, additional shims should be placed under the coil springs but the total shim pack thickness must not exceed 0.375 in (9.5 mm) otherwise the spring may be dislodged from its seat during very bumpy road conditions.
7   If the correct height cannot be obtained after fitting additional shims, renew the springs (as a pair).

16 Suspension height - (3500 and 3500S models) checking

1   Set the car on level ground with a full fuel tank and two persons in the front seats and one sitting in the centre of the rear seating position.
2   Check that the tyre pressures are correct.
3   The dimensions given in Figs. 11.14 and 11.15 are based upon a hub centre to tyre tread surface dimension (wheel radius) of 11.593 in (294.0 mm). This should be the case with a tyre in good condition. Any variation in this dimension must be taken into account when carrying out the following procedure.
4   **Front suspension:** Check the dimension "3" from the centre line of the bottom link pivot to the ground.
5   Subtract the standard tyre radius from the dimension "3" adjusting if necessary where the tyre radius was not as specified in paragraph 3.
6   The difference calculated should lie within the trim height specified limits which are 1.562 in ± 0.250 in (39.7 mm ± 6.0 mm).
7   Where the trim height is not within the limits, add shims underneath the coil spring but the total shim pack thickness must not exceed 0.375 in (9.5 mm) otherwise the springs may be dislodged during exceptionally bumpy road conditions.
8   **Rear suspension:** Measure dimension "3" from the centre line of the top link pivot to the ground.
9   Subtract the standard tyre radius from the dimension "3" adjusting if necessary where the tyre radius was not as specified in paragraph 3.
10 The difference calculated should lie within the trim height limits which are 3.750 in ± 0.250 in (95.0 mm ± 6.0 mm).
11 Implement the procedure in paragraph 7 for front suspension height adjustment.

17 Wheels and tyres - general

1   Pressed steel wheels are fitted and secured with five nuts.
2   Tyre pressures should be checked weekly and in accordance with the pressures listed in Specifications.
3   The wheels should not be moved round the car in order to minimise tyre wear but at a stage when they are about half worn they should be re-balanced.
4   Any punctures should be mended professionally, using the permitted (internally fitted) mushroom headed plugs.
5   Do not rub or scrape the tyres along kerb edges.
6   When tyres have worn down to the minimum permitted tread depth, they should be renewed with those of similar type and size. Always fit a new valve assembly.

18 Steering box (manual steering) - adjustment

1   These details are only relevant when the steering gear is still in position in the car.
2   Chock the rear wheels, apply the handbrake, jack up the front of the car and support on axle stands.
3   Undo and remove the rocker shaft adjuster cap nut.
4   With the steering wheel very lightly held between two fingers, turn the steering wheel slightly to the left and right so as to ascertain the amount of backlash present in the steering box.
5   An assistant should now release the adjuster lock nut and then very slowly screw in the adjusting screw whilst the steering wheel is still being rocked, until a condition of zero backlash is achieved. This is when no free movement is felt on the steering wheel.

6 Tighten the lock nut securely.

7 Turn the steering wheel slowly from one lock and back to the other lock so as to check if there is any excessive tightness throughout the steering wheel movement range. If this is evident either the adjuster has been screwed in too far, or the steering box is worn and requires overhaul as detailed in Section 22 of this Chapter.

8 Refit the adjuster screw cap nut and finally road test the car.

19 Steering lock stops (manual steering) - adjustment

1 Chock the rear wheels and apply the handbrake, jack up the front of the car and support on axle stands.

2 Turn the wheels slowly onto one full lock position and with a long rule or steel tape measure the distance from the centre of the bolt securing the bottom link to the body along the line of the link to the front rim of the road wheel as shown in Fig. 11.17. This dimension should be exactly 18¾ in (476.0 mm). Take this measurement at several positions on the wheel rim to eliminate any error caused by a distorted rim.

3 If any adjustment is necessary refer to Fig. 11.18 and adjust the steering lock stop, working through the wing valance, until the required dimension is obtained.

4 Repeat the instructions given in paragraphs 2 and 3 for the opposite lock stop.

20 Steering relay/damper - removal and refitment

1 Release the bonnet and prop it wide open.

2 Jack up the front of the car so that the road wheels may be turned from lock-to-lock.

3 Remove the split pin from the steering side rod and track rod ball joints and remove the nuts and washers.

4 Release the two ball joints using a suitable extractor.

5 On rhd cars, remove the bolts which secure the accelerator bracket to the relay bracket.

6 On lhd cars release the clip from the bracket on the steering relay which secures the fluid hose and then remove the power steering fluid reservoir to one side.

7 Remove the three bolts which secure the relay unit mounting bracket to the bodyshell and remove the assembly, retaining any spacing plates (photo).

8 Remove the mounting and angle brackets from the relay damper.

9 Refitment is a reversal of removal, use new split pins for the ball joints and check the steering stop bolt adjustment (manual steering only).

10 Check the wheel alignment as described in Section 34.

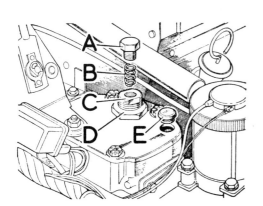

Fig. 11.16. Manual steering box adjuster

A Plug
B Spring
C Adjuster screw
D Locknut
E Filler plug

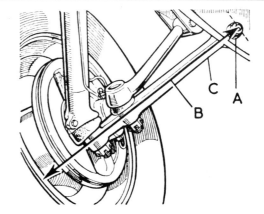

Fig. 11.17. Steering lock stops (manual steering) measurement diagram

A Bottom link bolt
B Measurement line
C Bottom link

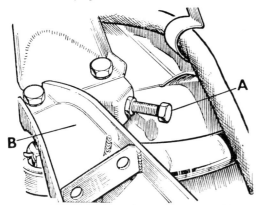

Fig. 11.18. Steering lock stop (manual steering LH side only shown)

A Adjustable stop bolt and locknut
B Relay arm

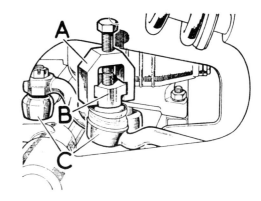

Fig. 11.19. Using a balljoint extractor (A) to remove a balljoint (C) from the steering drop arm (B)

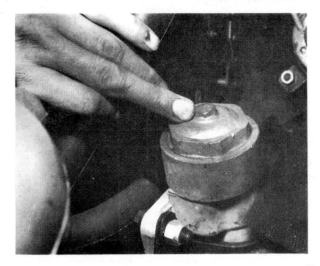

20.7 Steering relay, idler/damper unit

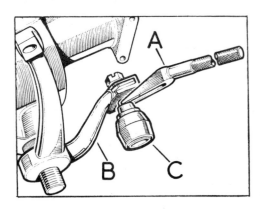

Fig. 11.20. Using a wedge type extractor (A) to remove a ball-joint (C) from the steering drop arm (B)

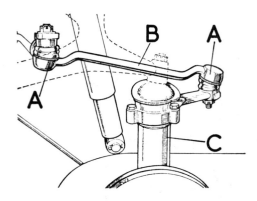

Fig. 11.21. Location of steering side rod (B) balljoints (A) and swivel pillar (C)

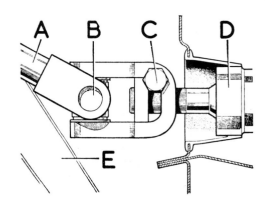

Fig. 11.22. Cross sectional view of the steering column joint

A Steering column	C Pinch bolt
B Universal joint	D Steering box
	E Bracket

22.9 Steering column universal joint pinch bolt

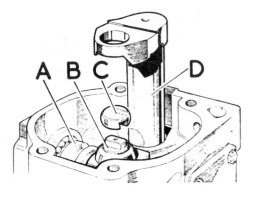

Fig. 11.23. Manual steering box components

A Worm shaft	C Roller
B Main nut	D Rocker shaft

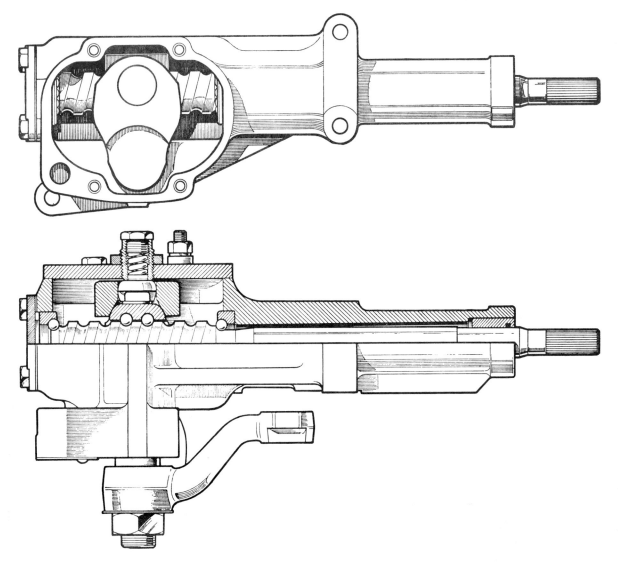

Fig. 11.24. Cross-sectional views of the manual steering box

21 Steering linkage - removal and refitment

1   Raise the bonnet and prop it open.
2   Remove the air cleaner.
3   Jack up the front of the car so that the wheels will turn from lock to lock.
4   Disconnect the two track rod end ball joints using a suitable extractor. It will be necessary to unbolt and move aside the anti-roll bar before the ball joint can be removed.
5   Remove the track rod from below the left-hand or right-hand wing valance.
6   The steering side rod may be removed in a manner similar to that used for the track rod (Fig. 11.21).
7   Refitment is a reversal of removal, use new split pins in the ball joints and when reassembly is complete, check the wheel alignment (Section 34).

22 Steering box (manual steering) - removal, servicing and refitment

1   Lift the bonnet and prop it open, remove the air cleaner.

2   Disconnect the lead from the battery negative terminal.
3   On rhd cars, remove the windscreen wiper arms and remove the wiper motor and linkage (Chapter 10).
4   Remove the brake fluid reservoir.
5   On lhd cars, remove the windscreen washer reservoir and the bracket (accelerator shaft from gearbox).
6   Jack up the front of the car so that the road wheels can be turned from lock to lock.
7   Disconnect the ball joints at the steering box drop arm using a suitable extractor.
8   Unscrew and remove the three bolts and one nut which secure the steering box to the bodyshell.
9   From behind the glove compartment (within the car) remove the pinch bolt from the steering column universal joint (photo).
10 The steering box may now be withdrawn but watch for and retain any spacers which may be fitted between the steering box and the bodyshell.
11 If it is necessary to remove the drop arm, bend back the tab washer and unscrew the nut from the end of the rocker shaft. Using a scriber mark the relative position of the drop arm to the rocker shaft end face so that they may be correctly fitted on reassembly. Use a two legged puller to remove the drop arm.
12 Clean the exterior of the steering box with paraffin or 'Gunk'

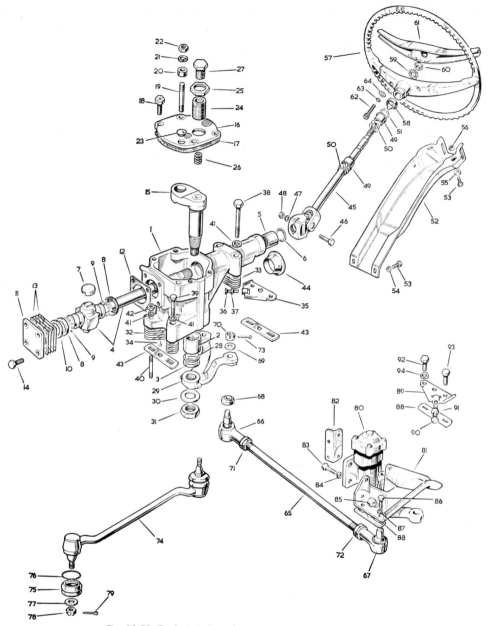

Fig. 11.25. Exploded view of the manual steering box and linkage

1	Steering box	24	Adjuster screw	47	Washer	71	Locknut
2	Bush	25	Nut	48	Nut	72	Locknut
3	Oil seal retainer	26	Spring	49	Bearing	73	Split pin
4	Shaft/nut	27	Bolt	50	Lockwasher	74	Side rod
5	Bush	28	Oil seal	51	Circlip	75	Rubber boot
6	Oil seal	29	Drop arm	52	Support bracket	76	Boot retainer
7	Roller	30	Tab washer	53	Bolt	77	Washer
8	Ball race	31	Nut	54	Lockwasher	78	Castellated nut
9	Ball	32	Shim	55	Plain washer	79	Split pin
10	Spacer	33	Shim	56	Nut	80	Relay idler/damper
11	End cover plate	34	Screw	57	Steering wheel	81	Damper mounting bracket
12	Paper jointing	35	Lock stop bracket	58	Striker for flasher switch	82	Accelerator bracket
13	Steel joint washer	36	Bolt	59	Lockwasher	83	Bolt
14	Bolt	37	Locknut	60	Special nut	84	Washer
15	Rocker shaft	38	Setscrew	61	Finisher	85	Self-locking nut
16	Top cover plate	39	Setscrew	62	Screw	86	Setscrew
17	Cover plate washer	40	Stud	63	Lockwasher	87	Lockwasher
18	Bolt	41	Lockwasher	64	Plain washer	88	Spacer
19	Stud	42	Nut	65	Track rod	89	Lock stop bracket
20	Washer	43	Spacer	66	Balljoint	90	Bolt
21	Lock washer	44	Grommet	67	Balljoint	91	Locknut
22	Nut	45	Shaft	68	Rubber boot	92	Setscrew
23	Oil filler plug	46	Pinch bolt	69	Washer	93	Setscrew
				70	Castellated nut	94	Lockwasher

and then clamp the unit in a vice using the moulded ribs provided for the purpose.

13 Slacken the adjuster locknut and then remove the three cover securing bolts and one nut and lift off the cover.

14 Withdraw the rocker shaft and slide the roller off the main nut (Fig. 11.23).

15 Remove the steering box end cover complete with shims and gaskets.

16 Check that the steering nut is in the midway position and then gently tap the splined end of the shaft to extract the bottom race complete with the ten 9/32 in (7.1 mm) diameter balls (Fig. 11.26).

17 Wind the wormshaft through the steering nut, remove the shaft, nut and further set of 9/32 in (7.1 mm) diameter balls from the steering box.

18 Tap the bottom end of the steering box to dislodge the top race.

19 Remove the 26 x 5/16 in (7.9 mm) diameter balls from the steering nut and recirculating tube. To facilitate their removal, tap the top face of the nut on a wooden block (Fig. 11.27).

20 Examine the worm nut ball tracks for indentations or scoring.

21 Examine the wormshaft for similar conditions, also the rocker shaft bush and oil seal for wear and renew components as necessary.

22 Drive the new rockershaft bush into position and renew the two steering box 'O' rings.

23 Fit the top bearing track into the steering box.

24 Insert the twenty-six balls into the steering nut using plenty of grease.

25 Support the steering box vertically in a vice and apply grease to the race just fitted to the box. Screw the worm shaft (splined end first) into the nut (held in position in the box) ensuring that the balls do not fall out of the nut (Fig. 11.28).

26 Raise the shaft so that the ten balls can be inserted into the top race.

27 Using plenty of grease to retain them, insert the ten balls and bottom bearing track into position.

28 Fit the end cover complete with shims and gaskets (one paper gasket each side of shim pack). Apply gasket cement such as 'Hermetite Red' (non-hardening) to the end cover bolts.

29 Adjust the worm shaft by adding or removing shims from below the end cover if necessary so that when the worm shaft is turned by hand, no endfloat exists, neither is it stiff to turn.

30 Adjust the steering box in the vice so that it is positioned horizontally and slide the roller onto the steering nut and insert the rockershaft so that it is located over the roller.

31 Fill the box with the correct grade of oil and then apply jointing compound to the steering box and top cover mating faces. Use a new gasket and fit the top cover.

32 Set the steering nut in the midway position of its travel and screw the adjuster on the top cover in by hand until there is no endfloat. Tighten the adjuster locknut, refit the spring and retaining plug.

33 Check the oil level, top up if necessary and fit the oil filler plug.

34 Turn the steering from lock-to-lock to check for free movement and then fit the drop arm with the marks made before removal in alignment. Bend up the tab washer.

35 Refit the steering box by inserting the shaft into the steering column universal joint. Before doing this, check that the steering

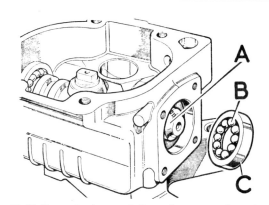

Fig. 11.26. Extracting bottom ball race from manual steering box

A Inner race   C Outer race
B Balls

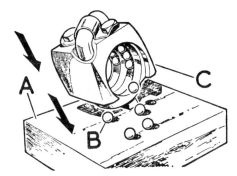

Fig. 11.27. Removing steering nut balls (manual steering box)

A Wooden block   C Steering nut
B Balls

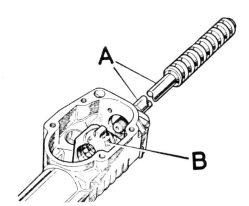

Fig. 11.28. Assembling wormshaft (A) and steering nut (B) to a manual steering box

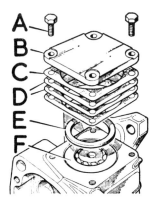

Fig. 11.29. Manual steering box end cover detail

A Securing bolts   D Shims
B End cover   E Spacer
C Gasket   F Bottom bearing race

wheel spokes are horizontal and the drop arm is in the 'straight ahead' position.

36 Check that the steering stop bracket is in place on the bodyshell and that any spacers used between the steering box and the bodyshell are refitted.

37 Fit the securing nut first to the steering box followed by the three bolts. Tighten the universal joint pinch bolt.

38 The rest of the refitting procedure is a reversal of removal but check the stop bolt adjustment and wheel alignment as described in the relevant sections of this Chapter.

23 Steering column/shaft - removal and refitment

1 It will first be necessary to remove the right-hand glove box (right-hand drive cars) or the left-hand glove box (left-hand drive cars.). To do this, open the glove box lid and detach one check strap end (right-hand box) or both strap ends (left-hand box) from the spring clips.

2 Undo and remove the two bolts that secure the hinges. The glove box may now be withdrawn from its location.

3 Slacken the bolt and nut that secure the journal to the steering box inner column.

4 On three thousand five models unscrew the two Allen screws (used on earlier cars) or the two self locking screws that secure the steering wheel finisher to the steering wheel. Lift away the finisher.
  On 3500 and 3500S models, prise the motif plate from the centre of the steering wheel.

5 Undo and remove the nut and spring washer that secure the steering wheel to the inner column and by using the palms of the hands on the rear of the steering wheel rim next to the horizontal spokes thump the wheel from the splines on the inner column.

6 Undo and remove the two bolts, nuts, plain and spring washers that secure the support bracket to the bulkhead next to the panel.

7 On late models, remove the bolts which secure the steering column lock to the facia.

8 On 3500S models disconnect the wiper delay switch vacuum pipe.

9 Make a note of the electrical cable connections at the steering column to the headlights and flashers so that they may be reconnected in the correct manner, and disconnect the cables.

10 The steering column shaft may now be lifted away, but take great care not to touch the headlining or trim which could be accidently damaged.

11 On late models remove the two crosshead screws from the steering lock switch and detach the switch from the lock body. Now spring off the plastic cover from the steering column nacelle - use a wide bladed screwdriver, hacksaw blade or knife so as not to break the plastic cover.

12 Extract the circlip and lift away the double spring washer from the top end of the steering column and withdraw it from the assembly.

13 Remove the lower double spring washer and circlip.

14 Note that on early produced models the steering column journal can be serviced and overhauled in the same manner as the universal joints on the propeller shaft.

15 On later produced models the steering column shaft is supplied complete with the journal and cannot be serviced.

16 Refitting the column shaft is the reverse sequence to removal but there are several additional points to be noted.

17 Take care to reconnect the electrical cables correctly and when the job has been completed, test the headlamps and flashers for correct operation.

18 When refitting the steering wheel, make sure the front wheels are in the straight ahead position and the steering wheel spokes in the horizontal plane.

19 If the car is a left-hand drive model the glove box compartment has a larger radius at the upper end so as to provide a clearance for the speedometer cable.

24 Steering column/shaft bearings - removal and refitment

1 Remove the steering column/shaft assembly as described in the preceding Section.

2 Remove the indicator and headlamp switches from the column.

3 Remove the steering column rake adjuster clip and Tufnol washer (Fig. 11.31).

4 Unscrew the rake adjuster and remove the nut and washers.

5 Drift the bearings from the steering column and install the new ones with recommended grease liberally applied.

6 Refitment is a reversal of removal and dismantling.

25 Steering box (power steering) - adjustment

1 Jack up the front of the car until the front wheels can be turned from lock-to-lock without touching the ground.

2 Gently rock the steering wheel (road wheels in 'straight ahead' position) and feel the amount of backlash (lost motion): this should not exceed 3/8 in (9.5 mm) at the steering wheel rim.

3 If the backlash is excessive, have an assistant slacken the adjuster locknut on the steering box and slowly tighten the adjuster screw while you continue to rock the wheel until the backlash has been reduced to that specified.

4 Tighen the adjuster locknut and check for tightness by turning the steering from lock-to-lock.

5 Lower the jack and remove it.

26 Steering box (power steering) - removal and refitment

1 Observe strict cleanliness during this operation, cleaning all external surfaces and fluid unions before any disconnection takes place. Never start the engine if the reservoir is empty or the system has been disconnected otherwise the pump will be damaged.

2 Remove the air cleaner from the carburettors and on rhd cars remove the brake fluid reservoir and its mounting bracket.

3 Remove the cap from the power steering fluid reservoir. Disconnect the pipes from the pump, drain and discard the fluid.

4 Disconnect the steering box flexible hoses.

5 Jack up the front of the car so that the wheels will turn from lock-to-lock.

6 Disconnect the two ball joints from the steering box drop arm. On lhd models, the accelerator bracket should now be detached from the steering box.

7 Remove the bolts, nut, lockplate and washers which secure the steering box to the bodyshell.

8 From inside the car at the rear of the glove compartment remove the pinch bolt from the steering column universal joint.

9 Withdraw the steering box, moving the position of the drop arm if necessary to facilitate the operation. Where spacer plates are located between the steering box and the bodyshell these must be retained.

10 Remove the drop arm if required, using a suitable extractor.

11 Refitment is a reversal of removal, but ensure that the original box to bodyshell spacer plates are installed and held in position by the securing bolts.

12 Fill the reservoir with specified fluid and bleed the system as described in Section 32.

13 Check the steering box adjustment, Section 25.

14 Check the wheel alignment, Section 34.

27 Steering box (power steering) - servicing

1 Remove the steering box as previously described in Section 26.

2 Remove the steering drop arm after first marking its relative position to the splined shaft.

3 Remove the coupling housing.

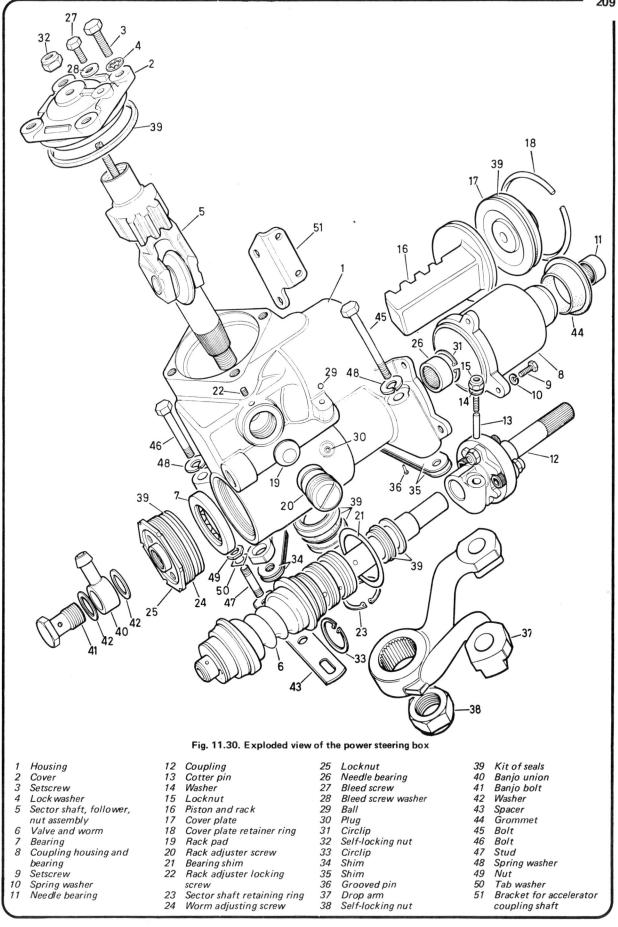

Fig. 11.30. Exploded view of the power steering box

1	Housing	12	Coupling	25	Locknut	39	Kit of seals
2	Cover	13	Cotter pin	26	Needle bearing	40	Banjo union
3	Setscrew	14	Washer	27	Bleed screw	41	Banjo bolt
4	Lock washer	15	Locknut	28	Bleed screw washer	42	Washer
5	Sector shaft, follower,	16	Piston and rack	29	Ball	43	Spacer
	nut assembly	17	Cover plate	30	Plug	44	Grommet
6	Valve and worm	18	Cover plate retainer ring	31	Circlip	45	Bolt
7	Bearing	19	Rack pad	32	Self-locking nut	46	Bolt
8	Coupling housing and	20	Rack adjuster screw	33	Circlip	47	Stud
	bearing	21	Bearing shim	34	Shim	48	Spring washer
9	Setscrew	22	Rack adjuster locking	35	Shim	49	Nut
10	Spring washer		screw	36	Grooved pin	50	Tab washer
11	Needle bearing	23	Sector shaft retaining ring	37	Drop arm	51	Bracket for accelerator
		24	Worm adjusting screw	38	Self-locking nut		coupling shaft

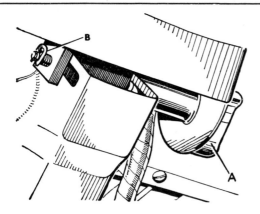

Fig. 11.31. Steering column rake adjuster (A) and clip (B)

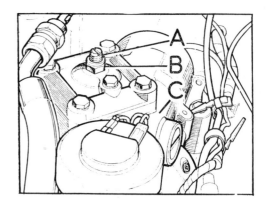

Fig. 11.32. Power steering box adjustment

A   Adjuster screw   C   Steering box
B   Locknut

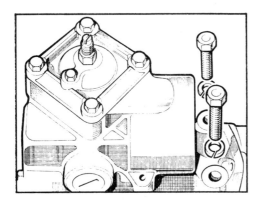

Fig. 11.33. Power steering box upper mounting bolts

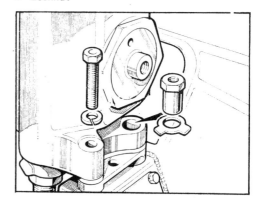

Fig. 11.34. Power steering box lower mounting bolts

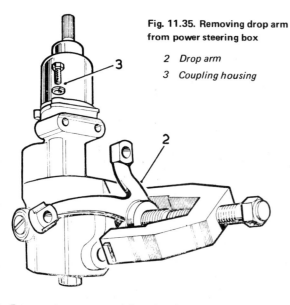

Fig. 11.35. Removing drop arm
from power steering box

2   Drop arm
3   Coupling housing

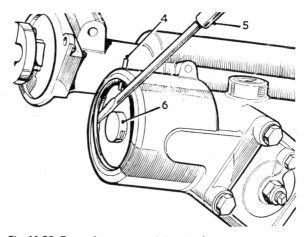

Fig. 11.36. Extracting cover retaining ring (power steering box)

4   Drift   6   Cover boss
5   Screwdriver

4   Extract the cover retaining ring from the cylinder bore groove by using a probe inserted through the hole provided (Fig. 11.36).
5   Withdraw the cover "6" using a pair of grips on the centre boss.
6   Refer to Fig.11.38 and rotate the input shaft coupling so that the rack piston rises to provide a distance between its crown and the top of the cylinder bore of approximately 1.75 in (44.5 mm).

7   Slacken the rack pad adjuster grub screw and turn the adjuster back two turns.
8   Remove the sector shaft adjuster locknut and withdraw the cover bolts. Lift off the cover tapping gently with a wooden mallet and screwing in the adjuster screw if necessary.
9   Withdraw the sector shaft just enough to disengage the sector teeth from the piston and rack teeth and then withdraw the piston and rack by screwing in a bolt (½ in UNC) into the tapped hole provided in the piston.

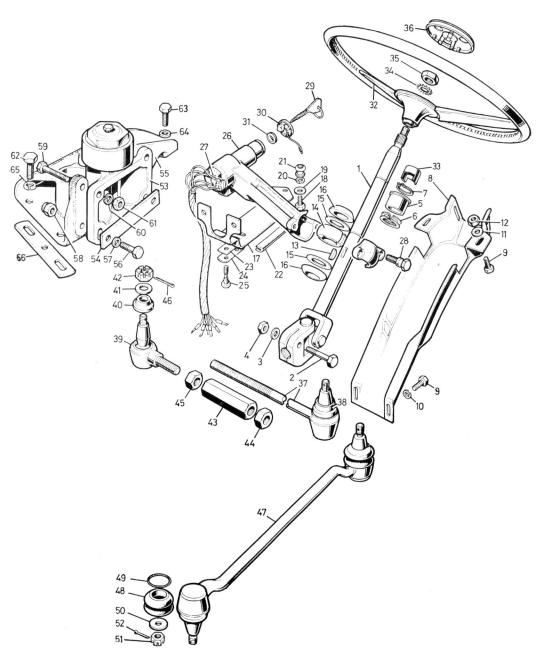

Fig. 11.37. Power steering linkage

1	Steering column shaft	18	Bolt	33	Flasher switch striker	50 Washer
2	Pinch bolt	19	Plain washer	34	Lockwasher	51 Castellated nut
3	Washer	20	Spring washer	35	Nut	52 Split pin
4	Nut	21	Nut	36	Finisher	53 Idler damper unit
5	Bearing	22	Plastic strip	37	Balljoint	54 Idler damper strap
6	Spring washer	23	Mounting plate	38	Rubber boot	55 Idler damper mounting
7	Circlip	24	Spring mounting plate	39	Balljoint	bracket
8	Support bracket	25	Bolt	40	Rubber boot	56 Bolt
9	Bolt	26	Steering column lock	41	Plain washer	57 Washer
10	Spring washer		assembly	42	Castellated nut	58 Self-locking nut
11	Plain washer	27	Combined ignition/lock	43	Adjuster sleeve	59 Bolt
12	Nut		switch	44	Locknut	60 Spring washer
13	Woodruff key	28	Shear bolt	45	Locknut	61 Nut
14	Collar	29	Ignition/lock key	46	Split pin	62 Setscrew
15	Thrust washer	30	Warning buzzer switch	47	Side rod	63 Bolt
16	Bearing	31	Grommet	48	Rubber boot	64 Plain washer
17	Lock mounting bracket	32	Steering wheel	49	Boot retaining ring	65 Spring washer
						66 Spacer

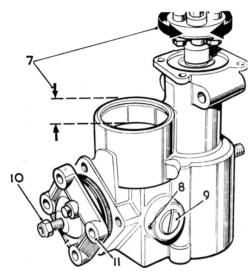

Fig. 11.38. Rack piston setting prior to sector shaft cover removal (power steering)

7 Rotation of input shaft	9 Rack pad adjuster
to provide rack piston	10 Sector shaft adjuster
height setting	locknut
8 Grub screw	11 Cover

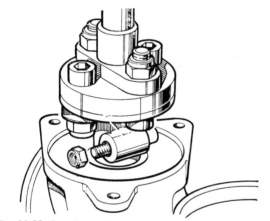

Fig. 11.39. Coupling to input shaft cotter pin (power steering box)

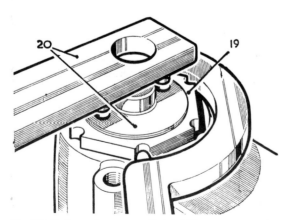

Fig. 11.40. Removing worm adjuster with a peg spanner (power steering box)

19 Locknut	20 Adjuster screw and peg spanner

10 Withdraw the sector shaft and lift out the rack adjuster thrust pad.

11 Remove the coupling assembly from the input shaft by withdrawing the cotter pin (Fig. 11.39).

12 Remove the worm adjuster locknut, using a 'C' spanner.

13 Remove the worm adjuster screw - a peg spanner will be required for this. One can be made up quite simply using a flat bar and two small bolts (Fig. 11.40).

14 Tap the input shaft to release the outer bearing cup at the opposite end of the housing.

15 Withdraw the outer bearing cup, the caged balls, the valve and worm assembly (Fig. 11.41). **Do not dismantle the latter or touch the trim screw otherwise the calibration of the unit will be upset.**

16 Withdraw the inner bearing ball race and remove the circlip and seals from the sector shaft housing bore.

17 Remove the circlip and seals from the input shaft housing bore (Fig. 11.42).

18 Unscrew the thrust pad adjuster grub screw and withdraw the thrust pad adjuster.

19 With the unit now dismantled, discard all rubber seals and obtain new ones. Renew the rubber seal and plastic ring fitted to the rack piston.

20 Inspect the needle bearing and rubber bush in the coupling housing and renew if worn. When refitting the bush, its outer diameter must be smeared with 'Bostik type 771' sealant, or similar material.

21 Examine the coupling flexible rubber disc and renew if perished. When refitting, tighten the coupling bolts until the rubber joint starts to compress.

22 Check that there is no side play on the sector shaft roller (Fig. 11.43) also that the adjuster screw retainer is well secured by its staking. If the adjuster screw end-float exceeds 0.005 in (0.12 mm) it should be reduced by screwing in the retainer and then re-staking.

23 Examine the sector shaft bearing areas for wear; also the gear teeth. If evident, renew the component.

24 If the sector shaft cover, bush and seat assembly is worn or damaged it can only be renewed complete.

25 Renew the sector shaft adjuster locknut as a matter of routine as it also acts as a fluid seal.

26 Inspect the steering box casing. If the cylinder bore is scored the casing must be renewed. If the bush or seat is worn or damaged drift them out and press in new ones.

27 Check the valve and worm assembly. The rings must be smooth and a sliding fit in their grooves. New rings may be fitted after expanding them in hot water.

28 Check the worm for scoring or wear, also to ensure that the input shaft to worm securing pins are tight and no movement between the two components is apparent.

29 Check the ball races and cups for wear and renew as required.

30 Examine the adjuster thrust pad for wear and renew as necessary; also the condition of the rack teeth and piston.

31 If the input shaft bearing is worn it must be renewed. Press the bearing into the bore with its numbered face uppermost and until this face is flush with the top of the housing bore.

32 Commence reassembly by fitting the seals dry to their components. When reassembling the components, dip them in clean hydraulic fluid of the specified type.

33 Fit the input shaft oil seal (lip leading) into the housing, followed by the extrusion washer and circlip (Fig. 11.46).

34 Fit the sector shaft oil seal (lip leading), the extrusion washer, dirt excluder (flat side leading) and the circlip (Fig. 11.47).

35 Refit the valve and worm assembly using the original shims and inner bearing cup. If new shims are used they should be of 0.030 in (0.76 mm) nominal thickness. Fit the inner cage and ball race, the valve and worm assembly (taking care not to damage the input shaft oil seal), the outer bearing assembly and cup (Fig. 11.42).

36 Loosely fit the worm adjuster and sealing ring, also the adjuster locknut.

37 Fit the coupling to the input shaft.

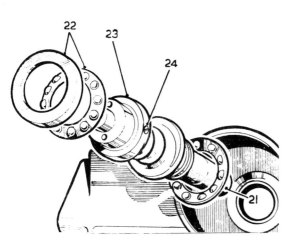

Fig. 11.41. Power steering box input shaft (21) outer bearing assembly (22) valve and worm assembly (23) trim screw (24)

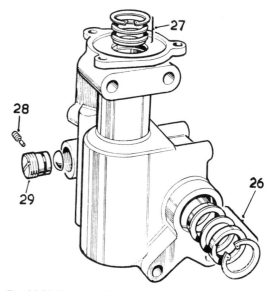

Fig. 11.42. Power steering box components

26 Sector shaft seals and circlip
27 Input shaft seals and circlip
28 Thrust pad adjuster grub screw
29 Thrust pad adjuster

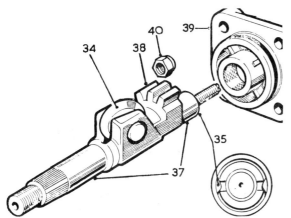

Fig. 11.43. Power steering sector shaft components

34 Roller
35 Adjuster screw and retainer
37 Shaft bearing surfaces
38 Gear teeth
39 Cover/bush/seat assembly
40 Locknut/seal

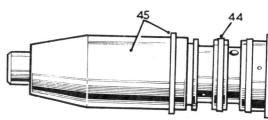

Fig. 11.44. Power steering valve/worm assembly

44 Valve rings
45 Sliding ring into position using chamfered tube as ring expander

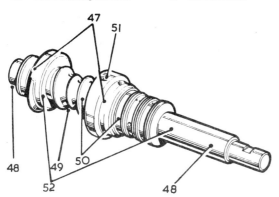

Fig. 11.45. Power steering valve/worm wear inspection diagram

47 Bearing surfaces
48 Seal surfaces
49 Worm track
50 Worm to sleeve end-float
51 Trim pin
52 Torsion type assembly pins

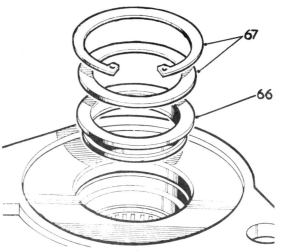

Fig. 11.46. Fitting input shaft oil seal (66) extrusion washer and circlip (67) to power steering box

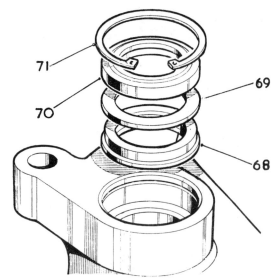

Fig. 11.47. Fitting sector shaft oil seal (68) extrusion washer (69) dirt excluder (70) and circlip (71) to power steering box

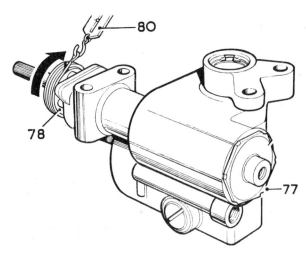

Fig. 11.48. Measuring input shaft bearing pre-load (power steering box)

77 Worm adjuster   80 Spring balance
78 Coupling

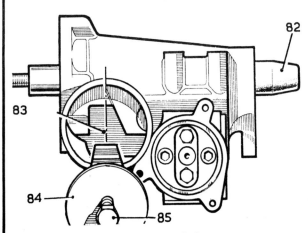

Fig. 11.49. Assembling sector shaft (82) to power steering box

83 Roller, sector shaft gear teeth in alignment with centre of rack piston housing bore
84 Seal and plastic ring
85 Bolt used as assembly tool

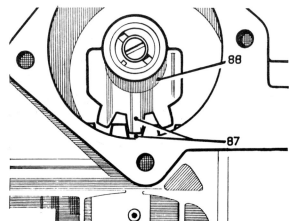

Fig. 11 50. Rack (87) and sector shaft (88) tooth alignment during reassembly (power steering box)

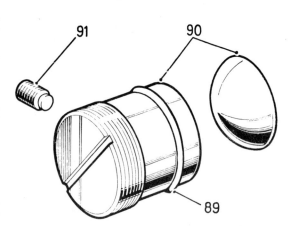

Fig. 11.51. Rack adjuster sealing ring (89) adjuster and nylon pad (90) grub screw (91) — power steering box

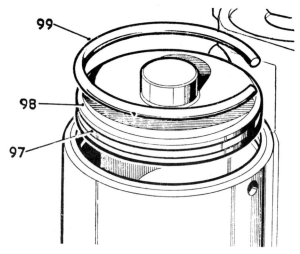

Fig. 11.52. Power steering box cylinder cover seal (97) retainer ring groove (98) retainer ring (99)

38 Screw in the worm adjuster until input shaft end-float just disappears. Now measure the preload of the bearings by wrapping a cord round the rubber coupling and attaching a spring balance to it (Fig. 11.48). Note the reading on the spring balance and then screw in the worm adjuster until the figure recorded on the spring balance is increased by 5 lbs (2.2 kg); this is required in order to settle the bearings. Back off the adjuster until when the cord is pulled the reading is only 3 lb (1.3 kg) in excess of that originally recorded. Tighten the adjuster locknut using the peg and 'C' spanners.

39 Insert the sector shaft into the casing (with the roller towards the worm) and taking care not to damage the oil seal (masking tape is useful to avoid this).

40 Locate the sector shaft as shown in Fig. 11.49.

41 Fit the rubber seal and plastic rings to the piston groove.

42 Fit the piston and rack so that the rack passes between the roller and gear teeth on the sector shaft. Align the rack and sector shaft teeth as shown in Fig. 11.50.

43 Push in the sector shaft and at the same time rotate the input shaft so that the sector roller engages the worm.

44 Fit the seal to the rack adjuster and then locate the rack adjuster and thrust pad so that they engage the rack. Unscrew the adjuster half a turn. Fit the nylon pad and adjuster grub screw so that they engage with the rack adjuster (Fig.11.51).

45 Install the sector shaft cover seal and screw it fully on to the adjuster screw. Locate the cover so that the bleed screw will be nearest the engine when the steering box is fitted to the car and tap the cover into position on the steering box casing. Tighten the cover bolts to a torque of 42 lb/ft (6.0 kg/m).

46 Fit the square section seal to the cylinder cover plate and press the cover plate into the cylinder so that it just clears the retainer ring groove. Locate the retainer ring in its groove so that one end of the ring is at a distance of 0.5 in (12.4 mm) from the extractor hole (Fig. 11.52).

47 Adjust the sector shaft by rotating the input shaft 1½ turns from either of the full lock positions. Unscrew the sector shaft adjuster screw so that there is some backlash between the input and sector shafts and then screw it in until the backlash is just eliminated. Using a cord and spring balance check the preload in a manner similar to that described in paragraph 38. The final setting should not exceed 16 lb (7.25 kg). Lock the rack adjuster with the grub screw.

48 Refit the coupling housing.

---

28 Pump drive belt (power steering only) - removal, refitment and adjustment

1 Open the bonnet and remove the cooling fan blades.

2 Remove the alternator drive belt.

3 Remove the compressor driving belt for the air conditioning system (if fitted) (see Chapter 12).

4 Unscrew and remove the steering pump mounting bolts from the support bracket and move the pump aside. Detach the driving belt by pulling it off the pump and crankshaft pulleys.

5 Fitting a new belt is a reversal of removal but it must then be adjusted in the following way.

6 Check the deflection at a point midway between the crankshaft and pump pulleys, reaching the belt from underneath the car. The total deflection should be between 0.025 and 0.375 in (6.0 to 9.0 mm). Adjust with the mounting pivot bolts and the adjuster strap bolts loose, then moving the pump as required. Finally tighten all bolts.

---

29 Pump, power steering - removal and refitment

1 Open the bonnet and remove the cap from the power steering fluid reservoir. Disconnect the reservoir to pump hose and drain the fluid into a suitable container and discard it.

2 Disconnect the outlet pipe from the steering pump.

3 Unscrew and remove the pivot mounting and adjuster strap bolts and after slipping the belt from the pump pulley remove

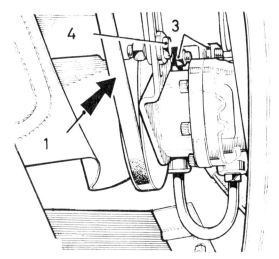

Fig. 11.53. Power steering pump drive belt adjustment

1 Deflection testing point   *4 Adjuster strap bolt*
3 Pivot mounting bolts

the pump.

4 Refitment is a reversal of removal but adjust the belt tension (Section 28) and bleed the system (section 32).

---

30 Pump, power steering - servicing

1 Thoroughly clean the pump exterior surfaces.

2 Remove the pulley by removing its centre bolt and spring and plain washers.

3 Remove the front mounting bracket and body end plate, also the rear bracket.

4 Secure the pump body in a vice and remove the adaptor screw, adaptor, fibre washer and rubber seal. Do not remove the venturi flow director which is pressed into the cover.

5 Remove the six Allen screws which secure the cover to the pump body and remove the pump from the vice, holding it vertically as the cover is removed so that the internal components do not fall out.

6 Remove the 'O' ring seals from the groove in the pump body and discard them.

7 Tilt the pump and extract the six rollers.

8 Draw the carrier off the shaft and remove the drive pin. Withdraw the shaft, the cam and the cam lock peg. If essential, remove the shaft key and draw off the sealed bearings.

9 Extract the shaft seal from the pump body and then withdraw the valve cap, valve and valve spring.

10 Wash all components in methylated spirit, or clean pump hydraulic fluid and renew all seals.

11 Examine all components for wear or damage and renew as appropriate.

12 Reassembly is a reversal of dismantling but observe the following points. The shaft seal is fitted to the pump body so that its lip is towards the carrier pocket. The vane carrier is fitted to the shaft so that the greater vane angle is as shown in Fig. 11.54.

13 Check the end-clearance of the carrier and rollers in the pump body using a straight edge and feeler gauges. If it is more than 0.002 in (0.05 mm) renew carrier and rollers.

14 Tighten the valve cap to a torque of 35 lb/ft (4.9 kg/m).

---

31 Reservoir, power steering system - removal and refitment

1 Unscrew and remove the filler cap, disconnect the fluid return hose (steering box to reservoir) at the steering box and drain and discard the fluid.

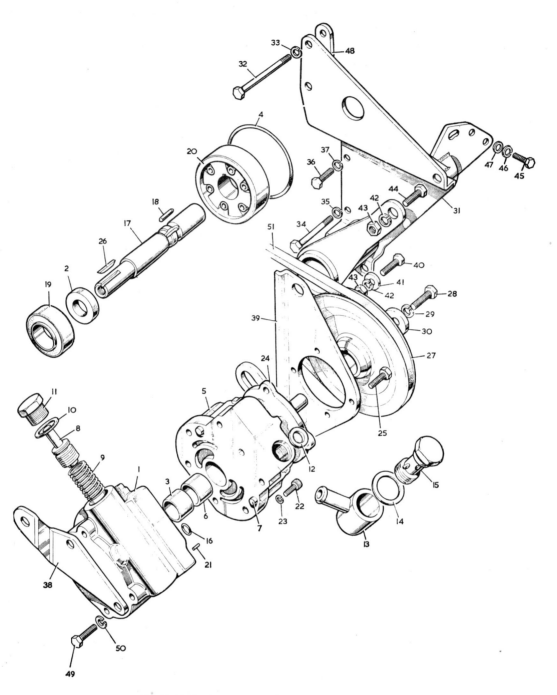

Fig. 11.54. Exploded view of the power steering hydraulic pump

1	Body	14	Fibre washer	26	Key	40	Nut
2	Oil seal	15	Banjo bolt	27	Pulley	41	Mounting bracket
3	Bush	16	'O' ring	28	Bolt	42	Bolt
4	'O' ring	17	Shaft	29	Spring washer	43	Bolt
5	End cover	18	Pin	30	Plain washer	44	Spring washer
6	Bush	19	Bearing	31	Pump mounting arm	45	Spring washer
7	Dowel	20	Vane carrier and roller	32	Bolt	46	Bolt
8	Valve assembly		vane	33	Spring washer	47	Spring washer
9	Spring (flow control)	21	Cam lock peg	34	Mounting bracket	48	Nut
10	'O' ring	22	Screw	35	Bolt	49	Bolt
11	Valve cap	23	Lockwasher	36	Plain washer	50	Plain washer
12	Adaptor seal	24	End plate	37	Spring washer	51	Spring washer
13	Banjo	25	Screw and washer	38	Bolt	52	Nut
				39	Spring washer	53	Drive belt

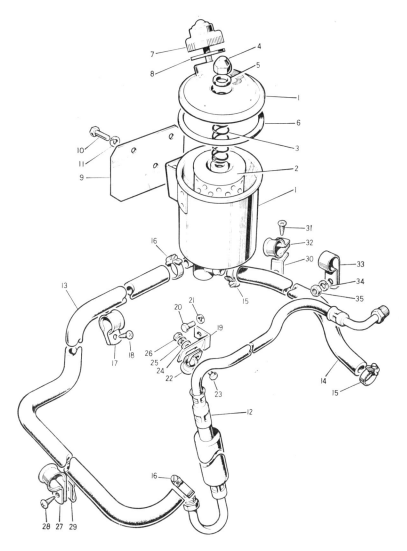

Fig. 11.55. Power steering fluid reservoir and pipe layout

1	Oil reservoir
2	Filter element
3	Spring
4	Domed nut
5	Seal
6	Sealing ring
7	Dipstick/cap
8	Seal
9	Support plate
10	Bolt
11	Spring washer
12	Pump to steering box hose
13	Reservoir to pump hose
14	Steering box to reservoir hose
15	Hose clip
16	Hose clip
17	Support clip
18	Screw
19	Bracket
20	Bolt
21	Spring washer
22	Clip
23	Bolt
24	Plain washer
25	Spring washer
26	Nut
27	Clip
28	Screw
29	Spire nut
30	Support clip bracket
31	Screw
32	Clip
33	Clip
34	Spring washer
35	Locknut

2 Disconnect the reservoir to pump hose at the reservoir and then plug all open pipes tp prevent the ingress of dirt.

3 Remove the reservoir and remove the top cover and extract the filter element. The latter should be renewed at intervals of 20,000 miles (32,000 km).

4 Refitment is a reversal of removal but always bleed the system (Section 32) and use fresh fluid for filling the reservoir.

32 Power steering system - filling and bleeding

1 Fill the reservoir with clean new fluid of the recommended type.

2 Start the engine and run until normal operating temperature is reached.

3 With the engine idling, slacken the bleed screw "A" (Fig. 11.56). As soon as fluid is ejected, tighten the bleed screw. Jack up the front of the car.

4 Top up the reservoir to the "F" mark on the dipstick and then turn the steering at full lock in both directions. Do not hold the full lock positions for more than 30 seconds otherwise overheating may occur. The steering movement should be smooth over its complete range of travel with no leaks at unions or connections. Repeat the bleeding process if necessary to smooth the action.

5 Switch off the engine and remove the jack.

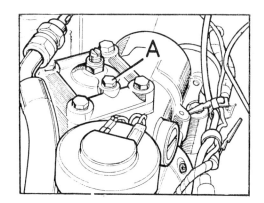

Fig. 11.56. Power steering bleed screw (A)

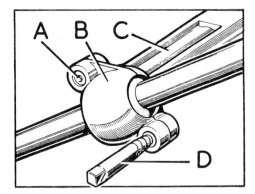

Fig. 11.57. Removing a shear bolt from steering column lock

A Drilled hole
B Lock half body clamp
C Body
D Extractor

Fig. 11.58. Fitting steering column lock to steering shaft

A Half clamp
B Lock shaft
C Lock body
D Steering column assembly
E Shear bolts
F Shim washers
G Collar
H Woodruff key
J Plastic bearings

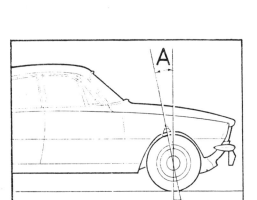

Fig. 11.59. Castor angle. For angle A see Specifications Section

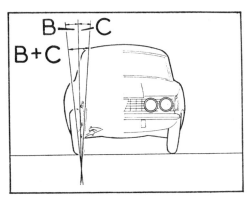

**Fig. 11.60. Camber (B) and steering inclination (C) angles.
For angles see Specifications Section**

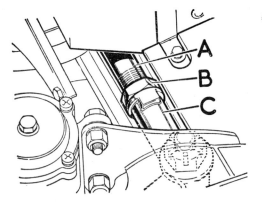

Fig. 11.61. Track rod adjustment (Three thousand five models)

A Track rod
B Locknut
C Balljoint

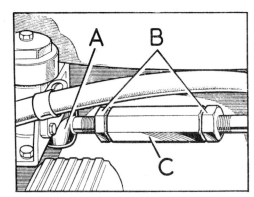

Fig. 11.62. Track rod adjustment (3500 and 3500 S models)

A Balljoint
B Adjuster
C Locknuts

33 Steering column lock - removal and refitment

1 Remove the steering column/shaft assembly (Section 23).
2 Centre punch the sheared ends of the lock securing bolts and either drill a hole to accept an extractor or drill the bolts out to a point below the mating faces of the two halves of the lock body. Remove the components of the lock.
3 Refitment is a reversal of removal but obviously if the original lock is being installed, new shear bolts will be required. Ensure that the column lock shaft engages in the slot in the metal collar and then tighten the securing bolts until the heads shear.

34 Wheel alignment

1 Accurate front wheel alignment is essential for good steering and slow and even tyre wear.
2 Before checking wheel alignment, ensure that the tyre pressures are correct, that the road wheels are not buckled, that the front hub bearings are not worn and are properly adjusted and that the steering linkage is in order.
3 There are four steering angles to be considered, only toe-in being adjustable.
   Camber, which is the angle at which the front wheels are set from the vertical when viewed from the front of the car. Positive camber is the amount (in degrees) that the wheels are tilted outwards at the top from the vertical.
   Castor is the right angle between the steering axis and a vertical line when viewed from each side of the car. Positive castor is when the steering axis is inclined rearward.
   Steering axis inclination is the angle, when viewed from the front of the car, between the vertical and an imaginary line drawn between the upper and lower suspension swivel pins.
   Toe-in is the amount by which the distance between the front inside edges of the road wheels (measured at hub height) is less than the diametrically opposite distance measured between the rear inside edge of the front road wheels.
   Front wheel tracking (toe-in) checks are best carried out with modern setting equipment but a reasonably accurate alternative and adjustment procedure may be carried out as follows;
4 Place the car on level ground with the wheels in the straight ahead position.
5 Obtain or make a toe-in gauge. One may be easily made from tubing, cranked to clear the sump and bellhousing, having an adjustable nut and setscrew at one end.
6 With the gauge, measure the distance between the two inner wheel rims at hub height at the front of the wheel.
7 Rotate the road wheel through 180° (half a turn) and measure the distance between the inner wheel rims at hub height at the rear of the wheel. This last measurement should be greater by 1/8 in (3.0 mm) with a tolerance of $\pm$ 1/16 in (1.5 mm).
8 Where adjustment is required, slacken the locknuts at each end of the track rod located at the rear of the engine and rotate the track rod. Turn the track rod only a quarter of a turn at a time before checking the toe-in as previously described.
9 When the setting is correct, tighten the locknuts without moving the track rods and ensuring at the same time that the ball joints are in the centre of their arcs of travel. Recheck the toe-in once again.

For 'Fault diagnosis' see next page.

35 Fault diagnosis - Suspension and steering

Symptom	Reason/s	Remedy
Steering feels vague, car wanders and floats at speed	Tyre pressures uneven	Check pressures and adjust as necessary.
	Shock absorbers worn	Test, and renew if worn.
	Spring broken	Renew spring.
	Steering gear ball joints badly worn	Fit new ball joints.
	Suspension geometry incorrect	Check and rectify.
	Steering mechanism free play excessive	Adjust or overhaul steering mechanism.
	Front suspension and rear axle pick-up points out of alignment	Normally caused by poor repair work after a serious accident. Extensive rebuilding necessary.
Stiff and heavy steering	Tyre pressures too low	Check pressures and inflate tyres.
	No oil in steering gear	Top up steering gear.
	Seized steering and suspension ball joints	Renew.
	Front wheel toe-in incorrect	Check and reset toe-in.
	Suspension geometry incorrect	Check and rectify (Rover dealer)
	Steering gear incorrectly adjusted too tightly	Check and re-adjust steering gear.
	Steering column badly misaligned	Determine cause and rectify (usually due to bad repair after severe accident damage and difficult to correct)
Wheel wobble and vibration	Wheel nuts loose	Check and tighten as necessary.
	Front wheels and tyres out of balance	Balance wheels and tyres and add weights as necessary.
	Steering ball joints badly worn	Replace steering gear ball joints.
	Hub bearings badly worn	Remove and fit new hub bearings.
	Steering gear free play excessive	Adjust and overhaul steering gear.
	Front springs weak or broken	Inspect and overhaul as necessary.

Additionally, for power steering:

Symptom	Reason/s	Remedy
Heavy steering at low speeds	Lack of oil	Top up.
	Idling speed too low	Increase speed
	Drive belt slipping	Adjust.
	Defective pump	Remove and service.
Poor handling under normal driving conditions	Rocker shaft adjuster over-tightened	Adjust.
Light or over-sensitive handling	Valve and worm assembly connecting pins worn	Dismantle box and renew worn components.
Noisy operation	Fluid hoses in contact with bodyshell	Alter route.
	Low oil level or air in system	Top up and bleed.

Chapter 12 Bodywork and bodyframe

Contents

Specifications

Dimensions		Three thousand five	Early 3500S (up to Oct. 1968)	3500 and 3500S (after Sept.1970)
Overall length	... ...	14 ft. 11¾ in. (4.56 m)	15 ft. 1 in. (4.59 m)	14 ft. 11¾ in. (4.56 m)
Overall width	... ...	5 ft. 6 in. (1.68 m)	5 ft. 6 in. (1.68 m)	5 ft. 6 in. (1.68 m)
Overall height	... ...	4 ft. 8¼ in. (1.42 m)	4 ft. 8¼ in. (1.42 m)	4 ft. 8¼ in. (1.42 m)
Wheelbase	... ...	8 ft. 7 3/8 in. (2.63 m)	8 ft. 7 3/8 in. (2.63 m)	8 ft. 7 3/8 in. (2.63 m)
Track (front)	... ...	4 ft. 5 3/8 in. (1.35 m)	4 ft 5 3/8 in. (1.35 m)	4 ft. 5 3/8 in. (1.35 m)
Track (rear)	... ...	4 ft. 3¾ in. (1.31 m)	4 ft. 3¾ in. (1.31 m)	4 ft. 3¾ in. (1.31 m)
Ground clearance (from final drive)	...	8½ in. (216.0 mm)	7 in. (177.8 mm)	8½ in. (216.0 mm)

* Weight with water, oil and 5 gals (22½ litres) of fuel	Three thousand five	Early 3500S (up to Oct. 1968)	3500	3500S
	2862 lbs (1298 kg)	3090 lbs (1461 kg)	2862 lbs (1298 kg)	2915 lbs (1322 kg)

* With air conditioning system add 110 lbs (50 kg).

1 General description

The body -with the exception of the bonnet and boot lid - is of welded steel construction. The bonnet and luggage boot lids are of aluminium alloy.

The structure comprises a basic bodyframe to which all mechanical units are attached. The body panels are secured to the body frame as separate painted units and this reduces the cost of repair in the event of damage. The doors are hinged at their forward edges and the locks are of the anti-burst type.

The difference in body style and equipment between the different models since introduction, is explained, and illustrated in the Introductory Section at the front of this manual.

Certain optional equipment has always been available during the production run and includes a full air conditioning system.

2 Maintenance - bodyshell

1 The condition of your car's bodywork is of considerable importance as it is on this that the secondhand value of the car will mainly depend. It is much more difficult to repair neglected bodywork than to renew the mechanical assemblies. The hidden portions of the body, such as the wheel arches, the underframe and the engine compartment are equally important, although obviously not requiring such frequent attention as the immediately visible paintwork.
2 Once a year or every 12,000 miles (19000 km) it is a sound scheme to visit your local main agent and have the underside of the body steam cleaned. This will take about 1½ hours. All traces of dirt and oil will be removed and the underside can then be inspected carefully for rust, damaged hydraulic pipes frayed electrical wiring and similar maladies. The car should be greased on completion of this job.
3 At the same time the engine compartment should be cleaned in a similar manner. If steam cleaning facilities are not available then brush 'Gunk' or a similar cleanser over the whole engine and engine compartment with a stiff paintbrush, working it well in where there is an accumulation of oil and dirt. Do not paint the ignition system, and protect it with oily rags when the 'Gunk' is washed off. As the 'Gunk' is washed away it will take with it all traces of oil and dirt, leaving the engine looking clean and bright.
4 The wheel arches should be given particular attention as undersealing can easily come away here and stones and dirt thrown up from the road wheels can soon cause the paint to chip and flake, and so allow rust to set in. If rust is found, clean down to bare metal with wet and dry paper, paint on an anti-corrosive coating such as Kurust, or if preferred, red lead, and renew the paintwork and undercoating.
5 The bodywork should be washed once a week or when dirty. Thoroughly wet the car to soften the dirt and then wash the car down with a soft sponge and plenty of clean water. If the surplus dirt is not washed off very gently, in time it will wear the paint down as surely as wet and dry paper. It is best to use a hose if this is available. Give the car a final wash down and then dry with a soft chamois leather to prevent the formation of spots.
6 Spots of tar and grease thrown up from the road can be removed by a rag dampened with petrol.
7 Once every six months, or every three months if wished, give the bodywork and chromium trim a thoroughly good wax polish. If a chromium cleaner is used to remove rust on any of the car's plated parts remember that the cleaner also removes part of the chromium, so use sparingly.

3 Maintenance - upholstery and carpets

1 Remove the carpets or mats and thoroughly vacuum clean the interior of the car every three months or more frequently if necessary.
2 Beat out the carpets and vacuum clean them if they are very dirty. If the upholstery is soiled apply an upholstery cleaner with a damp sponge and wipe off with a clean dry cloth.
3 Where leather upholstery is fitted, an occasional application of leather soap followed by an application of wax polish is all that is required.

4 Maintenance - PVC external roof covering

Under no circumstances try to clean any external PVC roof covering with synthetic detergents, caustic soaps or spirit cleaners. Plain soap and water is all that is required with a soft brush to clean dirt that may be ingrained. Wash the covering as frequently as the rest of the car.

5 Minor body repairs

1 At sometime during the ownership of your car it is likely that it will be bumped or scraped in a mild way, causing some slight damage to the body.
2 Major damage must be repaired by your local Rover agent, but there is no reason why you cannot successfully beat out, repair and re-spray minor damage yourself. The essential items which the owner should gather together to ensure a really professional job are:-
a) A plastic filler such as Holts 'Cataloy'.
b) Paint whose colour matches exactly that of the bodywork, either in a can for application by a spray gun, or in an aerosol can.
c) Fine cutting paste.
d) Medium and fine grade wet and dry paper.

3 Never use a metal hammer to knock out small dents as the blows tend to scratch and distort the metal. Knock out the dent with a mallet or rawhide hammer and press on the underside of the dented surface a metal dolly or smooth wooden block roughly contoured to the normal shape of the damaged area.
4 After the worst of the damaged area has been knocked out, rub down the dent and surrounding area with medium wet and dry paper and thoroughly clean away all traces of dirt.
5 The plastic filler comprises a paste and hardener which must be thoroughly mixed together. Mix only a small portion at a time as the paste sets hard within five to fifteen minutes depending on the amount of hardener.
6 Smooth on the filler with a knife or stiff plastic to the shape of the damaged portion and allow to thoroughly dry, a process which takes about six hours. After the filler has dried it is likely that it will have contracted slightly so spread on a second layer of filler if necessary.
7 Smooth down the filler with fine wet and dry paper wrapped round a small flat block of wood and continue until the whole area is perfectly smooth and it is impossible to feel where the filler joins the rest of the paintwork.
8 Spray on from an aerosol can, or with a spray gun, an anti-rust undercoat, smooth down with wet and dry paper, and then spray on two coats of the final finish using a circular motion.
9 When thoroughly dry polish the whole area with a fine

cutting paste to smooth the resprayed area into the remainder of the wing or panel and to remove the small particles of spray paint which will have settled round the area.
10 This will leave the area looking perfect with not a trace of the previous unslightly dent.

6 Major repairs to bodyframe

Upon reference to the 'General Description' at the beginning of this Chapter, it will be seen that the body design is of a rather unusual form whereby there is a basic bodyframe and it is to this that all the external panels are bolted. This means that major repair work cannot be successfully undertaken by the average owner and should be entrusted to a Rover body repair specialist who will have the necessary jigs, welding and hydraulic straightening equipment as well as skilled panel beaters to ensure a proper job is done.

If the damage is severe it is vital that on completion of repair the chassis is in correct alignment. Less severe damage may also have twisted or distorted the chassis although this may not be visible immediately.

7 Maintenance - locks and hinges

Regularly lubricate the bonnet, boot and door hinges with a few drops of engine oil from an oil can. The door striker plates should be given a thin smear of grease so as to reduce wear and ensure free movement (photo).

8 Door rattles - tracing and rectification

1 The commonest cause of door rattles is a misaligned, loose or worn striker plate but other causes may be:-
a) Loose door handles, window winder handles or door hinges.
b) Loose, worn or misaligned door lock components.
c) Loose or worn remote control mechanism.
2 It is quite possible for door rattles to be the result of a combination of the above faults so a careful examination must be made to determine the cause of the fault.
3 If the nose of the striker plate is worn as a result of door rattles, renew it and adjust the plate as described later in this Chapter.
4 If the nose of the door lock wedge is badly worn and the door rattles as a result, then fit a new lock as described later in this Chapter.

P7. Oiling a door hinge

5 Should the hinges be badly worn then they must be renewed as a complete assembly.

9 Door - removal and refitment

On 3500S models fitted with electric window lifts, the electrical leads must first be disconnected at their snap connectors by (front doors) peeling back the carpet at the door sill or (rear doors) by removing the door pillar trim in order to gain access to them.
1 Remove the locking cap from the check strap locating peg (Fig. 12.1) on the body.
2 Slacken the bottom hinge pin nut "D" and screw up the hinge pin "B" far enough to allow the door to be lifted off the top hinge pin. For this an Allen key will be required.
3 Do not slacken or remove the top hinge pin as this will locate the door when it is being fitted.
4 Very carefully lift the door from the hinge pin. Lay a blanket on the door and place the door so that it is leaning up against a wall out of the way to prevent any possible damage to it.
5 To refit the door, first locate the door on the top hinge pin and position the check strap onto its peg. Fit a new locking cap "A".
6 With an Allen key screw down the lower hinge pin until all play has been eliminated. Make sure that the door closes correctly and make any adjustment necessary as detailed in Section 10 of this Chapter.
7 Lubricate the hinge pins and check strap pivots with a little engine oil.
8 Reconnect the window lift leads (where appropriate).

10 Door - adjustment

1 To ensure that it is possible to fit the door correctly to its aperture there are three separate adjustments:-
a) Shims may be added or subtracted between the door hinge and the body so as to move the door either into or out of the door aperture (Fig. 12.2).
b) Shims may be added or subtracted between the door and hinge so as to move the door either forwards or rearwards in the door aperture (Fig. 12.3).
c) Raising or lowering the hinge pin which will raise or lower the door in the door aperture.
2 The correct method of adjusting the door position is to first check that the striker plate has not been distorted by placing a metal rule or straight edge across the two outside faces as shown

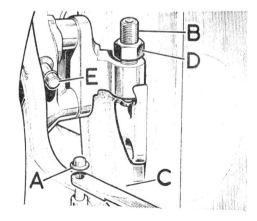

Fig. 12.1. Door (bottom) hinge

A Check strap post cap   D Locknut
B Pin   E Courtesy light switch
C Arm

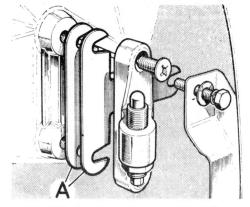

Fig. 12.2. Door hinge adjustment shims (A)

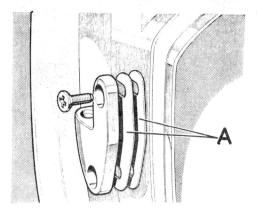

Fig. 12.3. Hinge to door shims (A)

Fig. 12.4. Testing door lock striker plate surfaces (A) for
alignment

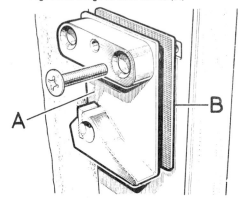

Fig. 12.5. Door striker plate (A) and adjustment shim (B)

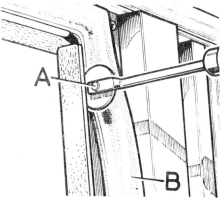

Fig. 12.6. Fitting door sealing rubbers

A Tool   *B Rubber strip*

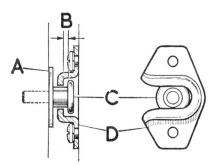

Fig. 12.7. Door anti-burst device

A Washer   *C Pin*
B Clearance   *D Striker plate*

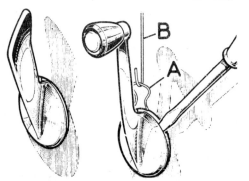

Fig. 12.8. Removing an interior door handle

A Spring clip   *B Wire hook*

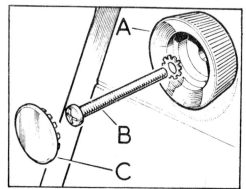

Fig. 12.9. Quarter light ventilator control knob

A Knob   *C Chrome blanking*
B Retaining screw   *plate*

in Fig. 12.4.

3   If distortion is evident, undo and remove the three crosshead screws and lift away the striker plate. Lower the seating face on the pillar so as to allow the plate to sit squarely.

4   If there is any distortion evident the sliding wedge will foul the bottom of the striker. Refit the plate and lightly tighten the screws to hold it in an approximately vertical position on the pillar.

5   With the door push button fully depressed, gently close the door on the striker. If necessary move the striker up or down until the dovetail does not foul either the nylon block or the bottom of the sliding wedge.

6   If movement of the striker is required but is not possible because the striker is at the limit of its movement, the door must be raised or lowered by adjusting the height of the hinge pins.

7   Tighten the three crosshead screws in the striker plate and close the door fully. Next check that overtravel exists by pushing the door aperture sealing rubber so that a little movement is felt after the rotary arm has been engaged. This movement should be about 0.060 inch which may be adjusted by moving the striker inwards or outwards relative to the door pillar.

8   The vertical and horizontal alignment of the lock and striker faces is independent and these should be kept as near parallel as possible.

9   To make sure that the rotary cam of the door lock is fully engaged with the latch plate, ensure that there is push button free play. With the door open make a pencil mark on the side of the button adjacent to the escutcheon.

10 Close the door and make a second mark on the side of the button. Open the door again and check if the two pencil marks coincide which is in fact what they should do.

11 If the clearance when the door is closed is more than when the door is open, the rotary cam of the lock is not fully engaged with the latch of the striker plate. Move the striker plate outwards slightly until this is rectified.

12 Make sure that the lock is fully engaged with the striker plate and also that the striker plate does not foul any part of the lock. Any further adjustment may be made by adding shims between the striker plate and the door pillar (Fig. 12.5).

11 Door sealing - renewal

1   Before the door sealing rubbers can be removed it is necessary to remove the doors (see Section 9).

2   Undo and remove the screws securing the sill plate and lift away the sill plate.

3   Undo and remove the screws and metal strip that secure the door apertures sealing rubber to the sill.

4   The door sealing rubber may now be carefully pulled out working from each end and meeting in the centre.

5   To refit the door sealing rubber prepare it first by applying a little Silicon MS4 to the seating face of the rubber.

6   Position the rubber at the door sill channel and secure it to the sill with the metal strip and screws.

7   The remainder of the door sealing rubbers may now be refitted using either the special tool as shown in Fig. 12.6 or a piece of tapered wood with the corners rounded. If the latter method is used, lubricate the wood with a little Silicon grease MS4.

8   Wipe away any excess Silicon grease and refit the sill plate.

9   It will now be necessary to refit the door in the reverse sequence to removal. Any adjustment to its positioning in the aperture may be made as detailed in Section 10 of this Chapter.

10 Lubricate the hinge pins and check strap pivots with a little engine oil.

12 Door anti-burst device - removal and refitment

1   This is simply a matter of unscrewing the large headed pin and washer from the door edge and the striker plate from the door pillar.

2   Refitment is a reversal of removal, but adjustment is very important and the striker plate adjustment must first be checked as being correct (Section 10) before centralising the anti-burst pin in its own striker plate while the door is being gently closed.

13 Door trim - removal and refitment

1   Carefully slide the veneer out of the waist moulding if the car is an early produced model. On later produced models remove the retaining clips.

2   Undo and remove the crosshead screws that retain the waist moulding.

3   On early 3500S models remove the setscrews from the underside of the door pull handle (front doors only).

4   On all models, remove the setscrews from the underside of the armrests.

5   Remove the window regulator handle and door lock handle by withdrawing the retaining clip as shown in Fig. 12.8.

6   Prise out the chrome plate from the ventilator control knob, remove the exposed retaining screw and withdraw the knob.

7   With a wide bladed screwdriver very carefully ease the door trim panel so as to release the clips from the door panel. When all are free, lift away the door trim and the plastic waterproof sheeting. On early 3500S models, the plug for the window lift switch must be disconnected as the trim is withdrawn.

8   Refitting the door trim is the reverse sequence to removal, but the following additional points should be noted:-

a) With Bostik or other suitable adhesive secure the plastic waterproof sheet to the door inner panel.

b) Care must be taken in refitting the veneer retaining clips on the later produced model.

9   Place veneer retaining clips with the convex side outwards and the chamfered sides facing towards the rear over the waist moulding fixing screw. The veneer may now be slid into position.

10 Reconnect the window lift plug (early 3500S models).

14 Door lock remote control mechanism - removal and refitment

1   Remove the door trim (Section 13), detach the spring clip and release the remote control arm from the door lock.

2   Unscrew and remove the three screws which hold the mechanism in position and lift it from the door.

3   Refitment is a reversal of the removal procedure but the mechanism must be adjusted as described in Section 19.

15 Front door lock - removal and refitment

1   Remove the door trim (Section 13).

2   Remove the closing panel.

3   Disconnect the remote control arm from the lock.

4   Remove the spring - loaded link eyebolt from the pushbutton locking arm (Fig. 12.11).

5   Remove the lock and dovetail with the lower link. The latter may then be detached if necessary.

6   Refitting is a reversal of removal but adjust as described in Section 19.

16 Rear door lock - removal and refitment

1   This is very similar to the operations described in the preceding Section except that a cranked link is fitted to the lock instead of a remote control arm (Fig. 12.12).

17 Door pushbutton - removal and refitment

1   Remove the door trim (Section 13).

2   Either remove the blanking panel, the door glass frame or

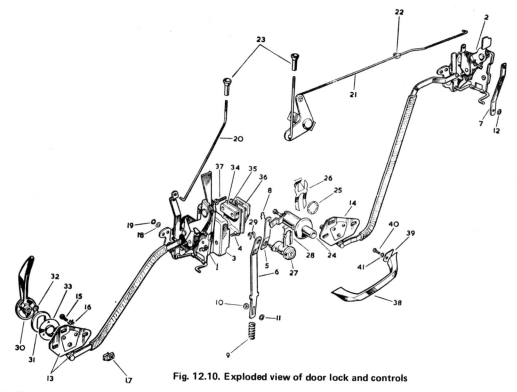

Fig. 12.10. Exploded view of door lock and controls

1	Front door lock assembly	10	Washer
2	Rear door lock assembly	11	Lockwasher
3	Dovetail	12	Lockwasher
4	Screw	13	Remote control, and link
5	Upper link	14	Remote control, and link
6	Lower link	15	Screw
7	Connecting link	16	Lockwasher
8	Clip	17	Spire nut
9	Spring	18	Wave washer
		19	Circlip
		20	Locking rod

21	Safety catch bellcrank
22	Steady bracket
23	Interior knob
24	Push-button
25	Washer
26	Clip
27	Front door private lock
28	Clip
29	Link clip
30	Interior door handle

31	Escutcheon
32	Clip
33	Wear plate
34	Striker
35	Shim
36	Plate
37	Screw
38	Exterior handle
39	Washer
40	Set bolt
41	Lockwasher

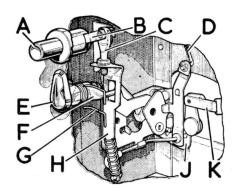

Fig. 12.11. Front door lock

A Push-button
B Locking arm
C Eye bolt
D Control rod
E Private lock
F Arm
G Retaining wire
J Door lock
K Link

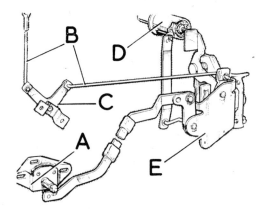

Fig. 12.12. Rear door lock

A Remote control
B Linkage
C Bellcrank link
D Push-button
E Lock assembly

the door strut according to model.

3 Release the upper link from the pushbutton lever (Fig. 12.13).

4 Remove the leaf spring retaining the pushbutton to the door panel and withdraw the pushbutton.

5 Refitment is a reversal of removal but adjust as described in Section 19.

18 Private lock with pushbutton - removal and refitment

1 Remove the door trim (Section 13).

2 Remove the blanking panel and the remote control arm from the lock.

3 Withdraw the wire rods which retain the private lock and remove the lock enough to detach the pushbutton securing leaf spring. Both components may then be withdrawn from the door together.

4 Refitment is a reversal of removal but adjust as described in the next Section.

19 Door locks - adjustment

1 The remote control handle and pushbutton have the same amount of free movement before they contact the rotary cam. Although this is a small amount, if it does not exist the door will open by the slightest touch and move onto the safety catch.

2 To adjust the remote control, slide it along its fixing hole slots so that the lever connecting the remote control with the lock has a slight amount of free movement before the lock begins to operate. This means that the lever "D" (Fig. 12.14) has a slight amount of movement and therefore the lock system is not loaded.

3 The push button adjustment bolt governs the clearance between the bolt head "A" (Fig. 12.15) and the lock contact plate "C". Clearance at this point should be between 1/16 and 3/32 in (1.6 and 2.4 mm). Once this condition has been achieved the push button should be fully depressed.

4 With the door in the open position check that the rotary cam of the lock is fully retracted to within 3°. This will ensure clearance of the striker plate latch when the door is opened.

5 To adjust the linkage for the key lock, first disconnect the link that connects the pushbutton to the lock and also the lower link.

6 Position the index hole in the pushbutton backplate with the hole in the operating arm by inserting a 1/8th in (3.2 mm) diameter rod as shown in Fig. 12.17.

7 Now with the key turn the arm on the key lock to the fully locked position. Then push the sill locking knob to the locked position and engage the lock arm in the cutout in the spring loaded link (Fig. 12.18). Adjust the eyebolt to take up any slack in the pushbutton locking arm and also ensure that the lock operated arm is not in contact with the frame of the cutout either in the locked or unlocked mode.

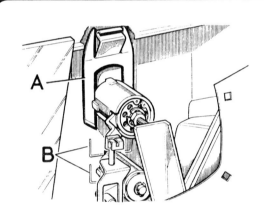

Fig. 12.13. Upper link clip (A) and lock clip (B) — push button lock

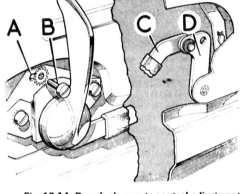

Fig. 12.14. Door lock remote control adjustment

A Elongated bolt holes   C Link
B Securing screws   D Lever

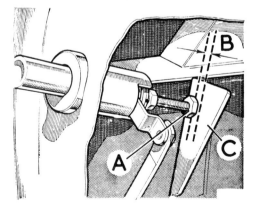

Fig. 12.15. Push-button adjustment

A Bolt head   (1.5 to 2.3 mm)
B Clearance 1/16 to 3/32 in.   C Plate

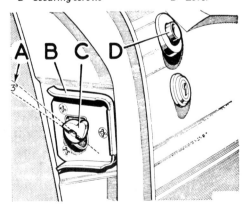

Fig. 12.16. Checking rotary cam

A 3° maximum movement   C Rotary cam
   (push-button fully depressed)   D Push-button
B Dovetail

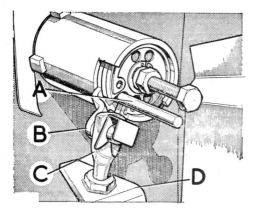

Fig. 12.17. Link adjustment

A   Rod   C   Link adjuster
B   Lever   D   Link

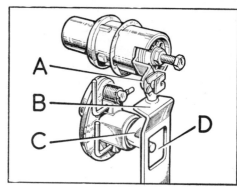

Fig. 12.18. Push-button locking arm

A   Push-button   C   Operating arm *in locked
B   Spring-loaded link   position*
                             D   Cut-out

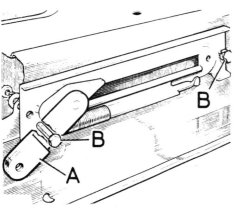

Fig. 12.19. Door check-strap

A   Arm   B   Securing bolts

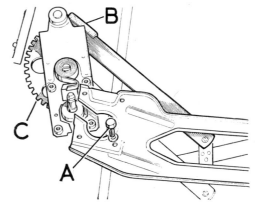

Fig. 12.20. Removing window regulator

A   Bolts   C   Mechanism
B   Anti-rattle pad

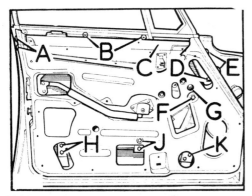

**Fig. 12.21. Door and electric window lift attachment points
(early 3500 S)**

A & B   Screws   bolts
C   Blanking panel   G   Motor bolts
D   Frame bracket bolts   H   Channel bracket screw
E   Bolts   J   Window stop bolts
F   Inner panel to frame   K   Channel bracket bolts

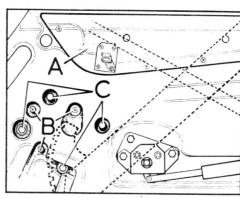

Fig. 12.22. Removing front window lift motor gear (early 3500 S)

A   Blanking panel   C   Gear assembly bolts
B   Motor bolts

20 Door check straps - removal and refitment

1 Remove the door trim (Section 13).
2 Remove the cap from the check strap pin and withdraw the check strap arm from the pin.
3 Remove the bolt and nut which secures the check strap to the door and remove the strap.
4 Refitment is a reversal of removal.

21 Window regulator - removal and refitment

1 Remove the door trim (Section 13).
2 Unscrew and remove the nine screws from the blanking panel and withdraw the panel.
3 Temporarily refit the window regulator handle and raise the glass to its fullest extent.
4 Unscrew and remove the four bolts and spring washers "A" which secure the window regulator mechanism (Fig. 12.20).
5 Separate the window regulator mechanism from the glass support channel and remove the mechanism from the door cavity.
6 Refitting is a reversal of removal but ensure that the anti-rattle pad is in position and smear a little grease on the moving parts of the regulator assembly.

22 Window regulator (electric - 3500S) - removal and refitment

1 Remove the door trim (Section 13).
2 Remove the blanking plate.
3 Unscrew and remove the bolts and screws which secure the window lift electric motor in position.
4 With front doors, disconnect the wiring and remove the motor.
5 With rear doors, leave the motor suspended until the leads are disconnected from the operating switch.
6 The regulator mechanism may now be withdrawn from the door cavity after having disengaged it from the glass support channel.
7 Refitment is a reversal of removal.

23 Front door glass frame - removal and refitment

1 Refer to Section 12 and remove the door trim.
2 Undo and remove the nine self tapping screws that secure the closing panel at the top of the door. Lift away the panel.
3 Undo and remove the crosshead set screw with star washer

that secures the glass stop to the bottom of the door.
4 Temporarily replace the window regulator handle and lower the glass as far as it will go without straining the regulator. This will give access to the five crosshead set screws with plain and spring washers, that secure the window frame cross rail to the top edge of the door.
5 Undo and remove the two crosshead set screws and shakeproof washers that retain the window frame channel to the rear edge of the door and the two set bolts, flat and spring washers retaining the channel at the front edge.
6 Undo and remove the four set bolts, flat and spring washers retaining the bottom of the window channel, access to which will be gained through the aperture in the bottom of the door.
7 Undo and remove the two long through bolts, flat washers and cage nuts located at the front top of the inside of the door. Access to these is gained through the aperture in the door.
8 Remove the complete window frame, mechanism and rubber weather seal from the door.
9 Wind up the window again and remove the four bolts and spring washers that secure the window regulator. Also slacken off the glass steady pad locknut and unscrew the bolt. Do not however, completely remove. This is shown in Fig. 12.24.
10 Remove the window regulator from the door. Take care that the glass does not fall down by supporting with a piece of wood.
11 Carefully slide the glass down the channel and remove from the inside of the door.
12 If necessary the glass support channel and glazing strip may be removed from the glass.
13 On 3500S models with electric window winder motors, remove the motor (preceding Section) and the frame and shims adjacent to it.
14 To refit the door glass carefully manoeuvre the complete assembly into position together with the weatherseal.
15 Refit the regulator assembly and connect it to the glass frame. Raise the glass and refit the glass regulator securing bolts loosely.
16 Lower the glass and fit the four self tapping screws and star washers to the top of the frame.
17 Replace all other bolts with their plain and spring washers as were used and noted upon removal, but do not tighten fully yet.
18 With the window frame height carefully adjusted so that it is a good fit in the bodyframe tighten the four set bolts into the two brackets located at the bottom of the glass runners.
19 Adjust the frame inwards so as to apply a little tension to the weatherstrip seal at the top of the door and then tighten all securing bolts.
20 Adjust the nylon glass steady panel so as to minimise door glass movement therefore checking glass vibration.
21 Replace the window glass stop bracket and rubber pad and secure in position with the four set bolts, plain and spring washers.

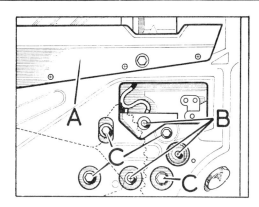

Fig. 12.23. Removing rear window lift motor gear (early 3500 S)

A Blanking panel   *C Gear assembly bolts*
B Motor bolts

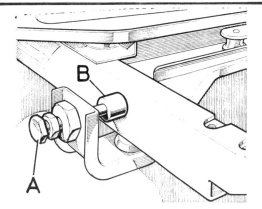

Fig. 12.24. Glass steady pad

A Bolt   *B Pad*

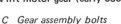

22 Fit the top closing panel and secure with the self tapping screws.

23 Refit the waist moulding with four self tapping screws and slide the veneer strip into position.

24 Refit the locking knob to the threaded rod.

25 Apply a little Castrol LM grease to all lock and window regulator moving parts to ensure adequate lubrication.

26 With Bostik or other suitable adhesive secure the plastic waterproof sheet to the door inner panel.

27 Refit the door trim panel and secure in position by pushing the clips fully home.

28 Refit the arm rest and secure with two crosshead set screws.

29 Refit the window winder handle and interior lock handle in their correct positions as was noted upon removal and secure with the retaining wire spring clips.

24 Front door quarter light (early models) - removal and refitment

1 Refer to Section 13 and remove the door trim.

2 Undo and remove the nine self tapping screws that secure the closing panel at the top of the door. Lift away the panel.

3 Refer to Fig. 12.25 and bend back the tab washer lock tab "B" undo the nut "A" and lift away the tab washer "B" plain washer "C", and spring "D" securing the front quarter light to the door. These are accessible through the door aperture.

4 The quarter light may now be lifted away from its location.

5 Refitting is the reverse sequence to removal. When the retaining nut for the quarter light has been locked in position apply a little Castrol LM grease to the spring washers and nut to prevent corrosion in the future.

25 Front door quarter light (later models) - removal and refitment

1 Refer to Section 13 and remove the door trim.

2 If the glass only is to be removed, pull off the spindle retaining clip and withdraw the glass and frame upwards.

3 Where the operating mechanism is to be removed, the door glass frame must first be withdrawn as described in Section 23.

4 Remove the bolts which secure the front quarter light mechanism to the frame and lift off the quarter light complete.

5 Refitment is a reversal of removal.

26 Rear door glass frame - removal and refitment

1 Refer to Section 13 and remove the door trim.

2 Unscrew and remove the nine self tapping screws and the two crosshead screws which secure the blanking panel and remove the panel. On 3500S models, the rod support will first have to be released before the panel can be removed.

3 Undo and remove the four crosshead set screws with star washers that secure the glass stop to the door and lift away the stop.

4 Temporarily replace the window regulator handle and lower the glass to its fully down position.

5 Wind the window down to give access to the six crosshead screws, plain washers and spring washers that secure the channel rails to the top of the door.

6 Undo and remove the two bolts, plain and spring washers that secure the side frame at the rear side of the door.

7 Undo and remove the two crosshead screws and shakeproof washers next to the lower door hinge.

8 With a screwdriver ease out the rubber grommet. Undo and remove the nut, spring and plain washer adjacent to the top hinge.

9 On 3500S models, raise the glass, remove the crosshead screws which secure the window lift motor and remove the motor letting it hang by its electrical lead.

10 Withdraw the spring clip that secures the bell crank link and disconnect the link from the door lock mechanism.

11 The complete window and mechanism may now be lifted away from the door together with the weather seal rubber.

12 Wind up the window glass and remove the bolts that secure the window winding mechanism, which may be lifted away.

13 Carefully slide the glass down its channel and lift away the glass.

14 The support channel and glazing strip may be removed from the glass.

15 To refit the glass, first reassemble it to the channel and then refit the window winding mechanism.

16 Slide the glass assembly into position with the top external weather seal rubber in place.

17 Wind the glass down so as to give access to the six crosshead screws in the channel cross rail.

18 Replace all bolts, crosshead screws, nuts and washers located as noted during dismantling but do not tighten at this stage.

19 Adjust the length of the window so as to be a correct fit in the body panel aperture and then tighten the four set bolts into the two brackets located at the bottom of the runners. Adjust the position of the frame inwards slightly so it will apply tension to the seal at the top of the door and now tighten all securing bolts.

20 Apply a little grease to all mechanical moving parts and check the window for ease of movement.

21 Refit the window glass stop bracket and secure with the four set bolts, plain and spring washers.

22 Replace the top closing panel and secure in position with the nine self tapping screws, and the door locking mechanism secured by crosshead screws and star washer to the closing panel.

23 Refit the door trim panel.

27 Rear door quarter light (opening type) - removal and refitment

1 Remove the door trim as detailed in Section 13.

2 Undo and remove the nine self tapping screws, two crosshead screws and star washers securing the blanking panel to the door locking mechanism. Lift away the panel.

3 Unscrew the plastic knob from the door lock remote control and lift away the door frame bracket.

4 Slacken the pinch bolt that secures the bottom of the quarter light spindle located as shown in Fig. 12.27.

5 Remove the spring clip that secures the remote control lever to the lock.

6 Unscrew the spindle from the bracket in the glass frame.

7 Undo and remove the screw and fibre washer that secures the catch to the quarter light.

8 The quarter light may now be removed from the frame in the door.

9 Refitting the quarter light is the reverse sequence to removal. The bottom hinge pin should be adjusted so there is no up or down movement and then locked in position with the bolt.

10 Apply a little grease to the moving parts of the hinge and pivot to ensure ease of movement.

28 Rear door quarter light (fixed type) - removal and re-fitment

1 Remove the door glass frame (Section 26).

2 Drill out the pop rivets and remove the blanking panel and channel.

3 Withdraw the glass and rubber surround.

4 Refitment is a reversal of removal.

29 Door strut - removal and refitment

1 Remove the door trim (Section 13).

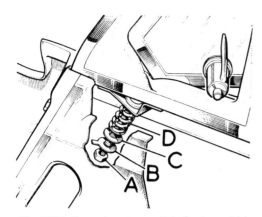

Fig. 12.25. Front door quarter light (early models)

A   Nut   C   Plain washer
B   Tab washer   D   Spring

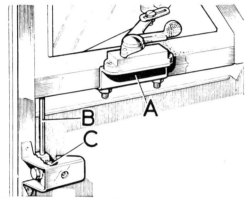

Fig. 12.27. Rear quarter light attachment (opening type)

A   Catch   C   Pivot pin lockscrew
B   Pivot pin

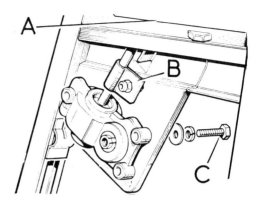

Fig. 12.26. Front door quarter light (later models)

A   Glass and frame   C   Bolts
B   Spindle retaining clip

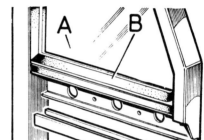

Fig. 12.28. Rear quarter light attachment (fixed type)

A   Glass   C   Sealing panel and
B   Rubber surround   channel

2   Remove the door glass frame (Sections 23 and 26).
3   Remove the bolts which secure the strut end brackets to the door panel.
4   Withdraw the strut by lowering the forward end into the door cavity and then lifting it out through the top of the door.
5   Refitment is a reversal of removal.

***

30 Bonnet - removal and refitment

***

1   Open the bonnet and secure in the open position. Place some old blankets over the rear of the wings and below the windscreen so that the paintwork is not damaged.
2   Disconnect the screen washer hose from the bottle. With the assistance of a second person take the weight of the bonnet (it is made of aluminium so it is not very heavy but take care because it is easily scratched or damaged). Undo the two retaining bolts to each hinge and lift away the bolts, spring and plain washers. These are located as shown in Fig. 12.30.
3   Note that the forward hinge securing bolt also secures the front wing rear mounting bracket which is 'Pop' riveted to the wing panels.
4   With the bolts free, carefully slide the bonnet rearwards about 2 inches from the hinges to clear the wing upper mounting brackets. Lift the rear of the bonnet up and then lift away the complete bonnet from the front of the car. Put in a safe place where it will not be damaged.
5   Refitting is the reverse sequence to removal. Inspect the sealing around the hinge mounting plate and if rusted clean off and re-seal with Bostik 692.

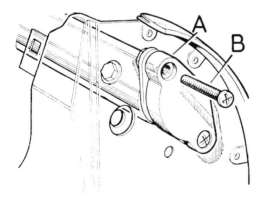

Fig. 12.29. Door strut

A   Distance piece   B   Bolt

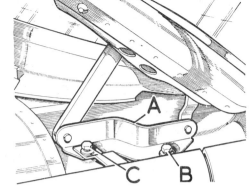

Fig. 12.30. Bonnet hinge detail

A   Hinge   B & C   Bolts

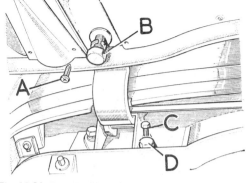

Fig. 12.31. Boot lid hinge detail

A   Self-tapping screw   C   Hinge steady post
B   Bolt   D   Bolt

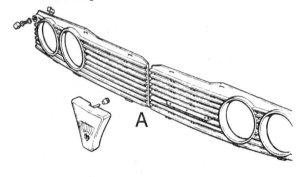

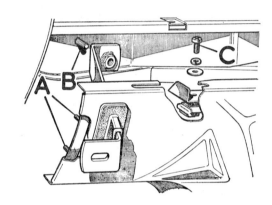

Fig. 12.33. Front valance attachment

A   Bolts to front wing   C   Valance to bodyshell
B   Bumper bracket to bodyshell   bolts
    bolt

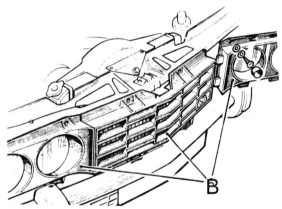

Fig. 12.32. Early style (A) and late style (B) radiator grilles

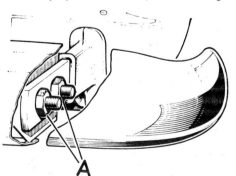

Fig. 12.35. Rear valance bolts

A   To wing   C   To rear jacking point
B   To bodyframe   D   Reverse lamp connectors

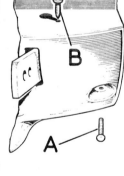

Fig. 12.34. Rear bumper bolts (A) (Three thousand five models)

31 Boot lid - removal and refitment

1 Open the boot and remove the metal hinge covers on the boot lid.
2 An assistant must support the weight of the boot lid in the fully open position as otherwise it can be easily damaged by the securing bolts.
3 Place an old blanket under the rear screen and along the forward edges of the rear wings so that they will not be scratched.
4 Undo and remove the four bolts and plain washers that secure the hinge to the boot lid (Fig. 12.31).
5 Very carefully lift away the boot lid.
6 To remove the hinge undo and remove the three bolts which secure the rear edge of the lower decker panel, so as to allow the panel to be eased out of its normal position.
7 Slacken the hinge bracket steady bolts.
8 Undo and remove the four bolts that secure the hinge to the body and lift away the hinges and torsion bars as a complete assembly.
9 Refitting the hinge and torsion bar assembly and also the boot lid is the reverse sequence to removal. To adjust the position of the boot lid in the aperture, the bolts securing the hinge bracket to the base should be slackened and adjusted as necessary.

32 Radiator grille - removal and refitment

1 Open and prop the bonnet.
2 With early style grilles, remove the badge by tapping the knurled studs at its rear.
3 Prise the plastic caps from the grille screw heads and remove both sections of the grille.
4 With later style grilles, remove the screws from the head-lamp bezels and the radiator grille and withdraw the component sections.
5 Refitment is a reversal of removal but ensure that the rubber insulators on the latest style grille engage correctly in their lower slots (see Chapter 10 - headlamp sealed beam unit - renewal).

33 Front valance and bumper (Three thousand five models) - removal and refitment

1 Undo and remove the six bolts with spring and plain washers that secure the bumper bar to the brackets. Lift away the bumper.
2 Undo and remove the two bolts, spring and plain washers and nuts that secure the two outer brackets to the body.
3 Remove the radiator grille as described in the preceding Section.
4 Undo and remove the six crosshead screws and shakeproof washers that secure the two sections of the grille to the frame and lift away the grille.
5 Remove the six self tapping screws that secure the valance to the front member of the base unit.
6 Undo and remove the four nuts, plain and spring washers that secure the wing to the valance. (Fig. 12.33) Remove the stud plates.
7 The front valance may now be removed from the base unit.
8 Refitting the valance and the bumper bar is the reverse sequence to removal. When refitting the two grille halves mount them loosely in position and then centralise to suit the badge clips.

34 Front valance and bumper (early 3500S) - removal and refitment

1 The procedure is similar to that described in the preceding Section but with 3500S models, disconnect the wing from the

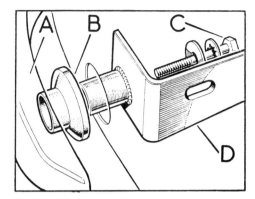

Fig. 12.36. Rear bumper side bolts (early 3500 S models)

A Bumper   C Side bolt
B Grommet   D Side bracket

front flashers and remove the towing eye bracket.

35 Rear valance and bumper (three thousand five models) - removal and refitment

1 Undo and remove the six crosshead set screws that secure the rear valance to the bodyshell. Also undo and remove the two special bolts "A" (Fig. 12.34) that secure the valance to the rear wing.
2 On early produced models note the reverse light cable colours at their connections as shown in Fig. 12.35 and disconnect the cables.
3 Undo and remove the reverse lamp brackets (early models only).
4 Remove the two drive screws that secure the rear valance panel to the base unit behind the reverse light mounting bracket.
5 Undo and remove the four bolts, nuts and washer "A" that secure the bumper to the mounting bracket.
6 The bumper bar and valance may now be lifted away whilst taking care that the two cables without the connectors are fed through the rubber grommet.
7 Refitment is the reverse sequence to removal.

36 Rear valance and bumper (early 3500S models) - removal and refitment

1 The procedure is similar to that described in the preceding Section except that the bumper side bracket bolts must be removed.
2 The towing eyes and stiffener may be removed if required.

37 Front wing - removal and refitment

1 Should it be necessary to remove the front wing because of corrosion subsequent to the fitting of a new panel or to give better access to the front suspension as detailed in Chapter 11, first open the bonnet and support in the fully open position.
2 Disconnect the battery earth terminal for safety reasons.
3 Clean the electrical cables and connections located behind the front wing and identify the cable coding. If this is difficult use strips of insulation tape so that the cables may be re-connected correctly. Release the three cables.
4 Undo and remove the bolt, spring washer and flat washer "A" (Fig. 12.37) that secure the rear top edge of the panel to the base unit. It will be seen that this bolt is also used to secure the hinge
5 Remove the nuts, washers and spring washers together with stud plate from the valance.

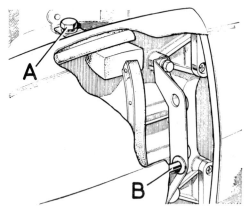

Fig. 12.37. Front wing attachment at rear end

A Bolt   B Dowel

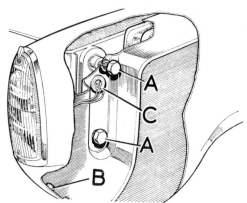

Fig. 12.38. Front wing attachment at front end

A Bolt   C Flasher and side lamp
B Bolt   connections

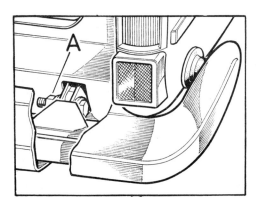

Fig. 12.39. Rear bumper bolts (A) — (early 3500 S models)

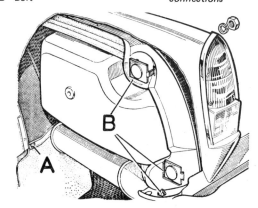

Fig. 12.40. Rear wing attachment bolts (B) mud flap bolts (A)

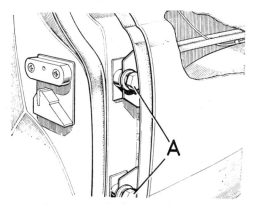

Fig. 12.41. Rear wing attachment at front end (A) bolts to door
pillar

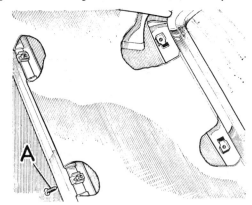

Fig. 12.42. Rear quarter panel attachment screws (A)

6   Undo and remove the two bolts fixing the top front of the
wing, working underneath the wheel arch.
7   Refer to Fig. 12.38 and undo and remove the two screws "A"
from the underside of the wing.
8   Ease the wing forwards so as to bring it clear of the dowel
"B", and lift it away from the side of the car. If the panel is being
removed to give better access to the front suspension system,
take great care not to scratch the wing on the front bumper by
suitably marking off the area with masking tape or wrapping the
end of the bumper bar in a little cloth.
9   The rear edge of the front wing is located by a dowel in a
rubber grommet. Soak the dowel in penetrating oil and remove

the securing nut and spring washer.
10 Fit the dowels to the new wing panel.
11 Undo and remove the four crosshead screws that secure the
front light lens to the light body. Lift away the lens and foam
rubber seal.
12 Undo and remove the three screws that secure the light body
to the front wing. The light body may now be withdrawn from
the front wing.
13 Fit the wing into position on the body taking care not to
scratch the paintwork on the bumper. If necessary wrap a little
cloth around the end of the bumper bar.
14 Insert the special nuts into the wing. These nuts are a nylon

equivalent of the speed nut variety. They are positioned in the wing so that when the bolt is entered and screwed up the nut will grip tighter.

15 Refit the wing securing bolts, screws and nuts.

16 A new wing panel may be obtained either factory painted in a standard colour or finished in primer.

17 It is recommended that all exposed bolts and nuts are coated with an anti-corrosive paint.

18 Rub down the primer with some wet and dry flatting paper and any bare metal areas should be given a coat of undercoat.

19 Insert the three nylon caps into the front light aperture.

20 Refit the light body and foam rubber backing and secure with the three screws. Replace the light lens and foam rubber backing and secure with the four crosshead screws.

21 Reconnect the light cables in the same positions as were noted upon removal from the connectors under the front wheel arch.

38 Rear wing - removal and refitment

1 Open the boot lid and support in the fully open position.

2 Disconnect the battery earth terminal for safety reasons.

3 Make a note of the cable connections at the connectors, located within the boot compartment, to ensure correct re-assembly. Disconnect the cables at this point. On early 3500S models, disconnect the leads to the number plate lamp, remove the four bumper to rear bracket bolts and the bumper side bracket bolts.

4 Remove the trim from the inside panel within the boot compartment which will give access to the rear wing mounting bolts.

5 Undo and remove the two bolts with spring and plain washers that secure the wing to the body side panel. One will be found inside the boot and the second one located on the underside of the car at the rear corner.

6 Note that on later produced models studs mounted onto plates are used instead of bolts. It may be necessary to soak the nuts in penetrating oil as they will probably be well rusted in position.

7 Undo and remove the special bolt and shakeproof washer that secures the rear valance to the rear wing.

8 Remove the two bolts, spring and plain washers that secure the forward edge of the rear wing to the rear door pillar. These are accessible once the rear door is opened.

9 Refer to Fig. 12.40 and remove the nut and bolt "B" adjacent to the mud flap.

10 Remove the rear wing and at the same time withdraw the rear light cluster cables through the rubber grommet in the side of the boot inner panel.

11 Next remove the crosshead screws that secure the lens to the light cluster and lift away the lens and foam rubber seal.

12 Undo and remove the screws that secure the lamp body to the rear wing and lift away the lamp body and foam rubber seal.

13 Refitment is a reversal of removal but make good any joint seals and undersealing and respray to match the remainder of the bodywork.

39 Rear quarter panel - removal and refitment

1 Remove the complete rear seat assembly by first lifting out the rear seat cushion. Undo and remove the two self tapping screws that secure the bottom of the rear seat squab to the body, and lift away the squab from inside the car.

2 Undo and remove the two crosshead drive screws that retain the rear quarter trim. Carefully ease the trim panel forwards so as to release it from its retaining clips. When free lift the trim panel away.

3 Undo and remove the three crosshead screws adjacent to the edge of the rear screen.

4 Undo and remove the three chrome plated crosshead screws that are located in the body adjacent to the rear edge of the door

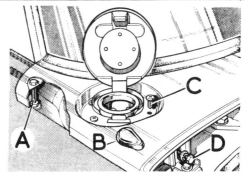

Fig. 12.43. Decker panel and fuel filler cap attachment

A Panel bolt   screw
B Fuel cap lock   D Panel bolt
C Filler cap assembly

glass surround.

5 Carefully lift away the rear quarter panel.

6 Refitment is the reverse sequence to removal. It is necessary to seal the three rear screw heads with a little sealing compound.

40 Rear decker panel - removal and refitment

1 Open the boot compartment lid. Undo and remove the four screws that secure the trimmed boot inner panel covering the petrol tank. Lift away the panel.

2 Slacken the hose clips that secure the top petrol filler hose and cut the hose to remove it.

3 Undo and remove the four screws "C" that secure the petrol filler unit. These are visible once the filler cap has been opened.

4 Remove the complete filler unit from the rear decker panel.

5 Release the rubber grommet retaining spring clip and remove the rubber grommet from the filler cap orifice.

6 Undo and remove the two nuts with plain and spring washers that secure the decker panel to the base unit. These are located at the right-hand and left-hand corners of the decker panel and are readily accessible through the boot.

7 Undo and remove the three nuts and bolts "D" (Fig. 12.43) that secure the rear edge of the decker panel and carefully lift away the panel.

8 Refitment is the reverse sequence to removal. It will be necessary to fit a new fuel filler hose.

9 To give a good seal apply a little sealing coumpound to the filler end of the top hose and a little round the mounting bolts.

41 Fuel filler cap - removal and refitment

1 Refer to the preceding Section and remove the rear decker panel.

2 Open the fuel filler cap and place a large rag in the filler pipe neck to stop dirt ingress.

3 Undo and remove the special set bolt "H" (Fig. 12.44) and shakeproof washer "G" that secures the lever "F" to the lock. Lift away the lever and shaped washer "E".

4 Remove the large nut "D" that secures the lock "A" to the decker panel and withdraw the lock "A" washers "B" and distance piece "C" from the panel.

5 To refit the lock place it in the decker panel with a washer each side of the panel and the distance piece on the underside and secure in position with the large nut.

6 Refit the special washer and the lever making sure that it will engage in the filler cap catch. To do this temporarily fit the filler cap to the decker panel.

7 Lock the lever in position with the shakeproof washer and special set bolt.

8 The rear decker panel should now be refitted.

9 Lubricate the lock by placing a little thin oil on the key and inserting and withdrawing it several times.

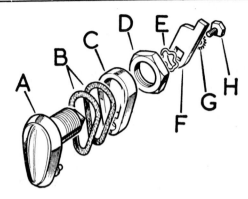

Fig. 12.44. Exploded view of fuel filler cap lock

A Lock
B Washers
C Distance piece
D Nut

E Special washer
F Lever
G Lockwasher
H Set bolt

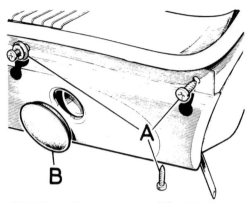

Fig. 12.45. Body sill securing screws (A) and jacking point plug (B)

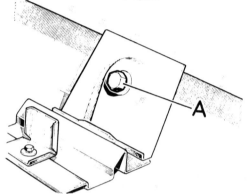

Fig. 12.47. Rear screen centre support bracket

A Securing bolt

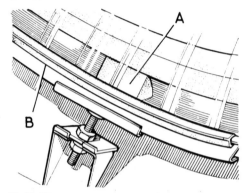

Fig. 12.46. Windscreen spacer blocks (A), support channel (B)

42 Body sill panels - removal and refitment

1 Refer to Fig. 12.45 and remove the crosshead set screws and also the drive screws that secure the valance to the bodyshell.
2 Lift away the body sill panel.
3 Refitment is the reverse sequence to removal.

43 Through-flow ventilation flap valve - removal and refitment

1 The valve is made of fibre-glass cloth and operates quite automatically. Access to it is obtained by carrying out the following operations.
2 Remove the rear seat and seat belt outer anchorage bolts.
3 Remove the interior quarter trim panel and the rear exterior quarter panel (Section 39).
4 Drill out the pop rivets which retain the flap valve and the drain channel.
5 Refitment will entail pop riveting and then resealing the drain channel. Ensure that the rubber strips which prevent the flap valve sticking in the open position are securely attached.

44 Face level vents - removal and refitment

1 Remove the instrument panel and facia top rail (see Chapter 10). On three thousand five models, remove the switch panel as well.
2 Remove the parcel shelf (Sections 49 and 50).
3 Remove the insulating felt pieces, the cover plates and vent outlet screws and withdraw the vents.
4 Refitment is a reversal of removal but reseal the vents to the bodyshell.

45 Windscreen - removal and refitment

1 Remove the bonnet (Section 30).
2 Remove the air intake valance (Chapter 10).
3 The stainless steel finishes must next be removed. It will be necessary to drill the 'Pop' rivets securing the finishes to the screen and door pillars before they may be removed. Finally remove the stainless steel finisher at the top of the screen by sliding to one side.
4 Undo and remove the centre windscreen support bracket securing bolts, spring and plain washers and then lift away the support bracket.
5 Release the lock nuts and lower the left and right-hand side support brackets.
6 The windscreen glass may now be removed together with the rubber surround. If the glass is to be renewed inspect the rubber surround for signs of perishing or damage and, if evident, a new rubber surround must be obtained and refitted. This is also applicable if the windscreen glass has shattered.
7 Now is the time to remove all pieces of glass if the screen has shattered. Use a vacuum cleaner to extract as much as possible. Switch on the heater boost motor but watch out for flying pieces of glass which might be blown out of the ducting.
8 Thoroughly clean off all traces of any sealing compound that may have been used on the glass and rubber seal.
9 Insert a little sealing compound such as Sealastik in the glass channel of the rubber seal and fit it to the glass.
10 Insert a length of cord to the rubber seal which will assist the fitting of the seal over the edge of the base unit.
11 Refit the bottom support channel to the glass.
12 Apply a little Sealastik to the screen channel in the body-shell.
13 Mix up a little soft soap solution to act as a lubricant and

apply to the exterior of the seal and insert the assembled screen into the aperture of the base unit.

14 Refer to Fig. 12.46 and fit the neoprene blocks "A" between the bodyshell and windscreen support channel at each jacking point so as to maintain the correct clearance between the windscreen glass and bodyshell.

15 Loosely fit the right-hand and left-hand side mounting plates with the jacking bracket to the bodyshell.

16 Adjust the brackets upwards to the angle support of the screen using the hinges only.

17 Check that the rubber seal is in position round the glass and lift the lip of the seal over the base unit using the cord previously inserted into the rubber surround.

18 Refit the centre clamp bracket to the bodyshell with the nylon spacer correctly fitted and tighten just sufficiently to support the glass.

19 The left-hand and right-hand brackets should be adjusted until the glass is fully seating in the rubber seal.

20 It is important that a gap of 1/8th inch exists between the rubber seal and the edge of the channel. The glass will be in a state of stress if the left-hand and right-hand brackets are over-tightened which could, in adverse weather conditions, cause it to break.

21 Lightly tighten the centre clamp bracket and lock in position.

22 Mask the area of the body next to the rubber surround to prevent scratching and fit the finisher along the top edge of the screen. Next refit the two screen side finishers and corner finishers and 'Pop' rivet the finishers so that they are secured in place.

23 Remove the masking tape and any excess sealing compound (using a paraffin soaked cloth) from around the rubber seal. Clean the windscreen both inside and out.

24 Refit the air intake valance and finally the bonnet.

46 Rear screen - removal and refitment

1 Refer to Section 40 and remove the filler unit and rear decker panel.

2 Undo the bolt securing the centre clamp bracket to the base unit and lift away the clamp bracket (Fig. 12.47).

3 Slacken the left-hand and right-hand jacking bracket locknuts and lower the brackets.

4 With the help of an assistant push the windscreen from the inside of the car in a downwards direction and then outwards.

5 Remove the rubber seal.

6 Inspect the rubber seal for signs of perishing or damage, and if evident, a new seal should be obtained.

7 Clean all traces of old sealing compound from the screen glass and channel.

8 Smear a little Sealastik onto the rubber seal and fit the seal to the glass.

9 Insert a length of cord to the rubber seal which will assist in fitting it over the edge of the stainless steel trim.

10 Refit the bottom glazing seal to the glass.

11 Mix up a little soft soap solution to act as a lubricant and apply to the exterior of the screen and insert the assembled glass into the aperture of the base unit.

12 Position the angle support channel centrally on the base of the glass.

13 Refit the left-hand and right-hand side retaining brackets to the base unit and adjust the position of the brackets so as to just take the weight of the glass.

15 Refit the centre clamp bracket to the base unit with the nylon spacer and tighten just sufficiently to nip the glass.

16 Check that the rubber seal is in position round the glass and lift the lip over the stainless steel trim using the previously positioned cord.

17 Carefully adjust the left-hand and right-hand bracket evenly until the glass is fully home in the rubber seal. Take extreme care not to overtighten the brackets as the glass will be stressed which could, in adverse weather conditions, cause it to break.

17 Lightly tighten the centre clamp bracket to the glass and lock the bracket in position.

18 Refit the rear decker panel and fuel filler neck.

19 Remove any excess sealing compound from around the rubber seal using a rag soaked in paraffin or white spirit, and then clean the windscreen both inside and out.

47 Gearbox tunnel - removal and refitment

1 Remove the front and rear ashtrays from the gearbox tunnel moulded cover.

2 Locate and remove the two nuts to be found under the rear ashtray location and the single nut under the front ashtray location. (Fig. 12.48).

3 Undo and remove the two crosshead screws at the front of the moulded cover.

4 Lift up the flap at the forward edge of the rubber grommet base and remove the self tapping screw.

5 Undo and remove the two crosshead screws securing the radio speaker grille to the console unit (Figs. 12.49 and 12.50). These screws are to be found between the petrol reserve control and choke control. Lift away the speaker grille. If a radio is fitted the loud speaker cables must be disconnected.

6 Remove the gearchange lever sleeve or the speed selector indicator plate (auto transmission).

7 Slide both front seats as far back as they will go and keep the locking levers in their raised position.

8 Carefully roll back the handbrake rubber grommet and to assist removal of the grommet smear the handbrake handle and the grommet with a little Silicone grease.

9 Lift the forward edge of the cover over and off the gearchange lever at the speed selector lever (auto transmission).

10 Apply the handbrake and slide the cover forward and upwards so as to enable the leading edge to protrude into the aperture at the front of the console. At the same time carefully

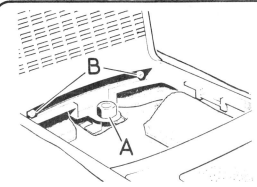

Fig. 12.48. Gearbox tunnel cover front securing nut (A) and screws (B)

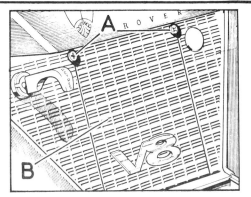

Fig. 12.49. Radio grille screws (A) grille (B)

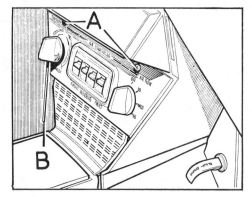

Fig. 12.50. Radio grille screws (early 3500 S)

A Self-tapping screws   B Releasing rod for
                               knob securing plungers

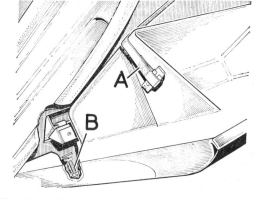

Fig. 12.51. Glove box check strap (A) and hinge screw (B)

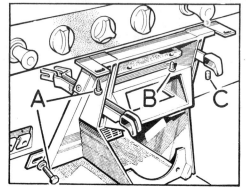

Fig. 12.52. Radio and heater control panel

A Securing bolts   C Knob screw
B Cover plate screw

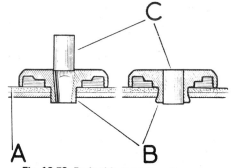

Fig. 12.53. Body side moulding clip

A Body panel   C Pin
B Hollow shank

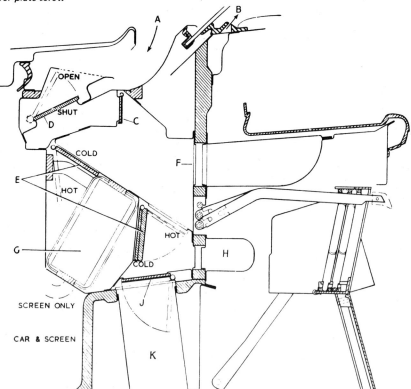

Fig. 12.54. Cross sectional view of heater

A Fresh air inlet
B Demister duct outlet
D Main valve
E Mixing valve
F Face level vent inlet
G Heater matrix
H Demister duct inlet
J Distribution valve
K Inlet to heater

push the handbrake grommet off the handbrake handle.

11 Release the handbrake fully and lift away the cover assembly.

12 Refitting the gearbox cover tunnel is the reverse sequence to removal. Take care to remove all traces of Silicone grease from the handbrake lever.

48 Glove box - removal and refitment

1 Open the glove box lid and detach one strap end for the right-hand box and two strap ends for the left-hand box from the spring clips as shown in Fig. 12.51.

2 Undo and remove the two bolts that retain the hinges on both the right-hand and left-hand glove boxes.

3 The glove box may now be lifted away.

4 Refitting is the reverse sequence to removal. If a new glove box is to be fitted to the driver's side of a lhd car make sure that the new glove box has a larger radius at the upper end of the large compartment so as to give the necessary clearance for the speedometer cable.

49 Parcels shelf (three thousand five) - removal and refitment

1 Remove the facia top rail (Chapter 10).

2 Remove the instrument panel (Chapter 10).

3 Remove the switch panel (Chapter 10).

4 Spring off the moulded finishers from each end of the parcels shelf.

5 Remove the three clips which secure the left-hand veneered panel to the screen rail clip and ease the panel out. Slide out the right-hand panel.

6 Remove the five set screws which secure the forward edge of the parcels shelf to the bodyshell, and then remove the shelf.

7 Refitting is a reversal of removal.

50 Parcels shelf (3500 and 3500S) - removal and refitment

1 Remove the facia top rail (Chapter 10).

2 Spring off the moulded finishers from each end of the parcels shelf.

3 Remove the two clips which retain the top edge of the veneer strip and lift the strip clear of the bottom groove.

4 Withdraw the instrument panel support bracket from the centre of the parcels shelf.

5 Remove the three screws and plain washers from the rear edge of the parcels shelf and then ease it up so that its front edge clears the face level vent controls.

6 Refitment is a reversal of removal.

51 Radio and heater console - removal and refitment

1 Disconnect the battery.

2 Remove the top cover from the gear box (Section 47).

3 Remove the glove boxes (Section 48).

4 Remove the four screws which secure the console to the dashboard bracket.

5 Disconnect the heater controls (Section 54).

6 Disconnect the fuel reserve control cable.

7 Withdraw the console unit. On early Three thousand five models, the choke cable must be disconnected.

8 Refitment is a reversal of removal but ensure that none of the cables is trapped.

52 Stainless steel body side mouldings - removal and refitment

1 The moulding is retained by nylon clips and it can be removed by gently prising with a hooked lever.

2 The clips are secured by the insertion of a pin at their centre which expands the clips and so secures them in their holes.

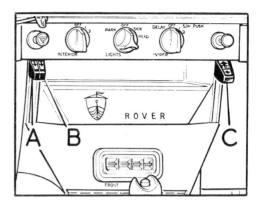

Fig. 12.55. Heater control panel

A Main control   C Distribution control
B Temperature control

3 When fitting new clips, tap the retaining pin into position until its head is flush with the clip face.

4 The stainless strip may be engaged with the clip by locating its top edge behind the clip and then striking it downwards with the palm of the hand to engage its bottom edge.

53 Heater and ventilation system - general description

A cross sectional view of the heater is shown in Fig. 12.54. It will be seen that the air flows through a built-in grille, assisted as necessary by a blower and passes to an air mixing chamber with various valves to control the temperature and direction of air movement.

The 'air inlet valve' is opened by means of the main control lever "A" (Fig. 12.55) in the right-hand side of the console and will allow air to pass into the air mixing chamber.

There is a 'wind blown' flap which is automatically opened by the ram effect of the air entering the mixture chamber as the car travels along the road. This air flow bypasses the blower fan.

The electric blower fan, when switched on, takes its air supply from the mixing chamber and increases the air flow above that effected by the forward motion of the car. The blower fan is controlled by a three position switch so as to give off, half-speed and full-speed conditions. When the blower is operating the windblown flap will close owing to the greater internal pressure.

The heater distribution "C", and temperature control "B" are located on the heater control panel and control the air blending valves, mixing the hot and cold air ready for passing to the car interior. These valves are positioned on either side of the heat exchanger radiator and are so connected that when one is open the other one is closed.

The air outlet valve is able to shut off the air flow into the car through the outlets at floor level. It is closed to increase the air flow through the demist nozzles when the car is being used during very cold conditions.

One of the features of the heater and ventilation system is the built-in face level ventilation ducts whereby a large outlet in the cold air passage allows fresh air to be directed to the instrument facia panel ducting.

As the heater matrix will not drain when the engine cooling system is drained, it is essential to maintain the correct strength of antifreeze solution in the system at all times.

54 Heater - removal and refitment

1 Remove both the glove boxes (Section 48).

2 Disconnect the heater controls from the adjustment forks underneath the instrument panel.

3 Drain the cooling system, retaining the coolant.
4 Remove the windscreen wiper arms and the air intake valance (Chapter 10).
5 Detach the accelerator coupling shaft bracket from the relay.
6 Mark the electrical leads to the heater and detach them.
7 Disconnect the heater hoses from the heater unit.
8 Unscrew and remove the four bolts which secure the heater unit in position and holding the air intake flap in the closed position withdraw the heater. It may be necessary to detach the insulation pad to facilitate the operation.
9 Refitment is a reversal of removal but check that the heater seats correctly on its mounting rubbers and before tightening the bolts make sure that the wires are not trapped between the heater and the bulkhead.

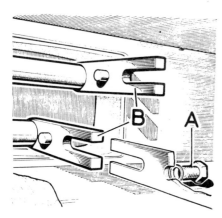

Fig. 12.56. Heater control connections

A *Securing bolt*
B *Levers*

55 Heater controls - adjustment of linkage

Upon reference to Fig. 12.57 it will be seen that the heater control linkages are all on the left-hand side of the unit so that if the performance is not satisfactory the linkage may be checked in the following manner:-
1 Slacken off the upper lever locking screw and move the main control lever on the control console approximately ¼ in (6.3 mm) below the upper detent position.
2 Move the upper link on the heater box in a clockwise direction and hold in this position with firm finger pressure so making sure that the valve is well seating onto the rubber pad. Tighten the locking screw.
3 Move the control knob to the 'ram air only' detent position. This will be approximately half way down the full travel. Look through the intake grille to see if the metal back of the inlet valve is almost touching, or actually touching, the small piece of foam rubber pad which acts as a stop.
4 If it is observed that the inlet valve is not in the correct position slacken the adjusting screw and slide the end of the spring link into the trunnion so as to increase the effective length of the link by between 1/16 to 1/8 in (1.5 to 3.0 mm). Re-tighten the screw firmly.
5 Now repeat the operations in paragraphs 1, 2 and 3. It is important that the length of the spring link is not increased more than necessary as otherwise there will be insufficient adjustment at the screw "A", to ensure that the flap can be shut when the control is in the 'off' position.
6 If the distribution of air is not corresponding to the control setting, slacken off the locking screw on the lower lever and then set the distribution lever on the console, approximately ¼ in (6.3 mm) below the upper detent position.
7 Apply firm finger pressure to the lower link on the heater box in a clockwise direction so making sure that the heater valve is well seating onto the rubber pad. Tighten the locking screw.
8 If the temperature of the air entering the car does not correspond to the position selected by the temperature control

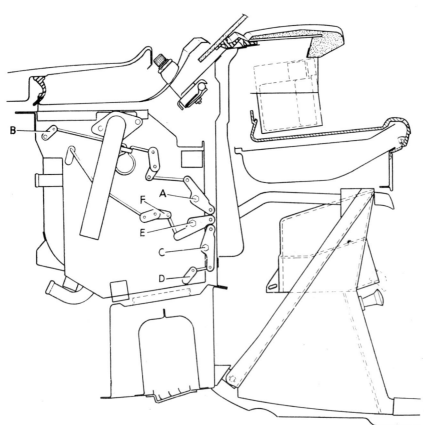

Fig. 12.57. Heater control linkage

A *Locking screw*
B *Upper link*
C *Locking screw*
D *Lower link*
E *Locking screw*
F *Centre link*

lever on the console, slacken the locking screw and set the temperature control lever to approximately ¼ in (6.3 mm) below the upper detent position.

9 Apply firm finger pressure to the centre link on the heater box in a clockwise direction and, maintaining this pressure, tighten the locking screw.

56 Air conditioning system - general description

A full air conditioning system (refrigerated) was fitted to early 3500S cars as standard and is a factory fitted option on all later models. The unit is designed to provide ideal interior temperatures under all climatic conditions.

The system includes a refrigeration circuit with thermostatically controlled air cooling and heat exchanger, the latter operating from the engine coolant. Both circuits are vacuum operated through a rotary control while a second control regulates the fan speed. Disconnection of the refrigeration lines or components is a job for experts with the necessary knowledge and equipment. The system will have to be de-pressurised, evacuated and finally recharged which is quite beyond the home mechanic. There is also a considerable safety risk in attempting to tamper with the refrigeration circuit.

In view of the foregoing, the servicing operations must be limited to those described in the following Sections.

57 Compressor driving belt (air conditioning system) - checking tension

1 Remove the windscreen washer reservoir.
2 Slacken the compressor adjuster and pivot bolts.
3 Move the compressor on its pivot until the total deflection of the driving belt is between 3/16 and ¼ in (4.0 to 6.0 mm) when checked at a point mid-way between the compressor and idler pulleys.
4 Tighten the securing bolts and re-check the belt tension.
5 If a new belt has to be fitted, then it should be installed working from below the car; also remove the radiator fan guard.

58 Vacuum reservoir (air conditioning system) - removal and refitment

1 The vacuum reservoir is located beneath the right-hand front wing.
2 Disconnect the pipes from the reservoir and blank the pipes to prevent the entry of dirt.
3 Refitment is a reversal of removal but ensure that dirt does not drop from the wing into the reservoir openings during reconnection.

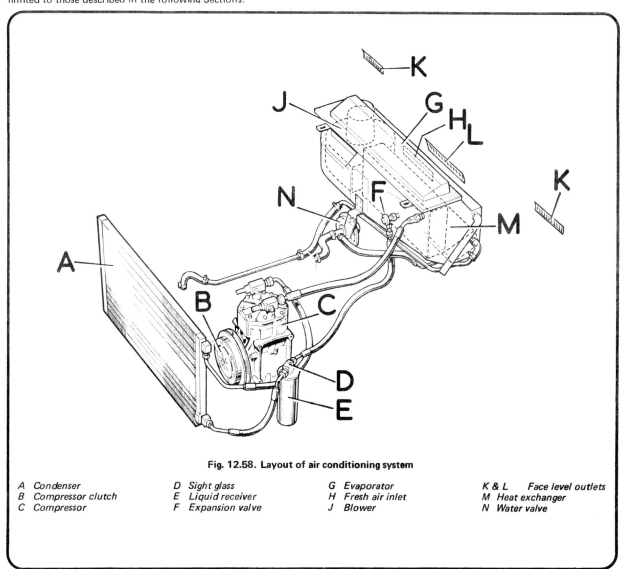

Fig. 12.58. Layout of air conditioning system

A Condenser
B Compressor clutch
C Compressor
D Sight glass
E Liquid receiver
F Expansion valve
G Evaporator
H Fresh air inlet
J Blower
K & L Face level outlets
M Heat exchanger
N Water valve

59 Water heater hoses (air conditioning system) - renewal

1   Drain the cooling system.
2   Remove the air cleaner.
3   Loosen the hose clips and cut the pipes from the metal connecting tubes. Do not try to twist the heater hoses from the metal pipes or they may fracture at the valve flanges.
4   Refitting the new hoses is a reversal of removal; refill the cooling system.

60 Radio - installation guide lines

1   Installation of car radio is best left to a specialist but where the operation is to be undertaken by the home mechanic, the following factors must be borne in mind. Provision for a radio is made at the top of the centre console just above the speaker grille.
2   Check that the set has the correct earth polarity.
3   Always include a fuse in the electric feed wire.
4   Ensure that the ignition system, the wiper and heater motors are all adequately suppressed.
5   Aerial types vary but generally the wing mounted extending type is satisfactory for normal reception. A short rod type for installation on the roof just above the windscreen is recommended by the manufacturers.

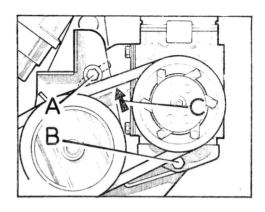

Fig. 12.59. Air conditioning system compressor driving belt adjustment

A   Adjuster strap bolt   (one of two)
B   Pivot mounting bolt   C   Belt tension check point

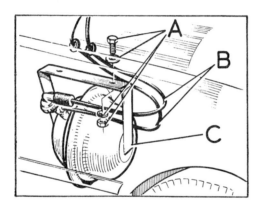

Fig. 12.60. Vacuum reservoir (air conditioning system)

A   Securing bolts   B   Vacuum pipes
                           C   Reservoir

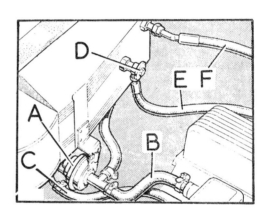

Fig. 12.61. Heater hoses (air conditioning system)

A   Water valve   D   Expansion valve
B   Inlet hose   E   Refrigeration inlet pipe
C   Outlet hose   F   Refrigeration outlet pipe

Metric conversion tables

Inches	Decimals	Millimetres	Millimetres to Inches		Inches to Millimetres	
			mm	Inches	Inches	mm
1/64	0.015625	0.3969	0.01	0.00039	0.001	0.0254
1/32	0.03125	0.7937	0.02	0.00079	0.002	0.0508
3/64	0.046875	1.1906	0.03	0.00118	0.003	0.0762
1/16	0.0625	1.5875	0.04	0.00157	0.004	0.1016
5/64	0.078125	1.9844	0.05	0.00197	0.005	0.1270
3/32	0.09375	2.3812	0.06	0.00236	0.006	0.1524
7/64	0.109375	2.7781	0.07	0.00276	0.007	0.1778
1/8	0.125	3.1750	0.08	0.00315	0.008	0.2032
9/64	0.140625	3.5719	0.09	0.00354	0.009	0.2286
5/32	0.15625	3.9687	0.1	0.00394	0.01	0.254
11/64	0.171875	4.3656	0.2	0.00787	0.02	0.508
3/16	0.1875	4.7625	0.3	0.01181	0.03	0.762
13/64	0.203125	5.1594	0.4	0.01575	0.04	1.016
7/32	0.21875	5.5562	0.5	0.01969	0.05	1.270
15/64	0.234375	5.9531	0.6	0.02362	0.06	1.524
1/4	0.25	6.3500	0.7	0.02756	0.07	1.778
17/64	0.265625	6.7469	0.8	0.03150	0.08	2.032
9/32	0.28125	7.1437	0.9	0.03543	0.09	2.286
19/64	0.296875	7.5406	1	0.03937	0.1	2.54
5, 16	0.3125	7.9375	2	0.07874	0.2	5.08
21/64	0.328125	8.3344	3	0.11811	0.3	7.62
11/32	0.34375	8.7312	4	0.15748	0.4	10.16
23/64	0.359375	9.1281	5	0.19685	0.5	12.70
3/8	0.375	9.5250	6	0.23622	0.6	15.24
25/64	0.390625	9.9219	7	0.27559	0.7	17.78
13/32	0.40625	10.3187	8	0.31496	0.8	20.32
27/64	0.421875	10.7156	9	0.35433	0.9	22.86
7/16	0.4375	11.1125	10	0.39370	1	25.4
29/64	0.453125	11.5094	11	0.43307	2	50.8
15/32	0.46875	11.9062	12	0.47244	3	76.2
31/64	0.484375	12.3031	13	0.51181	4	101.6
1/2	0.5	12.7000	14	0.55118	5	127.0
33/64	0.515625	13.0969	15	0.59055	6	152.4
17/32	0.53125	13.4937	16	0.62992	7	177.8
35/64	0.546875	13.8906	17	0.66929	8	203.2
9/16	0.5625	14.2875	18	0.70866	9	228.6
37/64	0.578125	14.6844	19	0.74803	10	254.0
19/32	0.59375	15.0812	20	0.78740	11	279.4
39/64	0.609375	15.4781	21	0.82677	12	304.8
5/8	0.625	15.8750	22	0.86614	13	330.2
41/64	0.640625	16.2719	23	0.90551	14	355.6
21/32	0.65625	16.6687	24	0.94488	15	381.0
43/64	0.671875	17.0656	25	0.98425	16	406.4
11/16	0.6875	17.4625	26	1.02362	17	431.8
45/64	0.703125	17.8594	27	1.06299	18	457.2
23/32	0.71875	18.2562	28	1.10236	19	482.6
47/64	0.734375	18.6531	29	1.14173	20	508.0
3/4	0.75	19.0500	30	1.18110	21	533.4
49/64	0.765625	19.4469	31	1.22047	22	558.8
25/32	0.78125	19.8437	32	1.25984	23	584.2
51/64	0.796875	20.2406	33	1.29921	24	609.6
13/16	0.8125	20.6375	34	1.33858	25	635.0
53/64	0.828125	21.0344	35	1.37795	26	660.4
27/32	0.84375	21.4312	36	1.41732	27	685.8
55/64	0.859375	21.8281	37	1.4567	28	711.2
7/8	0.875	22.2250	38	1.4961	29	736.6
57/64	0.890625	22.6219	39	1.5354	30	762.0
29/32	0.90625	23.0187	40	1.5748	31	787.4
59/64	0.921875	23.4156	41	1.6142	32	812.8
15/16	0.9375	23.8125	42	1.6535	33	838.2
61/64	0.953125	24.2094	43	1.6929	34	863.6
31/32	0.96875	24.6062	44	1.7323	35	889.0
63/64	0.984375	25.0031	45	1.7717	36	914.4

1   Imperial gallon = 8 Imp pints = 1.16 US gallons = 277.42 cu in = 4.5459 litres

1   US gallon = 4 US quarts = 0.862 Imp gallon = 231 cu in = 3.785 litres

1   Litre = 0.2199 Imp gallon = 0.2642 US gallon = 61.0253 cu in = 1000 cc

Miles to Kilometres		Kilometres to Miles	
1	1.61	1	0.62
2	3.22	2	1.24
3	4.83	3	1.86
4	6.44	4	2.49
5	8.05	5	3.11
6	9.66	6	3.73
7	11.27	7	4.35
8	12.88	8	4.97
9	14.48	9	5.59
10	16.09	10	6.21
20	32.19	20	12.43
30	48.28	30	18.64
40	64.37	40	24.85
50	80.47	50	31.07
60	96.56	60	37.28
70	112.65	70	43.50
80	128.75	80	49.71
90	144.84	90	55.92
100	160.93	100	62.14

lb f ft to Kg f m		Kg f m to lb f ft		lb f/in^2 : Kg f/cm^2		Kg f/cm^2 : lb f/in^2	
1	0.138	1	7.233	1	0.07	1	14.22
2	0.276	2	14.466	2	0.14	2	28.50
3	0.414	3	21.699	3	0.21	3	42.67
4	0.553	4	28.932	4	0.28	4	56.89
5	0.691	5	36.165	5	0.35	5	71.12
6	0.829	6	43.398	6	0.42	6	85.34
7	0.967	7	50.631	7	0.49	7	99.56
8	1.106	8	57.864	8	0.56	8	113.79
9	1.244	9	65.097	9	0.63	9	128.00
10	1.382	10	72.330	10	0.70	10	142.23
20	2.765	20	144.660	20	1.41	20	284.47
30	4.147	30	216.990	30	2.11	30	426.70

List of illustrations

Chapter 2/Cooling system

Chapter 3/Carburation, emission control and exhaust system

Chapter 4/Ignition system

Chapter 5/Clutch

Chapter 6/Manual gearbox and automatic transmission

Chapter 7/Propeller shaft and universal joints

Chapter 8/Rear axle

Chapter 9/Braking system

Chapter 10/Electrical system

Chapter 11/Suspension and steering

Chapter 12/Bodywork and bodyframe

Index

Printed by
J. H. HAYNES & Co. Ltd
Sparkford Yeovil Somerset
ENGLAND